THIRD COAST

Also by Roni Sarig

The Secret History of Rock: The Most Influential Bands You've Never Heard

THIRD COAST

OutKast, Timbaland, and How Hip-Hop
Became a Southern Thing

Roni Sarig

Photographs by
Julia Beverly

Da Capo Press
A Member of the Perseus Books Group

First Da Capo Press edition 2007

Library of Congress Cataloging-in-Publication Data
   Sarig, Roni.
   Third coast : Outkast, Timbaland, and how hip-hop became a southern thing / Roni Sarig.
       p. cm.
Includes bibliographical references and index.
ISBN-13: 978-0-306-81430-3 (pbk. : alk. paper)
ISBN-10: 0-306-81430-7 (pbk. : alk. paper) 1. Rap (Music)—Southern States—History and criticism. 2. Hip-hop—Southern States. I. Title.
ML3531.S27 2007
782.4216490975—dc22

                                              2007005231

Published by Da Capo Press
A Member of the Perseus Books Group

http://www.dacapopress.com

Da Capo Press books are available at special discounts for bulk purchases in the U.S. by corporations, institutions, and other organizations. For more information, please contact the Special Markets Department at the Perseus Books Group, 11 Cambridge Center, Cambridge, MA 02142, or call (800) 255-1514 or (617) 252-5298, or e-mail special.markets@perseusbooks.com.

1 2 3 4 5 6 7 8 9

To Danielle

CONTENTS

WHAT GOES AROUND 249

WHAT YOU PEOPLE KNOW ABOUT THE DIRTY SOUTH?

Sometime between first conceiving the idea for a history of Southern hip-hop and actually getting it all down on paper, I left the South—where I'd lived for a decade—and moved to New York, just a few miles up the Bronx River from where hip-hop began. Up here, the culture's foundation myth is held sacred: Kool Herc immigrated from Jamaica to the Bronx and, in the early '70s, began translating his native country's reggae-oriented sound-system DJ culture to the more funk-centered tastes of his Bronx neighbors. In the process, he developed the elements that would become hip-hop—isolating and looping breakbeats, MCing over instrumentals, and so on.

And so, the story goes, Herc and his successors developed the first African American music form *not* born in the South. Somehow, though, my relocation to the north north Bronx (OK, Westchester County) did not feel like a homecoming or arrival in an ancestral homeland, the way an Eric Clapton fan might be inspired by a trip to the Mississippi Delta. In fact, there was a sense that I was—to put it dramatically—behind enemy lines. That's because, despite the assuredness with which New Yorkers explain hip-hop's local birth, much of what I knew about the development of African American music suggested something else: That rap music was born in the South.

To be clear, I don't claim that *hip-hop* was born in the South. No, the culture that combined the musical innovations of Kool Herc, Grandmaster Flash, Afrika Bambaataa, and the rest with graffiti art and break-dancing—that stuff all certainly came together in the Bronx to create something revolutionary. But, let's face it, hip-hop music today isn't much connected to graffiti or breaking or even turntable trickery. What generally distinguishes hip-hop music from R&B or any other genre is the presence of rapping. And rap, as far as I can see, came from the South.

WORD UP: THE AFRICAN AMERICAN ORAL TRADITION

Of course, rapping could certainly be traced back beyond America, to the griots—West African storytellers—and other African cultural practices. But looking only at the black experience in America, one would have to begin a cultural anthropology of rap with the oral traditions that rose out of slavery. While slavery initially existed in all of colonial America and the early United States, the numbers of Southern slaves always dwarfed the black population in the North. And the type of community that fostered a black American oral tradition—large numbers of slaves living communally, as on a plantation—existed mainly in the South. Anyway, by the first decade of the nineteenth century, slavery was all but gone above the Mason-Dixon line. So, when we talk about American slavery, we're generally talking about the South.

Oral tradition was central to slaves because it was the only way memories of their African heritage and new American experience could be processed into cultural expression. For the most part, slaves were not allowed to gain literacy, and the tools to create visual art were often beyond reach. But the mind and spirit of African Americans could not be killed as long as slave masters valued their physical labor. So the voice became the primary instrument of expression—talking, rhyming, singing. And because even certain types of oral communication between slaves raised the suspicion of masters, blacks developed a tradition of codes, metaphors, and euphemisms that was both a matter of creative expression and survival.

All of the spoken forms that are recognized as precursors to rapping—playing the dozens, signifying, testifying, toasting, shuckin' and jivin'—have roots in slavery. For instance, the name of the dozens—the game of volleying "ya mama" insults back and forth—refers to deformed and dismembered slaves who were sold at a discount, by the dozen. According to Mona Lisa Saloy of New Orleans' Dillard University, "For a black to be sold as part of the 'dozens' was the lowest blow possible. In an effort to toughen their hearts against the continual verbal assault inflicted on them as part of the 'dozens,' blacks practiced insulting each other indirectly by attacking the most sacred 'mother' of the other. The person who loses his 'cool' and comes to blows loses the contest. The person who outwits and out-insults the other while keeping a 'cool' head is the winner."

Shuckin' and jivin', which today refers to the practice either of "acting a fool" or of hanging out with friends and boasting—in other words, "talkin' shit"—goes back to the days when slaves would entertain and motivate one another with exaggerated tales while shucking corn. Testifying involves proclaiming a belief or emotion—generally concerning God—and, while not limited to the black tradition, took on a unique declarative style and call-and-response cadence among black churches. And signifying refers to the larger concept of indirect communication—wordplay, or changing the meanings of words, or "sampling" the speech of others—as a means of protection and, later, a form of art.

Signifying, toasting, jiving, testifying, and the dozens all came together in the most formalized of the slave's oral traditions, and the most directly reminiscent of rapping: toasting. These were essentially epic rhymes told and retold, adapted and expanded over generations, as a form of entertainment. Toasts—the most famous of which include "The Signifying Monkey," "Stackolee," "Shine and the Titanic," and "Dolemite"—could involve explicit language, sexuality, and violence, as well as plenty of humor and folk wisdom. And the performance was as important as the rhymes and stories told in the toasts. A good toast needed to be recited with drama and flair, and audiences responded best to the most energetically performed toasts.

GO DJ, THAT'S MY DJ: JIVE TALKING TO REGGAE TOASTING

The forms of African American oral tradition that came out of slavery—the dozens, toasts, up to double Dutch jump-roping rhymes—are part of a folk culture developed organically over generations and practiced apart from commercial concerns. By contrast, today's practice of rapping is a form of commercial mass communication—rhyming over beats as a way to make money and engage in popular culture. The bridge between the two—the point where the black oral tradition entered the popular culture—came when blacks earned just the nominal amount of social power to start speaking freely on the radio. Black radio DJs—most either located in the South or transplanted elsewhere from origins in the South—became, essentially, the first rappers.

The first popular radio programming to be created by and for blacks arose in Chicago in the 1930s. A radio announcer named Jack Cooper on the city's WSBC was the best-known black radio personality of his day. Cooper played sophisticated jazz music and enunciated his words without any trace of blackness. According to William Barlow in his book, *Voice Over:*

The Making of Black Radio, Cooper represented—for the many black Chicagoans who'd recently arrived from the South—the community's aspirations to become assimilated.

In the South, the thought of putting black voices—"white-sounding" or not—on the air was still beyond the pale in the '30s and '40s. But black-geared programming did begin cropping up, including the "King Biscuit" hour on Helena, Arkansas's KFFA, which featured a band led by blues great Sonny Boy Williamson and aired at noontime, during the lunch break of many Mississippi Delta field hands. On Nashville's powerful WLAC—whose fifty-thousand-watt signal could be heard over much of the country at night—jive-talking white DJs continued to play rhythm & blues music into the '50s.

By the mid-40s, however, things were starting to change. The great black migration—which brought millions of blacks from the South to other regions, including nearly a million to Chicago alone—was in full bloom, with the promise of jobs during wartime and then postwar prosperity. The influx fostered huge changes in urban life and African American identity. Into this environment, with so many newly arrived Southern blacks homesick and trying to find their way in Chicago, stepped a radio personality named Al Benson. Benson, known as the Ole Swingmaster, was a preacher from Jackson, Mississippi, who came to Chicago and wound up on the radio in the mid-40s. When he started playing secular urban blues and rhythm & blues—on WGES at first, then expanding to WAAF and WJJD—he quickly became one of the city's most-loved men.

Unlike assimilationist African American radio announcers such as Jack Cooper, Benson had no use for standard English. With his Southern black drawl and slang, Old Mushmouth (as his fans called him) spoke to—and for—the black masses that identified with him. It was a voice, after all, that they recognized: Benson and the many disc jockeys he inspired brought the oral traditions that had flourished in the black South—rhyming, testifying, and signifying—and put them on the radio for all to hear. This leap—elevating black street talk to where it was acceptable in the realm of mass communication—was, in a sense, the genesis of rap.

According to William Barlow, Benson was unusually outspoken on racial issues—on the eve of the 1956 election, for instance, he flew a plane over Jackson, Mississippi, and dropped five thousand copies of the Constitution to "wake up the citizens of Mississippi." Though not many DJs of his era were as politically engaged, Benson's homespun style formed the template by which young black voices in radio operated. Through the late '40s and '50s, famous "black-talking" radio personalities popped up all over the country: Daddy-O in Chicago, Jocko Henderson and Dr. Jive in New York, Dr. Feelgood and Jockey Jack (aka Jack the Rapper) in Atlanta, and so on.

Some of the most colorful black DJs of the era actually spoke in rhyme, crafting a style that was rap in all but name. Among the most beloved was Lavada Durst, aka Doctor Hep Cat, who worked out of Austin, Texas's KVET. Barlow's *Voice Over* transcribes this Durst aircheck from 1948: "All the cats are hipped to the tip and draped on down/Here are a few of the crazy cats who came to town./There's Daddy Rabbit with the do-rag habit, and Ice Cube Slim in his pork pie brim./My man Jivin' Joe with Charlie the Blowtop, check out Frantic Fred and Heavy Hiphop. . . . "

Probably the most famous of hepcat DJs of the '50s was Jocko Henderson, who got his start in Baltimore and Philadelphia before bringing his "Rocket Ship Show" to New York in the mid-50s. Jocko was perhaps the first black DJ to syndicate his shows, and at the height of his popularity he was on air in D.C., Detroit, and St. Louis, in addition to Philadelphia and New York. He also hosted a three-hour program in Miami that—along with rhythm & blues shows broadcast out of New Orleans by DJs Doctor Daddy-O and Poppa Stoppa—reached far enough into the Caribbean to be heard in Jamaica.

These were the voices—Southern and black, in fact or in spirit—that influenced Jamaica's earliest toasters, such as U-Roy and Sir Lord Comic, to perform their rhythmic rhymes over reggae dubs. In fact, U-Roy's "Ace From Space" and Comic's "The Great Wuga Wuga" were lifted directly from Jocko's shtick. These toasters and their successors then inspired Kool Herc, who brought the style back to New York.

But there was not just one line leading from Southern oral traditions to Southern radio DJs to Jamaican toasters to South Bronx DJs. Many other crosscurrents impacted the sound and style of early New York hip-hop, and nearly all had roots in the South. There were the performers—musicians and comedians—who carried on the toasting and signifying traditions, including Arkansas native Rudy Ray Moore (aka Dolemite) and Georgia native Clarence "Blowfly" Reid. There were revolutionary black celebrities—most notably, Louisville, Kentucky's Cassius Clay, the boxer later known as Muhammad Ali, who crafted outrageous boasts and rhymes to taunt his opponents. And there were politically outspoken poets who brought those same folk traditions into the Black Power movement, including New York's Last Poets and L.A.'s Watts Prophets (some of whose members were among the migrants who left the South as children), Gil Scott-Heron (raised in Tennessee) and Black Panther "Minister of Justice" H. Rap Brown (born in Louisiana, attended college in Alabama).

Rap Brown, in fact, earned his nickname as a young man for his great skill at playing the dozens. Some of his rhymes later showed up in the lyrics to the Sugar Hill Gang's "Rapper's Delight," the first national rap hit. Other early rap recordings—including the Fatback Band's "King Tim III (Personality Jock)" and Jocko Henderson's own late-career novelty, "Rhythm Talk," both from 1979, had direct ties to the era of "soul-talking" radio DJs. All of these influences were floating in the air at the time rap music—or hip-hop—was invented. In essence, it was never really invented at all.

RAISE UP, THIS ONE'S FOR YOU: SOUTHERN RAP EXPLOSION

Having established rap's Southern roots, it would be unfair to suggest that the current hip-hop landscape in which Southern artists reign supreme is a direct inheritor of the region's oral traditions. Without question, early Southern hip-hop was predominantly, and directly, influenced by New York and, later, by West Coast rap (with the partial exception of Miami, which may have inherited its own mobile DJ culture in the '70s directly from Jamaica). Mostly, things like toasting and the dozens only touched Southern hip-hop inasmuch as they were distilled through the ages into rap music as a whole. Besides, by the time Southern hip-hop came around, the Great Black Migration of the twentieth century had already occurred, spreading black oral traditions throughout the country. Unlike in the nineteenth century, black culture was no longer a Southern culture.

And yet, there is to some ears a sense that, with the South's ascension, hip-hop has come home. That's one way to explain Southern hip-hop's enduring popularity. There are other theories as well—we'll get to them. The only thing for certain is that, starting in the late '90s and continuing to the present day, Southern rappers, musicians, songwriters, producers, and labels have contributed far more than their share to hip-hop's commercial and artistic success—and extending hip-hop's hold as pop music's dominant sound by introducing new sounds and fusions.

While Southerners were virtually absent from the national hip-hop landscape through the '80s, they started showing up in the early '90s and, by the end of the decade, they were involved in the creation of 30 to 40 percent of the singles on the hip-hop charts. Then, around 2002, the market share exploded and the figure went up to 50 to 60 percent, if not higher. In the week of December 13, 2003, for instance, the top six slots (and ten of the top twelve) on the *Billboard Hot 100*—that's the pop chart that includes all genres of music, not just hip-hop—were occupied by Southern urban artists, labels, or producers: OutKast (two singles), Ludacris, Kelis (Neptunes-produced), Beyoncé, and Chingy (on Ludacris's Disturbing Tha Peace label).

In fact, during the stretch from October 2003 to December 2004, the number one position on the *Billboard Hot 100* pop chart was held by a Southern urban artist fifty-eight out of sixty-two weeks (if you add in songs written or produced by people either born or currently living in the South, it becomes sixty-five out of sixty-five weeks during that same period). And a year later—December 11, 2004—the South's grip on the top ten had not subsided. That week, seven of the top ten featured Southern artists as primary or featured performers. That year, *Vibe* magazine reported that 43.6 percent of urban radio airplay featured Southern artists—that's just artists and doesn't account for songs that feature Southern producers and labels—compared to 24.1 percent East Coast and just 2.5 percent West Coast. (And the Midwest, where many artists—Chingy, J-Kwon, Nelly—had strong Southern connections, accounted for 29.7 percent.)

But despite all evidence to the contrary, the old East Coast/West Coast paradigm continued to thrive in hip-hop, at least in the larger culture. That's due, in part, to the intense media coverage around the Tupac and Notorious B.I.G. murders, and the relative lack of big-picture coverage of Southern hip-hop in the mainstream press. The feud, which peaked a decade ago, combined with the hugely influential, hugely galvanizing force that was L.A.-centric gangsta rap to create an impression that the West Coast had, in the early and mid-90s, somehow taken over from—or at least achieved parity with—New York–centric hip-hop. East Coast/West Coast was a story that worked well for the media; it was centered on the country's two media/entertainment hubs. But in fact, West Coast—the Bay and L.A. combined—never contributed more than 25 to 35 percent of acts on the rap charts, even at its peak.

The rise of Southern hip-hop, then, represents the first large-scale break from New York's dominance. Individual artists have cropped up from just about everywhere, but never has a region other than the East Coast been the primary influence. Indeed, rappers from other regions now look to the South for stylistic cues, the latest slang, and the talent pool of guest rappers and producers. Fifteen years ago, who could've imagined that New Yorker rappers would someday feel like underdogs in hip-hop? "A lot of people [in New York] seem to be mad that the South is gettin' all the attention right now," wrote Juelz Santana, of New York's popular Diplomats crew, in the November 2005 issue of *XXL*. "I guess people are takin' it personal, like, the South is not playin' our music but we play their music." My, how the tables have turned.

And so we return to the obvious question: Why has Southern hip-hop proven so successful? There's no definitive explanation—and with so many different strains emerging from Florida to Texas to the Virginia coast, it's nearly impossible to pinpoint one single factor that has attracted mass audiences to Southern hip-hop as a whole. But let's consider some sweeping generalities and unprovable theories.

Southern Heritage

If hip-hop has truly come home in the South, that's because of its innate connection to earlier forms of black music—field hollers, the blues, gospel, jazz, and rock—that have all come from the South. And if you consider that these music forms—combined with white styles like country and European folk—have collectively provided a blueprint for all of American popular music, then it's possible to imagine that Southern-flavored hip-hop simply sounds more familiar to our ears. It emerged from a place closer to the bedrock of music we all grew up hearing.

Social Music

The intent of the Bronx DJs, when they first picked up the mic to emcee over instrumentals, was simply to motivate the crowd, to enhance the music's excitement. That function has mostly disappeared over the decades, as New York rapping evolved through the '80s from crowd motivation to playground battling to political rhetoric to insular storytelling. Rapping went from being about the crowd, to being about the competition, to being about the rapper (with audience members left to stand still and cooly nod their heads).

That breakdown is less apparent in the South, where chanting and unabashed party songs are still part of hip-hop's social fabric. The music's foundation—from booty dancing in Florida to gangsta walking in Memphis—has always been tied to its listeners, and fulfills a social function. Unlike the too-hip-to-dance stance of New York hip-hop heads, the provincials down South are still unselfconscious enough to enjoy the music. Compare, for just one example, a popular New York rap hit, Terror Squad's "Lean Back," which is a dance song that claims "my niggas don't dance," to Out-Kast's "Hey Ya" (not strictly a hip-hop track, but still), a song about the impossibility of monogamy that has inspired dancing everywhere from clubs to weddings to elevators and supermarkets. There's a joyful spirit to Southern hip-hop that doesn't exist in even the most popular hip-hop acts, from Eminem to 50 Cent to Jay-Z (except, of course, when he's rhyming over a Southern track).

The social aspect of Southern hip-hop reflects, perhaps, a degree of connectedness that seems to exist among Southern blacks but is less apparent in the North. Because most Southern black families have been in the region—often in the same local area—for generations, the networks of extended relations (and the feeling that they're all tied, in blood or in suffering) have stayed in tact to a greater extent than in the North, where migration broke apart many extended, even immediate, families. With wider family connections and stronger church ties, Southern blacks may benefit from a greater sense of belonging—and imparting that sense of Southern hospitality into their music could be part of what makes it so infectious. We all want to belong, and we've all been invited.

Inversion

The achievement of Southern hip-hop may be, in part, a matter of demographics. At the start of World War I, almost 90 percent of all American blacks lived in the South. With a booming war economy and white males off fighting, Southern blacks migrated north, to Chicago, Detroit, New York, Philadelphia, and other industrial cities. The flow continued, gaining intensity again during and after World War II, up through the '60s. By the end of what is known as the Great Black Migration, more than six million blacks had left the South. As they migrated, they brought their folk music to northern cities, where it flowered into sophisticated works of genius.

So New Orleans' dixieland and hot jazz came to New York and became big-band swing and virtuosic be-bop. Mississippi Delta blues traveled up to Chicago and became the province of electric blues masters like Muddy Waters, Willie Dixon, and Howlin' Wolf. Rock 'n' roll left Memphis and reached its artistic peak in places as far-flung as California and the U.K. And the soul music of Georgia, Alabama, and Tennessee wound up in Detroit, where Motown unleashed the visions of Marvin Gaye and Stevie Wonder. By the end of the migration, the cities of the North and West Coast became the center of black cultural life.

By the late '60s, with conditions looking up for blacks in the South and the inner cities of the North and West in disrepair (and often in flames), the Great Migration ended. This is the landscape into which hip-hop emerged—the first form of black American music not born in the South. And certainly, if black music has always been born out of suffering, there were few places more in need of relief than the South Bronx of the 1970s.

Then in the mid-70s, as part of a general exodus from the industrial North and West, the tide of black migration reversed. As Gladys Knight sang in the surprisingly relevant 1973 song, "Midnight Train to Georgia":

"L.A. proved too much for the man/So he's leavin' the life he's come to know/He said he's goin' back to find what's left of his world/The world he left behind not so long ago/He's leavin' on that midnight train to Georgia/Said he's goin' back to find the simpler place and time. . . . " From then on, and continuing today, more blacks have been moving (back) to the South than leaving—more than a million reverse migrants in the past three decades.

Inverting the pattern of the earlier migration, it follows that Northerners coming south brought with them their music—in this case, hip-hop—where in the hands of artists such as OutKast and Timbaland the genre reached its creative zenith. We know that seminal Southern hip-hop artists such as Atlanta's Shy-D and Speech, and Houston's DJ Ready Red, were, in fact, Northern transplants, and that most of Florida's 2 Live Crew came from California. But more than specific individuals bringing their music south, a more subtle, ineffable shift took place: A switch from the North and West Coast as the cultural nexus of black creativity (back) to the South.

Just as Southern music's journey out of the region produced profound changes in the sound of jazz, rock, and other genres, the same evolution characterizes hip-hop's move southward. Indeed, it's often the case—in art, as with anything—that making advances requires a dislocation, that you can't really see where you can go with something until you've stepped out of your familiar landscape. Certainly Southern hip-hop has benefited by not being tied to notions of hip-hop orthodoxy—to Northern concepts of what does or does not qualify as hip-hop. *We'll just make our music*, Southern hip-hoppers seem to be saying, *and it'll be as melodic, sonically adventurous, and non-lyrical (or outlandishly lyrical) as we want it—you can decide if it's hip-hop or not; as long as people like it, we don't really care what it is.*

And so, breaking from hip-hop's traditional source material (jazz and funk loops), Timbaland and the Neptunes created exciting new sounds. Disavowing hip-hop's requirement that you limit melodies and musicality to a brief moment in the hook, OutKast made pop-music history. And forgoing the requirement that hip-hop contain sixteen-bar raps, Lil Jon made irresistibly primal, repetitive chanting a mainstream sensation.

Southern Strategy

There's one more thing about the strange alchemy of the South in this era. As Peter Applebome writes in his book, *Dixie Rising: How the South Is Shaping American Values, Politics, and Culture*, "We all need a calm in our storm, divine or otherwise. In ways both real and illusory, the South these days seems to promise one. It offers a sense of history, roots, place, and community when the nation desperately is seeking all four." It's probably not a coincidence that, in the last thirty years, every president except one has been a Southerner (Southern transplants count—given enough time, the region tends to make Southerners out of anyone); and the one exception, Ronald Reagan, chose to launch his campaign for president with a speech about states' rights in Philadelphia, Mississippi. It's a place where our country's values converge—you can't win the nation unless you've won the South.

Generally when we talk about the South setting our cultural discourse these days, we're referring to the white, conservative South. But what's so amazing about the complex relationship between black Southerners and white Southerners is how so many of the values are shared across racial lines. The same regional characteristics that the country finds so attractive—a sense of hospitality and courtesy, the importance of family and community, an awareness of history and heritage, a connection to the land, and that blend of rebel and traditionalist—can be claimed as much by regional hip-hop as it is claimed by the Christian right.

At the very least, down South rap is a populist effort. Deftly balancing its influences and loyalties in an almost political strategy, Southerners cherry-picked elements of the East Coast and West Coast hip-hop that came before. And by reflecting those influences through the prism of the South's own history and strongly defined identity, Southern artists have been able to create sounds that are simultaneously familiar and new, proudly regional but also easily accessible, irreverent while also tradition-bound. In fusing together other regional styles and breaking rules as it sees fit, Southern rap has been both musically inventive and also willing to embrace mainstream pop audiences. The result: Southern hip-hop has not only pushed the genre further aesthetically, it has also opened it to a wider audience.

DOWN TO THE CROSSROADS

Ultimately, this book is a map of the Crossroads, a term used in these pages both for its age-old blues connotation, but also in much newer terms of globalism and technology. Southern hip-hop developed, like so many things, through a series of fusions that traveled from different directions and collided to create something new.

The South's original style, Miami bass, resulted from the convergence of old-school rap from the North and a Caribbean spirit from the South. Houston's early rap involved a collision of gangsta rap from the West with soul, blues, and murder ballads from parts of the South further east. Atlanta hip-hop's pop breakthrough—everyone from Jermaine Dupri to OutKast to

Lil Jon—involved various distillations of hard-core sounds from the west (both the West Coast and the western South), bass beats from down in Florida, and assorted styles and imagery from up north.

Southern hip-hop, like the South as a whole, is in large part a product of all the external forces that have played upon it. In that way, the story of hip-hop in the South is not only a chronicle of one region's contributions to a larger artform, but—to the extent that the South has defined the genre during this era—a history of recent hip-hop, and urban pop music, as a whole.

Quoted by Applebome in *Dixie Rising*, the historian Howard Zinn long ago said that the South "is not a mutation born by some accident into the normal lovely American family. It has simply taken the national genes and done the most with them." Whether you're from the South Bronx, South Central L.A., or South Dakota, the South is part of us all. If the Hip-Hop Generation seems, at times, to have lost all sense of historical perspective, the South has risen to remind us who started this shit—and, perhaps, who's gonna finish it.

PART ONE

REGIONALISM AND EARLY CROSSCURRENTS

chapter 1

THE RISE AND FALL OF MIAMI BASS

SOUL TALKING: CLARENCE REID AND HENRY STONE

"Junior" Reid made the crackers laugh. It was a handy trick for a little black kid growing up in South Georgia in the early '50s. It would serve him well throughout his life.

The town was Vienna, in the area of Andersonville—once home to a brutal Confederate prisoner-of-war camp. Vienna is also close to Plains—where a peanut farmer grew up and would later leave for Washington, heralding the arrival of the New South. In terms of the tides of history, Junior's Vienna was somewhere between those two destinations.

Junior's mother had given birth to him in 1945, when she was sixteen, and then left to find a better life for herself in Florida. His dad had gone off to war against the Nazis—who, Junior learned, didn't like black folks either—and he died in a prison camp. So Junior lived with his grandparents on a farm they rented from their redneck neighbors.

As a kid, Junior loved listening to the hillbilly songs coming from the radio station up the road in Cordele. But on clear nights he could also catch the latest in "race" records—that is, black music—coming from WLAC in Nashville. In those formative years of the early '50s, when the more rhythmic "jump" blues were evolving into early R&B and then rock 'n' roll, WLAC was *the* station to hear the latest sides, and its fifty-thousand-watt signal was powerful enough to spread the new gospel (secular or otherwise) throughout much of the country.

Tuning in at night, Junior heard the famous DJ John R—a white guy you'd have sworn was colored—pattering between songs in his smooth, rhythmic hepcat rap. Back then they called it "soul talking."

It made a great impression on Junior, who, before he'd had a chance to learn to read, was imitating the soul-talking DJs and rattling off rhymes of his own. They were pretty damn funny, everyone agreed.

Then, when Junior was just seven, his granddaddy died. With no one to work the land, the neighbors gave him and his grandma three months to leave. They had nowhere to go, really, so Junior got the idea that he could work and support the family himself. "Get your little black ass in school and sit down," was what everyone thought about that proposal. Except Caldy, an ornery white guy that just about nobody liked—"niggers, crackers, rednecks, Klans, they all hated him," Reid recalls.

"He asked, 'Boy, do you know what a nigger is?'"

"A black person."

"He said, 'No, a nigger is a person so fucking stupid, you can't tell them nothing, you have to show it to them. You want to show these fuckers something?'"

"Yeah."

"'C'mon, hook up the mule yourself.'"

Now, most mules, once they saw that bridle in your hand, didn't want to come anywhere near you—they knew you were going to work them. But Junior had a way about him, and the mule came to him.

When the rednecks saw that Junior could work, they let him and his grandmother stay. So he left school in the third grade and went into the fields.

To keep his spirits up during the long hours on the farm, Junior made up his rhymes. He'd listen to songs on the radio and think up raunchy versions of the lyrics. "I'm walking the floor over you" became "I'm jerking my dick over you."

The crackers, catching this little kid with the nasty mouth, ate it up. But his grandmomma was appalled. She'd call him by his real name, saying, "Clarence, you're a disgrace, I'm ashamed of you. You ain't no better than a damn blowfly."

Junior didn't know what a blowfly was, but it sounded bad. He asked around and found out: they were the kind of flies that lay maggot eggs on dead things.

But Caldy was there with another dissenting view. Junior recalls him saying, "You tell your grandmomma, if it wasn't for fucking blowflies, none of our asses would be here. Blowflies clean the world of germs."

It sounded good to Junior, so he told his grandmomma, "I gotta be free to be me," and he began calling himself Blowfly Clarence Reid.

And he got by OK for a while in Vienna as the town crack-up. But life as an eleven-year-old tenant farmer wouldn't do. So Reid left Vienna and hitchhiked down to south Florida. He found a job stacking records for Hunter's Music in West Palm Beach, a shop that supplied records for juke-boxes throughout the area. He kept singing while he worked—both his nasty parodies and some more straightforward R&B things he'd started making up. One day Mr. Hunter noticed and asked what he was singing.

"That's something I made up," Reid answered. It was called "Gotta Be Free to Be Me."

Mr. Hunter beckoned Clarence into his office and asked him to sing some more.

Clarence crooned, "You and I are lovers, but girl we don't own each other, so get it out of your mind. . . . "

Mr. Hunter listened, then spoke. "That's fantastic. I want you to go to Miami, look up this guy named Henry Stone. Tell him Hunter sent you."

Henry Stone was born in 1921 in the Bronx, part of the interborough migration that took Jews out of the Lower East Side shtetl and into lower-middle-class confines to the north. He picked up the trumpet as a kid, inspired by Louis Armstrong, and got to be good enough to wind up in a military band during World War II, stationed at an embarkation center in New Jersey. And that's where, through his black band mates, he picked up his love of the blues.

After the war, Stone headed west to L.A. to work as a musician, but he wound up in the record business. He did some artist and repertoire (A&R) work finding songs for Mel Tormé, but soon veered toward the world of race records and began selling blues 78s for Modern Records. Back then, there wasn't yet a system in place for distributing records—you just got them out however you could. Stone drove around and sold them out of his car; to get records out to Chicago, he sold a stack to train porters heading in that direction.

When it was time to stake out some territory of his own, Stone found a largely uncharted land in south Florida. So, in 1949, he moved to Miami and set up his own record distribution company, which became known as Tone.

Distribution was Stone's bread and butter—he carried records from all the great independent labels of the time: Modern, Specialty, Savoy, King. But he also kept a small recording studio in the back of his warehouse, and one day in late 1950, a blind black kid from northern Florida named Ray Charles came by looking to do a session. He was young and still finding his sound, but Stone could tell he had uncommon talent. They cut four sides, including "St. Pete Blues." To put them out, Stone created his first record label, Rockin' Records.

The track was successful enough to keep Stone in the business of releasing records. As the 78 rpm record gave way to 45s and 33s, Stone landed his first million seller: Otis Williams and the Charms' "Hearts of Stone," on his DeLuxe label. As a distributor, he knew how to get his records out there. The best way was to get them played on WLAC in Nashville—on shows like "Ernie's Record Mart" hosted by DJ John R.

On a tip, Stone drove up to Augusta, Georgia, to check out a rising young singer named James Brown. By the time he got there, Brown was already signed, but Stone befriended Brown—an ornery badass even back then—and brought him down to Miami to play his first out-of-town gigs. Stone recorded Brown's band, Nat Kendricks and the Swans (otherwise known as the JBs), and scored a hit on his Dade Records with "(Do The) Mashed Potatoes."

Where none had existed before, by the late '50s, south Florida had a small, though vital, record industry brewing. Its name was Henry Stone.

If the boomtown that was Miami in the 1950s held some sort of promise to be any less racially segregated than Vienna, Georgia, Clarence Reid didn't know about it. He couldn't much tell the difference when he first came to town.

The postwar boom had drawn thousands of workers—black and white—to the city, doubling Miami's population over the course of two decades (the following decade, the massive influx of Cubans would further stretch the city's waistline). The blacks, who'd been restricted to an area called Colored Town (later known as Overtown) when they arrived en masse as railroad builders in the last decade of the nineteenth century, had stayed put and turned the neighborhood into a bustling center of black cultural life—the Harlem of the South. By the late '50s, though, Overtown was poised for a quick decline—spurred on by the decision to decimate the heart of black Miami by constructing the major north-south highway (I-95) and east-west highway (I-395) straight through it.

By then, however, many Overtown refugees had taken shelter farther north and west, in a new development called Liberty City. They were attracted there beginning in the late '30s by the new Liberty Square housing project—one of the largest of its kind in the nation, and considered quite nice at first. By the '50s, though, the area's white neighbors to the east had constructed a nine-block-long, five-foot-high brick wall to keep Liberty City residents away. As things got really bad at Liberty Square, the residents would nickname the projects Pork-N-Beans—who knows why, exactly, but it was not likely a term of admiration.

Reid arrived in Miami and joined his mother in Liberty City sometime in 1958. Soon after, he made his trip to see Henry Stone. Mr. Hunter had sent him, so Stone greeted the teenager kindly and listened to his songs. When Reid finished, Stone offered him a job: stacking records in the warehouse.

On days off from the warehouse, Reid picked up extra work carrying people's bags into ritzy Miami Beach hotels like the Fountainbleu and Eden Roc. He met all sorts of stars that way: Ella Fitzgerald, Count Basie, Duke Ellington. But, like Reid, they were just working at the beach, not staying there. Miami Beach hotels were for whites only.

He tells a story about one notable white guy he met in front of the Fountainbleu when Reid was barely out of his teens. A nattily dressed cat pulled up with an entourage in tow. A girl stopped the guy to ask for an autograph, and when he reached into his pocket for a pencil, his wallet fell on the ground. As the group turned to walk away, Reid noticed the wallet was still on the ground. He reached down and grabbed it.

"Hey mister, you dropped your wallet."

The man's bodyguards turned around ready to whip out their guns, which pissed Reid off. "Cracker-ass motherfuckers, he lost his wallet!" Reid yelled as he threw the wallet toward the man and took off running around the corner.

A few minutes later, the cops pulled up in front of Reid. "You're a mean little motherfucker, ain't ya," they said. "Mr. Sinatra wants to see you."

Frank was sitting in the lobby. "Why didn't you take it?" he asked.

"I'm not a thief," Reid answered.

Sinatra told Reid to come back later that night; he had some work for him. Then Sinatra motioned to his coat pocket. "Reach in there and get something."

Elated, Reid took the cash and headed down to the store. But at the register, the lady stopped him. "Kid, I don't have no change for a five-hundred-dollar bill."

So Reid had to go back to the hotel. "Now what?" Sinatra asked.

"Could you give me something like a ten or a twenty, so my mama won't think I stole this?"

Sinatra made change for Reid. And within a few years he was fostering change for all blacks. Just as he'd done in Vegas, Sinatra muscled the Miami Beach hotels into ending segregation. He'd asked the hotels: So, Ella and

Basie and Sammy are good enough to play here, but not good enough to stay? Then he made the hotels an offer: They play, they stay.

In the early '60s, Reid started performing as a singer himself. Between songs, he'd tear up the crowd by channeling his Blowfly persona. "How you motherfuckers doing?" he'd ask. "Your pussy looks like it's ruined." It was the blossoming of a double career—as soul songwriter Clarence Reid, and twisted rapping parodist Blowfly—that verged on Dr. Jekyll/Mr. Hyde, if not clinical schizophrenia.

Reid started going over to Criteria Studios in North Miami Beach, sweeping up the place for a month in exchange for a recording session. There, he cut his first Blowfly tracks. Though it would be another decade before the X-rated songs would be formally released, Reid pressed these early records and sold them wherever he could—at his shows, or in small record shops throughout the South. The records included songs like "Odd Balls" and "Rap Dirty"—the latter being one of the clear transitional moments between the soul-talking DJs of the South and the advent of rap music as a genre, which wouldn't happen for more than a decade.

Reid also started releasing more straightforward R&B for a small Miami label called Deep City. That's when Reid met Willie "Peewee" Clarke, a schoolteacher who was dabbling in the music business as an artist manager. The two formed a partnership and began developing new acts for Deep City. They were rehearsing a girl act in the Liberty Square projects one afternoon when a beautiful voice came wafting through the window. They looked out the window to find a thirteen-year-old girl named Betty Wright.

Wright had been singing in her family's gospel group, the Echoes of Joy, but she'd never performed secular music before—particularly the gritty soul music Clarke and Reid came up with. After convincing Wright's mother it would be OK, the songwriters took her under their wing. And when the relationship with Deep City soured over money issues, Reid and Clarke brought Wright over to Henry Stone—along with the hit single he'd been looking for, "The Girls Can't Do What the Guys Do." Released in 1968 on Stone's Alston label, it soared up to number fifteen on the R&B chart. The following year, another Reid/Clarke composition, "Nobody But You Babe"—this one recorded by Clarence Reid himself—also broke the Top 40. Convinced of their potential, Stone brought Reid and Clarke onboard full-time. This time, however, Reid was not expected to stack records in the warehouse. Stone gave Clarke and Reid full access to his recording studio and charged them with delivering hit records.

Reid and Clarke's biggest hit with Betty Wright came in late 1971, when "Clean Up Woman" shot up to number two R&B, number six pop. But by then, Alston's days—like the classic Southern soul that was its trademark—were waning. Stone had formed Alston back in 1961 to put out the first-ever single by Miami duo Sam & Dave (later made famous by hits like "Soul Man"). Since then, Alston Records—like Stax in Memphis, and the scene around Fame Studios in Muscle Shoals, Alabama—served as a regional feeder for the powerhouse independent label Atlantic Records, which in the '50s and '60s almost single-handedly brought the world a set of legendary Southern soul acts, from Ray Charles and Solomon Burke to Wilson Pickett and Aretha Franklin. This was down-home soul—not the lighter, more urbane and pop-oriented sound coming from Motown, but the sweat-and-blood sound of Southern black folks coming into their own, stretching wings and yelling out, "Here I am, now gimme a little respect." Among the most salient features of Southern soul was its prominent, undeniable bass, rooting the music in the soil and rumbling into the gut of its listeners.

Once Warner Bros. Records bought Atlantic and other popular indies, it grew into a major label with national distribution. So Atlantic no longer needed the help of regional operations like Stone's. As Alston folded, Stone embarked on a whole new musical direction—and a new label he called TK.

Alston's final single through Atlantic pointed Stone in the direction that would earn him his greatest success. On a trip to the Bahamas, Stone fell in love with a band called The Beginning of the End, whose music was Caribbean in feel, but more heavily percussive and horn-driven than calypso or reggae. The group's song, "Funky Nassau," was a contemporary take on the Bahamian traditional music style called junkanoo. In 1971, Alston released "Funky Nassau" through Atlantic, and it shot up to number six on the R&B chart.

Because Miami always had as much claim to being a Caribbean city as it had to being an American one, it wasn't a huge leap for fans of "Funky Nassau" to associate the record's sunny, party vibe with south Florida (it wasn't completely off base, in fact, given the Bahamian community in Miami, which brought junkanoo to the streets of Coconut Grove). As Stone got TK off the ground, its first release came from Herman Kelly and Life, a Miami group with a decidedly Bahamian influence (heard on the group's biggest hit, 1978's "Dance to the Drummer's Beat," which became a favorite sample for early hip-hoppers).

In 1973, Clarence Reid hired a junkanoo band to play his wedding, and it was there that a young TK staffer named Harry Wayne Casey—KC for short—first heard the unadulterated style. KC was a local white kid who, like Reid, had shown up at Henry Stone's doorstep and was put to work stacking records. But late at night, KC and a young TK engineer named Rick Finch would head into the studio. With Reid's help, they made a record rich with junkanoo's raucous percussion and parade spirit called "Blow Your Whistle." To release the single, KC and Finch put together KC and the Sunshine Band, and the track reached a respectable number twenty-seven on the Black Singles chart. In 1974, KC and Finch made a record, "Rock Your Baby," that TK artist George McCrae took to number one—it was one of the first twelve-inch singles to gain popularity not from radio play but from the discothéque, a sign of important shifts to come. When George's wife, Gwen McCrae, hit the top ten (number one Black Singles) the following year with the Reid/Clarke composition, "Rocking Chair," TK Records was on a roll. The label's signature style—remnants of '60s soul mellowed out and then pepped up with a Caribbean-inflected disco beat—became known as the "Miami Sound."

Then in 1975, things went nuts. KC and the Sunshine Band hit number one with "Get Down Tonight," then again with "That's the Way (I Like It)," and a third time in '76 with "(Shake, Shake, Shake) Shake Your Booty." The group would hit the number-one or -two spots four more times before the end of 1980, making it one of the most successful acts of the era—a defining force in the rabid music/cultural movement that was disco. By extension, TK—which also scored huge hits with Anita Warren's "Ring My Bell" and Ralph McDonald's "Calypso Breakdown" (from the *Saturday Night Fever* soundtrack)—became one of the disco era's signature labels, with twenty-three gold or platinum records. With the Miami Sound, south Florida music became a national focus for the first time, its lighthearted party jams closely associated with the tropical playland for which the city had come to be known.

Meanwhile, Blowfly was still buzzing around. When Reid wasn't holed up in the TK studio, he was on the road with the likes of Redd Foxx, bringing his brand of profane musical humor—think Weird Al Yankovic mixed with Richard Pryor—to chitlin' circuit clubs and frat houses across the country. Finally, one day Henry Stone took note. He heard Reid banging out piano chords and singing "Shitting on the Dock of the Bay," and he agreed to put out Blowfly records. First came *The Weird World of Blowfly* in 1973, then

Blowfly on TV. In 1977, Blowfly released *Porno Freak*, notable for two reasons: First, because its title track featured one of the earliest raps of what was about to become the hip-hop era; and second, because the record made it onto the *Billboard* chart—thereby drawing enough notice to get itself banned. In 1978, a record clerk in Pineville, Louisiana, got arrested for selling *Porno Freak*—foreshadowing the trials that would befall Miami's 2 Live Crew more than a decade later.

Then, sometime in late 1979, the disco backlash kicked in. By 1981, TK was out of business, and Miami was once again a musical backwater. For Reid, TK's demise hit particularly hard. For most black artists that got started in the '50 and '60s, record contracts were either loose, grossly unfair, or nonexistent. While Stone collected royalties on Reid's hits, TK functioned like a bank for Reid. As he describes it, he withdrew money as needed—a couple thousand here, a few there—enough to keep him happy, but probably not as much as he actually had coming to him by today's standards. And when TK went away, so did Reid's "bank account." By then, though, black culture had caught up with Blowfly, and rap music was the hot new style. So Reid just kept on doing what he'd done for decades and started a new career as Miami's—and the world's—first "dirty rapper."

Henry Stone was also down but not out. By 1982 he'd formed Sunnyview Records and its more urban offshoot, Hot Productions. Disco's quick demise left Stone, and the many Miami record people who'd started out with him, looking desperately for the next big thing coming out of Miami. And of course, it had already been brewing on the streets for years.

HIP-HOP COMES SOUTH

The basic creation myth of hip-hop has been well codified over the decades: DJ Kool Herc moves from Jamaica to the Bronx, bringing Kingston's DJ/sound-system culture with him and applying it to the funk records blasting out of the mean streets of New York, circa mid-70s. It's simplistic by necessity, as all creation myths are. And, of course, it's by no means the entire story.

No doubt the musical revolutions going down in the Bronx were the key catalyst for hip-hop's birth, and no doubt the Bronx style was the single biggest influence as the music spread in the early '80s, birthing regional hip-hop. But Kool Herc was not the only guy with a direct line to Jamaica, and so it wouldn't be fair to discount the possibility that some regional hip-hop materialized, in some part, on its own accord. Or, at least, it imbued the music with its own unique alchemy that was not entirely dependent on New York.

Miami, of course, had plenty of direct links to hip-hop's Caribbean roots. Again and again, you find prime players in the story of Miami hip-hop with direct connections to the islands. But there's a connection that's more subtle than actual family ties—something all-pervasive in Miami. The climate, proximity, and culture—drawing elements from Cuba, Jamaica, the Bahamas, Haiti, the Dominican Republic, and Trinidad—imbue Miami with an atmosphere that is, at heart, Caribbean.

Like Caribbean music, Miami styles have always been a little bit faster, a little bit sexier, more concerned with the party than The Message. It is music as a release, and the more visceral the release—the more you can actually *feel* the music—the better.

No one involved in the early Miami DJ crews can recall being directly influenced by the Jamaica sound systems. But given that Miami crews sprung up around the same time as those in New York, it's possible that a direct Caribbean influence existed. Of course, it could simply be that the idea of mobile DJing—of setting up speakers and turntables in the park and rocking a party on the spot—is simply a good idea that developed independently in more than one city.

Whatever the case, by the late '70s, black Miami had at least a handful of popular DJ crews operating in the parks, at school dances, and at skate rinks. And just as Stone's TK alumni would go on to act as key players in Miami hip-hop, so too would the most popular Miami DJs move on to become artists and label heads in the South's first successful rap scene. The meeting of Stone's music industry with the early street DJs would go a long way in shaping Miami hip-hop.

There were the South Miami DJs, the International DJs, the Space Funk DJs, the Triple M DJs, the Party Down DJs, the South District DJs, the Pony Express DJs (which evolved into influential mix-tape DJs Jam Pony Express), and the Ghetto Style DJs. Each had its own sphere of activity—certain neighborhoods, certain schools. And strong rivalries existed. On the weekends, crews set up in local parks, or just on random street corners in Liberty City. If they didn't have a generator for power, they'd tap into the street lights or pay the owner of a nearby house twenty dollars to string an extension cord from it. And when more than one crew showed up, battles commenced.

The bottom line in battles was getting a response from the crowd—motivating the gathered people with chants and rhymes—and whoever did that best won. Moving the people involved making them feel the music—setting the bass knobs to full blast, rumbling the low end through their bellies, making their shirts move from the vibrations when they stood in front of the speakers. The DJs used special bass enhancers and played only the records with the most bass. They'd play whatever the crowd wanted to hear—funk, disco, freestyle, early New York rap singles—but from the start, bass asserted itself as the key hook that Miami DJs used to grab hold of audiences.

Weekend gigs in the park happened spontaneously, and the DJ crews usually did them for free—a promotional appearance to get the word out and score gigs at schools and private parties. The most popular crews translated success on the street to regular work in the roller rinks, where Southern black teens typically gathered in the early '80s.

Among the most popular Miami crews at the time was the Ghetto Style DJs, led by Luther Campbell, a DJ and party promoter just barely out of his teens. Campbell, who grew up in Liberty City as the youngest son of a Jamaican immigrant father, provided a gregarious presence behind the decks and on the mic. Along with his Ghetto Style cohorts, Campbell liked to make the records talk to the crowd by injecting his own tag to localize the records. He also remembers using dub reggae records like "Every Posse Get Flat" to knock the crowd out with heavy bass. He'd slow down the record to make the bass notes boom impossibly low. "Everybody lost it," he recalls.

After a stint at the teen disco Studio 183, Campbell and crew set up a regular party at the Sunshine skate rink on 199th St. and NW 2nd Ave.—they called the event the Pac Jam. Kids would start out skating to mixes delivered by the Ghetto Style DJs, then hang up their wheels and meet in the center of the rink to dance. These nights quickly became hugely successful, and Sunshine wasn't the only skate rink that had been invaded by the DJ crews.

The South District DJs had moved to Miami in the mid-70s from "Down South"—Homestead, Florida, a town forty-five minutes farther down the coast, in what Miamians considered the sticks. "They had funny looking speakers, and they were funny looking guys, country guys," Campbell recalls. Edward Meriwether and Charles "Pop" Young headed the crew until they decided to start a business selling pagers. One of their crewmates—a young Cuban named Norberto "Candyman" Morales—stepped up by buying their equipment and opened a skate rink of his own, the Bass Station.

A third rink, Superstars Rollertech, on 79th Street in Liberty City, soon emerged as the favorite. It was owned by members of the Miami Dolphins, including all-pro lineman Larry Little and a prominent local black entrepreneur named Willie Taylor. Superstars hired the Party Down DJs, led by a young electronics whiz named "Pretty" Tony Butler, as the in-house crew. Willie Taylor's nephew, Rick Taylor, also hung around the place and, after Pretty Tony dubbed him Disco Rick, he also got his start DJing at the rink.

By 1982, hip-hop had started to shift from being viewed as a novelty to becoming acknowledged as a new genre of music. Going back to 1979, dozens of rap songs had been released on New York labels such as Sugar Hill, Tommy Boy, and Profile, and they'd quickly reached all urban corners of the country, Miami included. But aside from picking up on the party chanting of the DJ crews, and besides Blowfly—who was by then nearly forty and a generation removed from the new hip-hop kids—there's little evidence that anyone at this point in Florida had actually taken up rapping as a form of expression or entertainment.

Still, the sound of hip-hop was beginning to make a very deep impact. The record that launched a million hip-hop producers (in Miami and elsewhere): "Planet Rock," Afrika Bambaataa & Soul Sonic Force's 1982 breakthrough. One of the original Bronx hip-hop DJs in the '70s, Bambaataa had always exhibited broader music tastes than the standard funk breakbeats. So when he discovered the electronic sounds being created by the German group Kraftwerk, he got the idea to appropriate the style on a rap record. He teamed with Tommy Boy's in-house producer, Arthur Baker, and borrowed liberally from Kraftwerk's hit "Trans-Europe Express." The result was hip-hop's first seismic shift: a move away from using previous recordings of live bands as backing, and toward the synth-and-drum-machine-generated electro-funk sound.

The essential tools of "Planet Rock": the synthesizer, which in the early '80s was still a fairly expensive and rare piece of equipment outside high-end recording studios; and the Roland TR–808 drum machine, one of the first programmable beat boxes, which first hit the market in late 1980. Unlike more realistic sounding drum machines, such as those being made by Linn, the 808's synthetic timbre proved much more appealing to people like Bambaataa, who were exploring the future in their attempt to tame technology—and make it funky. And the folks in South Florida—forever on the lookout for the future of party music—couldn't get enough of it.

Among the first Miami producers to pick up on the electro-funk sound was a white telephone technician from Broward County named James Mc-Cauley. Recording under a whole slew of aliases (foremost among them the

P-Funk-inspired Maggotron, as well as DXJ and others), McCauley first tried his hand at electro within months of the release of "Planet Rock," recording his track, "Computer Funk," as part of the duo Ose in 1982. His breakthrough came with 1984's "Invasion From Planet Detroit," released under the name Planet Detroit.

Pretty Tony, onetime head of the Party Down DJs, created the more noise on a national level, making him Miami's first post-disco act of note— and on some level, the first significant Southern black artist of the hip-hop era. From 1983 to '85, his group Freestyle released tracks like "Freestyle Express" and "Summer Delight," which featured a basic synth line and an 808 beat, accompanied by funky guitar chopping and an R&B vocal line. Tony's biggest hit, "Lookout Weekend," was a 1984 track credited to the vocalist Debbie Deb. When groups like New York's Lisa Lisa & Cult Jam began hitting the pop charts with a similar sound, the quasi-genre called itself freestyle (or Latin freestyle). Tony claims his group inspired the name, and there isn't much evidence to counter his claim.

But Pretty Tony's most significant record, 1984's "Fix It in the Mix," was not a freestyle track at all, but rather a "Planet Rock"-influenced creation of studio technology—including vocoder, laser sounds, and lyrics that suggest the utopian potential of the new digital world: "If you got a problem that you cannot really fix, let me hear your problem and I'll fix it in the mix."

Meanwhile, back up in New York, the "Planet Rock" phenomenon made the 808 the tool of choice among emerging artists. New York producers were particularly drawn to the 808's unrealistically low, booming bass-drum sound—ostensibly one of its many "flaws" that caused Roland (unaware of its street-level vogue) to discontinue production of the machine. DJ PappaWheelie, a one-time Miami bass producer who has since become one of the genre's historians, points in particular to Def Jam's co-founder Rick Rubin as the first big New York producer to explore the 808's potential for heavy, pounding bass. In that sense, he considers "It's Yours," the Rubin-produced 1983 track by T LaRock and Jazzy Jay, the first bass-music track.

There's no denying the huge influence records produced by Rubin (Run-D.M.C., LL Cool J, the Beastie Boys) had in the mid-80s, the point where hip-hop truly started to be performed and recorded throughout the country. South to Miami and west to California, the 808's resonant kick drum became an essential part of hip-hop's landscape. As it turned out, the sound wouldn't last long in New York: Samplers took over in the late '80s, blasting wide open the possibilities for drum sounds and moving hip-hop forward into yet another stage. But in Miami, at least, bass settled in for the long run and, even as new technologies were integrated, the boom never really left.

Billy Hines came to Miami from Brownsville, Tennessee, in 1959. He was nineteen and just looking for something more exciting than Brownsville. After a couple of decades working various jobs open to black men of limited education, he started his own operation selling records at the Swap Shop, a monster-sized flea market that still counts as one of Ft. Lauderdale's prime non-beach-related attractions. Around 1983, Hines expanded to an actual retail space, Royal Sounds in the Lauderhill Mall. His sixteen-year-old son, Adrian Hines, liked hanging around the record shop. When a new stack of records arrived, Adrian would take them over to the stereo and give each a test spin.

Most of these rap records came down from New York. But by 1984, Henry Stone's post-TK operation was also running strong. His Sunnyview label scored success that year with Nucleus' "Jam on It," while his Hot Productions was putting out records by Miami producer Noel Williams, a Jamaican who'd worked at Kingston's famed Studio One and appeared as King Sporty on records by Bob Marley and Dennis Brown. Relocating to Miami in the '70s, King Sporty had fallen in with Stone's circle, eventually marrying (and producing) Betty Wright. Starting around 1982, Williams made electro novelty records such as "E.T. Boogie" by the Extra T's.

Then a second Stone staff producer emerged to create what may have been Miami's first actual rap release—and the first to mine the 808 drum machine's potential for sustained bass sounds. Amos Larkin knew Stone because his father had been an artist manager in the '70s who represented TK acts. In the early '80s, Larkin worked as an assistant at Middle Ear, the Miami studio owned by the Bee Gees. He heard early rap records and decided to try his hand at making some; Henry Stone, learning quickly of rap's commercial potential, expressed interest in putting them out. So Larkin recruited a Puerto Rican rapper named Mighty Rock, who—recording under the various names Double Duce, Double Dose, and Heavy Dose—released a series of singles in 1985 that did very well regionally: "The Beat Is Fresh," "We Got the Beat," "School Breakdown."

Adrian Hines and his friends hanging out at Royal Sounds took note of Larkin's local creations. Billy Hines, meanwhile, watched the enthusiasm with which the kids snatched up these latest hip-hop records and were aspiring to make records of their own. He talked about it to his friend Frank Cornelius, a producer and part of the Florida family that brought the world the easy-listening soul of Cornelius Brothers and Sister Rose (whose two 1972 hits, "Too Late to Turn Back Now" and "Treat Her Like a Lady," remain standards on oldies radio). Together in 1984, they conspired for Billy to start up his own record label, 4 Sight, with Cornelius producing.

For 4 Sight's first single, Hines recruited a Royal Sounds customer named Ervin German, who rapped under the name MC Chief, and a store clerk they called Sexy Lady to record a song called "Beef Box." The track conflated two current vogues: the "beat box," or drum machine, and the popular mid-80s Wendy's hamburger ad slogan "Where's the beef?" Given early rap's penchant for novelty, 4 Sight's co-optation of the catchphrase seemed a safe bet, and sure enough, it became a regional hit.

The 4 Sight label followed with records by other Royal Sounds customers. First came "Radio Mars," another vocoder-driven man-machine electro jam from James McCauley (as Maggotronics). Then Gigolo Tony and Lacey Lace came with "The Parents of Roxanne," their entry into the flourishing line of "Roxanne, Roxanne" answer records. Then, while doing a show in Georgia, Gigolo Tony met an Atlanta rapper named MC Shy-D and introduced him to Hines. Shy-D was the Bronx-born cousin of hip-hop pioneer Afrika Bambaataa, and his relocation to Atlanta made him not only some sort of original hip-hop missionary, but also the first rapper to emerge from Georgia. (A year later, 4 Sight also released what was likely New Orleans' first national rap record: the Ninja Crew, featuring rapper Gregory D.)

Shy-D debuted on 4 Sight with his 1985 single "Rapp Will Never Die," a fairly straightforward electro-style track featuring a heavy 808 bass and an interpolation of "The Pink Panther Theme." The song's lyrics, which lionize New York hip-hoppers from Grandmaster Flash to Run-D.M.C. as if they were established history (rather than close contemporaries), gives an indication of just how fast things were moving at this point in hip-hop, and just how much Southern rappers took their cues from New York.

In late 1985, Billy Hines brought his son Adrian in to record as an eighteenth birthday present. By then, the idea of putting a heavy bass drum in the mix to intensify the beat was well established. From party DJs turning their bass knobs way up to rap producers laying down 808 kick drums, the boom had become ubiquitous. Locally, Amos Larkin was the master of this style, so Billy Hines hired him to produce his son's track.

Recording as MC A.D.E., Adrian Hines created his own barely disguised version of Kraftwerk's "Trans-Europe Express" as distilled through "Planet Rock"—with the obligatory novelty element: an intro and closing lifted from the theme to TV's *Green Acres*. He called the song "Bass Rock Express," and used the sparse, spoken lyrics to list the equipment used in creating and enjoying bass-heavy music. This may well have been the first time anyone had actually talked about the phenomenon of bass on a record and, in essence, put a label on the newly emerging genre. When A.D.E. scored a hit with the song (huge in the South, it even reached number forty-two on the national dance chart), bass music for the first time had a name. And as New York hip-hop began to move away from the sound, Miami asserted itself as the place for bass.

2 LIVE IS WHAT WE ARE: MIAMI BASS BOOMS

Chris Wong Won was born in Trinidad to parents of mixed Asian and African ancestry. In the late '70s, still in his early teens, Wong Won moved to Brooklyn, where he witnessed firsthand the formative years of hip-hop. After graduating from high school in 1982, Wong Won joined the military and ended up, two years later, stationed outside of Los Angeles, at March Air Force Base.

Without many hard-core hip-hop fans on the base, the few around bonded quickly. Wong Won, who worked in medical records on the base and had started writing rhymes, heard about a cook named David Hobbs, who DJed up in the dorms. Hobbs, a California native, had been inspired to start DJing while stationed in England the year before, when he first saw Afrika Bambaataa perform. Along with a second rapper, a New Yorker named Yuri Vielot, they began pooling their records together and throwing parties at the base and in nearby Riverside, California. Before the end of 1984, the trio had become the group called 2 Live Crew, featuring DJ Mr. Mixx (Hobbs) and rappers Fresh Kid Ice (Wong Won) and Amazing V (Vielot). They released a debut single—"The Revelation" backed with "2 Live" (sometimes called "It's Gotta Be Fresh")—on their own Fresh Beat label, distributed through Macola Records, the Southern California label that later brought the world early N.W.A. records.

"The Revelation," with its electro-synth line and hand claps, was typical of hip-hop records coming out of California in the mid-80s, and Amazing V's socially conscious lyrics are hard to square with the party music the group started making only a year later. Club DJs found "2 Live"—with Fresh Kid's lighter subject matter, Mixx's turntable scratching, and throbbing 808 beat—more attractive, despite its awkward rhymes. The track offers evidence that the sound that would evolve into Miami bass was being explored in California as well (further proof came with Rodney O's 1986 hit, "Everlasting Bass").

Back in Miami, the force was with Luther Campbell—Uncle Luke had even altered his stage name to Luke Skywalker (soon amended to Luke Skyywalker, as if the extra *y* might somehow fend off George Lucas' trademark lawyers). Building on the Ghetto Style DJs' popularity, Luke spun off a show-promoting business that provided a stage for up-and-coming local talent as well as rising national stars, including Run-D.M.C. And in 1985, Luke moved his Pac Jam party out of the skate rink up on 199th and into its own full-time space, more centrally located in Liberty City, dubbed the Pac Jam Teen Disco.

Luke now had a reputation as a DJ who could make or break a record in Miami. He figured if he could embrace a completely unknown record and make it a local hit by playing it in the clubs as a DJ, he could then bring the act to town for little money and earn more profits as a promoter. So when he found the group, he set the wheels in motion.

Luke discovered 2 Live Crew's single among a stack of new releases. He liked what he heard—particularly the self-promotional opportunity provided by "2 Live," with its line: "Like Luke Skywalker, I got the force/Whenever I rhyme I am the boss." He called the number listed on the record and told the group, "Your record ain't hot down here, but I can get it hot. All I want you to do is come down and do a show for me. You'll be selling records in the next three weeks."

In truth, Luke was the only one calling 2 Live Crew with an offer, so they took vacation time from the base and flew to Miami. The record took hold in Florida and they returned for more shows. While back in California, the group—now just Fresh Kid and Mr. Mixx, after Amazing V departed—recorded a second single, "What I Like." Its lyrics seem laughable now: "I need a girl that I can hold, cuddle in my arms till I grow old." It was the last 2 Live Crew track to feature anything close to this attitude toward female companionship.

Meanwhile, Luke slowly tested the waters of making records himself. With the Ghetto Style DJs, Luke had been at the forefront of shepherding new dance moves onto the floor, which amounted to something of an obsession for Miami kids, with new dances created—and named—at every lift of the needle. One bass producer recalls "The George Jefferson" and "The Robocop," and later, "The Cabbage Patch" and "The Prep," among dozens of other dances popping up. Ghetto Style parties were particularly sexually charged, with Luke on the mic encouraging the hormonally charged teens to get increasingly nasty. So his audience developed a dance called "Throw the Dick"—a move that, as it sounds, roughly simulated intercourse—and Luke asked 2 Live Crew if the group wanted to make a record of it.

So 2 Live Crew returned to the studio and created "Throw the D," a track based around a TK Records/Miami Sound classic, Herman Kelly and Life's "Let's Dance to the Drummer's Beat." The B-side, "Ghetto Bass," served as a tribute to the Ghetto Style DJs and further solidified "bass" as a focal point for this new hip-hop offshoot. To release the single in February of 1986, Campbell formed his own label, Luke Skyywalker Records.

Luke had all the tools he needed to make "Throw the D" a local hit. As one of the big club DJs, he played the record constantly. As a promoter, he made sure 2 Live Crew made the rounds in the clubs, including his own Pac Jam. And having been an intern at Miami's main urban station, WEDR 99 Soulstar (later renamed 99 Jamz), he had connections on the radio as well. At WEDR, on-air DJ Steven J. Grey got an edited version of "Throw the D" on the air. (Grey recorded his own single, "Miami," for Luke Skyywalker Records later that same year.)

At competing urban station Hot 105, DJ Laz also took to the track immediately. "The first time I heard 'Throw the D' I was like, this thing is a monster," Laz recalls. "And I just started playing it and playing it, and the response was ridiculous. It had all the elements: the hard-hitting bass, the lyrics, Mr. Mixx cutting and scratching in the background, everything that was becoming big. And they just took it to a whole other level."

Within a few months of the release of "Throw the D," both Fresh Kid Ice and Mr. Mixx got their releases from the air force and moved to Florida. They brought with them a Riverside teen named Mark Ross, aka Brother Marquis, as 2 Live's new third member. Upon arriving in the Sunshine State, the trio got working on 2 Live Crew's debut album.

The members of 2 Live Crew had heard their share of X-rated black Southern musical comedians like Blowfly and Rudy Ray Moore (Dolemite), but until "Throw the D," they'd never aspired to creating sexually explicit material on their own. But they noticed right away that the people of Miami responded much more enthusiastically to sexual stuff like "Throw the D" than they had to the group's first records. So they decided to focus on making up dirty rhymes.

A second change took effect in Florida: Luke's influence, already important as the group's de facto manager and record label owner, became even more primary. Because Mr. Mixx was more of a behind-the-scenes scratch

DJ—not the party-motivating DJ Floridians expected—Luke joined the group on stage, acting as the hype man and delivering his rhythmic chanting to get the crowd excited. Luke's style had always been nasty, so that's what 2 Live Crew became as well.

The dirty side of 2 Live Crew hit full steam with its debut album. After an introductory title track, *2 Live Crew Is What We Are* kicks off with what had to be one of the most explicit declarations heard in commercial music up to that point. The song starts with a bass boom, a half-note that echoes alone long enough to imply a slow tempo. But then the third bass boom kicks into quarter notes, revealing a tempo that's quite fast—noticeably faster than the early bass records from Amos Larkin or 4 Sight Records, if not quite as fast as Miami bass would eventually become. And then, the call and response bursts out: "Somebody say, Hey, we want some pussy! Hey, we want some pussy!" Miami bass—and, by extension, hip-hop—would never be the same.

No time was wasted by 2 Live Crew in following up with a second album, 1987's *Move Something*. It was possibly the first Miami bass record to feature on its cover the backside of a scantily clad black woman—a connection between bottom-heavy ladies and bottom-heavy music that would be drawn forever more. And on the back cover, where Luke had been listed only as "manager" on *What We Are*, he now got top billing as a member of the group.

Despite some surprises—the pro-female empowerment of "With Your Badself" and Mr. Mixx's finely scratched and densely compiled "Mega-Mix II"—the record mostly continues to play puerility and, at times, misogyny for laughs, with X-rated lyrics set, a la Blowfly, to familiar tunes. The group's rewrite of Manfred Mann's "Do Wah Diddy" earned 2 Live Crew its first spot on the *Billboard* hip-hop singles chart (sample lyric: "I met this bitch standing on the block/Singing doo wah diddy diddy dum diddy doo/She'll suck on my dick if I buy her a rock"), while "One and One" pulled a similar job on the Kinks' "All Day and All of the Night."

Though lacking charm, crowds certainly found infectious the exuberance and sheer brazenness with which the group chanted. One chant in particular—"H-B-C," or "Head, Booty, and Cock"—brought the term "booty" back to town (last heard in KC's "Shake Your Booty") and, in doing so, contributed to Miami bass' shift toward the dog-in-heat style known as "booty music." Even more than 2 Live's debut, *Move Something* raised the bar significantly for what could be said on a commercial record.

While no one dared rival 2 Live Crew in its taste for nastiness, other Miami bass groups embraced the sexual as well. Henry Stone's Hot Productions introduced the Gucci Crew II, a trio of friends from Miami Edison

High School in Liberty City, led by former Superstars Rollertech DJ Disco Rick. The group hit in 1987 with "Sally (That Girl)," a mildly naughty ditty with a sing-song rap that stands as one of the era's catchier moments. Gucci Crew got more explicit on later albums, and when Disco Rick broke away to form a second bass group, the Dogs, the explicit sexuality matched 2 Live Crew's in vulgarity, if not popularity.

Orlando DJ Magic Mike also emerged in '87 and would soon assert himself as the genre's aesthetic antidote to 2 Live Crew and booty music. As early Miami bass artists ventured beyond south Florida on tours, they'd pass through Orlando clubs like the New York Times and Electric Avenue. They'd encounter Michael Hampton, who was paying his way through college by working as one of the town's most popular club DJs. One rising bass artist named Clay D offered Mike a chance to come to Miami to record, and Mike—who'd already begun working with a group in Orlando, the Royal Posse—jumped at the chance for entry into Miami's now-flourishing hip-hop scene.

During Mike's week in Miami, he and Clay D busted out two tracks— "Boot the Booty" and "Creep Dog"—that, when released by rappers Cool Rock and Chaszey Chess, significantly upped the ante on bass music's sophistication. "Booty," along with 2 Live's "H-B-C," solidified the booty style as bass music's dominant flavor. Unlike later booty music, criticized as formulaic and one-dimensional, Clay and Mike lifted the genre with intricate scratching and nods to Pretty Tony's freestyle/electro sound. "Creep Dog" was even more impressive—a collage of CHIC and Michael Jackson samples, "Planet Rock" orchestral stabs, scratches, and an infernal bass rumbling and rolling below it all.

Mike and Clay's collaboration continued sporadically over the following year—most notably, on Clay D and the Get Funky Crew's influential 1988 booty bass record *You Be You and I Be Me*. But Mike was soon on the outs with Clay, and with the Miami music industry as a whole. Disappointed by his failure to get proper credit as a producer on the tracks he made with Clay, and unhappy with the record labels he dealt with, Mike headed back to Orlando to get his own operation going. But not before he contributed to one more seminal 1987 Miami bass track.

Like Luke, a DJ-turned-club-owner-turned-label-head, Norberto "Candyman" Morales had also spun off his skate rink, the Bass Station, into a record label. His secret weapon was a producer named Eric Griffin, or Eric G, a former WEDR DJ who'd been part of the Triple-M sound system and

Worse 'Em Crew. The Bass Station label's big break came when Griffin found a pair of white kids from Palm Beach with an undeniable track. Working together, Eric G and the duo, Dynamix II, created an electro-bass breakthrough called "Give the DJ a Break."

An ever-shifting collage of electro vocoder, sampled snippets, sound effects, scratches, and thumping bass beats, the song earned special interest because of its multitoned bass. They used the new technology enabled by the EMU SP–12 sampler to create a bass drum sound that changed tones in the middle of a measure and, in effect, turned the booming bass beat into a dynamic bassline. The song caused an immediate sensation, garnering near-constant radio play in Miami and going gold nationally by year's end.

Bass Station's success, however, was short-lived. At the time, Candyman rented a house in the Carol City neighborhood from his former South District DJs partners, Charles "Pop" Young and Edward Meriwether. Dynamix's David Noller recalls that the place "was in the heart of the ghetto, but it was a huge, lavish house with electric gates and statues, fountains, a huge basketball court." The guest house out back had been renovated with a recording studio, where Eric G worked on tracks.

One day in late 1987, however, a visitor came to the house and unloaded a pistol into Candyman's back, then into the belly of his pregnant girlfriend, killing both of them. While unsubstantiated, the common interpretation of Morales' Candyman nickname, and his reputation, involved a drug connection. This was, after all, Miami, where large segments of the music industry—large segments of lots of industries—tie in with the drug trade.

In fact, the same year, an Atlanta court convicted Miami bass pioneer Pretty Tony of drug possession. His incarceration, though he only served a year of his six-year sentence, effectively put the breaks on his career.

In the wake of Candyman's murder, Meriwether and Young stepped back into the music business and formed Suntown Records as a sort of successor to Bass Station. For Young, it became something of a family affair: His oldest son, Derek "Hollywood" Young, helped run the operation, while his second son, Charles Jr., appeared on Suntown as a rapper. Pop's third son, Maurice, who'd have only been about eleven or twelve during Suntown's heyday, liked to help out around the office. A decade later, after both he and his father endured prison stints and Hollywood was murdered, Maurice hooked up with Luke and emerged nationally as the rapper Trick Daddy.

Suntown happened to be located next door to the studio where Magic Mike and Clay D had been recording. Hanging around one day, Mike met Suntown producer Ron Whitehead and together they created another dynamic production—complete with a James Brown–style Southern funk guitar riff—tied to Magic Mike's brief sojourn in Miami. Mike, however, didn't like the money Suntown was offering and he walked away with the track unfinished. A few months later he started hearing his song on the radio—as "Give It All You Got," released on Suntown by the group Afro-Rican. By then, Mike had returned to Orlando and released an album, with his Royal Posse group, on a new label that catered to him called Cheetah.

If any doubt remained that a new style called bass music had arrived—the first hip-hop sound to emerge from the South—awareness of the subgenre exploded in the late '80s. Pandisc, a Miami label formed by former WEDR music director/DJ Bo Crane, recruited electro-bass pioneer DXJ to produce compilations such as 1988's popular *The Bass that Ate Miami* and scored success with the booty-style Splack Pack. In 1989, Henry Stone's Hot label put out the first of three *This Is Bass* compilations, featuring seminal bass tracks such as "Throw the D," "Bass Rock Express," and "Boot the Booty." Another label, Joey Boy, emerged as an outgrowth of Caribbean Manufacturing, which pressed records for all the bass labels and, as such, could see that this stuff was beginning to sell. Caribbean owner Jose Armada Sr. let his son Joey launch the label, which signed Disco Rick's The Dogs, Uncle Al, and the Miami Boys, among others.

"Bass" itself—in song titles, lyrics, or simply in the mix—was a constant theme in the music. While some New York acts, such as Original Concept, continued embracing bottom-heavy hip-hop even after Miami bass emerged, for the most part the Northeast left the sound to the Southerners. The Brooklyn group Stetsasonic acknowledged the genre with its 1988 tribute song, "Miami Bass." But to some degree, New Yorkers came to view bass music as provincial—or worse, as wack.

Meanwhile, between 1987 and 1990, the music of 2 Live Crew, Magic Mike, Clay D, Disco Rick, and others transformed Miami bass from its early reliance on "Planet Rock"-style electro and old-school novelties into something more unique: superfast (with beats-per-minute reaching up to 130 or higher), superlow (Magic Mike subtitled one of his seminal tracks the "Speaker Terror Upper"), and, of course, as nasty as they want to be.

AS NASTY AS THEY WANNA BE

As Miami bass grew in popularity, 2 Live Crew led the genre's charge into the national consciousness. But as the group's music reached white kids in suburbs far away from Miami—kids who derived from it the kind of salacious thrill once reserved for hidden copies of *Playboy*—trouble was bound to find Luke and the Crew. To understand one version of how so much trouble happened to find Luther Campbell and take him all the way to the Supreme Court, you need to go back to 1979—back when Uncle Luke was just getting started with the Ghetto Style DJs.

One day in December, five white Miami police found themselves in a high-speed chase with a black motorcyclist named Arthur McDuffie. When the chase ended in McDuffie's death, the police reported that he had crashed his motorcycle. The coroner's report questioned the cause of death and, when the policemen stood trial for McDuffie's death in May of 1980, a sixth police officer testified that the five had severely beaten McDuffie when he resisted arrest. Still, an all-white jury acquitted the police.

From black centers like Liberty City and Overtown, the black rage that had been simmering for decades erupted at the verdict. A riot—the first in the United States since the civil rights era and, up to that point, the most destructive ever—raged through the city. By the time police and the National Guard restored order, eighteen people had died and eighty million dollars' worth of damage had been done. Luther Campbell remembers the riot, but can't seem to recall whether or not he was among the looters.

In the aftermath, some in black Miami found a government official to blame: Janet Reno, then the Dade County state attorney, still fifteen years away from the Clinton administration appointment that made her the first female U.S. attorney general. Though she had come into office in 1978 as a popular figure among Dade liberals, controversy led the black community to believe that her handling of police-brutality cases indicated she was biased against them.

While Jesse Jackson came to town to join other black leaders in calling for Reno's resignation, Reno took her case into the neighborhoods that had grown to hate her. She went anywhere she could to speak to the people directly, and she learned about the concerns of the black community. In particular, women revealed to her the epidemic of deadbeat dads, and so she strengthened her office's efforts to crack down on them. By the mid-80s, Reno's reputation in the black community had made a dramatic turnaround, and when the next election arrived, she ran unopposed.

By 1988, Reno was a certified folk hero among black women. Enter Luther Campbell. During the election season that year, Campbell had led a voter drive in support of Reno. What's more, Luke's cousin Anquette—who'd made her name the previous year for her 2 Live answer song, "Throw the P," and her Liberty City–inspired dance, "Shake It, Do the 61st"—released a song on Luke Skyywalker Records called "Janet Reno." The chorus, sung to the tune of "Yankee Doodle," went: "Janet Reno comes to town collecting all the money/You stayed one day, then ran away, and started actin' funny/She caught you down on 15th Ave., you tried to hide your trail/She found your ass and locked you up, now who can't post no bail?"

But the religious right had coalesced in Dade County, and out of this group came Jack Thompson, a Christian conservative lawyer from Coral Gables who posed the most formidable Republican challenge to Reno since she'd been elected ten years earlier. The campaign got ugly, with Thompson openly questioning Reno's sexual orientation. In the end, Reno was re-elected by a comfortable margin, but Thompson's campaign against Reno and her supporters did not end there.

In 1989, one of the state attorney's more vocal boosters conveniently released one of the most (perhaps *the* most) sexually explicit recordings ever offered for sale: 2 Live Crew's *As Nasty as They Wanna Be*, the group's sixteen-track epic statement of X-rated humor, sexual aggression, and all-around depravity. *Nasty* was so dirty, in fact, that the group decided to go beyond simply releasing an edited version of the record—or one with a warning sticker on it, as the group had done with previous releases. The group also released an entirely different, but still relatively racy, album: *As Clean as They Wanna Be*, which combined toned-down versions of *Nasty* songs with additional tracks such as "Pretty Woman," a parody of the famed Roy Orbison rock standard (new lyrics: "Big hairy woman, you need to shave that stuff/Big hairy woman, you know I bet it's tough").

The cleaner version of *Nasty*'s lead track, "Me So Horny"—a catchy romp built around a vocal sample from the film *Full Metal Jacket*—shot up to number one on the *Billboard* Hot Rap Singles chart, and the group appeared on Arsenio Hall's popular late-night show. At this point, a lot of people who had never heard 2 Live Crew's music began to raise eyebrows. It was not the first time 2 Live Crew's music had become a point of controversy: Both *2 Live Is What We Are* and *Move Somethin'* had gotten record-store clerks—in Florida and Alabama, respectively—into trouble for selling them. But *Nasty*'s popularity hit a particularly raw cultural nerve. This was, after all, the period between 1985— when future second lady Tipper Gore's Parents Music Resource Center spurred congressional hearings on lyrics in popular music—and 1990, when the music industry diffused the censorship debate by voluntarily agreeing to put warning stickers on records with objectionable lyrics.

As conservative groups like the American Family Association began taking note of 2 Live Crew, Jack Thompson—still smarting from his loss to Reno, and undoubtedly offended by the music—decided to use his political connections to make trouble for the group. Of course, *Nasty* was an easy target—a record even liberals found distasteful, and one that clearly fell far beyond the line of what would pass FCC standards for radio or television broadcast. Thompson recruited Florida's Republican governor, Bob Martinez, in a campaign to ban the record statewide, and Martinez thought Thompson's best bet would be to pursue an obscenity ruling on the local level. So Thompson went to Nick Navarro, sheriff of Dade's northern neighbor, Broward County, who in March of 1990, got a ruling from County Court Judge Mel Grossman to restrict the sale of *Nasty* in the county. To get their record back in stores, 2 Live Crew filed suit against Navarro. In court that June, the group garnered expert testimony from the likes of Henry Louis Gates, a foremost scholar of African American Studies, who testified that 2 Live Crew's music fell into a black oral tradition that was often risqué and intended as parody—and therefore not obscene. Still, U.S. District Court Judge Jose Gonzalez found that the album was obscene—marking the first time in U.S. history that a sound recording had been ruled as such.

Two days after the ruling, when a record store in Ft. Lauderdale sold a copy of *Nasty* to an undercover sheriff's deputy, store owner Charles Freeman was arrested, charged with a misdemeanor, and given a one-thousand-dollar fine. Soon after, Broward County sheriffs got wind that 2 Live Crew would be doing a show in the county, at an adults-only club in Hollywood, Florida. The group knew full well they were putting themselves at risk, but as Fresh Kid Ice recalls, "We just did our thing. At that time we just thought we were right."

Sure enough, deputies nabbed the group after the show. Their freedom was never at stake—road managers were ready to post bail and get them out as quickly as possible—and four months later, the group was acquitted of the charges. But the world for 2 Live Crew had changed forever. The notoriety helped record sales—*Nasty* eventually sold more than two million copies—but touring became far more difficult. The arrest fostered the group's image as criminals, and clubs were either less willing to book them or required promoters to pay prohibitively high insurance rates.

Where once 2 Live Crew was a California rap trio being managed by Luther Campbell, now it was unequivocally Luke's group—its personality inseparable from Luke's own. Campbell's role as star, manager, label head, and spokesman earned him the lion's share of attention and financial reward, but ultimately it was a deal with the devil. While the other members of 2 Live Crew were able to keep a relatively low profile and some distance from the legal wranglings, Luke would spend the next five years in a relentless string of legal cases. He'd become more of a star in the courtroom than on stage.

As 2 Live Crew became a focal point of debate over culture and free speech, the group also became familiar well beyond those who'd actually heard—to say nothing of liked—its music. Among those discovering the group was *Star Wars* creator George Lucas, who didn't want his Luke Skywalker character being connected with Luther Campbell's brand of nastiness—extra *y* or not. Lucas sued Campbell, who settled out of court for $300,000 and immediately shortened his stage name to Luke.

In addition to the obscenity charge and trademark infringement suit, the summer of 1990 brought two more legal actions to Campbell's doorstep. First, the Nashville music publisher Acuff-Rose sued Campbell for using Roy Orbison's "Oh, Pretty Woman" without permission. In fact, Campbell had been denied permission the previous year but figured he didn't really need permission anyway—though to be safe, he gave Orbison and cowriter William Dees a full writing credit, despite 2 Live Crew's new lyrics.

As the "Pretty Woman" case appeared, Atlanta rapper Shy-D—who'd jumped over to Luke Records for his 1987 release *Gotta Be Tough*—sued Campbell for underpayment of royalties. This case would take four years to settle, but would ultimately hit Luke hardest.

In the meantime, 2 Live Crew appealed Judge Gonzalez's obscenity ruling and, while awaiting trial, took its case to the court of public opinion. They found one sympathizer in Bruce Springsteen, a voice of moral authority in music, who lent permission for Luke to rework his song "Born in the U.S.A." as "Banned in the U.S.A." The song led off the album by the same name—credited as "The Luke LP featuring the 2 Live Crew"—and made the freedom-of-speech argument (to reinforce, the album's cover featured the words of the First Amendment). Elsewhere, the rhetoric was not quite as lofty. "Fuck Martinez," consisted of little more than a series of chants—hilarious in their sheer audacity, if ridiculously juvenile—directed at Florida's governor and Broward's sheriff: "Fuck Martinez, fuck, fuck Martinez!" "Fuck Navarro, fuck, fuck Navarro!" "Martinez's wife you know she suck a mean dick!" And just to show that 2 Live Crew hadn't become a bunch of protest rappers, they offered up for good measure another raunchy club hit, "Face Down Ass Up" (". . . that's the way we like to fuck").

Before splintering in yet another lawsuit—this one pitting 2 Live Crew's Mr. Mixx and Brother Marquis against Campbell for, once again, underpayment of royalties—the group put out one more studio album, *Sports Weekend (As Nasty as They Wanna Be Pt. II)*. Having seemingly exorcised their political views on *Banned*, *Sports Weekend* stuck to the old script of obsessive raunch, including "A Fuck Is a Fuck," "Baby, Baby Please (Just a Little More Head)," and "Freaky Behavior," which featured a sample of the group's spiritual godfather, Blowfly. The album's single, "Pop that Coochie"—a somewhat less explicit version of the album track, "Pop that Pussy"—made it to number five on the *Billboard* rap chart. Like "Face Down Ass Up," it offered more of the fast, hard-driving dance beat and hypersexual chants that became the bass genre's trademarks. The heavy bass was still present, but with so much other titillation it actually became a secondary element in this strain of bass music.

These tracks—"Pop that Pussy," in particular—gave name to the dance associated with bass music and Southern black clubs. Surely inspired by moves invented in strip clubs, but embraced by any woman in any club interested in getting wild and showing off her stuff, the face-down-ass-up, butt-jiggling, thong-revealing gyrations became known as "pussy-popping"—or "p-popping" in polite company. Though closely tied to bass music at first, p-popping has endured as Southern hip-hop's unofficial hoedown, from New Orleans' bounce music up through Atlanta's crunk sounds.

By 1992, 2 Live Crew had fallen apart and, though the group would reform in various incarnations over the years, it was never again the platinum-selling cultural lightning bolt it had been from 1989 to 1991. Still, the ruling made in May of '92 by the 11th Circuit Court of Appeals in Atlanta came better late than never. The court decided that Judge Jose Gonzalez had wrongly ruled *As Nasty as They Wanna Be* obscene and noted that he improperly took on the role of determining community standards himself rather than heeding expert advice. Thus, after a battle that cost Broward County a reported $100,000 to prosecute—and seemed to have little popular support—stores could once again sell the record in the county.

Luke scored some solo success with 1992's *I Got Shit on My Mind*, which introduced the turbo-fueled production work of Devastator on the superfast "I Wanna Rock" (Devastator also worked with Luke Records' Poison Clan on their high-speed, X-rated hit, "Shake Whatcha Mama Gave Ya"). Empowered by his free-speech victory, Luke had no qualms about dissing on record, whether it was the pop rappers Kid and Play ("Pussy Ass Kid and Hoe Ass Play") or Dr. Dre and Snoop Dogg ("Cowards in Compton" from 1993's *Luke in the Nude*). Fresh Kid Ice, Brother Marquis, and Mr. Mixx also released solo records during this period, though none made much noise. And in 1994, Luke and Fresh Kid reunited—along with a new member, Verb (Larry Dobson)—as the New 2 Live Crew and released *Back at Your Ass for the Nine-4*.

But at this point, where the group seemed mired in irrelevant releases that were largely ignored, Luke and 2 Live Crew made their most lofty contribution to American jurisprudence. Acuff-Rose had initially lost its 1990 lawsuit regarding Campbell's use of "Oh, Pretty Woman," but won on appeal. Campbell then appealed that ruling, which sent the case to the United States Supreme Court. There, in May of 1994, the justices ruled that 2 Live Crew's "Pretty Woman" was indeed a parody, and its use fell within the limits set by copyright law. The ruling sent out a sigh of relief throughout the community of writers, musicians, and comedians who make careers out of parody.

Of 1990's spate of lawsuits, only the Shy-D case remained unresolved. When Shy-D wound up in jail in 1991 on an aggravated assault charge, his lawyers offered to settle with Luke for $150,000, but Luke declined. Instead, Luke's lawyer bungled his defense and, in October 1994—just months after Campbell's Supreme Court triumph—a Dade County Circuit Court judge ruled that Campbell owed Shy-D $2.3 million, more than Campbell could afford to pay.

To make matters worse, Luke Records' in-house lawyer, Joe Weinberger, claimed he'd loaned Campbell $400,000 of his own money. When it became clear he would not get his money without some legal wrangling, Weinberger and two other of Campbell's creditors moved to send Campbell into involuntary bankruptcy. So Campbell made a deal with Weinberger: In exchange for $800,000 and forgiveness of Luke's $400,000 debt, Weinberger bought Luke Records' assets, including the 2 Live Crew albums and Luke's early solo records. Weinberger launched Lil' Joe Records to reissue the catalog. Campbell, meanwhile, was all but finished in his ride from street DJ to celebrity hit maker and champion of free speech. Though he'd relaunch Luke Records and get into the adult video business, he'd never regain the fame and fortune of the past.

MAXIMUM BOOM: BASS IN THE CAR AND ON THE CHARTS

While the 2 Live Crew drama played out nationally, the local Miami bass scene continued to evolve. By the late '80s, bass began to take on another cultural association beyond women with big booty: It became a focus of the subculture obsessed with car audio.

Ask people around Liberty City, and they'll tell you that car audio bass actually started far earlier, back in the early '80s. People like Disco Rick and Luther Campbell remember an eccentric dude from the 'hood named Big

Jim. "He had a white Lincoln Continental, used to ride around," Campbell recalls. "He was a big old muscle guy, real flamboyant, had all kinds of shit on his car."

When Big Jim was driving down the street, the whole block knew it. He had somehow gotten the idea to install eighteen-inch woofers in the trunk of his car and play whatever music he could find that would accentuate the low end for maximum boom. "Everybody looked at him like he was crazy," Campbell says. But eventually, big-bass car audio caught on—ushered in by technological advances in car audio in the late '80s that made it possible to pack an awful lot of sound into a fairly limited space. The technology coincided with the rise of Miami bass, when producers very consciously started pushing the levels of low end further and further. Inevitably, those who liked the visceral experience of booming bass discovered that it was all the more intense when confined inside a car. And with the bass pulses reverberating down the block as you drove by, it was a way of impressing others with your sonic power.

By 1988, car audio bass received its first tribute song. Courtesy of Henry Stone's Hot Productions, two teenage friends from Miami named Lady Tigra and Bunny D.—recording together as L'Trimm—hit with "Cars with the Boom." Far from 2 Live Crew's raunch and chauvinism, the song was cute and innocent, with a female perspective: "We like the cars, the cars that go boom/We're Tigra and Bunny and we like the boom." On the other hand, it probably encouraged the growth of car audio bass—to the annoyance of urbanites forevermore plagued by the inescapable pulsations from cars down the block—by suggesting that girls were somehow turned on by big car stereo systems. (This was Henry Stone's final hit, capping seven decades of recording Florida artists since Ray Charles. Before retiring in the '90s, Stone also earned notice for the parody album *As Kosher as They Wanna Be*, by 2 Live Jews, which featured his son, Joe Stone.)

Car audio bass caught on fast throughout the South, and then west through Texas to California. This was, logically, a phenomenon that resonated most in places reliant on cars—which explains in part why subway-riding New Yorkers never had much use for this brand of bass music. Car bass was most popular in places where driving counted as an activity in and of itself—in the warmer climates along the southern borders of the United States, where kids cruised year-round.

At first, the bass tracks getting the most play in cars were the same ones hitting big in clubs. Among the most popular acts was DJ Magic Mike, the second best-known bass artist after 2 Live Crew. In 1989, Mike and his Orlando-based crew released their debut album, *DJ Magic Mike & The*

Royal Posse, followed the next year with a solo album, *Bass Is the Name of the Game*—both considered classic statements of the powerful possibilities of bass music.

An early hit, "Drop the Bass," became a car stereo favorite; Mike recalls that people used to slow down the song to achieve even lower levels of bass. "I hated hearing my song like that, it kind of made me mad," Mike says. "So I went to the studio and designed a song that, if they slowed the bass down, it would tear the speakers up. It was done pretty much as a joke." Nevertheless, that track—"Feel the Bass (Speaker Terror Upper)"—became a sensation among car audio freaks. It was, essentially, the first track created specifically for use in cars, a practice that would soon launch an entire industry.

Leading the charge of this new car-centric bass music offshoot were two labels: Miami's Pandisc and Sarasota's Newtown. Newtown's franchise artist was Techmaster P.E.B., whose 1991 album, *Bass Computer*, warned on its cover: "Caution: Ultra Low Bass—May damage speakers." Pandisc's car-audio breakthrough came a year later, with *Techno-Bass*, by Beat Dominator, the alias of engineer Neil Case, a white Jamaican who had worked with DXJ and other electro-bass artists and later recorded as Bass Mekanik. In contrast to ghetto-style bass that tended to be more centered on vocal chanting and booty concerns, these records were more instrumental and synth-heavy—a throwback to the electro era, more closely related to emerging techno styles than to street hip-hop.

These records sold astoundingly well, some in the hundreds of thousands. A flood of compilations followed, including Pandisc's three volumes each of *Maximum Boom for Your System* and *Bass: Lo and Slo*. Many of these releases featured test sections that provided various tones to help listeners tune their car stereos for maximum impact. By its mid-90s peak, car audio bass had moved far from its Miami bass roots and became more the province of white kids at car shows than young blacks in booty clubs.

By the time booty bass reached the top of the pop charts, it had inched its way up I-95—in a ride with a booming system, no doubt—to Jacksonville, then on into Georgia. While Miami remained the place that still churned out the gutter variety of bass—groups like Splack Pack, Poison Clan, and 2 Live offshoots—acts farther north figured out that they could go mainstream by toning down the language and slicking up the production.

Leading this breakthrough were two labels led by veterans of Southern black music: First was John Abbey, an Englishman who'd started *Blues &*

Soul magazine in the U.K. before moving to Atlanta and working as advisor/manager for R&B and soul greats Clarence Carter, William Bell, and Curtis Mayfield. In 1984, he founded Ichiban Records and scored quick success with Carter's career-reviving hit, "Strokin'." But his biggest hit came once Ichiban stumbled into the world of Southern hip-hop and, in early 1993, hit number eleven on the *Billboard* singles chart with "Whoot, There It Is," by Jacksonville's 95 South. It was bass music's strongest chart showing up to that point.

The other soul-music veteran to get in on the action was former Stax Records executive Al Bell. Bell had left Memphis for Los Angeles in the '80s and, after a stint running Motown Records, started up his own label, Bell-mark Records. Like Abbey, Bell also had concentrated mostly on seasoned R&B acts but found a monster hit in 1993 with a bass song. Released one month after 95 South's "Whoot, There It Is," Atlanta duo Tag Team's "Whoomp! (There It Is)" soared even higher—to number two on the pop chart and number one on the R&B/hip-hop chart. The cumulative impact of both created a pop-culture phenomenon: "Whoot/Whoomp, there it is!" became an almost-mandatory replacement for "Well, alright!" among sportscasters and suburban housewives alike.

The obvious similarities between the two hits—the choruses were, in fact, identical—could easily have sparked lawsuits large enough to wipe away the profits from both. Questions of who ripped off whom were sure to arise: Tag Team, in fact, had recorded "Whoomp!" in Ichiban's studio, and Ichiban had considered signing the group before it discovered the similarity between the two songs. But amazingly, it was all love between the groups— they even performed together on *The Arsenio Hall Show*. It was agreed that "Whoot/Whoomp, there it is" was a black Southern catchphrase, and both songs simply adopted the cadence with which it was spoken.

In the end, the two songs proved an interesting case study for bass music producers. The fact that "Whoomp!" with its slicker, more R&B-oriented production, sold more than twice the copies of the more street-oriented "Whoot" underscored the possibilities that awaited more radio-friendly bass tracks.

While 95 South lost the battle for "Whoomp" supremacy and soon faded from sight, the producers behind "Whoot" emerged as bass music's most commercially successful artists. A pair of high school friends from Jacksonville, producers Nathaniel Orange (aka C.C. Lemonhead) and Johnny McGowan (Jay Ski) had from the start been the brains behind 95 South. When the group's two MCs broke away, Jay and Lemonhead simply created new groups to record their songs. In 1994, the 69 Boyz hit the top ten with

"Tootsie Roll," and the following year the producers scored a top-ten rap single with "Freak Me Baby," by female duo Dis-N-Dat. Then in 1996, recording as the Quad City DJs, Jay and Lemonhead scored a top-five single with "Come on Ride that Train," their most melodically sophisticated hit, as much funk and R&B as it was bass music.

As northern Florida became bass music's nexus—with Magic Mike in Orlando and Quad City DJs in Jacksonville—Georgia stepped up with a string of its own bass hits. It was an unlikely center for hip-hop: the conservative, military/industrial city of Augusta hadn't seen much musical success since James Brown emerged from there in the '50s. But that's where a half-Panamanian army brat who called himself Tony Mercedes moved as a teen. He didn't get into the music business until he was nearly thirty—before that he worked for a decade at the city's nuclear power plant, the Savannah River Site, until a radiation incident earned him a round of scrubbing down and decontamination that he didn't care to ever repeat. So he quit the plant and opened Augusta's Club Mercedes.

One day in 1992 a couple of military guys going by the name L.A. Sno and Creole D—collectively Duice—approached Mercedes with their demo and he agreed to spin it at the club. Called "Dazzey Duks," the booty bass record paid tribute to the short-shorts worn by that icon of Southern womanhood, the *Dukes of Hazzard*'s Daisy Duke. The response was immediate and overwhelmingly positive at the club, so Mercedes sent the track around to record labels. No one saw the potential, so he founded Tony Mercedes Records to distribute the song himself. Mercedes paid a visit to James Brown's Augusta office to ask the godfather's advice on starting a label. "Don't do it," was Brown's warning.

But Mercedes did it anyway, and soon he was spending weekends driving a rented van around the South to personally sell the record store-to-store. It spread, quicker than one might imagine possible. Copies wound up at radio stations, and airplay sold the record even faster. When he couldn't keep up with the distribution, he made a deal with Al Bell's Bellmark label to distribute the record. By the summer of '93, "Dazzey Duks"—with the help of a video that starred Catherine Bach (aka Daisy Duke) herself—had become one of bass music's earliest, and biggest, national pop successes.

In 1994, Mercedes hit again with a second Augusta act, 12 Gauge, whose "Dunkie Butt" mined similar territory. Mercedes' success led him to Atlanta, where he became an integral part of the city's late-90s rise as urban music's dominant city. Working behind the scenes, he brought "post-bass" hits to Atlanta's biggest hit makers: to Jermaine Dupri's So So Def (Playa Poncho's "Whatz Up, Whatz Up"); to Dallas Austin's Freeworld Records

("Who Dat," by former Poison Clan rapper JT Money); and to L.A. Reid's LaFace Records (the novelty hit "My Baby Daddy"). Reid was so enamored with Mercedes' magic touch that he hired Mercedes in 1997 to be an A&R director at LaFace.

As Atlanta put its own spin on bass music, it also contributed its own dance sensation: the Bankhead Bounce. Named for the rough west-side neighborhood, the Bankhead Bounce became a signature move for Atlanta superstars TLC. Unlike Miami booty dances, the Bankhead Bounce was rather mild and nonsexual. It involved shoulder shrugs and arm sways—a more genteel precursor to the "throw them 'bows" moves of the next decade. The dance also generated at least three 1995 singles that earned regional success: The first, "Bankhead Bounce," came from producer Diamond and up-and-coming Atlanta rapper D-Roc, who'd later become one of the Ying Yang Twins (the song's success was undercut when Diamond was arrested, and later convicted, of child molestation). The second was Kilo's "Dunkey Kong," produced by future Ying Yang Twins guru DJ Smurf (features the odd chorus: "Well, this is my pinky and this is my thumb, Bankhead Bounce, Dunkey Kong"). The third was another "Bankhead Bounce" by the A-Town Playaz.

Atlanta bass acts scoring hits in 1996 included Freak Nasty, whose "Da Dip" went to number fifteen on the pop charts, and Ghost Town DJs' "My Boo," which melded slow-jam-style R&B singing with bass beats. "My Boo" was also a single off the first *So So Def Bass All Stars* compilation, a collection of Atlanta-centric bass tracks released on Jermaine Dupri's label and A&R'd by Jonathan Smith (aka Lil Jon).

And then, bass was pretty much over. Make no mistake, the style continues in some form—as dance-club nostalgia, in the cars of the still-thriving car-audio genre, or in bass revivalists: including New York's Fannypack, whose 2003 track "Camel Toe" channeled L'Trimm; OutKast, whose bottom-booming smash of the same year, "The Way You Move," asked, "I know you're wanting that 808, can you feel that B-A-S-S bass?"; in the minimalist multitoned bass pulsations of the Ying Yang Twins' 2005 hit, "Wait (The Whisper Song)"; and in the unlikely appearance of a Brazilian music style called "Funk Carioca" or "baile funk," which is essentially Miami bass music with Portuguese lyrics, born out of the *favelas* (shantytowns) of Rio de Janeiro.

But for historical purposes, the bass era finally petered out in 1996, when tracks like "Come On Ride that Train" and "My Boo" so far diluted the bass sound as to make it almost unrecognizable. It was also the year that Luke, bass music's biggest icon, passed the baton to a new generation of

Miami hip-hoppers. Suntown Records' Pop Young was in jail at the time, but his son, Maurice "Trick Daddy" Young, decided to go straight. He won an open-mic contest that got him a guest appearance on one of Luke's tracks. The song, "Scarred," had all the elements of the bass music Luke had helped define. But when Trick Daddy launched his verse, it was clear that Miami—and the South as a whole—was ready for a harder form of hip-hop to take hold.

chapter 2

HOUSTON AND THE GANGSTA GOTHS

TEXAS HIP-HOP: LIFE ON THE HUMAN RANCH

Texans like to spread out. Of the most populated states, it's by far the roomiest—50 percent larger than California, with 50 percent fewer people. Even the Lone Star State's so-called urban areas are less like actual cities than immense human ranches: To compare, about 3,400 people on average live in each of Houston's 549 square miles, while New York City houses an average of more than 26,000 in each of its 303 square miles. Statistically, Atlanta's metro area has more sprawl, but that's because its suburbs go on forever. In Houston, however, the city *is* the sprawl. No wonder Houston is the country's fourth most populous city—it's more than half the size of the state of Rhode Island.

In part, the sprawl of Houston—and also Dallas, a smaller city, but with a larger and equally far-flung metro area—is the product of a frontier Texas-era brand of individualism. Unlike all other large U.S. cities, Houston has no zoning laws: If you own the land, you can pretty much build whatever you damn well please wherever you damn well want. So you have a skyscraper next to a residential neighborhood next to a warehouse next to a shopping center—a mass of enclaves with no real center.

And that's how Texas hip-hop has been, at least until recently: A whole lot of different things, without one dominant identity. Take, for example, three of the earliest hip-hop artists to stretch out beyond the Texas borders: DJ Premier, the D.O.C., and Vanilla Ice. None of the three was ever really associated with Texas, and their backgrounds could not have been more disparate: New York bohemian (Premier), L.A. gangsta (D.O.C.), and Miami wanksta (Vanilla Ice).

Chris Martin—the kid who'd become DJ Premier, one of New York hip-hop's most influential producers of the '90s—had family roots in Brooklyn, so New York was never the faraway spectacle it seemed to most Southerners growing up on the first generation of hip-hop. And, while he grew up in Houston, Premier wasn't a guy you'd find in the rougher 'hoods of H-Town. His mother was an art teacher and his father was a distinguished biology professor and longtime dean of Arts and Sciences at Prairie View A&M, a historically black college forty-five minutes outside of Houston.

Premier first picked up his turntable techniques from watching DJ R.P. Cola, an early Houston DJ who used to spin at the Rhinestone Wrangler, a popular hip-hop spot. After high school, Premier enrolled at Prairie View, but never took to academia. By then he had little on his mind beyond hip-hop. He started DJing at college parties as Waxmaster C and spending as much time as possible visiting his grandfather in New York. Up there, he'd check out the newest acts, then report back to his friend Carlos Garza, aka DJ Styles, who ran a record store in Houston. Garza would note Premier's recommendations and call the New York labels to have them send their records.

When Premier decided to move in with his grandfather, Styles called his label contacts to see if anyone could hook Premier up with work in New York. Stu Fine, owner of seminal hip-hop label Wild Pitch, reported that the MC for his act Gang Starr was looking to find a new DJ. So Fine hooked Gang Starr's Guru up with Premier, and the famous twosome was formed. After one album with Wild Pitch, 1989's *No More Mr. Nice Guy*, Gang Starr took off with classic records like '91's *Step in the Arena* and '92's *Daily Operation*.

Unlike the hip-hop circulating in Houston at the time—mostly car bass and gangsta rap—Premier's innovative tracks sampled heavily from jazz and played a large part in sparking the early '90s trend of jazz-inflected rap. Branching away from Gang Starr in the mid-90s, Premier became one of the genre's key producers, crafting tracks for stars like Nas, Biggie, and Jay-Z. Along the way, Premier's Houston roots have been all but forgotten, or at least deemed irrelevant.

To a large degree, the same could be said of Robbie Van Winkle, the rap phenom who, for a brief pop moment in 1990 and 1991, threatened to make rap music the territory of suburban white kids, much the way Elvis had done for rock music in the '50s. Despite his claim of having grown up in the Miami 'hood—a fiction that, when debunked, hastened Ice's meteoric fall from grace—Van Winkle actually grew up in Carrollton, a suburb just north of Dallas. Still, those who came into contact with MC Vanilla, as he was known in Dallas' late-80s rap scene, recall a guy who held his own on the mic, could break-dance as well as anyone, and who wasn't intimidated by his lack of melanin.

Performing locally at places like the City Lights, Vanilla was frequently booked as opener for groups coming through town (the other Dallas rap act to make a dent nationally in this era, the group Nemesis, was Vanilla's primary competition). After Vanilla opened for Public Enemy, Chuck D was impressed enough to try to hook him up with a record deal. Vanilla also made regular trips to Houston, where he rocked the MC weekly competitions at the Rhinestone Wrangler. There, he was a frequent combatant of William Dennis (aka future Geto Boy Willie D).

"He was OK," Willie recalls. "What I liked about him was his cockiness. He was always the one white guy in a sea of black. He just rolled, he didn't care. He'd come up and battle anybody."

After Vanilla put out a record through Atlanta indie label Ichiban in 1990, New York labels started making offers. But, as he told the zine *Backwash*, that's where everything went wrong: "I had two record deals on the table . . . one for Def Jam for thirty thousand dollars. Hank Shockley was going to produce my album, Public Enemy was going to appear on my record. And I had another deal with SBK to cross my hip-hop record to the pop market for $1.5 million. So I took the money. . . . It was like winning the lottery overnight. I didn't see the consequences. The consequences [were] being turned into a novelty act."

In his transition from local Texas battle rhymer to major-label rap crossover, Vanilla Ice traded in his standard hip-hop gear for garish genie pants and sculpted hair, and concocted easily discredited stories about his background. While his SBK debut, *To the Extreme*, still counts as one of the biggest-selling rap records of all time—and his song, "Ice Ice Baby," dominated the pop and rap charts in late 1990—within a year or so, Van Winkle's run as pop star had devolved into a long-standing gig as the butt of many '90s pop-culture jokes.

Around the same time Vanilla Ice emerged straight out of Carrollton, another MC was making moves across town in the projects of West Dallas. Tracy Curry, the rapper best known as the D.O.C., stayed out of trouble as a kid by keeping to himself and staying at home reading the dictionary. He liked rap from the time he heard "Rapper's Delight," but after checking out Run-D.M.C. and, later, Rakim, he was inspired to write. He started spitting out the dozens of songs with a neighborhood friend named Kurtis and, as he began to get positive feedback from friends and devote long hours to writing raps, Tracy—who became Dr. T—and Kurtis—who became Fresh K—formed a group, the Fila Fresh Crew.

After appearing in a local TV commercial, the group earned the notice of local club and radio mix DJ Dr. Rock, who became the Fila Fresh Crew's DJ. Dr. Rock had recently moved to Dallas from Los Angeles, and one weekend he invited a friend from L.A., the World Class Wreckin' Cru's Dr. Dre, to make a special appearance at one of his parties. Dre then invited Fila Fresh to L.A. to record with him. By then, Dre had begun collaborating with Eazy E and the group of rappers who'd appear on 1987's *N.W.A. and the Posse* album. More a compilation than a proper group debut, the record featured four Fila Fresh tracks (as many as N.W.A. contributed), including "Drink It Up," a drunken bit of fun set to the tune of "Twist and Shout," and a trio of Dr. Dre–produced hip-hop cuts.

As N.W.A.'s profile rose, Dr. T—who became Doc-T, then the D.O.C.— moved to L.A. and became part of the group's inner circle. D.O.C. was seen as a solo artist for Eazy E's Ruthless Records, but he was also recruited to write verses for Eazy and Dr. Dre on N.W.A. tracks. Aside from the lyrics Ice Cube wrote for himself, the D.O.C. is said to have penned a good part of the lyrics to *Straight Outta Compton*, N.W.A.'s 1988 classic. He also wrote lyrics for Eazy's 1988 solo debut, *Eazy-Duz-It*. Though thuggish street rap had already been brewing in New York and elsewhere, *Compton* and *Eazy-Duz-It* codified gangsta rap as a subgenre of its own. What's more, N.W.A.'s brutal tales inspired a sea of hard-core rappers and changed the language of hip-hop forever. As much as anyone, this was the work of Dallas wordsmith the D.O.C.

Respected for his N.W.A. lyrics, the D.O.C. hit the top of the R&B/hip-hop chart when he released his debut solo album, 1989's acclaimed *No One Can Do It Better*. Not nearly as explicitly violent as N.W.A., the D.O.C.'s solo material presented him as an MC on par with his East Coast heroes—a first for the West Coast, which (like the South later) was initially disparaged for its lack of strong lyrics.

A rising rap star, the D.O.C. seemed destined to become one of the great hip-hop MCs. But soon after *No One*'s release, the D.O.C. found himself on the way home from a video shoot, and the combination of fatigue and inebriation drove him off the highway. With his car totaled and his body battered, the D.O.C. was lucky to survive the accident. But, in a cruel turn of fate, the wreck crushed the D.O.C.'s larynx and took away the clear, forceful voice that had put across his lyrics with gangsta authority. His career as a major rapper was effectively over.

As the D.O.C. told Charlie Braxton in *Murder Dog*, "It started a 10-year healing process that I wouldn't understand for years to come. . . . I think that shit hurt me deeper than words can ever say."

During his years of recuperation, the D.O.C. stayed close to Dr. Dre. He ghostwrote lyrics for N.W.A.'s album *Niggaz4life*, and it was the D.O.C. who led his defection, with Dr. Dre, from Eazy's Ruthless Records, toward a partnership with Suge Knight and Death Row Records. The D.O.C. also played a pivotal role in the making of Dre's classic, *The Chronic*, and contributed to Snoop Dogg's debut, *Doggystyle*. But eventually the D.O.C. got fed up with giving his lyrics away; he broke from Dre and put out 1996's *Heltah Skeltah*. Coming seven years after his debut, *Heltah Skeltah* reflects the dark period when the D.O.C. struggled to come to grips with his misfortunes and missed opportunities. Fans were shocked and disheartened to hear the D.O.C.'s voice scratching and cracking through the record, a shadow of its former power. *Heltah Skeltah* disappeared after a short stay on the charts.

The D.O.C. more recently returned to Texas and, it seems, has begun to put his troubles behind him. Founding his own label, he released a compilation of sorts, 2003's *Deuce*, which featured his roster of Texas artists (including 6Two and Cadillac Seville) and reconciled West Coast cronies like Dre, Snoop, and Ice Cube. The record also showed that the D.O.C.'s voice had largely recovered—if not back to its original power and clarity, at least it was far beyond the scratching and cracking on *Heltah Skeltah*.

With each passing year, the chances get more remote for the D.O.C. to ever get the fame or fortune he likely deserves for his role in defining gangsta rap. But for those who know, his legend is secure. In 2004, the D.O.C.'s girlfriend, neo-soul icon and fellow Dallas native Erykah Badu, gave birth to their daughter, Puma. Even OutKast's Andre Benjamin, who now shares a "baby mama" with the D.O.C., considers him a hero. As Benjamin told *Sister2Sister* magazine, "As far as Southern rappers . . . he was like the first real rapper that we looked up to that could really rap."

HOUSTON STARTS MAKING TROUBLE

The D.O.C. was no doubt an inspiration to the Texas rappers who were discovering their voice through street poetry in the late '80s. But even before then, things were brewing in the 'hoods of Houston. And, aside from its earliest rap records, Houston's dominant flavor has always been gangsta.

H-Town's first hip-hop was, in Willie D's term, *real puffy*—that is, not the hard-core street stuff that would soon take over. Rapper K-Rino, himself one of Houston's first recorded MCs, remembers a song from the early '80s called "McGregor Park" that celebrated the place where black kids gathered on Sundays to socialize, show off their cars, and bump bass music out of their speakers. The huge stretch of streets on the south side of town below McGregor Park was, fittingly, named South Park. Largely black, South Park encompasses both hard-core slums and middle-class streets. Of Houston's two largest black centers—the Fifth Ward to the north being the other—South Park is newer, more sprawling, and less urban. And this is where much of the town's earliest hip-hop was created.

One of the earliest South Park groups was K-Rino's original trio, Real Chill, which put out a song called "Rockin' It" in 1986. Like other early Houston rap acts, such as Royal Flush and Triple Threat, Real Chill had an old-school New York flavor, but none of these acts enjoyed much success.

Curiously, while Miami bass music became popular in Houston's clubs and prominent car culture, there's little evidence of H-Towners adopting the style in their own music (Dallas, on the other had, used bass to a greater extent, as can be heard in the music of Nemesis and Ron C). The car culture surrounding bass, however, played a key role in jump-starting the group that would come to define Houston rap for a decade.

Around 1986, local entrepreneur James Smith—aka Lil' J, James Prince, or J Prince—got the idea to put out some rap music. Given his day job as the owner of a luxury used-car lot on the north side, it's possible that the first song he released—a single called "Car Freaks" by three teen rappers known as the Ghetto Boys—was meant as little more than self-promotion. Smith teamed up with a white computer software engineer from Seattle named Cliff Blodget and formed Rap-A-Lot Records.

Lil' J also brought Houston's other black center, the Fifth Ward, into the hip-hop game. Located northeast of downtown across the Buffalo Bayou, it was one of the six wards created in the nineteenth century as districts for the city's alderman (South Park is roughly part of the Third Ward, though that name usually refers to the older area closer to downtown, just north of South Park). A more historic neighborhood than its southside rival, Fifth Ward has had a distinctly African American character since the 1860s, when freed blacks settled there to work in the nearby harbor and downtown area. Fifth Ward was home to Houston's pre-rap music industry—most notably the famed rhythm & blues label Peacock Records, one of the country's earliest black-owned record companies of note and home to acts such as Bobby "Blue" Bland and Big Mama Thornton. But after decades of decline, Fifth Ward earned its reputation as the roughest spot in H-Town.

As the story goes, J encountered his little brother Thelton and some kids hanging around on the corner of the Fifth Ward's Trinity Gardens neighborhood during school hours. When J asked why they weren't in school, they told him they were working on becoming rappers. So J made them a deal: If they finished high school, he'd help them put out a record. They took him up on it and, by graduation, they'd recorded "Car Freaks." J adopted Thelton's original rap alias, Sir Rap-A-Lot, as the name of his new label, Rap-A-Lot Records, while Thelton became known as K-Nine. Featuring K-Nine and fellow rappers Jukebox and Raheem, "Car Freaks"—a bass-inspired track about girls more interested in a guy's car than in the guy himself—became a local sensation in the sprawling town that was (and is) even more automobile-obsessed than Miami.

But neither the bass influence nor the original lineup would last. Raheem went solo first, and in 1988 scored Rap-A-Lot's first national distribution when A&M Records released his album *The Vigilante*. Soon after, K-Nine dropped out as well. He tried going solo, then wound up involved with drugs (he's currently serving time in Beaumont, Texas). That left only Jukebox, and a need to recruit some new members for the Ghetto Boys.

In January of '87, DJ Ready Red moved from Trenton, New Jersey, to Houston to help out his sister, who was living in town. Out in the clubs, Red discovered a new world of music: 2 Live Crew and other bass acts coming out of Florida, as well as a local song he kept hearing that sounded like it went "corn flakes, corn flakes"; it was, he soon realized, "Car Freaks."

Within a month of arriving in Houston, Red hooked up with a group of MCs relocated from Brooklyn and Chicago called Def IV. But he was also making his rounds at the Rhinestone Wrangler, which held regular Battle of the DJs contests. In the crowd one night was a Ghetto Boys associate named NC Trahan (the group dedicated its *Grip It!* album to Trahan after he was murdered). Impressed by Red's skills on the turntables, Trahan brought Red over to Lil' J's car lot in the Heights, and Red played some of Def IV's demos for J. J liked the backing tracks more than the group (though he later signed Def IV as well), and asked Red to serve as DJ for the Ghetto Boys shows. By March of '87, the twenty-one-year-old Red was the group's official DJ.

As work started on the album that would become the Ghetto Boys' debut, Red called an MC friend from Trenton, Prince Johnny C, who moved down to Houston to become part of the Ghetto Boys' new lineup. While J and Trahan worked on lyrics, Red moved into the upstairs room at J's car lot and began constructing tracks with his Roland 909 drum machine and a pair of Technics 1200 turntables. *Making Trouble*, featuring Johnny C and Jukebox, was released in 1988. It featured New York–style old-school rap, mostly Run-D.M.C. knockoffs ("I Run This," "Making Trouble"); a Kurtis Blow–style message rap ("Why Do We Live This Way?"); innocent teen rebellion ("No Curfew"); and the kind of high-profile samples that would never fly these days ("Ghetto Boys Will Rock You" uses Jimi Hendrix's "Purple Haze" guitar intro, while "You Ain't Nothin'" lifts the guitar riff and vocal hook from Elvis' "Hound Dog"). The Ghetto Boys' one attempt at gangsta, "Assassins," stands out for its uncharacteristic brutality and misogyny, though even there the rappers refrained from using profanity and broke character at the end (laughing and saying, "we just was buggin'").

The one link connecting *Making Trouble* with the group's subsequent work is the preponderance of samples lifted from the 1983 Al Pacino movie *Scarface*. Four of the record's eleven tracks feature *Scarface* samples—sound bites of Pacino's Tony Montana saying things like, "All I have in this world is my balls and my word" and "Say hello to my little friend"—including the rap-less "Balls and My Word," which is built entirely around snippets from the film.

While working on *Making Trouble*, the Ghetto Boys met a badass dwarf named Little Billy who danced at a club called Flames. The idea of hiring a three-foot eight-inch break-dancer to romp around on stage and act as hype man seemed like a surefire attention getter, so the Ghetto Boys invited Billy into the fold. Billy was, in fact, Richard Shaw, a Jamaican-born high school dropout who grew up in the rough Brooklyn neighborhood of Bushwick. As a kid, he got involved in his neighborhood's Linden Crash Crew break-dancers, but at sixteen was sent off to Bible school in Minnesota. Bill moved down to Houston around 1985 and was living with his sister and brother-in-law at the time he became part of the Rap-A-Lot crew. Though he was not officially a member of the Ghetto Boys at that point, his presence became an important part of the group's image. Bushwick Bill, as he came to be known, appears on *Making Trouble*'s album-ending skit, "The Problem," and is even featured on the album cover. And, as Red explains. "I started putting together these Scarface concepts—'Say hello to my little friend' and all that stuff. Bill became the 'little friend,' so everything started working out for us."

As an independent release in a state that had not yet developed channels to get local rap music out to the public, *Making Trouble* did relatively well in spreading the group's name throughout Texas and the Southwest. Granted, the record's modest success was likely more a function of the area's dearth of credible acts at the time, rather than any original vision or regional flavor being offered in the music. Still, it was a start that put Rap-A-Lot on the map as Houston's most accomplished hip-hop label. For fans in Texas and surrounding states, Rap-A-Lot was revolutionary.

"Before them, they just talked about East Coast, West Coast. Nobody respected us down here," K-Rino says. "They viewed us down here in Texas as country hicks who don't know nothing about nothing. But J did something that none of these other cats did, he started an independent label, pushed it independently, didn't care nothing about radio play, worked the underground. It was dope and it sold itself. That's what put Houston on the map. It laid the blueprint for every independent record label to ever come out of the South: No Limit, Cash Money. It gave us an identity and made other cats believe we could do it."

GETO BOYS GET A *GRIP*

Willie Dennis was a product of the Fifth Ward at its most degraded. Born to unwed parents he describes as alcoholics, Willie had to raise himself from as far back as he can remember. "I had a mom who was very abusive and neglectful. Back in the neighborhood, parents preferred their kids to stay outside while they stayed inside in the cool air and did their drinking and smoking. That was my experience and I've seen my friends experience the same thing. So that had to account for a lot of the turmoil that young people experienced. No real connection, no positive interaction with their parents on a consistent basis."

But Willie was fortunate if only in that his mother's twin brother, Melvin Dennis, was a middleweight boxer of national stature. And in 1977, he watched his uncle fight Wilfred Benitez on ABC's *Wide World of Sports*. "He gave me a glimmer of hope that I could succeed on a major level," Willie says. "To see someone I knew on TV who was doing something positive, not being arrested on the nightly news, it was something special."

By giving a fake address, Willie was able to attend a better high school—Forest Brook, north of the Fifth Ward. On his way to the bus stop early each morning, he'd steal a *Houston Chronicle* from a doorstep and read it on the way to school. "I always knew that the world was bigger than Houston. It always interested me, the people who pulled the strings."

Willie heard hip-hop from its start and became a huge fan once Run-D.M.C. came around. Hanging out in the neighborhood singing songs evolved into rapping, and the more positive feedback Willie got for his rhymes, the deeper he got into it. He starting performing in other places and perfecting his improvisational freestyle skills. Then Willie learned about the Rap Attack contests held every week at the Rhinestone Wrangler, the popular southside club near the Astrodome. The event became the city's premier showcase for up-and-coming MCs, and it was here that Willie Dee discovered he was among the best rappers around.

"I used to kick ass every Sunday," he says. "The last thirteen weeks in a row that the club was open, I won all thirteen." Ready Red recalls Willie was given the title "Rankmaster" because of his skill at ranking on his opponent during freestyles.

J Prince would check out the Rap Attack contests and was certainly familiar with Willie's skills, but it wasn't until they were introduced by the barber they shared at Harvey's Barber Shop in the Fifth Ward that J invited Willie over to the car lot to audition for Rap-A-Lot. *Making Trouble* had just been released, and J told Willie he wanted to make Willie's solo album the label's next release. As J heard the material Willie was creating for his 1989 debut, *Controversy*, J asked him to also write material for the Ghetto Boys next album. Taking the group's name to heart, Willie came up with material that dealt with the lives of "ghetto boys"—hard, grimy street tales delivered with intensity and explosive anger.

By this point, N.W.A.'s *Straight Out of Compton* had hit big nationally and, Willie admits, West Coast gangsta rap "had the streets on lock" in Houston. While locals pride themselves on the Geto Boys being among rap's original gangstas—arriving earlier or simultaneous with N.W.A.—evidence suggests that Willie D and his Rap-A-Lot cohorts were intimately familiar with N.W.A. and earlier L.A. rappers like Ice-T before their own gangsta stance had fully formed. Such was N.W.A.'s monumental influence: *Straight Out of Compton* opened a Pandora's box for inner cities throughout the country that enabled people to express their own rage and depict the everyday violence and depravity as explicitly as they wanted—even reveling in the opportunities to embellish and inflate the depictions in the name of entertainment. It just happens that Houston was among the first cities to pick up the torch (and use it to set the slums on fire).

As Willie began introducing new rhymes to group members Jukebox and Prince Johnny C—hard-core tracks like "Do It Like a G.O." and "Let a Ho Be a Ho"—Lil' J became more and more convinced this was going to be the group's new style. Willie's creations went far further in terms of depicting street realities in frank, hateful language than Johnny C wanted to go, so he quit the group. J took this as an opportunity to reconfigure his Ghetto Boys as the Geto Boys: The first step was to make Willie a member of the group.

But there was another change J wanted to make. He'd been hearing a local track circulating called "Scarface" by a southside MC named Akshun, and he figured Akshun would be a perfect fit for the Geto Boys, given Red's arsenal of *Scarface* samples.

Akshun was, in fact, an eighteen-year-old rapper named Brad Jordan. His mom worked two jobs and often left her son at his grandmother's house in South Acres. He picked up playing guitar and bass from his uncles. He was a troubled kid—a loner by admission who, according to later press reports, had attempted suicide by slitting his wrists at fourteen and spent two years in and out of psychiatric care facilities. While he had a longtime passion for rock music, particularly heavy metal, by age sixteen Brad was focused on being the rapper Akshun.

He met a local producer named John Bido, who was working with a South Park street hustler named Lil' Troy Birklett to get a record label off the ground. Lil' Troy's parents had been musicians in the Third and Fifth Ward clubs, and he was trying to convert some of the money he'd made as a drug dealer into the music business. With the help of Bido and other aspiring producers from the Dead End—an infamous 'hood in the lower reaches of South Park, where (symbolism noted) Martin Luther King Jr. Blvd. dead ends—Troy set up his Short Stop label and brought DJ Akshun on board as one of its first signings.

In 1988, Akshun recorded "Scarface," a gripping gangsta tale full of movie-like action and detailed storytelling. The track caused an immediate sensation on the streets of Houston, and Lil' J set about recruiting Akshun to be one of the Geto Boys. Akshun was more than happy to get involved with Rap-A-Lot, which was at that time by far the most successful Houston hip-hop label. And Lil' Troy, who still made the majority of his income from dope dealing, was not concerned about losing Akshun—Short Stop was little more than a hobby at that point (though the fallout between Troy and Akshun would play itself out over decades in lawsuits and smear campaigns). So the deal was made and the new lineup of the Geto Boys—*Making Trouble*'s Jukebox, along with Willie Dee and DJ Akshun—started work on the group's second album, *Grip It! On That Other Level*.

"The first day I met Scarface [Akshun] was the day J picked me up to go record the album," Willie recalls. Despite the northside/southside rivalry that simmered in Houston even back then, southsider Akshun's entry into the largely northside Geto Boys went smoothly. Willie and Akshun didn't exactly hit it off as buddies, but they respected each other's abilities and shared the goal of making the Geto Boys succeed.

But the group's lineup was still not secure. Ready Red recalls that Jukebox quit the group because he didn't get along with Willie. As Willie recalls it, however, Jukebox quit after the first day of recording, when he received a letter from his girlfriend informing him that she was pregnant with twins. "I heard she put some kind of voodoo shit on the letter," Willie says, "some perfume or pubic hairs or something. The man quit the group that night."

In the restructuring that turned the New York–styled Ghetto Boys into the gangsta-rapping Geto Boys, Lil' J had decided to do away with the hype-man/dancer concept. Going into the recording of *Grip It!*, Bushwick

Bill's status had become little more than a friend of the group. But with Jukebox's sudden departure, there was now a slot open in the group.

As Willie recalls, "While we're in the studio, Bushwick is just hanging out. At this point we're not considering him a member at all. And I overhear him recite Public Enemy, and I looked at him and a light just went off in my head: That would be some trip shit to see a midget rap."

Lil' J was apprehensive at first. "I said, 'Let me write him a rap, and if he can do the rap let him be in the group,'" Willie says. "So I took Bill downstairs, asked him some personal things about himself, and I wrote 'Size Ain't Shit' that night. About three days later, Bushwick Bill recorded his first record."

Grip It!, which appeared on Rap-A-Lot in late 1989, showed a drastically changed Geto Boys. Despite the clear influence of *Straight Outta Compton* on its urgent flows and funky beats, locals understood that *Grip It!* was an authentic expression of Houston street life. Besides the occasional references to the Fifth Ward, there was music that drew largely from samples of Southern soul, including numerous bits lifted from James Brown and his JB's group.

"Trigga Happy Nigga," for example, rewrote the spoken intro to Texas-born saxman King Curtis' 1967 hit "Memphis Soul Stew," with J Prince's voice replacing the original's soul-food metaphors with gangsta and drug references: "Today's special is ghetto dope processed in Fifth Ward, Texas." Meanwhile, "Life in the Fast Lane," another brutal drug tale, features a blistering harmonica blues riff. And the opener, "Do It Like a G.O.," rolls on a bassline borrowed from Curtis Mayfield's "Superfly." That song also features what may be Southern hip-hop's first expression of frustration at the resistance its artists confronted in breaking into the New York–centered rap mainstream: Willie raps, "The East Coast ain't playin' our songs/I want to know what the hell's goin' on/ . . . Everybody knows New York is where it began, so let the ego shit end."

The lyrics that drew the most attention, however, were far more outrageous than that. In the militant "No Sell Out," Willie and Akshun express support for Public Enemy's Professor Griff, who'd been recently dismissed from the group after making anti-Semitic statements. "Gangsta of Love" explicitly depicts violent and extreme sex acts to the catchy backing of a Steve Miller Band sample. And Willie's solo piece, "Let a Ho Be a Ho," is a scathing portrait of greedy, deceitful women (set to the backing of Pink Floyd's "Money") that was ripe for charges of misogyny.

"I felt like, shit, we're Geto Boys, let's tell some ghetto stories," Willie says. "Let's talk about the shit that really go on in the ghetto. If you're from the street, there ain't no happy shit. I wrote 'Let a Ho Be a Ho' because, at that point in my life, all the women that I had personal experiences with were low-down. The women I knew had five babies by eight different men. The majority of women around me that I knew were playing men. So I wrote my experience."

But Willie concedes that the Geto Boys also rapped about things that weren't actual experiences, for shock and entertainment. Partly, it was a game of one-upmanship: N.W.A. had already created a world where gats get pulled on a whim and blood pours freely over drug wars and police harassment. So with *Grip It!*'s "Mind of a Lunatic," the attempt was to take it even further. "It was like, 'What's the worst shit that can happen?'" Willie says. "It's like making a movie. Let's take it one step beyond what came before. Well, shit, he killed ten people, I'm going to kill twenty."

"Mind of a Lunatic" goes much further than gangland murder, with graphic descriptions of rape and mutilation and cop killing and casual racism thrown in for good measure. And it's all told in the first person, with Willie promising "this is fact, not fictional." In the way it presents psychopathic behavior without any context and without a wide-angle view that could take in the perspective of the victims, the song certainly goes beyond anything found in even the bloodiest of movies. The sole intent is to shock and disgust in a way that popular music has never done before, and in this it surely succeeds. But the track's antisocial expression is not just a sign of depravity. The Geto Boys' disinclination to self-censor or take responsibility for their creation, and their contempt for listeners (who, quite often, are not consenting adults), points to something more disturbing: the rappers' complete alienation from and lack of interest and participation in society.

"I really didn't give a fuck," says Willie (who wrote his verses, as well as Bill's) about people's reaction to the song. "I didn't feel like anyone respected us anyway, so I was trying to piss them off. At that point, I was willing to say or do anything to make some money and get people to pay attention."

Anticipating the protests that would come, Bill (again delivering Willie's lines) offers a weak rationalization for the group's rewrite of James Brown's "Talkin' Loud Ain't Saying Nothin'": "You don't want your kids to hear songs of this nature/But you take 'em to the movies to watch Schwarzenegger"; "Call me a bad guy, but in reality/Most you muthafuckas curse worse than me." If action, violence, and profanity were all that was objectionable about "Mind of a Lunatic," Bill would have a point. But those were the least of the issue.

Still, it's worth noting that a musical tradition of depicting gruesome killing—sometimes told graphically in the first person, and sometimes without any cautionary elements or consequences—has existed in folk traditions for centuries. Murder ballads were popular in nineteenth-century England and found a home in the Appalachian hills of Kentucky, Tennessee, and North Carolina. Though largely a white tradition, murder ballads did pop up in black folklore as well—most notably with "Stagger Lee" (also "Stag O Lee"), a true story embellished in song as a toast to St. Louis pimp "Stack" Lee Sheldon.

Whether the Geto Boys were just a bunch of modern-day Stagger Lees is up for interpretation. More certain was the way *Grip It!* introduced Brad Jordan as a hard-core lyricist on par with anyone from L.A. or New York. Akshun shines in the sharply observed, rapid-fire bravado of "Seek and Destroy," and the album's reprisal of his pre–Geto Boys single "Scarface"— now retrofitted with Ready Red's *Scarface* movie samples and N.W.A. sound bites. By the time the album exploded on the streets, Akshun was so identified with the character of *Scarface* that, he'd begun referring to himself as Scarface.

Despite being released without major distribution, *Grip It!* spread like contraband. The way it out-gangsta'd the gangstas helped it travel by word of mouth all the way to the San Francisco Bay Area, where rappers like Too Short had been among the earliest to adopt a gangsta persona. When the Geto Boys hit the road to promote the record, they found pockets of rabid fans all over. In fact, *Grip It!* sent ripple effects throughout the South, inspiring street rappers from New Orleans to Memphis and beyond to follow the Geto Boys' lead.

While the group had not yet achieved mainstream success, among the Geto Boys' early admirers was Rick Rubin, who had already influenced Southern hip-hop through his bass-heavy early Def Jam productions, and had gone on to produce everyone from Public Enemy to Danzig. Rubin saw the potential for the Geto Boys to become a national sensation, so he signed them to his label, Def American, which could offer major distribution through Geffen Records.

Rubin and the Geto Boys quickly put together a self-titled record that was essentially a remixed and remastered version of *Grip It!* with three new songs, two cuts removed, and some important cosmetic changes: To avoid a lawsuit from Steve Miller, "Gangsta of Love" replaced its original sample of

Miller's "The Joker" with Lynyrd Skynyrd's Southern rock anthem, "Sweet Home Alabama." The group also revamped the lyrics to "Mind of a Lunatic" with a description of necrophilia and other heinous acts, making the track significantly more shocking.

But when executives at Geffen Records reviewed the album's content, they declined to distribute the record. Some have cited pressure exerted on Geffen by the Parents Music Resource Center or crusading politicians like Bob Dole, though company executives may have simply taken personal offense at the lyrics or feared possible negative publicity. Indeed, the Geto Boys became controversial as soon as they began to receive national exposure—from having shows and records banned in some cities to being blamed for inspiring a Kansas man to commit murder. Without Geffen, Rubin decided to release the record independently. In the end, *The Geto Boys* actually performed slightly worse on the charts than *Grip It!*, but the publicity generated from the Geffen fallout established the group nationally at the forefront of gangsta rap.

SOUTHERN GANGSTA CAN'T BE STOPPED

Riding the momentum of the group's self-titled album, the Geto Boys returned to the studio and, with the help of J Prince and early Scarface producer John Bido, recorded *We Can't Be Stopped*. While the group initially bonded over their shared mission, signs of wear began to show: With group members spending little time in the studio together, nine of the album's fourteen tracks are solo performances, and only one features all three rappers.

"We didn't even know each other," Willie says. "You're kind of forced together and you actually spend more time together than people on a regular nine to five. You're just forced to bond. But I can count the times that we actually hung out on one hand, besides doing music business stuff."

DJ Ready Red, who'd been in the group longer than any of the rappers, was first to leave. Frustrated over what he calls "funny money" and concerned that "famous don't pay your bills," Red quit during the recording of *We Can't Be Stopped*. While he appears on the record—most notably, his album intro "Rebel Rap Family"—there's no mention in the credits of his involvement.

As Red recalls, the night he quit the group he got a call at three a.m. that Bushwick Bill was in the hospital. Group members rushed to the hospital to find Bill in serious condition with a gunshot wound to his eye. According to the lyrics to "Ever So Clear"—a track from Bill's 1992 solo debut, *Little Big Man*—here's what happened that night in May of 1991: A depressed Bill, stoned and blackout drunk on Everclear (a highly potent grain alcohol), went to his girlfriend Mica's house with the idea of shooting her, but then decided he'd rather if she shot him. To provoke her, he physically assaulted Mica and then threatened to throw her baby out the door if she didn't shoot Bill. As they struggled, Bill put his gun to his eye and, the lyrics explain, "the gun went off." In press reports, Mica is often described as having pulled the trigger.

After Bill's condition stabilized, Scarface and Willie D joined him at the hospital to lend support. Some enterprising individual affiliated with Rap-A-Lot got the idea to shoot a photo of the Geto Boys in their self-inflicted glory, and so it was immortalized: Bushwick Bill, in his hospital gown and "5th Ward Posse" hat, first-generation cell phone in hand, being wheeled down the hospital hallway by a pimped-out Willie D, in a purple denim outfit, and gangsta-clad Scarface, in black leather pants and porkpie hat. The shot became the cover image for *We Can't Be Stopped*.

It was, in fact, the essence of the Geto Boys captured in one frame: the absurd, the grotesque, the hardcore, the pathetic, the black comedy. If these guys had little else in common with William Faulkner and Flannery O'Connor, they were at least firmly in a territory that Dixie artists had cultivated for generations: *We Can't Be Stopped* was as Southern gothic a tableau as hip-hop had ever seen, then or since. The playwright Tennessee Williams, one of the style's paragons, described Southern gothic as capturing "an intuition, of an underlying dreadfulness in modern experience." Tranported to the inner city, decades later, the description fit the Geto Boys perfectly.

We Can't Be Stopped's gothic qualities go beyond its cover. They're in the bloodbath of "Another Nigga in the Morgue," and even more so in two of the album's key tracks. The first, "Chuckie," is a rap written for Bushwick Bill by Rap-A-Lot label mate Ganksta N-I-P. Invoking the campy horror movie character, Chuckie, an evil animated doll, Bill plays a serial-killing psycho who commits mass murder and eats the brains of children for a cocktail. It was, for many, their first taste of a rap sub-subgenre called horror-core—a style N-I-P and Bill would explore before it was picked up by mid-90s New York–based acts like the Gravediggaz. With twisted juvenalia on par with B-list slasher movies, it evoked the Southern gothic tradition in the way that it offered a disorienting, nightmarish conflation of ugly fantasy and actual street life.

Far more impressive was "Mind Playing Tricks on Me," which turned out to be the Geto Boys first chart hit—a number-one rap single. Set to the woozy, hypnotic groove of Memphis soul man Isaac Hayes' "Hung Up on

My Baby," Scarface, Willie, and Bill take turns elucidating the afflictions of their troubled minds: from paranoia and schizophrenia to loneliness, regret, and depression, and finally—in Bill's Halloween ghost tale—delusion. There's compelling storytelling and even sad vulnerability—something the group had never tried before. Scarface raps: "I often drift while I drive/Havin' fatal thoughts of suicide/Bang and get it over with/And then I'm worry-free, but that's bullshit/I got a little boy to look after/And if I died then my child would be a bastard/I had a woman down with me/But to me it seemed like she was down to get me/ . . . Now she's back with her mother/Now I'm realizing that I love her/My mind is playin' tricks on me."

But *We Can't Be Stopped* does not sustain this introspection. There are X-rated romps (Scarface's clever "Quickie"; Bill's awful "The Other Level"); Willie D's portrayal of the worst boyfriend ever ("Homie Don't Play That"; "I'm Not a Gentleman"); and self-conscious dissections of the group's controversies (the defiant "We Can't Be Stopped"; the funny "Trophy"). And with "Fuck a War," the group crafts a verse that stayed relevant across two decades: Bill raps, "They put niggas on the front line/But when it comes to gettin' ahead, they put us way behind/I ain't gettin' my leg shot off/While Bush's old ass on T.V. playin' golf/ . . . I ain't fightin' behind no goddamn oil/Against motherfuckas I don't know/Yo Bush! I ain't your damn hoe/The enemy is right here, G, them foreigners never did shit me."

We Can't Be Stopped's range of memorable tracks made it the Geto Boys' creative high point, a critical favorite and commercial breakthrough. But there was too much turmoil surrounding the group to sustain the success. Encouraged that the group's success might segue into a high-profile solo career, Willie quit the group in 1992 and released his second solo album, *I'm Goin' Out Like a Soldier*. By then, Scarface has also dropped a solo debut, *Mr. Scarface Is Back*, which solidified his reputation as the South's best hardcore lyricist. Six more solo albums followed—including the 1994 standout, *The Diary*, and 2002's *The Fix*, which marked a late-career revitalization.

The Geto Boys carried on as well. They replaced Willie with Big Mike from the Rap-A-Lot act, The Convicts, and released 1993's *Til Death Do Us Part*. Willie returned to the group for 1996's *The Resurrection* and 1998's *Da Good Da Bad & Da Ugly*. By '98, though, Bushwick Bill quit and was replaced by DMG (Detrimental Ganxta), who'd appeared on Rap-A-Lot as a solo act and as part of Scarface's spinoff group, Facemob. After *Da Good*'s lukewarm reception, the Geto Boys seemed done for good, but the classic trio—Scarface, Willie, and Bill—reformed for 2005's *The Foundation*.

Despite some great tracks scattered through their later albums, the Geto Boys owe most of their reputation to *Grip It! On That Other Level* (redone as *The Geto Boys*) and *We Can't Be Stopped*. Those two records put Texas on the hip-hop radar and set a precedent for down-South hip-hop—at least for the western part of the South, including Tennessee, Mississippi, and Louisiana—for being gangsta in tone, bluesy in feel, and independent in business. Developing simultaneously with bass music on the South's eastern side, Texas gangsta offered an entirely different view of the South than the party-charged Miami flavor. To some extent, the meeting of those two poles has defined the essence of Southern hip-hop.

THE SOUTH'S TRUE UNDERGROUND KINGS

The Geto Boys' breakthrough in the early '90s opened a door for other Houston acts, though none attained their popularity, or infamy. But other Rap-A-Lot acts made an impact locally and regionally. Many Rap-A-Lot releases relied on the same set of producers, the best known being Bido, N. O. Joe and his Gumbo Funk productions, and the multi-instrumentalist sound engineer Mike Dean. Collectively, they crafted the sound of the label.

Among the Rap-A-Lot acts in the label's early '90s heyday were the Convicts, featuring Lord 3–2 and future Geto Boy Big Mike; the "bad ass bitch" Choice, whose 1990 album *The Big Payback* prefigured the likes of Lil' Kim; the 5th Ward Boyz, who debuted in 1991 with *Ghetto Dope* and released four more records on Rap-A-Lot through the '90s; the six-piece group O. G. Style; and the Terrorists, a duo whose 1991 album *Terror Strikes: Always Bizness, Never Personal*, closes with a track called "South Park Coalition," a tribute to Houston's longest-running rap crew.

The South Park Coalition (SPC) went back to rapper K-Rino, whose group Real Chill was among H-Town's earliest recorded hip-hop groups. K-Rino came out of the Dead End section of South Park and formed his Coalition in 1987 around Real Chill and friends C-Rock, Rapper K, MC Ice, and a beat boxer named Beat Controller. The original crew battled other South Park rhymers like Klondike Kat and Ganksta N-I-P, who joined up with the SPC around 1988.

More came aboard over time: Dope-E, then Point Blank, then the quartet Street Military (which actually represented four different Houston neighborhoods, only one being South Park). Street Military became one of the few post–Geto Boys groups to spread its name beyond the South when it signed to New York's Wild Pitch Records in 1993.

The South Park Coalition was never a label or a group, though more recently it created a series of posse records—including 2002's *Personal Vendetta*. Mostly, the SPC has functioned as a collective of aligned hip-hop artists who support one another and appear on each other's records. Two Rap-A-Lot debuts brought the SPC early visibility: *Terror Strikes* by the Terrorists, a group featuring producer Egypt E, who helped create the SPC's sinister sound; and Ganksta N-I-P's 1992 debut, *The South Park Psycho*. N-I-P, who ghostwrote "Chuckie" for Bushwick Bill, released his own horror-core album with songs such as "Horror Movie Rap" and "Slaughter." With his early melding of street rap with horror-movie themes, N-I-P has been credited as being the "father of horror-core."

Klondike Kat also debuted in '92, with his *The Lyrical Lion* EP, as did Point Blank (*Prone to Bad Dreams*), while K-Rino's first solo album, *Stories From the Black Book*, appeared the following year. The best-known SPC acts managed to support themselves by selling thousands of CDs independently and touring regionally. While the SPC still exists, its popularity diminished in the mid-90s, as Houston hip-hop's next wave kicked in.

Meanwhile, the two most significant rap acts to emerge from Texas in the wake of the Geto Boys—UGK and Eightball & MJG—were neither Rap-A-Lot acts nor part of the South Park Coalition. And while both started out recording for Houston labels, neither was actually from Houston. But thanks in part to the Geto Boys and Rap-A-Lot, the city became a magnet for this first wave of hard-core Southern rap, as others tried to replicate the formula that had put the region into the hip-hop mix.

Port Arthur, Texas—a Gulf Coast oil-refining town on the Louisiana border, about an hour and a half east of Houston—was an unlikely home for a hip-hop group, particularly back in the late '80s. Perhaps it took an extreme backwater to define what some Southern rap fans consider the essence of "country rap."

Chad "Pimp C" Butler and Bernard "Bun B" Freeman started out in separate groups, but as less-dedicated rhymers weeded themselves out, Bun and his partner, Jalon Jackson, joined forces with the duo Mission Impossible, which featured Pimp C and a rapper named Mitchell Queen. The new quartet called itself 4BM, or 4 Black Menacesters (combining "ministers" and "menace"), and recorded an early version of "Cocaine in the Back of My Ride" around a Bob Marley sample. Soon, Jackson and Queen quit, leaving Pimp and Bun as the sole members of the renamed group, Underground Kingz.

As Pimp and Bun got more serious about music, they began spending more time in Houston. One day in the summer of 1991, while checking out Kings Flea Market in South Park, they spotted Russell Washington's record booth. Washington was starting his own label, Big Tyme, and had posted a sign in his shop asking for demos. Pimp and Bun brought theirs and Washington fell in love with their track, "Tell Me Something Good," a hip-hop spin on Rufus and Chaka Khan's Stevie Wonder–penned 1974 hit. Big Tyme signed the Underground Kingz, who became UGK and put together a six-track cassette called *The Southern Way*.

After the group entered "Tell Me Something Good" in a radio contest, 97.9 The Box added the song to their playlist. By the time *The Southern Way* arrived in early 1992, UGK was among the most highly touted new acts in Houston. Despite its title, *The Southern Way* was not particularly South-identified—the cassette included UGK favorites such as "Short Texas," "Cocaine in the Back of My Ride," and "Trill Ass Nigga," fairly generic gangsta tales and sex romps. But there was a sense of language in UGK that evoked the region more than the Geto Boys had. In particular, "Trill Ass Nigga" introduced a classic bit of down-South hip-hop vernacular: *trill*. Simply defined, it combined the words *true* and *real*—or else it contracted *too* and *real*, or implied "three times as real"—and the term described someone who was particularly hard and worthy of respect. It eventually became so much a part of hip-hop language that, a decade later, when an Atlanta group decided to call itself Trillville, it felt no need to cite (or else didn't even know to credit) UGK as its progenitor.

With sales reportedly around forty thousand copies—impressive for an independent cassette—the group drew attention in the music industry. Labels such as Priority and Select were calling with offers, but Jive wound up with the deal and quickly put together *Too Hard to Swallow* using six tracks that were edited and remixed from *The Southern Way* and added five new songs. But the label rejected two new tracks for being too offensive. To release those, Big Tyme put together an extended CD single that it called *Banned*.

The title was not quite accurate, but it served to pique the curiosity of fans; plus the two "banned" tracks were plenty offensive. One, "Mutha Ain't Mine," degrades and threatens women who claim the rapper is the father of their children. The second, "Pregnant Pussy," is truly sick—albeit comically so—with a frat-house puerility that showed the depths one had to reach to be more outrageous than peers such as the Geto Boys or Ganksta N-I-P.

Still, it's hard to understand how "Pregnant Pussy" is much more offensive than songs on *Too Hard to Swallow*, including "I Feel Like I'm the One Doin' Dope," with its Bushwick Bill–inspired psychotic criminality, including rape, murder, and drug-addled delusion. Or how the "banned" tracks were more ridiculously obscene than *Swallow*'s "I'm Bad," which lifts a classic boast (if you'd call it a boast) from LL Cool J: "I'm so bad I can suck my own dick." The Jive debut had plenty of hard-core gangsta-rap bite, even if die-hard fans were disappointed by the way the tracks carried over from *The Southern Way* had been watered down, both lyrically and musically.

UGK's jump from Houston indie label to national urban-music power-house didn't send the duo to the top of the charts. Rather, the group's growth came steadily, through an ever-enlarging cult following. UGK's albums sold well enough to keep making more, but the group's singles never hit the pop charts—UGK didn't even break into the rap Top 40 until its fourth album. But by the mid-90s, UGK had established itself among those in the know as one of the key acts defining Southern hip-hop, and its influence spread among other groups.

Lyrically, 1994's *Super Tight . . .* didn't offer much beyond the crime and sex tales UGK had already offered on *Too Hard to Swallow*. But the music was more revelatory. Pimp C had already handled production on earlier material, but with the higher production values afforded by a major label and two more years of experience, he widened UGK's sonic palette considerably. "The Return" and "Underground" both suggest a reggae influence, with "Underground" also adding an elegant grand-piano sound. "It's Supposed to Bubble" presents an East Coast mellow-jazz vibe, "Three Sixteens" cops a West Coast *Chronic* style, while "Stoned Junkee" keeps it regional with a psychedelic blues riff (Port Arthur, after all, was hometown to Janis Joplin). Meanwhile, "Front, Back & Side to Side" became the group's most successful single to date by celebrating H-Town's car culture with a classic cruising song that rides on bluesy organ swishes. (In 2006, T.I. celebrated UGK by borrowing the song's hook for his track "Front Back.")

UGK's partnership didn't come to full fruition until 1996's *Ridin' Dirty*, where Bun B steps up his game considerably, revealing himself as one of hard-core hip-hop's most creative wordsmiths. In the blend of Pimp's rich production and Bun's dense rhyming, the duo reached a newfound sophistication and maturity. Long after *Ridin' Dirty* had pushed UGK into the upper reaches of the charts (pop number 15, and R&B/hip-hop number 2), the record remained for many the ultimate statement of Texas hip-hop, as powerful a representation of the South's "Westside" as OutKast's early records would be for the Southeast.

Pimp and Bun had not given up flexing their gangsta muscles, but they discovered perspective and depth in their portrayal of street life—they found that real people caught in the game are far more interesting than psychos and cold-blooded killers. So while the title, *Ridin' Dirty*, suggests bravado and glory, the record actually laces in recurring sound bites from prison inmates, as if to remind listeners where this dirty ride ultimately ends. And while they rip through dark capers like "Murder" and "Touched," they also accept life's impermanence with "One Day"—which samples Ron Isley's doleful wail—and express regrets and family concerns on "Hi Life," another down-tempo cut punctuated by producer N.O. Joe's subtly ironic chorus.

Among the more up-tempo tracks, "Pinky Ring" presents a good taste of Pimp C and Bun B at their best: Pimp's smooth, Curtis Mayfield–sampling funk backing Bun B, who twists through verses filled with internal rhyme and swagger: "Flashin' cop lights keep a playa dashin'/Cash in on the crack 'cause paper stashin'/Wit a passion for high-priced fashion/My dank is closin', and my 84 is clanky/Goddanky, muthafuckas actin' cranky/Stanky attitudes be janky/I thank [think] he gon' have to feel the stang [sting] from the rang [ring] of my panky [pinky]."

As much as the music, *Ridin' Dirty* earned classic status through its highly influential language—Texas slang that the group didn't necessarily invent or record first, but was key in disseminating through the South and beyond. Terms such as *swisha* and *sweets* (like the Northern term *blunt,* a hollowed-out cigar filled with marijuana); *candy paint* (bright colors used to paint Cadillacs and other *pimpmobiles*); *leanin'* (being under the influence of codeine cough syrup); *plex* (having a beef with or hating someone); and *third coast* (a term once claimed by the Midwest's Great Lakes region, but adopted more recently by the South's Gulf coast, and to Houston specifically).

The song "3 in the Mornin'" runs down many of these terms while the chorus serves as a tribute to Houston's DJ Screw, whose distinct slowed-down mixing style was just beginning to bubble beyond the region. The track—along with UGK's "Diamonds & Wood," which samples a Screw mix tape—likely provided "screw music" its first widespread national exposure, laying the groundwork for a mainstream Houston crossover sound in the decade to follow. With its artistry, terminology, and embrace of regional styles, it's no wonder that *Ridin' Dirty* is lauded as the bible of Houston-area hip-hop.

Amazingly, UGK never got the chance to build on *Ridin' Dirty*'s success. Between label problems and legal issues, the group took five years to release a follow-up, *Dirty Money.* By then, the Southern style they pioneered had become well established, and the group no longer sounded fresh. The album's opening track did, however, introduce a term often associated with UGK: *country rap.* "This ain't no muthafuckin' hip-hop records, these country rap tunes," Pimp C says at the end of "Let Me See It." The group adopted the tag in response to Northerners who said the South wasn't making real hip-hop.

"Since we ain't real hip-hop, you right, we make country rap tunes down here," Pimp C told Matt Sonzala in a 2005 interview. "We rappin' and we country and they done already told us they don't want us. The attitude has changed a lot in the past seven or eight years, but New York had an attitude for a long time."

Ironically, UGK's biggest success came in 2000, as the guest of New York's hip-hop king, Jay-Z. The song, "Big Pimpin'," seemed to find Bun and Pimp far outside their element, accompanying Jay on an Indian-influenced track created by the Virginia producer Timbaland. It was so far from a country rap tune that Pimp C initially resisted doing it for fear it would hurt UGK's credibility as Southern hip-hop leaders.

"We put the ['Big Pimpin''] reel on and we hear these flutes and this happy music . . . and I'm like *maaan*. I'm not doing it. I called [Jay-Z] and said, 'Hey man, are you trying to sabotage me?' He said, 'Look fam, it's gonna be the biggest record of your career.'"

After much convincing, Pimp agreed to record his verse, which complemented Bun's and Jay's intricate rhymes with a straight burst of energy and local references such as "lean up in my cup," "car got leather and wood," "Texas boys," and "candied toys." Sure enough, it wound up being the group's biggest hit—top ten rap and R&B/hip-hop, and number eighteen pop. For Jay-Z, it was a canny move: By bringing UGK aboard, he was able to co-opt the fast-rising tide of Southern hip-hop by showing he was down with the trillest cats around. For Bun and Pimp, it not only meant a big paycheck, it brought the UGK name out to millions of hip-hop fans who'd never heard of them—and it set the precedent that UGK was a Southern legend worth having on your track.

UGK's guest appearance also helped Memphis' Three 6 Mafia score its first national hit, when the Houston-inspired anthem "Sippin' on Some Syrup" hit the charts around the same time as "Big Pimpin'." Though Jive tried to push UGK to continue in this more pop-oriented direction, *Dirty Money* showed little sign of crossover potential. By the time the group was ready to promote the album, though, the question was moot: Pimp C got hit with a parole violation from a previous conviction for attempted aggravated assault. By 2002 he was behind bars serving four years on a seven-year sentence.

While Pimp's incarceration put the breaks on UGK's recording career, his years away saw the group's legend grow tremendously. Bun B was more visible than ever—always ready with a refrain of "Free Pimp C!" in songs and interviews. In 2005 alone, Bun made appearances on records by fellow Texans Lil' Keke and chart-topper Paul Wall, Louisiana's Webbie, Georgia's Ying Yang Twins, Tennessee's Tela, Alabama's Dirty, and Lil' Kim in New York. In 2005, Rap-A-Lot released Bun B's first solo album, *Trill*, which hit number one on the R&B/hip-hop chart (the same year the label also put together a Pimp C record, *Sweet James Jones Stories*, though he'd remain in jail until early 2006). With Pimp's release and Bun's mainstream crossover, prospects look great for a UGK comeback.

Eightball & MJG, the other key hard-core rap act to emerge from Houston in the wake of the Geto Boys' success, developed parallel to UGK. Like UGK, Eightball & MJG came out of H-Town but were not from there; and like UGK, the duo attained legendary status as Southern hip-hop innovators without finding the mainstream national success that usually comes with hit singles. And as New York's hip-hop industry awoke to Southern hip-hop in the new millennium, the duo found itself similarly embraced as high-cred elder statesmen of their region.

Despite having moved to Houston in 1992 to record for upstart H-Town label Suave (later Suave House)—and despite the Houston skyline on the cover of the duo's 1993 debut album, *Comin' Out Hard*—Eightball & MJG were never shy about revealing the city they actually represented: Memphis. And while they spent much of their early career in exile from their hometown, to understand Eightball & MJG's music it's necessary to view them in context, as Memphis hip-hop's breakthrough act.

chapter 3

MEMPHIS—PIMPED OUT OR BUCKED UP

WHEATSTRAW'S GANGSTER BLUES

Like jazz and rock and everything unique about American culture, the myth popularly tied to blues legend Robert Johnson—the one about him selling his soul to the devil at the crossroads in exchange for guitar virtuosity—has its roots in both African and European cultures. The notion of a devil was largely European, being loosely based in Christianity and manifested in literature, most popularly in the Faust tale. But the idea of making a deal with a deity in exchange for extraordinary skills—that's African. And the concept of the crossroads as a place where ghosts and devils lurk seems to have precedents in both Europe and Africa, though the African roots are more directly drawn.

So the devil-at-the-crossroads myth wasn't something just made up to justify Robert Johnson's extraordinary talent—it far predates him. Among the most popular characters to appear in the African American oral tradition was Peetie Wheatstraw, "the devil's son-in-law." It's impossible to know where the name came from (possibly from the wheatstraw paper commonly used for rolling joints). Whatever the case, Peetie Wheatstraw was one of the badasses who ran in the devil's posse in Southern black folklore.

William Bunch was born in 1902, just down the road from Memphis in Ripley, Tennessee, and he grew up on the other side of the Mississippi River, in Cotton Plant, Arkansas. By the time he'd left Cotton Plant in the late '20s and started his career as a traveling bluesman, Bunch adopted the stage name Peetie Wheatstraw, the devil's son-in-law—or, alternately, "the high sheriff of hell." He appeared on the scene a few years before Robert Johnson, but like Johnson, he wasn't the first to boost his reputation by shrouding his past in dark lore. But the Wheatstraw image certainly fit Bunch's music.

The dozens of sides Peetie Wheatstraw recorded during the '30s and '40s contain no shortage of sex, alcohol, and violence, as befit a man in league with the devil. There was the circa 1937 proto-bass-music anthem "Shack Bully Stomp" ("stomp" being the term for the barrelhouse piano style Wheatstraw used, emphasizing the left hand's heavy pounding bass notes): "I used to play slow/But now I play it fast/Just to see the women/Shake their yass, yass, yass." Or "Gangster's Blues," a cold-hearted number from the early '40s: "I'm gon' take you for an easy ride/Drop you off on the riverside . . . /I'm gonna bound yo' mouth so you can't talk/Tie yo' feet so you can't walk . . . /I'm gonna tear you a-pieces and put you back again/I got the gangster's blues/Boys, I'm feelin' mean."

Peetie Wheatstraw, the blues singer and pianist, died at thirty-nine, in 1941, in a manner suiting his legend: at a crossroads in East St. Louis, where a passing train barreled into his car. But the Wheatstraw of folklore lives on, now often conflated with the real man. In the early '50s, he showed up in Ralph Ellison's masterpiece, *The Invisible Man*, as a colorful character who dazzles the narrator with his quick-fire rapping: "All it takes to get along in this here man's town is a little shit, grit, and mother-wit. And man, I was bawn with all three. . . . I'll verse you but I won't curse you—My name is Peter Wheatstraw, I'm the Devil's only son-in-law."

And right around the time Peetie Wheatstraw the bluesman laid down his classic recordings, not far from his own hometown another Wheatstraw was born. Rudy Ray Moore came out of Fort Smith, Arkansas. Long before making his name as an X-rated comedian, recording artist, and C-list blaxploitation film star, Moore grew up hearing about the great figures of the black South's oral tradition—characters like Dolemite and Peetie Wheatstraw. In the '60s, those toasts became a key part of Moore's nightclub act—in fact, Moore became so associated with the Dolemite toast that fans took to calling him Dolemite.

In the '70s, Moore released albums such as *Eat Out More Often* and *This Pussy Belongs to Me* that gained a huge cult following and even made the black album charts, despite the way their unprecedented profanity and semi-nude cover photos made it necessary for record stores to keep his records under the counter. Moore made a series of low-budget films in the mid- to late '70s, including his first and best-known, *Dolemite*. In 1977, he starred in *Petey Wheatstraw: The Devil's Son-in-Law*, loosely based on the toast he had already recorded. As hip-hop took root, Moore's style of reciting explicit rhymes over musical backing made him a hero to everyone from old-school rhymers like Big Daddy Kane to gangsta rappers like Ice-T and X-rated acts such as 2 Live Crew (who sampled Moore over a dozen times).

And so it was that *Peetie* Wheatstraw, a folk legend of the black South, was transformed to *Petey* Wheatstraw, a hip-hop inspiration. But back in Memphis, where Arkansas and Mississippi meet up with Tennessee, it was not just the thirdhand distillation of Wheatstraw folklore that informed the area's conception of rap music. It was also Wheatstraw himself, the legend and the homegrown blues pioneer. Memphis was, after all, the blues' first stop on its way north out of Mississippi. The fabled Highway 61 rambles up from New Orleans, through the Mississippi Delta, and creeps into Memphis, where it becomes South 3rd St. The ghost of Peetie Wheatstraw still haunts western Tennessee, and that's at least part of the story of why the sound of Memphis hip-hop has always been the gangster's blues, as conceived by the devil's son-in-law.

But there's more to it. Even before Memphis became forever scarred in the black consciousness as the place where, in 1968, Martin Luther King Jr. was assassinated, it was known as a dark, desperate kind of town. It's no accident a New York rapper seeking to evoke his hardness would adopt the name Memphis Bleek. And it's not just bluster that locals have assigned the city the acronym M-E-M-P-H-I-S, for Making Easy Money Pimpin' Hoes in Style. It's no coincidence that the first major movie to depict the world of Southern hip-hop, 2005's *Hustle & Flow*, would have as its main character a Memphis pimp. No one remembers how or why exactly, but Memphis has long been associated in black street lore with pimping. It's seen as a city of pimps, home to some of the biggest and baddest hustlers around.

True enough, back in the '70s—the city's darkest days—hookers lined the way down Lamar Boulevard in Orange Mound, the city's oldest black neighborhood. But there's no definitive evidence that there are more pimps per capita in Memphis than in comparable cities. Some say it's just the city's vibe, part of an economic deprivation that has long bred street hustling. Some say the tie to pimping goes back to the time of slavery, which casts its legacy over Memphis more than other major Southern cities that are either younger (Atlanta, Houston) or where blacks had experienced more freedom (New Orleans).

"Memphis was one of the first cities where all of these cathouses and whorehouses set up in back in the day," says Patrick Hall, aka Gangsta Pat, the city's first rapper to release a record nationally. "Because pimping derived from slavery. From the slavemaster coming in, fucking the black women, and there wasn't nothing the black man could do about it. So he started to teach the black women to don't just give your pussy up, ask for some food or something."

It's also possible that hustlers were attracted to Memphis for its geographical features: halfway up the country's major waterway, roughly halfway between the East and West Coasts. For traffickers—whether legal ones like FedEx, which set up shop in town in 1971, or illegal ones—settling in Memphis had its advantages.

Perhaps its centralized location is part of what made Memphis a key crossroad for American music. The road from Mississippi to Chicago brought the blues to town. The route from Arkansas to Nashville carried hillbillies like Johnny Cash. The road from Tupelo to the rest of the world passed through Memphis, where Elvis Presley fused country and blues to make rock 'n' roll.

Memphis was also one of the main places where Southern blacks built on the blues and early R&B to create a sound so affecting and spiritually centered that they called it soul music. Stax Records began its life in the early '60s, when Jim Stewart and his sister Estelle Axton combined the first two letters of their names to create a new label, and moved into an old movie theater on McLemore Avenue. They hooked up with R&B powerhouse Atlantic Records and scored hits by locals such as Rufus Thomas, his daughter Carla Thomas, and Booker T. and the MGs. At its height, Stax hit the charts with Otis Redding, William Bell, the Bar-Kays, and the Dramatics—with some of the label's best work written by in-house producer Isaac Hayes, who later became a star in his own right.

Compared to the refined, mannered soul music being created up in Detroit by Motown Records, Stax's music was rougher and heavier. Memphis soul was ghetto music—that it caught on nationally among whites and blacks was merely a testament to its quality and universality. Soul music provided the soundtrack to the Civil Rights Movement, and its success as a form of black music being accepted by whites was a sign of the country's changing cultural landscape.

Before things could get better in Memphis, however, the city had to crash and burn. In 1968, Memphis' black sanitation workers went on strike to protest poor work conditions. Dr. Martin Luther King Jr. went to Memphis to support the strike, and he was assassinated by a gunshot as he stood on the balcony of the Lorraine Motel in downtown. The city, along with the rest of the country, exploded. But Memphis never really recovered. By late 1978, when police and firefighters went on strike and citizens were put under curfew, central Memphis was a depressed shell of its former self: The neighborhood of Whitehaven was informally renamed Blackhaven; Hickory Hill became known as Hickory Hood. And the idyllic dream of Orange Mound, which had been built on the land of a former slave plantation and was resurrected as one of the country's first centers of black home owner-ship, had devolved into an urban nightmare.

Along the way, Stax Records had made some bad deals and disappeared in 1975—with it went many of the recording studios and musicians that had become a fundamental part of the local music industry. Meanwhile, soul music—called so because of its ability to elevate—took a darker, moodier turn. The deep funk and cool groove of acts like Bobby Womack, the Del-fonics, and Curtis Mayfield rang out in the streets, but often, it was just blasting out of the Cadillacs of hustlers creeping down the avenue. Memphi-ans gave a new name to that type of sound: they called it "pimping music."

The names and the styles have changed over the years, but Memphis still makes pimping music. If it's not always about actual pimping—that repre-hensible exploitation of women for financial gain—then it's the more gen-eral sense of pimping, that pathetic illusion of living large in spite of facts that shout to the contrary. The pimp, that is, as the figurative slave celebrat-ing his extra piece of bread.

MEMPHIS GETS BUCK

By the late '80s, when local Memphis hip-hop began making itself known, so much time had passed since the days of Stax—to say nothing of Beale Street blues—that the music was more of a new beginning than any sort of evolution. And yet, plenty of links tied the hip-hop generation to Memphis' musical heyday. For one, the hit-making producer Jazze Pha (Phalon Alexander) is Memphis music royalty—the son of R&B vocalist Deniece Williams and James Alexander, bassist for Stax's later-era house band, the Bar-Kays. And Gangsta Pat, the first Memphis rapper with a national record deal, was born Patrick Hall—also the son of a Bar-Kays member, drummer Willie "Too Big" Hall (later a member of the Blues Brothers' band). He and Phalon played together as kids. In fact, Pat spent much of his early child-hood at Stax—"Rufus Thomas had to run across the street and get me a bottle so I'd stop crying," he says.

Another early Memphis rap act was M-Team, the duo of brothers Archie and Lawrence "Boo" Mitchell, who put out an album called *For Deposit Only* in 1991. Archie and Boo's father is Memphis soul great Willie Mitchell, who scored his own hits and also ran the Hi Records label—home to Al Green's classic recordings, and Stax's premier competition back in the day. Though M-Team went nowhere, Archie and Boo continue as producers at Willie's Royal Recording Studio, which was around in the soul era and records hip-hop acts today.

"Memphis is one of those cities where everyone has an uncle, or a dad, who's a member of a band or related to music somehow," says Devin Steel, program director for Memphis radio station K97 and a pioneer of the city's hip-hop radio (Steel's father worked for Stax Records and in local radio). Select-O-Hits, the local distributor that gets much of Memphis' independent hip-hop into stores regionally and nationally, is still run by the Phillips family—the same clan that sired Sun Records founder (and Elvis "discoverer") Sam Phillips.

Despite these connections, there was a near-total break of more than a decade between Stax's flameout and when any hip-hop of note arose. John "J-Dogg" Shaw, who works at Select-O-Hits and chronicles Memphis hip-hop history, points to Cool K's 1986 record "I Need Money" as the city's first rap release. Popular club and radio DJ Soni D produced the twelve-inch single, though it didn't make much impact in town. The first local rap track to receive radio airplay seems to be the 1989 single "Ain't Nothing Like the Bass" by W-Def (aka William Bratcher), who recorded the song as his prize for winning a Memphis Cablevision rap contest.

For the most part, it was the club DJs rather than the artists that drove early Memphis hip-hop. In addition to Soni D, Spanish Fly (who also rapped on songs such as "Smokin' Onion") and Ray the J were the top jocks. Both spun at local clubs and broadcast live late-night radio shows, where those too young for clubs could check out the latest hip-hop. The happening spots included Club No Name on Lamar in Orange Mound; 21st Century, a church converted into an East Memphis teen club; and Studio G, located downtown at 380 Beale St., in what had once been the Muhammad Ali Theatre.

As in much of the South, early Memphis DJs spun East Coast hip-hop at first, then discovered bass-heavy acts like Miami's 2 Live Crew. With the arrival of Too Short's West Coast pimping sound and the gangsta rap of N.W.A., Memphis embraced what was, at the time, the closest reflection of the city's own grimy spirit. And when Rap-A-Lot made gangsta Southern, Memphis fell in love with that as well.

"Memphis was into it all, but we were a big Rap-A-Lot city," Eightball recalls. "Whatever they put out, from Ganksta N-I-P to the Geto Boys, just anything, Memphis was on it."

The first entirely unique expression of Memphis' hip-hop scene was not music, but dance. Sometime in the late '80s, in clubs like No Name and

Studio G, crowds began marching around in an aggressive strut to the high-octane party music being spun by Spanish Fly, Ray the J, and others. The local parlance for getting wild was "get buck"—as in, "buck wild"—so they called the step the buck jump. Akin to moshing in the punk subculture, the buck jump was merely a way to move aggressively—throwing elbows, stomping feet, pumping fists—to express the energy of the music. Performing the buck jump full-on often meant that anyone in the way had a good chance of getting hurt. Fights were common.

Just about any aggressive hip-hop song could spur the buck jump, but one early favorite was "Gortex," by Seattle electro-bass-oriented artist Sir Mix-a-Lot, a song that celebrated a kind of boots and evoked stomping. The connection was less clear with the song that became preeminent among tracks that launched club goers into a buck-jumping frenzy: "Drag Rap," by a New York duo called the Showboys and released in 1986 by early rap label Profile Records. Called "Drag Rap" because it sampled from the theme song of the TV show *Dragnet*, fans of the song came to know it by a key word in the crime-caper lyrics: "Triggerman."

It's not clear why that song had such a big impact on Memphis' buck music (and an even larger influence on New Orleans' bounce, discussed later). But it's a fine specimen of mid-80s New York rap, with its Run-D.M.C.-style flow and a musical bed that combines a recognizable sample with two distinct, shifting drum patterns. The lyrics, which take the bad-guy point of view and get more graphically violent than most New York rap at the time, could be seen as a precursor to gangsta styles that would soon arise. But it's hard to see how "Triggerman"—which didn't even make the charts when it was released—stood out enough to travel south, stick around for several years, and come to rule the dance floor in late-80s Memphis.

By the early '90s, the buck jump had evolved into a much more formalized ritual, and locals began making records inspired by—and designed to inspire—the step. In 1991, a local rapper named Pretty Tony (not the Miami freestyle artist) recorded a song called "Get Buck" that became a fixture in the sets of Soni D and Spanish Fly. Though the rare track was never released commercially, "Get Buck" has proven one of Southern hip-hop's most seminal songs. Pretty Tony's chanting of "get buck" at the end of each line ("I'm Pretty Tony, North Memphis get buck!") sparked later Memphis acts to adopt the chanting technique in their own music, which eventually unleashed the aggressive chanting style that became known as "crunk music."

As early Memphis hip-hop clubs shut down and new ones opened, Studio G became an alcohol-free establishment (allowing teens to enter) called Club 380, while Club No Name became Club Expo. By then, the buck jump had given way to a slightly more organized dance called the gangsta walk. It looked pretty much like the buck jump in the heavy stepping and arm swanging, but gangsta walkers tended to march in circles on the dance floor—a hip-hop mosh pit.

Theories abound as to how and why the buck jump and gangsta walk developed. Some point to the Crystal Palace skate rink in South Memphis, where young black Memphians attended skate jams that turned into dance parties. When the kids took off their skates to dance, they continued circling around the rink as they had while skating. Some say the gangsta walk was literally that at first: The city's big-time hustlers would strut around the dance floor, champagne bottle in hand, taking a victory lap after a long day of making easy money pimping ho's in style. Given the influx in gang membership around this time—most notably, the Black Gangster Disciples—it's possible that many of the kids doing the gangsta walk were actual gangsters. In fact, a gang-related shoot-out took place in front of Club 380 in 1992, resulting in two deaths.

Whatever its roots, the gangsta walk became a major component of the Memphis hip-hop scene. Within a year of Pretty Tony's "Get Buck," a Memphis-based artist named SMK created a song called "Da Gangster Walk." The dance/ritual spread into Arkansas and Mississippi but didn't make it to other big cities. Oddly, its biggest national exposure came from MC Hammer, the Oakland rapper whose radio-friendly confections took over the charts in 1990 and '91. Apparently, Hammer had a dancer from Memphis who introduced him to the buck jump/gangsta walk—and he saw it in action while on tour through the city. Hammer introduced the dance to a national audience when he appeared on the popular late-night program *The Arsenio Hall Show*, and then the title track to his *Too Legit to Quit* album featured the refrain "get buck, get buck." But Hammer faded too quickly to turn the gangsta walk into a national phenomenon.

While the gangsta walk died down with time—hastened by the violence that tended to accompany it—the dance still occasionally shows up in Memphis-area clubs. And in 2005, Mississippi rapper David Banner recorded a tribute song called "Gangsta Walk," which features Memphis' biggest acts, Eightball & MJG and Three 6 Mafia.

As Memphis began producing local rap acts in the early '90s, small short-lived labels like Kenina and Terry were able to release some records. The most successful of Memphis' early indie labels was called On the Strength and was run out of a little red house on Park Avenue in Orange Mound.

OTS's first artist was Gangsta Pat, the son of Bar-Kays drummer Willie Hall mentioned above. Before Pat was out of high school, he hooked up with a label called Good to Go, but one day he and the label's owner, a hustler named Fat Tony, were driving down Beale Street when a gunshot entered the car, killing Tony.

A guy named Reginald Boyland took over and renamed the label On the Strength. Over the next few years, OTS almost single-handedly put Memphis on the map by releasing records from the city's most significant early acts—the first of which was Gangsta Pat. Growing up the son of a famous musician, Pat traveled with his dad to shows and learned to play drums, keyboards, trumpet, and guitar. But he also went through rough times in White Haven and other deteriorating parts of Memphis. Though initially an LL Cool J adherent, Pat changed styles once he heard N.W.A. As a gangsta rapper, Pat fell in with the Geto Boys around 1989, when they made a promotional appearance at a local record store. He gave them his tape, and they liked it so much they invited Pat to join them on tour.

Pat's first single, "I'm the Gangsta" (backed with "Shootin' on Narcs") became a huge local club hit, the perfect soundtrack for gangsta walking. "Shootin' on Narcs," in particular, caused a stir by taking aim at Memphis' narcotics officers, who had a reputation for corruption. The local success spurred OTS to hook up with a Miami label called On Top Records (a subsidiary of bass label Joey Boy), which gave the single wider distribution. By the time Pat's album, *#1 Suspect*, was released in 1991, Atlantic Records had gotten word of the Memphis rap pioneer and signed on to release the record—making Pat Memphis' first rap act with a major label contract.

That distinction, however, wasn't enough to save *#1 Suspect* from quickly disappearing. Atlanta's Ichiban Records picked up Pat when Atlantic dropped him, and he has gone on to release ten more albums for various labels (including his own Select-O-Hits-distributed label Redrum) while living at various places in Atlanta and Memphis. Though he never reached the mainstream, Pat retains the special status of elder statesman of rap in Memphis.

Around the same time that OTS brought out Gangsta Pat, the label also released a single by the local duo Radical T: "Two Rapping Young Brothers" backed with "Gangsta Dream." Like Pat's, Radical T's debut, 1991's *Radical But Critical*, failed to earn much notice. But the record is significant because it featured the first recorded appearances of two important Memphis acts: MC Al (also known as Ska-face Al Kapone) and Eightball & MJG.

Alphonzo Bailey grew up in the Lamar Terrace projects of South Memphis and got into rapping when he first heard Run-D.M.C. By high school,

West Coast gangsta rap became Al's dominant influence and he took the name Ska-face Al Kapone before Houston's DJ Akshun became famous as Scarface. But when Scarface released his solo album, *Mr. Scarface Is Back*—which featured the line "There's a lot of wanna be Scarfaces, I heard the name in ninety-nine different places"—Al decided to drop "Ska-face" from his name. "He killed it, I couldn't use the name anymore," Kapone says.

Initially, Al was part of a group called Men of the Hour, yet another Memphis act hooked in with On Top Records through On the Strength. After dropping a single in 1991, "Cops Ain't Shit," the group was set to put out a full-length when the master tapes were stolen from the studio. Dispirited, the group broke up, and Kapone emerged as a solo artist the following year. He met the producer SMK over Phalon "Jazze Pha" Alexander's house, and together they recorded Al's first single, "Lyrical Drive By." The track, which lifts its beat from the D.O.C.'s "It's Funky Enough," got a major push when local DJs—most notably, DJ Paul and Juicy J—put it on their mix tapes, and established Al Kapone as a major local presence.

Kapone's first two cassette-only releases came out on Outlaw Records, run by Eli Ball, a local producer who'd had some success with Tennessee metal band Every Mother's Nightmare. Ball embraced local hip-hop but laced Kapone's debut, *Street Knowledge Chapters 1–12*, with rock backing tracks, while its follow-up, *Pure Ghetto Anger,* stuck more closely to gangsta rap convention and featured the Memphis Mafia (Al's cousins, later known as the Taylor Boyz). Though Outlaw had difficulty figuring out what to do with its rap acts, the label did cause a local sensation when it released *Pimps and Robbers,* a collaborative album by North Memphis rappers Kingpin Skinny Pimp and 211. When word got out that one of the album's songs called out specific Memphis police officers by their street nicknames, the story made local news and forced Outlaw to pull the track off the record.

For 1994's *Sinista Funk*, Kapone's first album on CD, he switched to Select-O-Hits' Basix Records label. The record further established Kapone as a local favorite and pioneer in defining Memphis' hip-hop sound. True to its name, *Sinista Funk* translated the grimy, malevolent vibe of the Memphis streets into musical terms, with creeping basslines in minor keys and eerie 6th chords, much of it played live. It was a sound that would become the standard in Memphis, reaching its largest audience through the music of Three 6 Mafia.

Sinista's follow-up, *Da Resurrection*, was even more consistently menacing and attracted a wider audience through a distribution deal with Priority Records. By 1995, when Kapone founded his own Alcatraz label and released the compilation *Memphis Underground Hustlas*, he was widely acknowledged as a leading figure in Memphis rap. But while he continued to release albums independently, Kapone has never been able to attract large audiences outside Memphis.

In 2000, however, Kapone met a local filmmaker named Craig Brewer, a fan of his who asked Kapone to contribute music to a new movie he was planning called *Hustle & Flow*. The invitation stood for years as Brewer struggled unsuccessfully to get financial backers, until 2004, when Brewer finally won the support of filmmaker John Singleton (*Boyz N the Hood*), who came aboard as producer.

Brewer asked Kapone to ghostwrite lyrics for the film's theme song, which would be rapped by lead character DJay, a low-level Memphis pimp who once showed potential to become something more, but had lost his way. Kapone, at thirty-two, could relate, so he wrote "Hustle and Flow," which convincingly imagines DJay's early life and expresses the defiant will to reach for something better: "It ain't over for me, it ain't over for me/I'ma step my game up and get what's coming to me."

Singleton and Brewer loved the rap and asked Kapone to contribute another song, "Woop that Trick," for actor Terrence Howard to perform. Kapone also landed one of his own performances on the soundtrack and appears in a small role as well. In a real-life story that echoed DJay's fictional tale, Kapone found himself—after fifteen years as a rapper—with more exposure and a larger paycheck than he'd ever seen. "So many people know my struggle," Kapone says, "they're like, 'Finally Kapone is getting his chance.'"

EIGHTBALL & MJG: PIMPS IN THE HOUSE

Around the time Al Kapone's "Lyrical Drive By" started making waves in Memphis, On the Strength Records dropped the debut of another one of M-Town's pioneering acts. The 1991 cassette—credited on the front as the work of Eightball and Organized Rhyme, and on the spine as Eightball & MJG—included just three songs: "Listen to the Lyrics" (aka "Lyrics of a Pimp"), "Pimp in the House," and "Got to Be Real." The cover depicts two guys in Jheri curls at a public phone, one slim and one not. It was the not-so-glorious arrival of the group that would, along with UGK in Houston, prove to be the most enduring and influential act of the down-South hardcore rap underground.

Premro Smith (Eightball) and Marlon Jermaine Goodwin (MJG) grew up just a few blocks from one another in Orange Mound—Ball on Tunstall St. and JG on Sample St.—but they didn't know each other until they met in the seventh grade, in 1985. Premro grew up alone with his mom and got into hip-hop from the days of Sugar Hill Gang. The mother of his best friend, Daryl, lived in New York, and when Daryl visited her he'd bring back mix tapes of all the latest East Coast stuff. He and Daryl formed a rap group and performed occasionally at talent shows and skate rinks. Premro met Marlon, a trumpeter in the Ridgeway Junior High marching band. They clicked right away around their shared interest in writing raps, but remained friendly rivals until high school. By sixteen, though, Eightball and MJG were a team.

As On the Strength started putting out music, word reached the duo about a new record label in their neighborhood. They looked for an opportunity to get in with OTS, and one day it walked right in the door. Eightball worked at Central Park, a Tennessee hamburger chain that had a joint in the neighborhood. One day, Gangsta Pat walked in, on break from recording at OTS, and Ball approached him. "Hey, man, I rap too. Here's my tape," he said. Pat passed the music along to Reginald Boyland, who signed Ball up.

Eightball and MJG originally called their group D.O.A., but soon started recording either under their own rap monikers or as part of an extended crew called Organized Rhyme. The spotlight track of their first single, "Listen to the Lyrics," defined the duo within the tradition of the Memphis pimp, but with a difference: these were real hip-hop lyricists, capable of stringing together lines with creativity and precision. And while they claimed pimpdom regularly, they also made it clear they defined it broadly: they were "pimping the rap game"; their "category is defined as being a hustler, and my territory just became a rhyme."

"Listen to the Lyrics" became the first local rap song to get into rotation on Memphis radio. By their second cassette, Eightball and MJG were fast becoming OTS's central focus. Many of the leading producers—Psycho, SMK, Gangsta Pat—made tracks for Ball & MJ, and a young northside DJ named Juicy J worked the turntables for them (Juicy's future Three 6 Mafia partner, DJ Paul, also hung around at OTS). But the deal with Boyland was going sour, and a young hustler from Houston was talking to them about recording for his new label.

Through a mutual friend, MJG met Tony Draper, a native Memphian who'd moved to Houston as a kid. He'd already launched his label, Suave, in Houston but was having trouble finding the right act to get behind. When he began hearing about the hot new duo in Memphis, he went there to check them out. After about a year of talking, Ball and JG decided to go with Suave. And to make it work, they'd relocate to Houston.

When Ball and JG left Memphis in 1992, Houston was the regional mecca for hip-hop—moving seemed like a smart career move. As MJG rapped years later in the song "Paid Dues": "I can remember in the past closin' down at fast foods/Strictly stickin' to my dreams, but feelin' like I'd be the last dude/Who can make it in this rap, I thought that they ain't gon' see me in Memphis/It was like a time they looked over Tennessee and didn't know hip-hop was in it."

Still, the move took its psychological toll on Memphis hip-hop. As J-Dogg says, "Not that they were obligated to carry Memphis on their shoulders, but if they had stayed here, kids could've watched them do it and they could've been more of an inspiration. They were an inspiration anyway, but it was done at such a distance, they didn't have the influence they could have."

When Eightball & MJG's debut album, *Comin' Out Hard*, arrived on Suave in August of 1993, there was grumbling that the group had become too Houston-ized, more sophisticated than they had been back in Orange Mound. But the more probable truth was that Ball & JG's musical vision had always extended past the limitations of Memphis. Except for the Houston skyline on the cover, *Comin' Out Hard* gave no indication the duo had forsaken their hometown. "When we heard their album, it was straight Memphis," Gangsta Pat recalls. "It was all about Memphis, not Houston. So people understood that they had to go do what they had to do."

In fact, the album's first words, delivered by MJG, are "straight out of Orange Mound." What's more, *Comin' Out Hard* brings Memphis pimping into the world of hip-hop. While West Coast rappers from Ice-T to Too Short had long celebrated pimping in their verses, Eightball and MJG took it to a new level. *Comin' Out Hard* uses the pimp game as a metaphor for life in general, but also treats it as a straight-up career option. Tracks like "The First Episode" and "Pimps" play out as lesson plans on how to "break a ho" and keep the tricks coming, with no attempt to temper the vicious misogyny. Eightball and MJG's pimps were not particularly fly—these were the down-home Memphis hustlers, proudly donning outdated Jheri curls and gold teeth (in the days before blinged-out grills became a standard Southern hip-hop accessory), sipping on "yak" (cognac), and riding vintage Cadillacs with Vogue tires. It could've been 1974, but in Memphis the look was timeless.

Comin' Out Hard is best, however, when it sticks to self-contained episodes of great gangsta storytelling. "Armed Robbery," an OTS-era favorite, reappears with a thrilling "Mission Impossible" sample and added verses that paint the action as vividly as any heist flick. Even more impressive is "Mr. Big," Eightball's classic tale of one man's passage from flipping burgers at McDonald's to being the top dog in town, impervious to police and rivals. With its catchy keyboard crawl and immediately accessible hook chant—"Mr. Big, Mr. Big, they call me Mr. Big"—this was quintessential pimping music.

Though it only peaked at number forty on the R&B/hip-hop album chart, *Comin' Out Hard* was, at that point, by far the most successful Memphis hip-hop record, so it largely defined the city's sound to outsiders. While seriously flawed, the record earned classic status as a seminal album of hardcore Southern hip-hop. But as Eightball & MJG grew more mature and experienced, their music only got better.

Though Ball & JG found their biggest commercial and critical success starting with their major-label debut, 1999's *In Our Lifetime, Vol. 1*, the record arrived after a four-year hiatus and sounds like the work of a group trying to get their slice of the mainstream success that had, in the intervening years, come to peers and fans. By 2004's *Living Legends*, the duo had signed with the New York–based Bad Boy label as P. Diddy's Southern "cred" act. However, the two records that followed *Comin' Out Hard*— 1994's *On the Outside Looking In* and 1995's *On Top of the World*—present the duo at their most exciting.

In some ways, it's tempting to view *Outside Looking In* as a companion to *Southernplayalisticadillacmuzik*, the debut by Atlanta duo OutKast. The two seminal down-South records rode the charts at the same time. And like OutKast's "Player's Ball," Ball & JG's "Player's Night Out" betrays an influence of Dr. Dre's *The Chronic*, but also glides with a laid-back funk soaked in the Southern milieu. Bubbling with all sorts of old-school soul and funk flourishes—wah-wah guitars, bongos, blaring trumpets, many of them played live—the record reveals a major leap in musical sophistication, thanks to their own production work and that of fellow Memphian T-Mix.

Lyrically, Eightball and MJG make an equally impressive jump. There's a newfound self-consciousness about the struggles of being Southerners, as Ball raps: "All I see is New York rappers back and forth on BET/See, I'm the first true Southern funkadelic preacher" ("No Sell Out") and "Me and MJG had to struggle just to hustle down in Tennessee/In Memphis, tryin' to be a rapper/But rappin' don't mean shit to Elvis Presley–lovin' crackers" ("Another Day in tha Hood").

The duo's perspective on the streets had evolved as well, to include root causes and tragic effects. *Outside Looking In* includes a pair of solo tracks dealing with jail—Ball's "No Mercy" and MJG's "On the Outside Looking In." They come late in the record, as if to bring down a harsh reality on the earlier smoking, balling, and hustling. Pimping recedes as the primary concern, and when it arises—quite memorably in "Break-a-Bitch College"—it's framed within a comedy skit. By *On Top of the World*'s "Space Age Pimpin'" the connotation of "pimping" has shifted entirely and become a metaphor for a smooth lover.

On Top brings a more soul-searching outlook, with tracks like "What Can I Do" crying for a "way out" of the game, full of confusion, regret, and—a novel emotion in a rap song—shame: "I was hauled away a sunny day on my street . . . /Embarrassed as fuck, my own kids had to watch while daddy was beaten and being drug by a cop," MJG raps. Elsewhere, they wonder aloud about who they can trust, how to overcome the legacy of racism in the South ("I'm supposed to love America but America don't love me/The son of a slave of the father of this country"), and "for-real" issues confronting regular black people. When things get really bad, they blame Satan ("Hand of the Devil"). Far from rap's typical modes of partying or playing tough, Ball and JG embrace a Memphis blues legacy as they wail, "When hard times seem to find you, when all your good days behind you."

As Eightball told *Murder Dog* magazine, "Being from Memphis and Memphis having that blues background—and blues and rap music being so closely connected—all of my music got a real blues feel. Everybody talking about the hard times in their life with blues. Right now rap just got on another page, with the jewelry and the Cristal and shit. . . . But all the time it ain't all about that. It's gonna be other feelings you gonna feel, and if you're a real artist you're gonna express that through your music."

While embracing the blues, Eightball takes on the mantle of a preacher. His lyrics are not the platitudes of so-called conscious rap, but rather a nononsense kind of plain-talk mixed with some Southern wisdom. As he raps in "For Real": "Here's this other fool with dreads growing from his head/He's trying to tell me 'bout some shit Farrakhan said/I tried to listen cause Eightball ain't the one to knock it/but I can't hear over the echo from my empty pocket/Instead of sweating me, fool, sweat Chuck D/'Cause I been true to playa shit since '83/Southern funkadelic preacher, I'm hear to reach ya/Don't be so prejudice and let my holy words teach ya." As Eightball and MJG connected with their musical legacy to bring a new soulfulness to hip-hop, the duo hit its peak.

It's possible to detect the influence of Houston creeping onto both *Outside Looking In* and *On Top of the World*—by the latter record, for instance, the "Intro" had been augmented to, "Straight out of Orange Mound, Memphis, Tennessee, Houston, Texas. . . . " But on the title track to *On Top of the World*, Eightball reconnects, emphasizing his distinctly Memphian drawl: "With versatile South-style rap ability/I had to catch a plane that took me far from my community/Made a lot of cheese, people say I changed/But if you thinking this you never knew me from the gate, mane."

Outside Looking In closes with "Lay It Down," a track that embodies the Memphis sound, with its chanted chorus, hi-hat-heavy 808 beat, and basic synth riff (a sound very close to the one Lil Jon would adapt in the late '90s). But until the twosome actually moved back to Memphis in 2000, Houston was very much a part of what they did, whether collaborating with Houston artists or incorporating screwed-up elements in their music. In that way, they rounded out the first era of Houston hip-hop that connects the Geto Boys to UGK to Eightball & MJG.

"Geto Boys, UGK, and Eightball & MJG laid the blueprint for Southern music," says MJG. "The hooks, the chords, the styles of the songs, what we're talking about and how we're talking about it. Before that, it was bass music and booty music." And in the confluence of the Houston/Memphis sound and booty music would emerge something new: crunk music.

chapter 4

NEW ORLEANS' SOLDIERS IN THE MURDER CAPITAL

IN NEW ORLEANS, THE WATERS RISE, BUT SO DO THE PEOPLE

When the levees broke in August of 2005, the raging floodwaters washed away much of the city of New Orleans and took a horrific toll—more than a thousand human lives, a million people displaced from their homes, and over $300 billion in property damage. This was an enormous tragedy made all the more shocking because it happened at home—not in a faraway third world country. Hurricane Katrina hit the Big Easy—the home of our grandest musical heritage and a place where America's heart beats loudest.

Before the rest of the United States was ever a cultural melting pot, the soul of New Orleans was already stewing in the city's great bowl of gumbo. Spanish, French, and Creole blacks made their marks before it became American soil, followed by Anglo-Protestants and African slaves, then Irish and Italian immigrants. And so it was here that the European classical tradition and its popular American adaptation, ragtime, collided with the tonality and improvisational techniques of the Africans. They met in the bordellos and burlesque halls of Storyville, the city-sanctioned no-holds-barred red-light district that once covered several blocks of downtown adjacent to the French Quarter. The Creole musicians—generally more light-skinned, better educated, and fluent in European culture—mixed with musicians who descended from more recently freed American blacks (who had closer cultural connections to Africa and the slave traditions that birthed the blues). And both groups mixed with white musicians. The resulting brew—a music that put European instruments and musical forms into an African context—was jazz, American character writ in sonic expressionism.

Even while Hurricane Katrina turned New Orleans into an extension of Lake Pontchartrain, the city's cultural heritage could not be washed away forever. That part of New Orleans was both already gone and immutably enshrined. The neighborhoods where jazz was born had disappeared long ago, replaced by—in Storyville's case—a now-derelict housing project. New Orleans' jazz heritage is a matter of history—captured on recordings and in the musical legacy passed down—that cannot be erased by natural disaster.

Far fewer tears were shed for the more current cultural and musical legacy that actually *was* swept away by Katrina—a world that the floods put into shocking focus, but that existed in squalor long before the levees gave way. Katrina didn't so much destroy this large segment of New Orleans as put it out of its misery. Before Katrina, 5 percent of New Orleans (about 20 percent of blacks) lived in one of the Housing Authority's ten projects—a figure that had already declined due to the number of dwellings that had become uninhabitable in recent decades. These were mostly old-style projects: rows of grim apartment blocks set apart from the rest of the neighborhood and crowded together to create a menacing urban jungle.

These projects—some just blocks from the tourist-friendly New Orleans of the Garden District and French Quarter—provided a population stuck in dire poverty with dehumanizing living conditions, and without enough law enforcement or programs to help anyone reach for something better. The result was, among other pathologies, a massive crack and heroin epidemic, fostered by an army of young dealers dedicated enough to make New Orleans the murder capital of the country, several years running.

Long before Katrina threatened, entire buildings in the C. J. Peete Housing Development—better known as the Magnolia Projects—were fenced off, lest they become the Taj Mahal of crack dens. Boarded-up windows lined the buildings—even in those still occupied. And it was pretty much the same story ten blocks east at the Guste (aka Melpomene) complex, and six blocks north from there, at the B. W. Cooper—that is, the Calliope Projects. This is Uptown New Orleans, the Third Ward, where the latest (last?) chapter in the Crescent City's musical evolution took root, and where—in the late '90s—it launched a surprise attack on the mainstream music charts. From a toxic environment of disenfranchisement, dysfunction, corruption, violence, struggle, and a determination to grab the American dream by any means necessary came a third wave of Southern hard-core hip-hop—one more successful than anything out of Houston or Memphis. This was the breeding ground of Master P and his No Limit soldiers.

Simon Bolivar Ave. is a wide Uptown boulevard running between the Magnolia and Melpomene projects, and on hot days residents set up folding chairs under the leafy trees that line the grassy median (when things get this rough, the median strip serves as a patch of parkland). There, along Bolivar, behind the Chicken Mart, where you get your turkey necks and pig's ears, you'll find a mural painted on the side wall of a community center that includes lines from the Maya Angelou poem, "Still I Rise":

> *Out of the huts of history's shame*
> *I rise*
> *Up from a past that's rooted in pain*
> *I rise*
> *I'm a black ocean, leaping and wide,*
> *Welling and swelling I bear in the tide.*
> *Leaving behind nights of terror and fear*
> *I rise*
> *Into a daybreak that's wondrously clear*
> *I rise*
> *Bringing the gifts that my ancestors gave,*
> *I am the dream and the hope of the slave.*
> *I rise*
> *I rise*
> *I rise.*

The Uptown projects—Magnolia, Melpomene, Calliope—survived Katrina with flood and roof damage, though they were already unfit for human habitation. Their residents became the masses of people broadcast on TV, dying on the sidewalk, using their front doors as rafts, and standing on their roofs—sometimes for days—until emergency help arrived. Most of the projects' former residents have been relocated to Houston, Baton Rouge, Atlanta, and other cities and towns throughout the United States.

City authorities talk of tearing down the projects and building more enlightened, affordable housing, such as the newly renovated projects St. Thomas (re-created as the mixed-income River Garden) and Desire (where Tennessee Williams' streetcar once led, now deluged with the rest of the 9th Ward). But just as those in extreme poverty didn't have the means to get out in time, they don't likely have the wherewithal to return anytime soon. It could be the world that created New Orleans hip-hop—not just No Limit, but also Cash Money and the style known as bounce—is gone forever.

But still—one way or another, if not here then over there—they rise.

FROM CALLIOPE TO CALI HOPE, AND BACK

Around the end of the Civil War, an inventor had the idea to apply the steam of steamboats to create a new musical instrument called the calliope (pro-nounced *ka-LIE-oh-pee*). Named after the Greek Muse of epic poetry, the calliope used the steam to sound the various tones of its pipe organ. Soon, many of the Mississippi River steamboats had calliopes; New Orleans' great jazz architect Louis Armstrong got his early musical training watching cal-liope players when he worked on steamboats as a teen. Calliopes would sound as the steamboats docked, and their circus-like swirl (calliopes were later used prominently by P. T. Barnum) could be heard throughout the in-ner city.

It's possible that, in the days before automobiles and tall buildings, one could hear the steamboat calliopes in the neighborhood known today as the Lower Garden District, and onto Calliope St. It's the first of nine parallel streets named, back in the city's French-dominated period, for the nine Muses: Calliope, Clio, Erato, Thalia, Melpomene, Terpsichore, Euterpe, Polyhymnia, and Urania. When Americans settled in, many of the classical pronunciations were lost and Calliope became *KAL-ee-ope*.

Calliope Street runs from the Convention Center by the river into mid-city (where it's now called Martin Luther King Jr. Blvd.). That's where, in 1941, the Calliope Housing Development opened. Originally created to provide affordable housing for middle-class workers struggling through the Depression, the Calliope evolved to exclusively house blacks living in deep poverty. Over the next four decades, the Calliope degraded like housing projects throughout the country, and it was quickly descending into a war zone of drugs and guns (even Aaron Neville, who grew up in the Calliope and is today one of the city's most respected musical ambassadors, did a jail stint for burglary in the '50s).

By the early '80s, things had gotten so bad that the Miller kids—Percy, Kevin, Corey, and Vyshonn (they have one sister as well)—had a rule: When they heard gunfire, they needed to run back home, or else face trouble with Big Ma. Their grandmother lived in a three-bedroom apartment at 3649 Er-ato St., in the heart of the Calliope, and she took care of her grandchil-dren—not just the Millers, but their cousins as well, sometimes ten or twelve at a time. The Miller kids knew their mom and dad, and they came around "when it was convenient," Corey says. Mostly, the kids spent time hanging out on the corner, riding bikes, shooting hoops, rapping along to songs, and collecting cans to earn some money.

Percy, the oldest of the kids, somehow managed to get through school. He earned decent grades at Booker T. Washington High and was a good basketball player, so he won a scholarship to attend the University of Houston. But a knee injury is said to have derailed P's hoop dreams, so he wound up back in the Calliope. By then, Kevin was deep into the drug trade, and P felt pulled toward it as well. But before he got sucked in completely, he escaped to Richmond, California, in the Bay Area. His mom had moved there, and he planned to live with her and attend classes at the local junior college. Just weeks after his arrival in California, Kevin was shot dead in a drug deal.

In 1989, shortly after arriving in Richmond, P's grandfather died. A malpractice settlement, the story goes, brought P a check for ten thousand dollars, which he invested by opening a record store called No Limit Records. In the Bay Area at that time, rappers like Too Short and Spice–1 were local heroes, and the store put P in contact with the world of record distribution. He observed what most appealed to record buyers and, within a year, figured he understood the business well enough to give it a shot himself. So he contacted In-A-Minute Records, a local distributor, and asked them to distribute the first release by his No Limit label. His first artist: Himself, of course.

From the start, P's motivation was money. He had no great need to express himself, and no musical ambition to take hip-hop somewhere new. He simply knew how cheap it was to make a record, how much he stood to earn, and what his customers were buying. With the goal of maximizing profits, he figured, why seek out an artist who'd want a cut? Master P—as he called himself—would be artist, producer, and record label, and pretty much every cent earned would wind up in his own pocket.

By 1991, P put together *Get Away Clean*, not simply a debut album but the work of an absolute beginner. Third-rate production values and stilted thug rapping suggest this was the creation of someone who'd never done anything like this before. No surprise, the record didn't make much noise, even locally. But *Get Away Clean* featured the first appearance of The Real Untouchables, No Limit's core group TRU. Though its lineup evolved considerably over the next fifteen years, even in 1991 it featured P's youngest brother Vyshonn—aka Silkk the Shocker—who probably wasn't even sixteen at the time.

Perhaps P realized he needed help, because 1992's follow-up, *Mama's Bad Boy*, fared much better. The Real Untouchables were more prominent on the tracks—P's other brother Corey had joined the family in Richmond and became the rapper known as C-Murder. *Mama's Bad Boy* relied on smooth '70s funk and familiar samples that had little connection to the later No Limit sound. Lyrically, P sounded more at ease—a lot like Eazy E, in fact—when rapping. But where *Get Away Clean* offered standard gangsta style with occasional social messages, *Mama's Bad Boy* wallowed in the kind of degenerate, hateful material that marked the Geto Boys at their most shocking—only without any of the more artful rhyming to redeem it.

That "Mama's Bad Boy" and "Dope, Pussy and Money" depict P as a violent drug dealer was all the more shocking given his brother's death just three years earlier, *and* given P's desire to distance himself from that world. His new persona suggested the depths of P's ambition: If selling records to the streets required a glorification of ghetto violence, he was willing to do it—even if it meant celebrating the thing that caused his brother's murder. The strategy, such as it was, seemed to work; P's music began gaining traction in the Bay Area.

As P's notoriety snowballed, he expanded No Limit's roster. But he kept his artists close, signing everyone in his immediate family: TRU—featuring P, C-Murder and Silkk, plus various Bay Area rappers—put out two albums during No Limit's Richmond era. And in 1993, the label released the one album by Sonya C—Master P's wife, who lived with P in the back of their record store (and they remain married today). But despite its New Orleans roots, early No Limit was definitely a West Coast label. It put out records by Richmond rappers Lil' Ric, King George, and E-A-Ski, and even the Millers represented for Cali at least as much as they did the Calliope. And, at this point, few down South knew anything about No Limit.

P's stature as an artist grew considerably when he put out his third album, 1994's *The Ghettos Tryin to Kill Me!* Having refined his sound and switched to Solar Music for distribution, this was P's first record to sell significant numbers locally. P's vocals took on the gritty, dreadful scowl that defined his later style and made tracks like "Hands of a Dead Man" and "Always Look a Man in the Eye" distinctive.

No Limit's West Coast days peaked in 1995, when P corralled the Bay Area's hard-core rap talent onto one popular compilation, *West Coast Bad Boyz: Anotha Level of the Game*. The disc features Rappin' 4-Tay, JT the Bigga Figga, C-Bo and E-40 on their way to becoming recognized names, and its success helped give No Limit a national profile. The same year, P offered his most polished record to date, *99 Ways to Die*, his first to reach the *Billboard* charts.

As he started selling records beyond the Bay Area, P's name was finally getting back to New Orleans. At the same time, the success of Third Coast gangstas like the Geto Boys and Eightball & MJG convinced him there might be some opportunity in the South where he'd seen none back in 1989. He began to wonder if he could replicate the success of *West Coast Bad Boyz* by creating a Southern compilation of rappers on the verge. With No Limit established as one of the Bay Area's most successful hip-hop labels, P finally had the resources to reach back home and try some things.

When P went through New Orleans promoting *99 Ways to Die*, he stopped at Peaches Records & Tapes on Gentilly, where local rappers met and sold their independent CDs. He picked up some local releases and met Mia X, who worked at the store. Mia was already a rap veteran, having started a decade earlier in New York Incorporated, one of New Orleans' earliest rap groups. P wanted her for No Limit.

P also visited Club Rumors, where one of the city's most popular DJs, KLC, worked. He'd met KLC the year before at the Jack the Rapper music convention in Atlanta. KLC was there with his friend, the rapper known as Mr. Serv-On, and Serv-On knew P through his brother, C-Murder. P asked Serv-On about a track he liked out of New Orleans—"Who produced it?" P asked. As fate would have it, the producer was KLC, and P was an immediate fan.

P had given KL his card in Atlanta, but a year later P still hadn't heard from him. When P came by Rumors, KL told him he'd lost P's info. In fact, KL had seen no pressing need to seek out P at that time. A year later, however, No Limit was getting big and KL decided to take P up on his offer to work with him.

Craig Lawson, aka KLC, grew up in the Melpomene projects, and then moved to a house off the Parkway, also in Uptown. Craig's dad was a saxophonist, and Craig took up music as well. Nicknamed the Drum Major even before he joined the band at Green Middle School, Craig became strongly attached to the cadences of the marching band's snare—the sound would later influence his hip-hop beats.

In the mid-80s, as Mannie Fresh emerged as the top DJ from Downtown, KLC established himself as Uptown's premier turntablist by spinning at school dances and project yard parties. By the late '80s, KL DJed for the early New Orleans rap group 3-9 Posse and, soon after, established his own label, Parkway Pumpin'. KL signed many of the artists (Mystikal, Serv-On, Fiend) that would later fill out No Limit's New Orleans roster—including his very first signing, a young rapper named Magnolia Slim.

Slim (James Tapp) was just thirteen in 1990, when KL first passed him a mic. He was living with his mom in the Magnolia, and had already begun earning the reputation as the most-loved hustler in the 'hood. On weekends, Slim set up a makeshift barbershop and earned money by giving fades to neighborhood kids. Though untrained, his style was so distinct that people named them Third Ward Fades. With the money he earned, Slim liked to buy black Reeboks—he called them his Soldier Reeboks.

In the summer of 1990, KLC was DJing in the Magnolia. Since Slim was already a neighborhood celebrity, KL handed him the mic and invited him back to the Parkway to work on his music. From the start, Slim talked about life in the ghetto in terms of being a soldier—his earliest songs included "Soldier 4 Life" and "These Soulja's Made for Walking," a tribute to his Reeboks set to the tune of Nancy Sinatra's "These Boots Are Made for Walking." Slim—with his camouflage apparel and combat-style high-tops—probably wasn't the first rapper to adopt a soldier conceit, but he might have influenced Master P, with his No Limit Soldiers and tank logo. P, in turn, influenced countless Southern lyricists to use solider imagery—even R&B sensations Destiny's Child hit in 2004 with "Soldier," a song featuring New Orleans rapper Lil' Wayne. More locally, soldier wear became Magnolia fashion and Slim, still a teenager, a project hero.

Slim put out two albums on KLC's Parkway Pumpin' label that helped move the city's early '90s bounce sound from its original party-chant style toward more gangsta-style lyrics. Slim pioneered the "gangsta-bounce" sound that the Cash Money label took to the top of the pop charts in the late '90s—Cash Money's biggest star, Juvenile, grew up with Slim, while the label's B.G. had been Slim's friend since elementary school. But despite his local influence, Slim's early records didn't get out much past the 'hood, due in part to Parkway Pumpin's limited distribution.

KLC believed Slim's intense popularity in the projects could be expanded regionally, even nationally, but Slim's habit of getting arrested made it difficult to grow his rap career. When KL finally decided to go to California and work with Master P, he had hoped that Slim would accompany him. But Slim was sinking into narcotics addiction and doing regular stints in jail. Soon, Slim earned himself two years in state prison.

By the time KL flew out to Richmond, Serv-On and Mia X had already made the trip—and both had touted KL as the guy P needed if he wanted to make New Orleans–style music. In California, KL found P putting together *Down South Hustlers*, a Southern compilation. P still had no plans of actually moving No Limit down South; instead, he gave KL equipment to take back with him to use in creating tracks for Serv-On.

The next time P came through New Orleans, he visited KL to hear what he'd created. P was looking for a track to use as a commercial for Wild Wayne, a popular local radio DJ. KL played him a slow crawling beat with a wheezing siren synth—a track intended for Mr. Serv-On. P liked it so much he quickly layed down a freestyle to use for the radio spot. The song, "I'm Bout It, Bout It," grew to become P's breakthrough single and his first overt reclamation of New Orleans as home. "I could never turn my back, I could never forget where I came from. Master P, native of New Orleans," P says in the song's intro. He's been out in Richmond doing his thing, he says, but, "Check out some of this down-South shit."

The song set the tone for Master P's transition from West Coast rapper back to Southerner: "I represent where them killers hang, Third Ward Calliope Projects, we got our own thang/It's a small hood, but it's all good." After Mia X drops local flavor with mentions of gumbo and étouffée, P and Mia namecheck the wards, the projects, the Southern states, local DJs, and P's brother ("Kevin Miller, rest in peace"). Along the way, the song adopts a Southern chant/sing hook that's oddly infectious despite being particularly raw and atonal: "You 'bout it? Well I'm 'bout 'bout it/If you 'bout it 'bout it, then say you 'bout it 'bout it." To audiences, it was an irresistible invitation to represent and claim how true—how "'bout it"—they were. A precursor to the crunk style, "I'm Bout It, Bout It" disavowed lyrical flow and tunefulness. It was hip-hop shredded to its core and lacking all sophistication—as far from mainstream hip-hop as the Mississippi country blues was from the elegant Chicago style.

Wild Wayne's listeners liked the commercial so much that he started playing "Bout It" in regular rotation, and P put the song onto TRU's third album, *True*. KLC returned to Richmond to work with P's cousin Mo B. Dick on a second TRU track, "Fuck Them Hoes," and P provided an apartment in Oakland that KL shared with Mia X and Serv-On.

In late 1995, KL's track, "Bounce that Ass," wound up on *Down South Hustlers: Bouncin' & Swingin'*. The compilation mostly featured New Orleans artists like Tre-8, Skull Duggery, and an incarcerated Magnolia Slim, as well as smattering of acts from Texas (UGK, DJ Screw, ESG). No Limit's leap into Southern hip-hop coincided with its first success in a new partnership with the major national distributor, Priority Records. With Priority's help, *Down South Hustlers* reached number thirteen on the *Billboard* R&B/hip-hop chart.

Clearly, No Limit's future pointed south. "We had to come and take over the hometown and represent," C-Murder says. "P came around and changed the whole program. He was like, 'This is what we want y'all to hear. This is what's happening right here.'"

KLC returned to New Orleans, but his short stay in California solidified a relationship with Mo B. Dick. They decided to join forces as production team and, because they churned out tracks so quickly, KL and Mo B. started calling themselves Beats By the Pound.

NO LIMIT TESTS THE LIMITS

Despite Master P's unique presence as a major figure in both the West Coast and Southern underground, by early 1996 he was still little-known nationally. But what had been brewing for six years was about to boil over with the release of P's *Ice Cream Man* album. The combination of Priority's promotional muscle and No Limit's own ever-expanding reach took the music industry by surprise: The first week of May 1996, *Ice Cream Man* debuted on the R&B/hip-hop chart at number three. It was a strong indication that the independent rap business had taken root in areas outside New York and Los Angeles, and had grown to become a powerful force in hip-hop. And Master P served as a poster child for this rising tide—part of a new generation of hip-hop CEOs who hadn't risen through the ranks of major labels (as folks like P. Diddy had), but rather built their own empires away from the power centers, by selling records straight out of their trunks.

It probably didn't hurt sales that *Ice Cream Man* was P's transition record, with one foot in the smooth *Chronic*-influenced West Coast style ("1/2 on a Bag of Dank," "How G's Ride") and one in the grittier Southern style ("Break 'Em Off Somethin'," "Back Up Off Me"), leading to P's new "catchphrase": the throat-clearing guttural groan, "hnngh." The effect was somewhat disorienting, with P repping entirely different regions depending on the song.

But *Ice Cream Man* was all over the place in another way: While P spends most of the record building himself up as the crack-dealing, cap-pealing, women-hating Ice Cream Man, he also breaks away to lament how "Things Ain't What They Used to Be" in the 'hood, and warns against following in the footsteps of "My Ghetto Heroes." He follows "No More Tears," which sings the praises of his mama, with a graphic sex skit; and while chanting the chorus to "Time to Check My Crackhouse," he'll add in a sound bite that goes, "Am I my brother's keeper? Yes I am!" Perhaps these are examples of P's sense of irony, or an expression of the contradictions faced every day by those who victimize their own community in order to survive. Certainly, P was not the first rapper to glorify antisocial behavior and warn against it on the same record.

Whatever its problems, *Ice Cream Man* easily went platinum and jump-started No Limit's golden age—from 1996 to '98—when the label relocated to the South and found massive success as a gangsta rap hit factory. While few would cite Master P—or any No Limit act—as being a great rapper, P nevertheless became one of the most influential figures in Southern hip-hop in the late '90s. He was, quite likely, the richest as well—which was the point all along. "I like to make money," P told *The Source*. "I don't want to be the best rapper. I want to be the best hustler in the game. If it don't make dollars, it don't make sense."

To whatever extent No Limit's appeal had on a musical basis, a lot of credit goes to Beats By the Pound. As No Limit left Richmond and set up offices and studios in Baton Rouge, the capital of Louisiana eighty miles from New Orleans, BBTP became the label's main production squad. With *Ice Cream Man*, Mo B. had established himself as a singer of hooks and KL as the creator of some of the record's most interesting tracks. BBTP also expanded with the arrival of Craig B., another local DJ-turned-producer, and Carlos Stephens. And following *Ice Cream Man*, a fifth BBTP member arrived: Odell, a session musician who began making tracks for Mia X's 1997 release, *Unlady Like*.

"When I first got there it seemed like a real family, and you had access to everybody," Odell told *Murder Dog* magazine. ". . . They welcomed me like I had been there forever. That made me incredibly loyal to P and the whole squad."

Through 1997 and '98, Beats By the Pound had a monopoly on No Limit production. The arrangement suited P, who liked to keep things tightly controlled and cost effective (as the name implies, BBTP dealt in volume more than painstaking precision). Plus, requiring everyone on the label to use the in-house crew created a unified sound across all No Limit releases that fit with P's vision for the company—an army of foot soldiers, all equal and equally undistinguished, with only one general leading at the front.

At its peak, No Limit churned out nearly one release per month. The albums were quickly assembled, garishly designed, filled with an endless stream of gangsta clichés and marginal rap talent—including guest appearances by other No Limit artists—and overflowed with twenty or more tracks crammed onto each CD. To maximize income, CD booklets featured No Limit advertisements for merchandise and 900-number phone lines. And despite the questionable quality of many No Limit releases, they sold re-markably well—even those by lesser-known acts—with virtually no national promotion or radio play.

P was, above all, a master of ghetto marketing, and his work at crafting a look and sound for No Limit—one that made clear the product was de-signed with the 'hood in mind—paid off beyond belief. An intensely loyal core of black and Southern fans gave No Limit credibility to attract out-siders in search of the "real thing." Album covers played a big part in con-veying this sense of authenticity. Like the music, they appeared technically unsophisticated, with Photoshop collages (no expensive photo shoots) and busy designs that reveled in ghetto fabulousness. For just one example, see Young Bleed's 1998 debut, *My Balls and My Word*. It's a minor release that retreads the most tired of Southern gangsta clichés, but the gold-framed cover art is an eye-catcher: Bleed, guarded by tigers, prepares to ascend a golden stairway to a mansion in the clouds, while three white doves soar off into beams of sunlight above. What does it mean? Who knows, but the dingy fatalism it conveys speaks volumes.

The visual aesthetic was unique to Southern hip-hop, the work of Houston-based designers Pen & Pixel Graphics. Aaron and Shawn Brauch, brothers who'd been involved in the early stages of Rap-A-Lot Records, started the firm. Though the company's earliest album designs involved Houston-based artists—including Eightball & MJG's 1993 debut, *Comin' Out Hard*—Pen & Pixel's Southern hip-hop style became most associated with the flood of No Limit releases.

P's greatest stroke of marketing brilliance was his less-is-more approach. Where the typical business equation holds that investing more in a product leads to a better product, No Limit found that cheaper worked better. Much of the label's authenticity derived from the impression that its releases were raw, even amateurish. Just as blues fans might perceive an old black street musician in tattered clothes as somehow more authentic than the same guy, tuxedo-clad in an expensive nightclub, No Limit fans valued the lack of pro-duction values.

To further the blues analogy, No Limit's image fit with people's notions of the South as low-rent and unsophisticated. But unlike blues iconography, No Limit never connoted poor. The label's shoestring approach had more to do with the hustler's mentality: maximizing profits while minimizing work. And with No Limit's look and sound so effectively advertising its 'hood creden-tials, the actual quality of the artists was secondary to the label's success.

Following on *Ice Cream Man*'s breakthrough, No Limit launched an all-out blitz that yielded hit after hit: In late '96, the self-titled debut from Silkk the Shocker reached number six on the R&B/hip-hop chart; then TRU's *Tru 2 Da Game* hit the top ten on both the pop and urban charts in early '97; in the summer of '97, Mia X's *Unlady Like* got up to number two R&B/hip-hop, while Mr. Serv-On's *Life Insurance* reached number five, and Steady Mobb'n's *Pre-Meditated Drama* got to number six.

That same summer, No Limit extended its reach to film with *I'm Bout It*, a semi-autobiographical account of the Miller family's struggles, with P's best friend and No Limit vice president Anthony Boswell playing the roll of Kevin (Silkk, C-Murder, Mia X, Serv-On, and Mack 10 also appeared). Though the film was terrible on just about every level—acting, story, production values—*I'm Bout It* went straight to video and earned a healthy profit. That No Limit could make a film the same way it made records was a revelation. Its financial success brought a string of Master P movie productions (including three in 1998—*Da Game of Life*, *MP da Last Don*, and *I Got the Hook Up*, which got a theatrical release)—and the birth of an entire genre of ultra-low-budget rap films. Among Southern rap outfits following P into moviemaking were Cash Money (2000's *Baller Blockin'*) and Three 6 Mafia (*Choices, Choices II*).

Capping off the first year of No Limit's domination in independent hip-hop was Master P's follow-up to *Ice Cream Man*, *Ghetto D*, which shot to number one on the *Billboard* 200 pop chart in late September 1997 and went on to sell more than two million copies. Unlike its predecessor, *Ghetto D* was a strictly Southern record, with guest appearances serving as a who's who of the label's New Orleans roster: Silkk and C-Murder, twin duo Kane & Abel, Mia X, Fiend, Mac, Mr. Serve-On, Big Ed. *Ghetto D* thus turned out far more cohesive—a defining statement of No Limit as a New Orleans label—with plenty of worthwhile hooks and even some impressive rhyming (from the underrated Mia X, among others).

Thematically, P was still talking about "ice cream"—including some very detailed instructions on how to turn cocaine into crack—as well as the usual rundown of sex, weed, and crime. "Gangstas Need Love" and the hit "I Miss My Homies" (featuring UGK's Pimp C) attempt to show off the thug's tender side, with the latter serving a real function in the murder capital: In the opening, P says, "I want y'all to play this at funerals in the 'hood, till all this black on black crime stops." But *Ghetto D*'s biggest hit supplanted "I'm Bout It" as Master P's theme song—"Make 'Em Say Ugh," possibly the weirdest, most constipated, and least tonal song to ever make the *Billboard* Top 20. Driven by synthesized orchestral stabs that hit odd notes at odd intervals, the track showcases P emoting his trademark grunt, "ugh"—a gut-wrenching groan that packs all the latent energy that exploded into crunk music. It also displays some decent rapping by Fiend, Mia X, and No Limit's new arrival, Mystikal.

Mystikal had come up in New Orleans, first as part of KLC's Parkway Pumpin' crew and then on Robert Shaw's Big Boy Records. Born Michael Tyler and raised in the Magnolia projects, Mystikal started rapping as a student at Walter L. Cohen High in the '80s. But he didn't record until his mid-twenties, after a stint in the military took him to Iraq for the first Gulf War and then some trouble landed him in prison. Big Boy released his self-titled debut in 1995, and it sold well enough independently to get major-label distribution with Jive Records. Jive added some new tracks and re-released the disc in '96 as *Mind of Mystikal*.

By then, Master P had his eye on scoring Mystikal for the hometown label and, after notable guest spots like his verse on "Make 'Em Say Ugh," Mystikal debuted on No Limit with his own album, *Unpredictable*. In late 1997, the record hit number one on the R&B/hip-hop chart (number three pop). But the relationship between Mystikal and Master P didn't last, and within a year Mystikal had landed back at Jive.

By 1998, No Limit had fine-tuned its hit factory to ultimate precision. All seventeen albums No Limit released in '98 landed in the top twenty of *Billboard*'s R&B/hip-hop chart, twelve in the top five, and six at number one (including albums by Silkk, C-Murder, Fiend, and Kane & Abel). On the pop chart, eleven of them made the top twenty, five landed in the top five, and two reached number one (including Master P's *MP da Last Don*). Even obscure and instantly forgettable releases by acts like Ghetto Commission, Magic, and Full Blooded sold far better than could be expected. Label revenues for the year were listed at $56.6 million, which put Master P at number ten on *Forbes* magazine's annual list of the forty highest-paid American entertainers.

As a symbol of how powerful Master P had become in just two years on the national scene, consider No Limit's signing of the legendary West Coast rapper Snoop Dogg in early 1998. As P told *Murder Dog*, when Snoop's label, Death Row, fell apart and its head Suge Knight went to jail, P merely called them up: "'What y'all want for Snoop?' They said what they wanted and the next day I sent the money to them."

In August, No Limit released Snoop Dogg's *Da Game Is to Be Sold Not to Be Told*, and it topped the pop and R&B/hip-hop charts. Snoop's resurgence on No Limit represented a major psychological leap for Southern hip-hop. For the first time, a major rap star left one of the music industry's centers to live and record in the South, for a Southern label. It was a sign the region had become a center in its own right—a place that could no longer be marginalized as an outlying region, but one that could compete on every level with the East and West coasts.

Among the seventeen records No Limit charted in 1998 was *Give It 2 'Em Raw*, the national debut by Soulja Slim—the former Magnolia Slim who, at just twenty-one years old, was already a New Orleans veteran. Though he'd appeared on the *Down South Hustlers* compilation in 1995, Slim had been locked up since then. While he was away, Slim had developed some powerful allies at No Limit—both KLC, his original producer, and Anthony "Boz" Boswell, his cousin, had become part of Master P's inner circle. Knowing Slim's talent and reputation in the N.O. 'hoods, they both pushed hard for P to sign Slim upon his release from jail. P, however, was wary of Slim's reputation as a cat that couldn't stay out of trouble.

"Before Slim got out, I sat down with P before and let him know I was bringing Slim up to the office," KLC told *Murder Dog*. "It was me, P, and Boz. . . . P said, 'Look here KL, you can bring the nigga up here, but I'm not gona be having all this bullshit up in here. Cause something go down, I ain't having it.' Boz said, 'Let me tell you something P. First of all, this boy [Slim] is not no hoe, you can get that out your head. This nigga is dope as fuck, but he ain't no hoe, so don't just think you can handle him like that.'"

P decided to give Slim a chance and released *Give It 2 'Em Raw* in May of '98. Given the soldier imagery and dress that both Slim and No Limit shared, shifting from Magnolia Slim to Soulja Slim made sense. It also suggested a desire to reach beyond the New Orleans projects to become a more universally recognized rapper. But by the time the record hit, a parole violation put Slim back in jail, making him unable to promote his record. *Give It 2 'Em Raw* still managed to do reasonably well, but a mainstream breakthrough would have to wait.

When Slim finally left jail and mustered the wherewithal to do another record, it was 2001 and No Limit was just a shell of its 1997 to '98 glory. A fall was inevitable—no operation the size of Master P's could sustain that level of success. But the fall also resulted from an over-extension of No Limit's—and P's—capabilities. At the height of his powers, in 1998, P decided to revisit an old dream: to become a pro basketball player. After doing well with the Fort Wayne Fury of the semi-pro CBA, he tried out for the NBA's Charlotte Hornets. Though P had been an all-state high school player, he found it difficult to keep up in the big game and was cut after just a few days. Undeterred, P spent much of 1999 bringing his ball skills up to speed and earned a second NBA tryout—this time for the Toronto Raptors. But after averaging just 2.2 points per game in the preseason, he was cut. He closed out the year back playing semipro in San Diego.

Spectators saw P's excursion as either a courageous adventure or a rich guy's lark, but No Limit insiders look to this as the point where the label began falling apart. With P away from New Orleans, communications broke down, and making music was no longer a priority.

"I started seeing that music wasn't as important to P as it was a hustle to him," Odell told *Murder Dog*. "I think if P could have made more money selling cartons of eggs then he would have stopped doing music in a second."

At the same time, Beats By the Pound's fame brought them the possibility of working outside No Limit, and the label's slowdown afforded the time as well. But P wanted to keep the architects of No Limit's sound to himself—lest other projects dilute the label's brand identity. According to KLC, one day in 1999 P gave the BBTP producers contracts to sign—their first—that formalized their relationship with No Limit. But their lawyers advised them against signing, so they set up a meeting with P. He wasn't in the office, but rather on the phone from L.A. KL says P gave an ultimatum: "If y'all ain't gonna sign the contracts then get the fuck out of my face."

And like that, Beats By the Pound no longer worked for No Limit. Though one of the five, Carlos Stephens, stayed, the rest—including P's cousin Mo B. Dick—formed the Medicine Men. Working together and individually, the Medicine Men scored hits with Ludacris (KL's track for "Move Bitch") and Mariah Carey (Craig B.'s "Did I Do That?"), and worked with artists from Mystikal to Brian McKnight. After some legal wrangling, the producers wound up with their royalties and rights to the Beats By the Pound name. More recently, they founded Overdose Entertainment, a label to release projects such as KLC's first album, *The Drum Major*.

Meanwhile, Beats By the Pound's 1999 departure from No Limit was just one of many exits around that time. Mystikal went back to Jive, Snoop left to form his own label, and in the spring of 2000, both Fiend and Mr. Serv-On announced their departures. Slim returned for 2001's *The Streets Made Me*, but once again landed in jail before he could promote it. Master P's own records continued to sell in respectable, if diminishing, numbers, and the label relied once again on the Miller family for hits: Silkk's "It Ain't My Fault," as well as "Wobble Wobble" by the 504 Boyz (mostly the Miller brothers with guests) and 2001's debut hit, "My Baby," by Master P's eleven-year-old son, Lil' Romeo.

When the label ended its fruitful relationship with Priority Records in 2001, its release schedule slowed to a trickle. The following year, P dissolved No Limit and started the New No Limit, with Romeo, Silkk, and himself as the marquee artists. In 2003, C-Murder was sentenced to life in prison for murder. Behind bars, he changed his name to C-Miller, though that did not likely play any part in his 2006 release, when a judge dismissed his conviction and ordered a retrial. While still in jail, C recorded and released *The Truest $#!@ I Ever Said,* and upon his release published his first novel, *Death Around the Corner.*

P, meanwhile, moved his family to Los Angeles, where in 2003 he and Romeo began appearing in the popular Nickelodeon sitcom *Romeo!* In 2006, P showed up on national television as a bizarre addition to the reality show "Dancing with the Stars." He also planned his own reality series, *America's Next Hip-Hop Stars,* and wrote, staged, and starred in *Uncle Willy's Family,* a gospel musical about a Louisiana family's post–Hurricane Katrina experiences (P's son, brother, and father also appeared in the show).

By the time Master P's label reverted back to the independent distribution it had left behind a decade earlier, No Limit had sold in the range of forty million records. Though he'd once again left his city behind for new opportunities, Master P had already attained the distinction of being the biggest-selling act—bigger than Louis Armstrong, or Jelly Roll Morton, or Fats Domino, or the Nevilles, or Marsalises—to ever emerge from the great musical city of New Orleans.

Indeed, even coming from the Calliope, occasionally they still rise.

PART TWO

SYNTHESIS AND THE NEW SOUTH SENSIBILITY

chapter 5

ATLANTA—FUSION AND FAMILY

THE GREAT SOUTHERN CROSSROADS

The devil of the Mississippi blues legend—the one who provided virtuosity in exchange for the bluesman's soul—has long since come to collect his due. So he moved on to other prizes, infecting the music's spirit into other Southern inventions, from rock to soul to funk. And today, it's hip-hop—perhaps not exclusively Southern, but rooted there and now warmly lavished in the Southern hospitality reserved for returning relations.

But the crossroads still exist—they only widened the lanes a bit, and added streetlights. Today, it's called Atlanta. Back in the 1830s, prospectors picked the spot on the Georgia piedmont as an ideal place for the terminal of a railroad that would connect the rail lines of the Midwest with lines from the Georgia coast. They called it Terminus until the governor renamed it Marthasville after his daughter. But that name was too wimpy, so it became, finally, Atlanta.

While most great cities are situated on the banks or shore of a great body of water, Atlanta tied its fortunes to land transportation, and has suffered the results of waterlust and traffic congestion ever since. But being a crossroads has advantages as well. After the Civil War, when Southern fortunes started looking up and the automobile age arrived, Atlanta was better positioned than any other city to assert itself and become a great hub of the South.

Today, instead of its railways, Atlanta is defined by its highways—geographically, politically, culturally, even psychologically. And it's also defined by air travel, with the busiest airport in the United States: Hartsfield-Jackson Atlanta International Airport (named, Atlanta-style, for one white mayor and one black mayor). As ever, the city is not some monolith wedged into finite space, but an organism made porous by the constant flow of capital in and out and through. What is Atlanta? It's eager to please. What do you want it to be?

"GOOD MORNING, ATLANTA. WE ARE HERE."

The voice, which rang out at six a.m. in October of 1949, barely contained its pride. It was Jack Gibson broadcasting from Auburn Avenue—or Sweet Auburn, as the vibrant artery of black Atlanta was known. Gibson was heralding the arrival of WERD, 1160 AM, the city's—and the nation's—first black-owned and -operated radio station.

A decade earlier, Gibson's friend J.B. Blayton Jr. had introduced him to a Georgia peach named Sayde. They married and settled in Chicago, where Gibson had grown up. But then J.B. called with some exciting news: His father, Atlanta's prominent black businessman J.B. Blayton Sr., had purchased a local radio station and asked J.B. Jr. to run it. J.B. didn't know anything about radio, so he called his old friend Jack, who did. Offered the chance to participate in this African American milestone, he and Sayde packed up and moved back down to Georgia.

Gibson got his start in Chicago radio on WJJD, as an actor on a black soap opera. When the station canceled the show, he switched over to being a disc jockey. His acting skills helped Gibson project the type of on-air character that the community expected: a down-home hipster, rattling off street slang to the thousands who'd moved up to Chicago from the South in the latest phase of the great black migration.

But being that kind of DJ wasn't something that came naturally. Gibson's maternal grandfather was of German descent, which made Jack's skin tone about as white as a black man could be. And Jack's father, a Caribbean immigrant named Dr. Joseph Deighton Gibson, was one of the most distinguished black doctors in Chicago (he had both medical and dental degrees and had served as Marcus Garvey's personal physician). So Jack was about as far as a brother could get from being a street-talking, newly urbanized migrant worker from Alabama.

No matter. Jack was a natural-born rapper, to use the term as it applied in pre-hip-hop days. Plus, he had a great teacher: the original "native talk" disc jockey, Al Benson. Though Gibson wasn't Southern himself, he brought the style he'd learned from Southerner Al Benson with him to Atlanta, where it was instantly recognizable. An early WERD listener might tune in to hear Jockey Jack, Gibson's on-air name, ranting between songs: "Look out, mama! We gone put one in ya' ear and get it on for the git-go! Here's the Queen, Miss Dinah Washington, tellin' it like it T-I-S is with 'Evil Gal Blues.'"

Gibson served two stints in Atlanta—1949 to '51, and '54 to '57. By his second run, WERD had relocated to the Prince Hall Masonic Temple building on Auburn. John Wesley Dobbs, the famed "mayor of Sweet Auburn" and grandfather to Atlanta's first black mayor, Maynard Jackson, served as Grand Master of the all-black Prince Hall Masons in the '30s and raised funds for the construction of the building. In addition to housing the nation's first black-owned radio station upstairs, downstairs it became the office of the Southern Christian Leadership Conference when it opened in early 1957.

Though the SCLC's president, Martin Luther King Jr., was still based in Montgomery, Alabama, he often returned home to Atlanta to strategize with other civil rights leaders. The Montgomery bus boycott victory had already made King a hero, so—as Gibson recalls in his unpublished autobiography—"When I knew he was in his office, I'd take a break from my program and say, 'And now, here's a word from the Reverend Dr. Martin Luther King.' Then I'd dangle the microphone down through an open window, and he'd grab it and say something inspirational to the listeners."

Over his long career, Gibson regularly found himself in the presence of greatness. In Miami in the early '50s, Jockey Jack broadcast from Miami Beach's only black hotel, the Lord Calvert, where he hung out with the likes of Nat King Cole, Sarah Vaughan, and Sammy Davis Jr. (Gibson once "passed" as white so he could bail out Davis when he was thrown in jail for the "crime" of being black after dark in Miami Beach). Gibson partied with Thurgood Marshall in his pre–Supreme Court days. Working on the air in Ohio in the late '50s, he hosted young acts sent down from Detroit by Berry Gordy, and from 1961 to '69 Gibson served as Motown's head of promotions, where he helped make stars out of Smokey Robinson, Stevie Wonder, Diana Ross, and the Jacksons. After moving to Memphis soul label Stax, Gibson helped Isaac Hayes and the Staple Singers break into show business.

While at Stax, Gibson created a promotional newsletter called "Jack the Rapper Says . . . ," adopting his new nickname because of his skill at "tellin' it like it T-I-S is." He discontinued it in 1972 when he moved to Orlando. After a promised radio job fell through, Gibson took a job at a gift shop in the newly opened Disney World. His charm with the tourists soon got him promoted into the park's conventions department, where he learned about putting together large-scale events.

But Gibson longed to get back into the music business, so Sayde suggested he revive his "Jack the Rapper" newsletter. This time, he went all out: He filled its pages with news and gossip for and about people working in the black music business. An important feature of the newsletter was the Rapper's brash editorials on the state of the industry, which always closed with the same line: "Stay black 'til I get back." From its start in 1975, the publication became required reading, and its bright yellow paper earned the newsletter its nickname, the Mellow Yellow. To keep it going, music companies contributed funds, and soon the Mellow Yellow earned enough to support Gibson and a small staff.

Within its first year, Jack and Sayde hatched an idea for a black music convention that would extend the newsletter's influence: the Jack the Rapper Family Affair. Though he lived in Orlando, there was no doubt where he'd hold the convention. "We chose Atlanta because I knew from first-hand knowledge that Atlanta was the birthplace of black radio," Gibson writes in his autobiography. "I had come full circle—back to Atlanta."

Jack the Rapper's first Family Affair, held in June of 1977, brought artists, producers, managers, record executives, and radio programmers to Georgia. The event, welcomed by Mayor Maynard Jackson, prospered and was held annually through 1994. It was a place to make deals and run wild through Atlanta's club scene. And it was a forum to get discovered—for Southerners, somewhere close to home. More than anything, the Family Affair provided a spark that helped turn Atlanta, by the late '90s, into the capital of urban music.

Ironically, the hip-hop industry Jack the Rapper helped build in Atlanta caused its undoing. As rap took over urban music in the early '90s, the convention got bigger than ever. Given the coincidence of its name, Jack the Rapper became known as a rap convention. But the new generation of gangsta rappers and independent label hustlers created image problems for the convention, which grew more unruly each year. Then in 1994, an ongoing beef between Suge Knight's Death Row label and Luther Campbell's Luke Records exploded into a melee that covered three floors of the convention hotel. Afterward, older black music executives lost interest in attending Jack the Rapper, and hotels were less hospitable. After moving the event to Orlando for two years, it ended in 1996.

Of course, Jack the Rapper wasn't the only thing that contributed to Atlanta's rise as a music mecca in the '70s. The city's reputation as a place where blacks could thrive financially and culturally arose in part through its association with Dr. King, and with Maynard Jackson's election in 1974. So when the south-to-north wave of the great black migration began to reverse in the late '70s, Atlanta was one of the largest and earliest beneficiaries. In fact, the same year Jack the Rapper held his convention there, another famous "pre-rapper"—the fiery Black Panther orator H. Rap Brown—also moved south and settled in Atlanta.

But, truth be told, Atlanta was far from a musical hotbed in the '70s and before. The city had birthed a few seminal artists—country-music progenitor Fiddlin' John Carson, blues pioneer Blind Willie McTell—but Atlanta was secondary as a home to emerging Southern styles: jazz (New Orleans), blues (Memphis), country (Nashville). Even Southern rock took root down the road, in the much smaller city of Macon. And Atlanta's most significant soul act, Gladys Knight and the Pips, did not achieve massive success until they left Atlanta and signed with Motown.

Things started to change in 1976, when a local group called Brick scored a number-one hit on the black-music chart with the disco/jazz-funk favorite, "Dazz." Along with the singer Peabo Bryson, Brick emerged after Bang Records set up shop in Atlanta in 1973. In the '60s, Bang was a New York pop label run by producer/songwriter Bert Berns, and the label found success with acts like Neil Diamond and Van Morrison. After Berns died in 1967, his widow took over and moved to Atlanta. While Bang did not particularly focus on Atlanta acts, Ilene Berns happened upon Brick, who'd found local success on the tiny Main Street label.

Brick's leader was a flute- and saxophone-playing multi-instrumentalist named Jimmy Brown who'd started in Savannah, Georgia, as frontman for '60s R&B group James Brown and the Mighty Sensations (he became Jimmy when another Georgian named James Brown took off nationally). Brown's mother was also a musician who played in Savannah's most prominent band of the era, Bobby Dilworth and the Blazers. Jimmy Brown settled in Atlanta in 1971 and joined the house band at Soul Expedition, a nightclub in the still-new Underground Atlanta complex. Brown and other Soul Expedition regulars formed a jazz group called Dawn's Early Light, which turned toward funk and became Brick. "Dazz" sent the group to national prominence on the road with acts like Parliament, the Gap Band, and Con Funk Shun. Brown occasionally brought his family on the road, and that's where his young son, Patrick Brown, got his first taste of the easy-flowing '70s funk-soul he'd incorporate, two decades later as part of the Organized Noize production team, to create OutKast's winning sound.

Patrick wasn't the only kid hanging around. In Atlanta at the time, bands that needed a stage manager to help them on the road turned to Michael Mauldin, a young North Carolinian at the start of what would become a long, varied career in the music business. Mauldin became Brick's stage manager, and he, too, would sometimes let his son, Jermaine, accompany him to rehearsals and concerts. Jermaine later adopted his mother's maiden name, Dupri, and turned tagging along with dad into a career as one of the South's first and most significant hip-hop moguls.

A second local funk outfit, The S.O.S. Band, went national in 1980 with the number-one hit, "Take Your Time (Do It Right)." In 1983, the group hired little-known producers Jimmy Jam and Terry Lewis, members of the Minneapolis-based, Prince-produced group The Time who were looking to branch out. While on a tour break, the two stopped in Atlanta to record The S.O.S. Band's "Just Be Good To Me," but a freak snowstorm stranded them in Atlanta and forced them to miss a Time concert. Prince promptly fired them from the group (some say they'd also violated Prince's rule against doing outside work). Now forced to focus only on production, Jam and Lewis became one of the biggest production teams of the '80s—and in doing so inspired similar duos, including L.A. and Babyface.

The reverse migration kicked into full swing in the early '80s and brought black musicians to town. R&B singer Millie Jackson personified the black migration experience, having been born in Georgia, moved to New York in the '50s, and returned to Atlanta in the late '70s. She collaborated on a 1979 album called *Royal Rappin's* with Stax soul legend Isaac Hayes, who also came to town in the late '70s. The record, though critically panned, united the two best-known purveyors of the "love rap" style in '70s R&B— that smooth-talking romantic (or raunchy) recitation over a slow jam or funk groove.

There were others as well: Hayes' fellow Stax songwriter William Bell set up Peachtree Records in Atlanta back in 1969. Clarence Carter moved to town in the '70s. Curtis Mayfield moved in the early '80s and brought his Curtom label with him. While these artists were not in their prime by the time they arrived, their presence in town encouraged the scene's development. In fact, the first local label to find success with rap acts got started in the mid-80s, when Bell, Mayfield, and Carter all found career-rejuvenating success working with Ichiban Records.

Ichiban was the creation of John Abbey, an English music journalist who'd founded the U.K.'s *Blues & Soul* magazine in the '60s and came to Atlanta in 1978 to launch an American version. Though the operation quickly folded, Abbey stayed and carved out a niche helping soul legends with overseas business. While planning European tours and distribution for guys like Mayfield, Bell, and Carter, Abbey heard about their frustration about not getting decent record deals in the U.S. Within two years of founding Ichiban in 1984, Mayfield released a comeback record called *We Come in Peace*, Bell hit with a single called "I Don't Want To Wake Up," and Carter scored a raunchy novelty hit, "Strokin'." But it would be local bass acts in the early '90s—Success-N-Effect, Kilo, and Tag Team—that would turn Ichiban into a major Atlanta presence.

One '80s Atlanta transplant was different from the mostly past-their-prime soul stars. Cameo, a thoroughly contemporary funk band, had been scoring hits since 1976, but it wasn't until the New York group relocated to Atlanta in 1982 that it hit its peak. With number-one R&B singles like 1984's "She's Strange" and 1986's "Word Up"—released on Cameo's Atlanta Artists label—the city found its first major urban act of the hip-hop era.

Though Cameo was not actually a hip-hop group, it embraced rapping ("She's Strange") and served as a progressive force in the local scene. At a time when future Atlanta hip-hop icons like Jermaine Dupri, Dallas Austin, and Organized Noize were getting started, Cameo was the biggest act in town, and the group's influence—its live instrumentation, its eccentric presentation, its rock and hard-funk flavors—loomed large.

ATLANTA ORIGINALS

While Jack the Rapper, Cameo, and Ichiban helped lay the groundwork for mainstream successes in the '90s, Atlanta had hip-hop early on. A local R&B label called Shurfine released a single called "Space Rap" by Danny Renee and the Charisma crew in 1980. But locals are more likely to remember the rapper Mojo as the first Atlantan to release a record, around 1983 or '84. Mojo earned his rep through "The Dog Show," an event broadcast on AM radio Tuesday nights from the popular Sans Souci nightclub. If favorites like "Let Mojo Handle It" and "Jump Stomp and Twist" got any kind of distribution at all, it was very limited and Mojo's career did not extend far beyond his early party jams.

The other name that dominated Atlanta's underground rap scene in the mid-80s was King Edward J. Not a rapper, Edward J was the leading mixtape DJ. He first sold his tapes on consignment at big record stores like Peaches in Buckhead, then at his own store on Candler Road in Decatur. J also led a DJ crew, the J Team, which produced many of Atlanta's early mixers, including DJ Man; DJ Len of Success-N-Effect; and DJ Smurf, who made his own records for Ichiban, then—renamed Beat-in-Azz and, later, Mr. Collipark—shepherded the Ying Yang Twins to mainstream success.

But the first Atlanta rapper to score anything resembling national, or even regional, success was MC Shy-D. He was Atlanta's original b-boy—the guy who likely had more to do with bringing hip-hop to Atlanta, and then spreading it, than any other individual. Born Peter Jones, Shy-D grew up in the Bronx River Projects of the 1970s. He lived a couple of buildings down from his cousin Afrika Bambaataa and was witness to hip-hop's seminal moments. When Bam set up a sound system in his ground-floor apartment and stuck his speakers out the window—or DJed across the way in the Bronx River Center—Jones was one of the kids who'd gather around. In 1978, when Jones' family moved to Ellenwood, Georgia, near Decatur, he brought with him the knowledge of a subculture that was still forming back home. With his older brother as DJ, and Peter break-dancing, they took their novel act to school playgrounds and talent shows.

"They were looking at us like, 'Man, these cats, where are they from?'" Shy-D recalls. "No one ever heard of it then."

Within a year of Shy-D's arrival in Georgia, "Rapper's Delight" had introduced hip-hop nationally. At Cedar Grove High School, Shy-D formed his first rap group, with his best friend Anthony Durham (aka Tony Rock) and two recent arrivals from Philadelphia. "Whenever the teacher would leave, he'd just beat on the desk and be rapping, and everyone'd be clapping," Tony Rock recalls of Shy-D. "That was his thing."

Later in high school, Shy-D and Tony formed a group—the Ultimate Krush MCs—with two rappers also originally from the Bronx. By graduation in 1984, the popularity of the movie *Beat Street* made all things Bronx must-haves on the streets of Atlanta—and Shy-D was the real deal. His big sister even dated Cowboy from the Furious Five.

Shy and Tony earned their biggest success not as rappers, but as dancers in a group called the Break Kings, which performed as an opening act at concerts and competed in talent shows with other dance crews like the New Rock City Breakers. Tony Rock recalls hanging out backstage at a show, and seeing the video for Gladys Knight and the Pips' "Save the Overtime (For Me)" on TV. The clip showcases the popular New York City Breakers, which fascinated an eleven-year-old kid hanging backstage with them.

"He was watching the video, like, 'How do they do this?' And I'm showing him all these moves. And he's asking, 'How do they do this?' And I'm thinking, 'God, this kid asks a lot of questions.'"

Just a year later, Tony recalls seeing the new video for Whodini's "Freaks Come Out at Night" and spying that same little kid he'd tutored backstage, Jermaine (Dupri) Mauldin, busting a move in the video. "I see this little kid with a Jheri curl break-dancing, doing all the moves that I taught him. I'm like, 'Oh my god, that's that kid!'" (After years away from music, Tony Rock reinvented himself as Woodchuck, the bass player in the Atlanta live rap-rock group El Pus. In 2005, El Pus released its major-label debut on Virgin Records, where Jermaine Dupri served as president of urban music.)

When Tony joined the army after graduation, Shy-D became a solo rapper. Soon after, Shy won a contest that enabled him to open up for Run-D.M.C. and Roxanne Shanté at the Omni Arena. There he met Miami rapper Gigolo Tony, who'd made a "Roxanne, Roxanne" answer record called "Parents of Roxanne," and Gigolo Tony's manager. They invited Shy to Miami to record for the seminal bass-music label, 4Sight.

Though Shy-D had been thoroughly oriented toward Bronx-style rap, his two 1985 singles for 4Sight—"Rapp Will Never Die" and "Shy-D Is Back"—took on some of the characteristics that defined early Miami hip-hop: 808 beat, novelty hook ("Rapp" sampled "The Pink Panther Theme"; "Back" used the *Sanford and Son* theme). At first, this was no great contradiction—early bass music, after all, took its cues from the Rick Rubin/Def Jam sound. But within two years, as Shy-D started spending time in Florida, his music transformed with Miami bass as a whole. Shy fell in with 2 Live Crew's Fresh Kid Ice, who enticed Shy to sign with Luke Records. With Shy's 1987 Luke debut, *Gotta Be Tough*, the music got faster and the bottom heavier. As he became a full-fledged bass artist, Atlanta began looking to Florida for that original Southern hip-hop flavor. And in 1988, Shy-D made Atlanta hip-hop official by repping his city on the track "Atlanta— That's Where I Stay."

While away in the army, Tony Rock kept up with his friend Shy-D's growing success. When Tony got out in 1988, Shy hooked him up with Luke Records, which released Tony's debut single, "She Put Me in a Trance" backed with "Still Doing It." The single did well enough that 2 Live Crew's Mr. Mixx brought Tony to Miami to make a full record, which Luke released in 1989 as *Let Me Take You to the Rock House* (the album cover credited "Tony MF Rock," which thereafter became his rap name).

Rock House not only introduced Atlanta's second bass artist on the national stage, it also marked an ambitious leap in Mr. Mixx's bass production. With samples that ranged from Queen to Average White Band to Yellow Magic Orchestra, the record (along with other Mixx tracks of that period) pointed to bass music's potential to be more than simplistic booty shakers.

By *Rock House*'s release, though, Shy-D has already broken from Luke Records in a royalty dispute, and Tony would soon follow as Luther Campbell slipped deeper into his legal morass.

As other rappers—Raheem the Dream, Kizzy Rock, Kilo—followed Shy and Tony into the world of Miami bass music in the late '80s, Atlanta became a sort of colonial outpost of Miami hip-hop. While the Atlanta act Success-N-Effect earned some national notoriety after signing with Miami's On Top Records, acts that stuck with local labels usually remained local. Raheem, for example, was a star in Atlanta clubs like My Brother's Keeper and Sharan's Showcase, but his records—put out on his own Arvis label beginning around 1988—never reached very far outside Atlanta.

More than a decade later, after Tony Rock left music, worked in the accounting department at Georgia Pacific, then took up playing bass and renamed himself Woodchuck, his band, El Pus, performed on a bill with Atlanta soul singer Joi. OutKast's Andre Benjamin had shown up to lend support to his friend Joi and, after watching El Pus' set, approached Woodchuck to ask him for bass lessons.

"'You look familiar. I know you from somewhere, I can't figure it out,'" Tony recalls Andre said.

"I said, 'Maybe you know the person I used to be: Tony Rock.'"

"He was like, 'Oh, shit, Tony MF Rock! You and Shy-D made it possible for us. We wouldn't be here without you. You're a legend.'"

YOUNG, FLY, AND FLASHY

While Miami bass took hold of Atlanta in the late '80s, a second stream of local hip-hop was taking shape. While bass had a raw, unrefined quality that made it work in the 'hood, Atlanta also felt a pull toward something more slick and upwardly mobile—something more in line with its reputation as the "Big Apple of the South." From the part of town that identified more with the cosmopolitanism of New York and the show-biz flair of Motown came something else, something—to borrow the title of Jermaine Dupri's 2005 So So Def compilation—"young, fly, and flashy."

Jermaine took his mother's name because it sounded better than Mauldin, but he planned to follow his father into the music business. He grew up in College Park, just across Atlanta's southwestern border, and by age twelve he was accompanying Michael Mauldin to shows whenever possible. Word spread of this preteen shorty who could pop and lock like crazy and eventually—at a Diana Ross concert, Dupri recalls—someone called Jermaine on stage to perform. His break-dance cameo became a regular fixture at local concerts, and it landed him a spot in Whodini's "Freaks Come Out at Night" video. The video, in turn, inspired Whodini to bring Dupri on the 1984 Fresh Fest tour, the first large-scale national hip-hop tour, which also featured Run-D.M.C. and the Fat Boys.

Jermaine had more in mind than dancing, though. He began selling mix tapes and developing his skills as a DJ and rapper (some recall that Michael Mauldin paid Shy-D to teach Jermaine to rap, though Shy has no recollection of this). Then he bought a drum machine and began learning production. By sixteen, Dupri had become the guru behind Silk Tymes Leather, a female rap trio he'd met through Whodini. The group signed to Geffen Records and released its only album, *It Ain't Where Ya From . . . It's Where Ya At*, in 1990.

"I don't know if the executives took me seriously, but the artists were paying attention to the fact that I was there, writing raps, trying to be on time," Dupri recalls. "I knew what I wanted to do and I was 100 percent serious about it."

The record flopped, but Dupri had earned his entry into the business of making records. Unlike Atlanta's bass music, his music was not the kind to be written off as strictly regional in appeal. Dupri's vision of Atlanta music was something more universal. "Even today, my records don't have super slang and they don't really sound hella country," Dupri says. "But when you look at me and see my style, it's Atlanta. I just didn't want to be stagnated as just a Southern artist. I want people to say my name the same way in New York as they say it in California. When you go too South, they got a section for you, like a smoking section in the airport."

Dupri made his ambitions clear from the start. In naming his production company, he looked to Russell Simmons' successful Def Jam label as the potential competition. So, as Dupri told the *Atlanta Journal-Constitution*, "It was like saying, 'Russell, he's def. OK, but I'm SO! SO! Def!'" Dupri's company, So So Def, was born.

Jermaine, it turns out, wasn't the only teenager in Atlanta making music-mogul moves. Dallas Austin arrived in 1986 as a fourteen-year-old music prodigy from Columbus, Georgia, about two hours south. Back in Columbus, Austin was surrounded by music from the time he was a baby: His mother owned a nightclub, and Austin has called the guitarist Jimmy Nolen, part of James Brown's famous late-60s backing band, his "stepdad." Dallas played in bands from an early age, including his school marching band. Relocating to Atlanta, Austin settled in College Park. He played in local groups, recorded some demos, and soon hit pay dirt when he fell in with Joyce "Fenderella" Irby.

Irby had been singing for the female R&B band Klymaxx, but she had recently left the group and relocated to Atlanta, where she planned to launch a solo career and start a production company. Irby sought out talented locals to collaborate with and found Dallas. The two cowrote and coproduced "I Will Always Love You," a minor hit for the California-based R&B group Troop. They also worked with the local band Princess and Starbreeze that featured Debra Killings, whose voice and bass playing later graced many important Atlanta records, including those by TLC and OutKast. But Austin's breakthrough came when he produced "Mr. D.J." for Irby's 1989 solo debut album for Motown Records, *Maximum Thrust*.

The song reached number three on the R&B chart and earned Austin the attention of Motown executives, who then hooked him up with an Atlanta-based, Jackson 5–inspired group of preteen new-jack swingers called Another Bad Creation. Austin wrote and produced the majority of ABC's 1991 debut album, *Coolin' at the Playground Ya Know*, which blended a bubblegum pop sensibility with hip-hop and scored two top-ten pop singles. Austin expanded his Motown success with Boyz II Men, a Philadelphia vocal quartet that had appeared on the ABC record. The group's 1991 debut, *Cooleyhighharmony*, went on to sell more than ten million copies worldwide. Within a year, the nineteen-year-old Austin had almost single-handedly recast the classic Motown brand as a contemporary hit factory and earned himself the distinction of being named *Billboard* magazine's producer of the year.

Jermaine Dupri, meanwhile, was building his career along a path nearly parallel to Austin's. After Silk Tymes Leather, Dupri had his eyes out for an act that would bring hip-hop's exploding popularity to the masses. Like Austin, Dupri found his answer by smoothing out hip-hop's rough edges and making it palatable for preteens and parents alike: kiddie rap. His first attempt at a teen rap act, Javier and the Str8jackets, never got off the ground. Then one day, Dupri found himself in Greenbriar Mall, a popular gathering place for black kids in the SWATs (the southwest quadrant of intown Atlanta, including the Cascade and West End neighborhoods, as well as the satellite cities of East Point and College Park). He spotted two young kids he thought were stars.

"They were getting more attention in the mall than I was," Dupri says. "I don't watch Nickelodeon, so I thought, 'Oh, they must be a group on Nickelodeon or on Disney or something.' So I had the girl [I was with] go up to them and ask, 'What y'all do?' And they were like, 'Nothing.' They didn't sing, they didn't rap, they didn't do nothing. But they looked very hip—they just had that look. So I got their number, called them, we kicked it a little, I just watched them and said, 'These kids could be stars.'"

And almost overnight, they were stars. Dupri took the two thirteen-year-olds, Chris Kelly and Chris Smith, renamed them Mack Daddy and Daddy Mack—collectively Kris Kross—had them wear their clothes backward (which, oddly, created a fashion sensation), and equipped them with a set of songs perfectly designed to achieve Dupri's goal. Released in March of 1992 on Columbia Records' Ruffhouse imprint, Kris Kross' debut *Totally Crossed Out* hit immediately with the infectious singles "Jump" and "Warm It Up." The signifiers were clear: "Jump" borrowed its riff from the Jackson 5's "I Want You Back," but also took a swipe at the kid-hop competition, rapping, "Don't compare us to Another Bad little fad." Elsewhere on the record, "Lil' Boys in Da Hood" samples N.W.A. without the gangsta sentiments, while "Party" lifts from Public Enemy without the politics. Here was a group determined to have it both ways: to be thoroughly hip-hop, but easily recognized as falling in the tradition of classic black bubblegum (Michael Jackson even took them out on the road with him for their first major tour).

The Kris Kross formula worked beyond Dupri's wildest dreams, selling in the neighborhood of five million records. It also made nineteen-year-old Dupri—the group's songwriter, producer, and manager—a major player in the music business.

L.A. AND BABYFACE MOVE SOUTH

The teen impresarios Dupri and Austin weren't the only things coming out of Atlanta at the end of the '80s. As Jack the Rapper's convention hit its second decade in town, it was stronger than ever. Ryan Cameron, who pioneered commercial hip-hop radio in Atlanta, recalls, "Jack the Rapper was the convention where everyone went to make it. It was just a big party. I remember seeing groups standing outside harmonizing, trying to sing to people. It was the premier convention for people in the music business to be seen and heard."

Jack the Rapper was where Jermaine Dupri unveiled Kris Kross, and where Puffy introduced Mary J Blige. It's where a fourteen-year-old Atlantan named Kandi Buruss (of Xscape) snuck in, hoping to get discovered. And in 1988, it's where Los Angeles–based songwriters/producers Antonio "L.A." Reid and Kenneth "Babyface" Edmonds brought their new artist Karyn White, whose debut album would soon go double platinum and solidify the team's reputation as urban music alchemists. Reid and Edmonds fell in love with the city.

Antonio Reid grew up in Cincinnati and started drumming when he was nine. By his early teens he played in rock and funk bands and earned the nickname L.A. because he wore a Los Angeles Dodgers T-shirt (though he'd never been to L.A. at that point). In the early '80s, Reid's R&B/funk band The Deele moved to Indianapolis, where they found a guitarist named Kenneth Edmonds. Edmonds was younger than Reid, but had already scored some national success as a member of Manchild, an Indianapolis funk-soul group that scored a minor hit in 1977 with "Especially for You." Since then, Edmonds had made the rounds in various groups of little note. When Reid spotted the left-handed guitarist he recognized an underutilized talent, so he invited Edmonds to join The Deele. Soon, the band was earning moderate success with hits like 1984's "Body Talk" and 1987's "Two Occasions." One day, Bootsy Collins, the flamboyant bassist who had backed James Brown and George Clinton, met Edmonds in a studio and bestowed upon him the nickname Babyface.

L.A. and Babyface both had ambitions to be more than working musicians. As Reid told *New York* magazine, "Neither of us were big party guys. While the other guys in the band would go out and have fun, he and I would sit at home and write songs." They took progressively larger roles producing The Deele's three albums—L.A. produced the second, and they produced the third together. Relocating to Los Angeles, they parlayed their modest success with The Deele into much larger success producing others: The Whispers' 1987 number-one R&B hit "Rock Steady"; number ones for Bobby Brown ("Don't Be Cruel," "Every Little Step"), The Boys ("Dial My Heart"), and Pebbles ("Girlfriend"), plus four number-one R&B hits for Karyn White ("Superwoman," "The Way You Love Me," "Love Saw It," and "Secret Rendezvous").

With those impressive accomplishments, record labels quickly responded to L.A. and Babyface's desire to take more ownership in the music they created. So in 1989, Reid and Edmonds entered into a joint venture with Arista Records to create their own label, LaFace Records. The vision was for LaFace to herald in a new wave of R&B, so they looked to set up shop where they'd find a lot of potential but still largely unexplored talent. What's more, L.A. had just married the singer Pebbles and they wanted to raise their kids away from the "Hollywood lifestyle," they told *Ebony* magazine, in a "black city with strong black politicians." So they moved to Atlanta.

LaFace moved slowly at first. Between L.A. and Babyface's arrival in Atlanta in 1989 and the release of the label's first record, by R&B duo Damian Dame, in 1991, both Jermaine Dupri and Dallas Austin had appeared on the scene. L.A. and Pebbles moved into a house far north of Atlanta, in the prestigious Alpharetta development called Country Club of the South. They worked out of the house before moving to an office in nearby Norcross (they eventually set up a full-scale label headquarters on Peachtree Road in Buckhead).

While popular artists like Bobby Brown, Keith Sweat, and briefly, Teddy Riley moved to Atlanta around the same time, L.A. and Babyface's arrival caused the most excitement locally because they were bringing a major-label-affiliated company with them. But false starts left Atlantans scratching their heads. Pebbles, who helped shape the style and image of LaFace while looking for artists to develop through her own company, Pebbitone, signed Devyne Stephens, a local dancer who'd made his name on the school talent show circuit (though he never made it as a singer, Stephens became one of the top video choreographers in urban music and, later, a talent manager responsible for shepherding Atlanta singer Akon to R&B stardom).

Ian Burke, who managed many top Atlanta acts of this era, says, "It was a huge deal that they were opening up a record company in Atlanta, and they had had a lot of success with different acts back then. It was exciting. But they kept signing the wrong kind of acts—stuff that wasn't cool, a bunch of Jheri curl acts. It took a while for them to get adjusted."

THE TLC TIP

L.A. and Pebbles were not yet finding acts that would redefine urban music in the '90s, but at least they were looking in the right place: the high school talent show. On weekend nights during the last few months of the school year, each school held a talent show that attracted performers and audiences from throughout the area. One of Devyne Stephens' talent-show rivals was Guess, a dance troupe that featured Patrick "Sleepy" Brown—the now-teenage son of Brick's Jimmy Brown—and Pat's friend Rico Wade.

Rico grew up with his mom and sisters in an apartment in East Point, and from the earliest he can remember, he was a hustler. Not a hustler in the illegal street sense, but rather a charmer, a go-getter. Before he was even a teen, he'd earn a few dollars by going down the street to Delowe Shopping Center, on the corner of Headland Dr. and Delowe Dr., and asking the owner of Lamonte's Beauty Supply if he could sweep up or take out the trash. Rico looked up to Charles Lamonte Willis—he was one of the few black men he knew who owned a business, and Rico didn't really know his own father. Willis gave Rico work whenever he could, and by the time Rico was nineteen, he was manager of Lamonte's.

Sleepy met Rico through a girl he was dating, and they formed Guess together. But Sleepy wanted to make music, so Guess evolved into a singing group called Uboyz. The fact that Rico couldn't sing didn't stop him. "I was just fly, a local celebrity," Rico says. "I had a car, girls liked me; I had a perm. I just danced and looked like I sang."

More than dancing or singing, Rico's real talent was being a connector and facilitator. Through Uboyz he met the local artist manager Ian Burke, and Burke told him about a female R&B/hip-hop hybrid group he was putting together. Burke was building the group, which he called Second Nature, around a local singer named Crystal Jones. Rico had a couple of young women to recommend: The first was a girl he was sort of dating; she'd come down from Philadelphia to be a dancer but was frustrated and planned to return home. Rico brought Lisa Lopes to audition for Ian, and Ian signed her up.

Rico had planned on bringing a second woman to audition—his neighborhood friend Tionne "T-Boz" Watkins—but she had to work and couldn't make it. So that night Lisa and Ian went to see T-Boz at home. "I got her up at two in the morning and she came to the door looking amazing," Burke recalls. "So that was it, it was the look I needed. So if she couldn't sing we were going to find a way to make it work."

T-Boz, it turned out, could sing, and Lisa knew how to rap. So Ian put them, along with Crystal, into a studio with Jermaine Dupri. They put together a demo and set their sights on getting it to Pebbles. Tionne worked as a manicurist in a salon with Pebbles' hairstylist, so when the hairstylist made her house call to Pebbles in Alpharetta, she took Second Nature's publicity photo with her.

Pebbles liked what she saw and contacted Ian about buying out his interest in the group. Ian walked away with a payout big enough "to buy a 1988 Chevy Nova" and Pebbles signed Second Nature to Pebbitone. Only she didn't like the group's name, so she wondered if the girls' first names spelled out TLC. And she didn't like Crystal, either, so she found a beautiful young woman named Rozonda Thomas, a backup dancer for Damian Dame (needing a "C" to replace Crystal, she nicknamed her Chilli). And she didn't want the songs on Jermaine's demo, so she hired Dallas Austin, whom L.A. Reid had lured away from Motown with the promise of a production deal with LaFace. Austin produced the bulk of TLC's debut (Jermaine got a track, and L.A. and Babyface contributed three), and also got a deal to release his own group, Highland Place Mobsters, on LaFace.

Reid signed TLC to LaFace, which—even by the music business' ethically lax standards—was astonishingly conflicted: Together, the Reid household triple-dipped into TLC's finances as the group's manager, production company head, and label head. At first, that was just fine with the group members, as long as L.A. and Pebbles were working hard to make them stars.

Released in February 1992, *Oooooohhh . . . On the TLC Tip* did indeed make the trio stars, and gave LaFace its first huge success. With three top-ten hits—"Ain't 2 Proud 2 Beg," "What About Your Friends," and "Baby Baby Baby"—TLC marked off their territory as a sassier Salt-N-Pepa, with their baggy clothes, their literally in-your-face safe-sex message (Lisa "Left Eye" Lopes' condom eye patch), and their mix of girl-group R&B with pop-oriented hip-hop.

Arriving on the heels of Another Bad Creation, and virtually concurrent with Kris Kross' debut, *TLC Tip* further defined Atlanta's new position at the forefront of hip-hop-inflected urban pop. Here was the sound of modern Atlanta: upwardly mobile and irrepressibly youthful, proudly black but friendly to all, and slick enough to compete with New York without the whiff of Northeastern elitism.

THREE YEARS, FIVE MONTHS, AND TWO DAYS IN THE BIRTH OF SOUTHERN-IDENTIFIED HIP-HOP

Of course, there was more to Atlanta—and the black South—that was about to surface. Like the city's urban pop, another stream also took cues from up north. But otherwise, it was completely different. Around 1989, a clique of New York–area hip-hop acts called the Native Tongues—including the Jungle Brothers, Queen Latifah, De La Soul, and A Tribe Called Quest—presented a gentler, more cultural nationalist approach to the political Afrocentrism espoused by Public Enemy. These groups redefined hip-hop's identity game, broadening it from mere signifying boasts to expressions of self-love and racial pride.

The approach proved influential beyond the African American community, and far beyond New York. Ethnic pride became a main ingredient in the cultural expansion of hip-hop: There were Irish rappers (House of Pain), Jewish rappers (Blood of Abraham), and South Asian rappers (Apache Indian). It was only a matter of time before there were Southern rappers as well—Southern, that is, as a cultural identification and source of pride, something that had not yet been explored by bass artists or urban-pop acts.

Todd Thomas was taking classes at the Atlanta Art Institute when the Native Tongues acts appeared, and he became an immediate fan. Their approach became a huge influence on Thomas, better known as the rapper Speech, when he formed the group Arrested Development. But it was not the only influence.

Thomas grew up in Milwaukee in a family with a strong African American cultural identity. His parents, Robert and Patricia Thomas, published black newspapers—his mother's *Milwaukee Community Journal* is still being published. As a child, Todd grew up in a house filled with foster siblings, including a legally adopted brother from Ghana and a natural brother named Terry. But while his family was educated and middle class, his father had grown up dirt poor in the South. Todd's parents wanted to instill in him a sense of his roots, so each summer they sent him down to live with his grandmother in Henning, Tennessee, a town with fewer than one thousand residents.

Todd recalls that his grandmother had indoor plumbing installed when he was eleven or twelve (that would be, roughly, 1980). So Todd's summers involved rounding up well water, trips to the outhouse, and outdoor baths with water heated over a fire. "It was a very old-school way of life, which I really liked," Thomas says. "I really learned a lot about nature and agriculture from that experience. That was a turning point in life. Just spending time in this small town learning about my family's history, culture—the South felt like home to me, I just embraced it."

Back home in Milwaukee, Todd fell in love with early hip-hop, particularly conscious raps such as "The Message." When his father opened a nightclub called the Fox Trap, the thirteen-year-old Todd became its DJ. Still, he felt drawn to the South. "I always wanted to be in the South, ever since my childhood experiences," he says. "As far as African Americans in this country, I feel like the cradle is the South, and so I always felt a deep connection." So as soon as he graduated from high school in 1987, Thomas moved to Atlanta to pursue music.

Thomas enrolled in the music business program at the Atlanta Art Institute and, wanting to start a band, posted flyers around the school to recruit suitable candidates. A fellow student, Tim Barnwell, answered the ad, and he and Thomas formed a group called Secret Society, which was soon renamed Arrested Development. Thomas' idea was highly conceptual: He wanted to draw a real, direct link between hip-hop and pan-African culture—and he saw the American South as the crossroads between black America and Africa. He envisioned a rap group that was a collective—a microcosm of a black community—making hip-hop that was both contemporary and spiritual. This was the Native Tongues idea, but expounded upon and relocated to the heartland of the American black experience, the South.

Initially, the group was open-ended, with Speech on the mic and Barnwell (aka Headliner) on turntables. They got a regular gig at a southside joint called Club Celebs, where they invited vocalists, djembe players, breakdancers, graffiti artists, and African dancers to join them onstage. As the group's following grew, Arrested Development performed out of town and played at the Georgia Congress Center during the Omega Psi Phi black fraternity's big step show.

Along the way, Speech and Headliner recruited drummer Rasha Don and Don's fiancée, the singer Dionne Farris, as well as other musicians. Playing shows back in Milwaukee, they recruited clothing designer/vocalist Aerle Taree and a sixty-year-old man whom Speech had befriended when they took an African history class together, Baba Oje. "From my African studies I knew I wanted to have an elder in the group," Speech says. That neither Taree's nor Oje's role in the group was predominantly as a musician was significant; Speech saw Arrested Development as a community more than strictly a music group.

Ian Burke, who had been Speech's roommate, was initially the group's manager. But as Arrested Development released an independent single, "Speed Limit 55," and started getting label interest, Michael Mauldin took over Burke's role. He got the group a development deal with Chrysalis Records and put them to work on beats over at Jermaine Dupri's home studio. "But we were on two different paths," Speech recalls. "I was more on a hip-hop vibe on a cultural level. He was starting to do Kris Kross, so we just kept doing our own thing."

Arrested Development's first recording was a somewhat didactic song called "Mr. Wendal" about a homeless man. Chrysalis was impressed, and the label agreed to contract a full album. Before "Mr. Wendal" could be released, however, two tragedies shook Speech's life. First, his grandmother died, breaking the tie that first connected him to the South. Then, Speech's older brother Terry, just out of medical school in Milwaukee, suffered an acute asthma attack and died at twenty-nine. In mourning, Speech reflected on the last time he'd seen his brother alive, at his grandmother's funeral in Tennessee.

Out of Speech's soul-searching over mortality, his connection to God, and the cyclical nature of life that had led him back to his family's Southern heritage, he conjured up the astonishing song "Tennessee." Part gospel, part metaphysical musing, it was hip-hop unlike any that had been heard before. Addressing God, Speech rap/sings both personal testimony and statement of purpose:

> *Then outta nowhere you tell me to break outta the country*
> *and into more country*
> *Past Dyesburg into Ripley*
> *Where the ghost of childhood haunts me*
> *Walk the roads my forefathers walked*

Climbed the trees my forefathers hung from
Ask those trees for all their wisdom
They tell me my ears are so young (Home!)
Go back to from whence you came (Home!)
My family tree, my family name (Home!)
For some strange reason it had to be (Home!)
He guided me to Tennessee (Home!)

"Tennessee" became the group's first single; it was popular on college radio first, then MTV picked it up. The black-and-white video showcased the
group—draped in a blend of African garb, down-home rags, and street
wear—hanging out in front of a rundown house, spinning records on a
turntable, washing clothes in a washtub. The video blended Southern and
hip-hop images in a totally new way. When black radio finally embraced the
single, it shot to number one on the rap and R&B/hip-hop charts (number
six pop).

Arrested Development's album debuted in March of 1992—less than one
month after *Ooooooohhh . . . On the TLC Tip*, and just one week before *To-*
tally Krossed Out arrived. In hindsight, early 1992 kicked off the golden era
of Atlanta urban music. Where TLC signaled LaFace Records' arrival, and
Kris Kross marked Jermaine Dupri's ascension, AD's *3 Years, 5 Months & 2*
Days in the Life of . . . —named for the time it took between the group's
founding and signing its record deal—marked the dawn of Southern consciousness in rap. "Hip-hop was still very urban," Speech says. "The country
thing, the Dirty South thing still hadn't been said yet. So the South didn't
really have an identity."

AD's second single, a rewriting of Sly Stone's "Everyday People" called
"People Everyday," was far less impressive. But with its familiar hook, the
song matched the chart success of "Tennessee" (number one rap, number
eight pop) and further established Arrested Development as one of the
year's biggest musical successes. The third single returned to "Mr. Wendal,"
which also reached the top ten on both pop and urban charts. In the end,
Arrested Development sold five million records, earned two Grammys—
Best New Artist and Best Rap Performance by a Duo or Group ("Tennessee")—was named Band of the Year in *Rolling Stone*, and won the
prestigious *Pazz & Jop* critic's poll in the *Village Voice*.

Still, from today's vantage point, it's easier to see *3 Years* as a commercial
peak for Native Tongues–style alternative rap than as a blueprint for Southern hip-hop. The record consciously, and often successfully, evokes Southern imagery and values: from the harmonica wails of "Mama's Always On

Stage" to the critique of the Baptist church on "Fishin' 4 Religion," to the quasi-agricultural focus of "Children Play with the Earth" and "Raining Revolution." But ultimately, AD's undoubtedly earnest love of the black Southern heritage was more academic than naturalistic—an aesthetic statement rather than a true expression of identity. And that's why, a decade on, Southern hip-hop doesn't sound much like Arrested Development imagined it.

After two years of touring the world, Arrested Development returned to Atlanta in 1994 and made a second studio album, *Zingalamaduni*, which sold shockingly few copies considering it was the follow-up to a multiplatinum sensation. Blame partly goes to the material—more ambitious in places, but generally less captivating musically—and partly to label problems, as Chrysalis' parent company, EMI, shut down most of the label's American operations. These problems exacerbated issues within the band, and after a 1995 tour of Japan, Arrested Development went on an indefinite leave. By the time they returned five years later, American audiences were no longer interested, and the group has released its records only overseas.

That AD's success was short-lived does not suggest its influence was not profound. Speech says, "I don't think that it would've been as easily accepted if we had not given the public a chance to get acclimated to what an Andre 3000 would later wear, or some of the imagery that would later have been seen with the Nappy Roots or Goodie Mob. Some of those things would've been harder to chew."

ATLANTA'S BASS SURVIVORS

Atlanta has long had two distinct faces to its black community: There's the upwardly mobile Atlanta—people who've moved from other places for educational and economic opportunities—along with the established black society; and there's the 'hood, which faces the same challenges that inner cities face everywhere. This kind of division exists in any large city, for whites and for blacks, but Atlanta's unusual features—its black colleges, its black political power, its large black middle class, its reputation as the black mecca— bring the number of haves and have-nots to more equal levels, accentuating the divides within a black community that is so often viewed monolithically.

In the early '90s, it was easy to see the two Atlantas manifested in music. Because while Another Bad Creation, Kris Kross, TLC, and Arrested Development defined what Atlanta meant to the rest of the country, huge stretches of the other Atlanta were still buying bass music.

While early Atlanta bass acts like Shy-D, Tony Rock, and Success-N-Effect were mostly offshoots of Miami bass, things started changing around 1990, when a Bankhead teenager named Kilo (born Andrell Demetrius Rogers) began putting out records on Raheem the Dream's local Arvis Records label. Within a year, Kilo was the biggest bass artist in Atlanta, which prompted Ichiban to expand beyond its soul roots and get into the bass game. Kilo was actually Ichiban's third hip-hop signing—it had already put out a single by a young white boy from Dallas, Vanilla Ice, and it inherited the Michigan-born, Atlanta-based rapper MC Breed when Breed's Ichiban-distributed label folded. Given Ichiban's success with Breed, it decided to make rap a priority. The label set up an imprint called Wrap Records for artists such as Kilo and Kizzy Rock.

While Kilo's huge local popularity never translated to more than a regional following, he's remembered as one of Atlanta bass' best MCs. He indulged in bass' usual themes of sex ("My Ding-a-Ling") and booming systems ("Hear What I Hear"), but also offered hard-charging street raps ("Kilo Don't Take No Mess") and even a social critique, "America Has a Problem (Cocaine)." A throwback to message-oriented rap of the '80s, it was downright progressive for bass music—and became one of Kilo's most popular songs.

Fellow Wrap artist DJ Smurf says, "For Kilo to make a bass record called 'Cocaine,' to be talking on some social shit, that was unheard of. And he was singing on records even back then. So he was like the OutKast of the bass game." (In fact, OutKast producers Organized Noize held Kilo in such high regard they signed him to their major-affiliated label to put out Kilo's 1997 album, *Organized Bass*, which featured appearances by members of OutKast and Goodie Mob. But after it failed to gain a national audience, Kilo's life became unhinged; he was sent to jail in 1998 for burning down his own house.)

Building on Kilo's modest success, Ichiban established itself as Atlanta's home for bass, scoring its biggest hit in 1993 with 95 South's "Whoot, There It Is." After Shy-D's prison stint, he wound up on Wrap for a 1993 album, *The Comeback*. Though Shy's recording career was winding down, the record introduced his mixer, DJ Smurf. Michael Crooms got his start as a DJ through King Edward J's J Team and earned the moniker Smurf because of his size. He started making his own music in college at Alabama A&M, where he did a bass record called "To the Wall"—containing the hook "to the window, to the wall"—that was borrowed a decade later by Lil Jon and the Ying Yang Twins for their massive hit, "Get Low."

Smurf signed his own deal with Ichiban and released the album *Versastyle* in 1995. By then, though, bass music was faltering, and, besides scoring a top-twenty rap single with "Ooh Lawd," Smurf's records never had much impact nationally. For Smurf, though, bass music was just the first act of a career that has changed as many times as his nicknames.

UP FROM THE DUNGEON

Rico Wade's friendship with T-Boz, and Sleepy Brown's music connections as Jimmy Brown's son, provided some opportunities for their singing group, the Uboyz. Sleepy had access to his father's recording studio and used it to record some Uboyz demos. And T-Boz got the demo to Pebbles. As Sleepy recalls, "Pebbles liked our music, but we weren't that great vocally. She just flat-out told us, 'I like y'all's beats, I think you should get more into production.'"

With the Uboyz looking like a dead end, Rico and Sleepy took Pebbles' advice. They'd recently met Ray Murray, a hip-hop producer from the Greenbriar area, who had his hands in a bunch of different neighborhood groups. With his rapper friend Cameron Gipp, Ray was a member of Sixth Sense, which was getting attention for a song it recorded during the Gulf War. As Murray recalls, "We had a record called 'Pray for Peace,' and we had talked to NBC's *Today Show* and they had us like we were going to perform. But the day the plane tickets were coming, the war stopped. So we didn't go."

Ray was also making tracks for a rapper named Reese, and a group called 66 Mello that featured two guys, Mello and Kawan Prather (KP). Ray and his artists came together with Rico and Sleepy through a guy who was "managing" most of them, and they bonded through their affiliation with Joseph Carn, a guy from Ray's neighborhood with a full studio in his house. Carn's mother was the vocalist Jean Carn, a Georgia native who'd sung with Earth, Wind & Fire and George Duke before recording a trio of solo albums for the Philadelphia International label. Joe had access to his mother's recording equipment and hoped to use it as home base for his own stable of artists. Ray worked over at Carn's house and, one night, their manager brought Rico and Sleepy over. They soon began to talk of collaborating.

But the situation at Carn's studio didn't last long. Ray thought Carn was taking credit for Ray's work, and so they all broke away. "His arrogance kind of made us come together," Ray says, "to unite against him, in the sense of: I do beats, you do tracks, you dance, you rap, let's get together."

The problem was that they didn't have anywhere to go, and no one could afford the kind of equipment Carn had. But a friend of Rico's, Ruben Bailey, or Big Rube, wanted to help. Rube had gotten into some trouble while at Tri-Cities High, and his father had died when he was young. Rube's mother, who knew Rico as the hard-working young man from the beauty supply shop, wanted to steer her son toward positive influences. So when Rube approached her asking for a couple thousand dollars from his father's insurance policy to buy an MPC60 sampler, she saw music as a hobby to keep Rube occupied. Rube bought the sampler and donated it to the collective efforts of this new production crew. Pooled together with some equipment Sleepy had, some that Ray had, and some turntables and mixers that Rico procured, they set up a studio inside Rico's cramped Delowe Gardens apartment.

"It was 24–7 after that," Rube recalls, "banging on the beat machine. And that's kind of the reason he had to move out of there, because we were doing beats real loud."

It wasn't long before Rico's mom, and the neighbors, had had enough of the loud music, so Rico found the crew a room to rent for cheap. It wasn't ideal: It was a storage room with no windows or ventilation. But the location couldn't be beat: inside of Jellybeans.

Jellybeans, a skate rink in the Ben Hill neighborhood off Cambellton Road, was an institution for black teens in Southwest Atlanta during the '80s and early '90s. It was where everyone went to see and be seen; Dallas Austin, Jermaine Dupri, members of TLC, Rico Wade, and others were all there before any of them knew each other. The Austin-produced 2006 film, *ATL*, is set around a rink modeled after Jellybeans—in fact, the movie's working title was *Jellybeans*.

Jellybeans was in decline by the time Rico, Sleepy, and Ray built a studio there, but it served well as a place to meet for the rappers, DJs, and producers who were coming together around the trio: The Uboyz were still nominally active; Big Rube was rapping; Ray's friends Mello, Reese, and KP formed Parental Advisory, or P.A.; Big Gipp had a group called Chain Gang, with an East Point rapper named Cool Breeze (Frederick Bell); and Ray and Gipp's friends from Benjamin E. Mays High School—Willie "Khujo" Knighton and Robert Terrance "T-Mo" Barnett—started their own duo, the Lumberjacks.

Meanwhile, Rico, Sleepy, and Ray bonded to form a production partnership. They adopted the name Rico and Sleepy had originally created for a girl group they were hoping to put together. The group never materialized, but the name stuck, so they used it for their production team: Organized Noize.

As a team, the threesome settled into complementary roles: Sleepy had an R&B background, while Ray was hip-hop through and through. It created a musical dynamism, which Rico integrated by focusing on the big picture.

"In the beginning, I did all the beats," Ray says, "Sleepy did all the melodies, and Rico had the vision. I'd be programming, Sleepy would do the arrangement, and Rico would be, 'OK, that sounds dope.' I'm a hip-hop purist, so I ain't sampling no other hip-hop shit, I ain't doing such and such—it's like a Bible a hip-hop dude would go by. Rico comes in, loves hip-hop, loves R&B, loves rock 'n' roll. So he taught me to say, 'Fuck the rules.' And I taught him the techniques to build tracks. Sleepy is the singer, and he can play every instrument."

Of the groups forming around Organized Noize, P.A. was the first to develop a real chance at scoring a record deal. Again, T-Boz was the hookup. Around the time TLC prepared to release its debut album, Pebbles held a casting audition for the group's "Baby, Baby, Baby" video. P.A. showed up and performed for Pebbles. She liked what she heard. KP, who was also cast in the video, recalls Pebbles telling the group she'd make them the "down South Naughty By Nature."

When TLC took off and proved Pebbles' eye for talent, MCA Records offered her a label deal. She set up Savvy Records and made P.A. her first signing. It was a small deal—KP says their advance was fifteen thousand dollars, split by P.A.'s three members—but for Organized Noize and crew, it meant their first professional deal.

Meanwhile, the studio at Jellybeans was getting difficult to sustain. Having earned nothing from their work yet, Organized Noize had trouble stretching Rico's paycheck at Lamonte's to help with rent at home and cover the studio space. With his family facing eviction, Rico asked his most powerful acquaintance for help: Eldrin Bell, who served as Atlanta's colorful police chief in the early '90s. Bell (also known as the father of *American Idol* also-ran Justin Guarini) helped Rico's family find a place that was big and private enough to hold a studio: a small corner house in the Lakewood area, on a quiet block of Lakewood Terrace.

Rico, Sleepy, Ray, and the rest of the crew set up their equipment in the unfinished basement of the Lakewood house. It wasn't glamorous, but the friends grew to love this refuge—a place all their own, where they could hang out and create their music.

"It was under the kitchen floor—a crawl space with a dirt floor," Ray says. "We had a table, chairs set up, an MPC with dust all over it, keyboards, records all over. We put crazy lights down there, so we had the whole atmosphere. When it flooded we had to take the shit upstairs, because it warped. But the vibes down there were otherworldly. Sometimes we'd be down there writing—everybody talking, smoking a joint—then the drum machine would go on, and we'd be like, 'What the fuck?' Because of the moisture in the machine, it used to go haywire. It would trigger samples, crazy shit."

The place cried out for a nickname and, given its location and near-squalid conditions, "the Dungeon" was the natural choice. No one recalls who thought of it, but the name stuck. "The whole idea of calling it the Dungeon came from the way the basement looked," says Big Rube. "There were red clay walls, pipes over your head, like a boiler room. And people didn't leave. You'd go over there and basically live there—almost like you was held captive. So it just fit perfectly."

As Organized Noize and P.A. laid down tracks for P.A.'s debut, Rico's house became a virtual youth hostel for the crew that was becoming known as the Dungeon Family. They'd scrape together change and share a three-dollar fried-chicken dinner from Church's, or the spaghetti special from the Citgo gas station. The guys would work into the night down in the Dungeon, then crash upstairs on the living room floor. In the morning, Rico's mom—who Rube describes as "the kind of person that, if she don't cuss you out, you know she probably don't like you"—would clear them all out, knowing they'd be back by the time she returned from work.

"Rico's mom didn't care because she knew we were going to do good," Sleepy says. "That's all we would do, work all night, work all day."

Though the close quarters and shared adversity turned the aspiring artists into a kind of family, all was not going smoothly with the work. "We thought we were the shit," KP admits of P.A., who grew increasingly unwilling to follow Organized Noize's musical lead. Pebbles' intention to make P.A. a Naughty by Nature–styled group—that is, without any discernible trace of Southernness—added to the tension.

It was true that, before Arrested Development's emergence, Southern acts did better nationally when emulating Northern styles (Dallas Austin's and Jermaine Dupri's approach) than when sticking to a Southern sound (such as bass music). But for P.A. and Organized Noize, the approach didn't fit. "Pebbles was telling us we needed to appeal to people outside of the South," KP says. "So we pretty much fucked the album up. It was just like some Southern cats trying to sound like they're from New York."

In frustration, Organized Noize started looking elsewhere for talent. A lot of the rappers hanging around—Gipp, Cool Breeze, Khujo, T-Mo, Big Rube—were developing material but had not yet grown into marketable artists. One day, Ray visited Rico at Lamonte's. "Man, we need another group," Ray recalls saying. "We need two young cats that's fire, who are from Atlanta, that we don't know, so our relationship can be entirely on a different level. It could be brand new."

Though it sounds more the stuff of legend than literal truth, Ray swears that just as he spoke, he looked down the street and saw two guys walking toward the shop, looking for Rico.

The first thing that brought Andre Benjamin and Antwan "Big Boi" Patton together was a shared impulse to get out beyond their familiar surroundings. In 1991, both were tenth graders at East Point's Tri-Cities High School, in the heart of the SWATs, and one weekend they both happened to take the MARTA train up to Buckhead, to the ritzy Lenox Mall on the north side of Atlanta, to have a look at how the other half lives. And there, standing in front of the Ralph Lauren store—window shopping, because neither had any money to spend—Antwan and his little brother ran into Andre.

They knew each other already from school—a mutual friend introduced them and they were both falling in with a small clique of guys who shared a more bohemian, worldly outlook than most students. They loved the music of Brand Nubian, De La Soul, and A Tribe Called Quest in addition to local bass stuff, while peers tended to stick with regional and West Coast rap. But they hadn't yet interacted a whole lot one-on-one. They rode the MARTA back to East Point together and bonded over talk about school, music, and girls. The conversation never ended; Andre called his dad, whom he lived with at the time, and asked if Antwan could sleep over that night. They were inseparable from then on.

Like all successful relationships, Andre and Antwan brought together common interests and backgrounds with different, but complementary, personalities and experiences. Antwan Andre Patton was the first child born to a teenage mother on the poor and black west side of Savannah, Georgia. He grew up surrounded by an extended family—his grandmother, as well as his aunts and uncles, and occasionally his father. In his early teens, 'Twan's mother, Rowena Patton, sent him to live with his Aunt Renee in Atlanta, where there were more opportunities for education and advancement. He was glad to be in the big city; as long as he kept good grades, his mother would let him stay.

Andre Lauren Benjamin was also born to unmarried parents in 1975, but in Atlanta. He was the accidental product of a short relationship between nineteen-year-old office secretary Sharon Benjamin and Lawrence Walker, a loan officer nearly ten years older who worked next door. They'd never intended to start a family together, but they tried to make it work. By the time Andre was a toddler, though, they'd split up for good. Lawrence would take Dre to stay with his family in Columbus, Georgia, during the summer, but

Dre mostly grew up alone with Sharon. Neither parent remarried while he was growing up, and neither had any more children, so Andre grew accustomed to being alone and self-sufficient. When he was about nine, Dre convinced his mother that he'd be OK if she left him home alone while she worked night shifts at General Motors. He cooked for himself, did his homework, and put himself to bed. Both parents described Andre as a quiet kid.

While Antwan distinguished himself as a good student in southwest Atlanta, Andre's mother had other plans for him. "My mom always used to say, 'Why you wanna be a typical everyday nigga?'" Andre recalls. "'Why don't you do something different? Why you wanna be like everybody else?'"

In the mid-80s, Sharon signed Andre up for Atlanta's minority-to-majority busing program, which offered blacks from low-performing schools the chance to transfer to better-performing white schools. Andre rode the bus each day into the heart of Buckhead, to Sarah Smith Elementary School and then to Willis A. Sutton Middle School. Kids from the neighborhood wondered why he didn't go with them to the school down the street, but Andre thrived in his new environment. At Sutton, he got involved in drama and served on the student council. "It let me see a lot of new things I probably wouldn't see at a neighborhood school," Andre says. "I grew up right across from the projects, but by going to school with white kids, I got into skateboarding and the music and everything. I listened to both. I'd come home and might hear Eric B & Rakim or Too Short, then go to school and hear another thing. I was influenced by both."

Antwan had his eclectic side, too. Where Dre got into Prince and George Clinton as a kid, Antwan found himself moved by the music of Kate Bush. By the time they met in high school, though, hip-hop was their focus and, stylistically, they were on the same page. But at first, their friendship wasn't about making music. They fell in with a crew that was stealing cars from the Old National Highway on the south side, until a close call scared them straight. And they tried peddling weed, but Big Boi recalls, "We were smoking it before we could sell it." Eventually, they gave up hustling and got jobs at shoe stores—Andre at Foot Action in Greenbriar Mall and Big Boi at Foot Locker in Underground Atlanta.

In eleventh grade, Andre dropped out of Tri-Cities and was taking classes at Frank McLaren High, an alternative school for kids who had jobs or children and wanted to get their GED. Andre and Big Boi stayed close, though, and their shared interest in music blossomed into a plan to form a group. They'd sit around the kitchen table and take turns saying rhymes, practicing and developing an act they could take to the clubs. They called themselves 2 Shades Deep.

One night Dre arranged for them to perform on a cable-access show, their first public performance. Big Boi had to work, however, so Andre turned to Thomas "Cee-Lo" Burton, an old friend from the third grade with whom he'd become reacquainted at McLaren. Cee-Lo was also interested in music, and he often joined Andre and Big Boi for their practice sessions. He knew the material, so Andre asked Cee-Lo to fill in for Big Boi.

It was not an illustrious start; as Andre recalls, "After we performed, some guy called in and said, 'I just wanted to let you know ya'll sounded like *shit!*'" Their first stage appearance didn't go much better—a high school party at the West End's Club Fritz (later known as Club 559). "Big Boi's uncle gave us weed and we smoked it in a napkin, so it was burning all wrong," Andre says. "Then we got to the party and just crunked it up. We was on one mic, passing it back and forth, busting each other in the lip."

When Andre and Big Boi learned of another local group called 4 Shades Deep, they ditched their group's name. Instead they chose Misfits, because, Big Boi says, "We didn't want to be compared to anybody. We wanted our name to mean 'apart from the norm.'" But there was a rock band by that name already established. So they looked in the dictionary for similar words, found "outcast," and adopted the phonetic spelling: OutKast.

By late 1992, Dre and Big were polished enough to present their rhymes to a label. So when a friend from Tri-Cities, Bianca, said she knew a producer, they asked her to set up a meeting. Bianca worked after school with Rico at Lamonte's. By then, Organized Noize was earning a reputation as an up-and-coming production team, through working with P.A. But for Dre and Big, it was just one of two meetings they planned for that day.

Years later, Andre would describe the meeting in the song "Elevators (Me & You)":

> *One for the money and two for the show*
> *A couple of years ago on Headland and Delowe*
> *Was the start of something good,*
> *when me and my nigga rode the MARTA through the hood*
> *Just trying to find that hook-up. . . .*

Having been immortalized in song—and being so significant in the Southern hip-hop story—the Dungeon Family has mythologized the scene. Just about all the early DF members remember being there the day OutKast showed up, though certainly not all were present.

While accounts vary, some details are consistent: When Bianca showed up at Lamonte's that afternoon, she told Rico that some rappers she knew were coming by to meet him. "Oh man, some more rappers," Rico recalls think-ing. But Rico liked Bianca, and she wasn't one to routinely send rappers to him, so he kept an open mind. Then, about an hour before closing time, he spotted two guys walking up the block from the direction of the MARTA bus stop. They immediately caught Rico's eye: Dressed in sweatshirts, cutoff jeans with thermals, and huaraches—and sporting bald heads—Andre and Big Boi looked like nothing Rico had seen coming out of Atlanta, more like the latest New York styles of Das EFX or Onyx. "They weren't no ghetto Atlanta niggas with gold teeth," Rico says, "They were hip-hop."

When Dre and Big got up in front of Lamonte's, Bianca introduced them to Rico. "What's up, y'all. Y'all got songs?" Rico asked.

Dre and Big hadn't recorded yet, so they wanted to rhyme live on the spot for Rico. They pulled out a cassette to rap over. Gipp had been hanging out in the parking lot in his Isuzu Trooper, and they all went over to put the tape into Gipp's system. It was the extended instrumental version of A Tribe Called Quest's "Scenario," and the track seemed to go on forever.

"They went back to back until the mufuckin' tape stopped," Rico recalls. "One of them would rap until his breath was out and then it was like, 'Tag!' It was just incredible—no hooks, no errors. They seemed like some battle rappers of something."

"I thought they were dope," Gipp says. "They sounded like Das EFX. And at that time, anyone who could rhyme fast I thought was dope. That wasn't something that was real popular with us. They could really spit like an up-north rapper."

"I just thought they rapped long as hell," says Sleepy, who remembers be-ing there as well. "Each one had a rap for like fifteen, twenty minutes. I was just standing there, like, 'Damn, when you gonna end?' I liked them, but Rico really believed in them and made us believe in them. He heard some-thing we didn't hear."

When Dre and Big finally finished, Rico told them to come back at clos-ing time. He was going to take them to the Dungeon. "Rico was the hus-tler, the mouthpiece of Organized Noize," Andre says. "He would say stuff like, 'Yeah, we can get you a deal next week.' And we believed him. So we went to the Dungeon."

Andre and Big Boi arrived at the house on Lakewood Terrace to find a cou-ple of young men already there. Both were sixteen, a few years younger than most of the Dungeon guys, but they fell in with the crew right away. "I thought it was going on over there," says Big Boi, who arrived to find a dozen or so people scattered upstairs in the family room and downstairs in the studio. "Niggas just writing on pads everywhere, smokin' their herb, forty ounces of Olde English and all kinds of shit everywhere. The atmosphere said, 'Damn, this is where we need to be.'"

Big Rube was one of the first to greet the new arrivals. "They looked real young," he recalls. "But the personalities were already there. Dre had the kind of quiet personality, Big Boi had this reputation for not giving a fuck—talking about you right in your face even if he don't know you. They were cool."

When Rico arrived in the Dungeon with Dre and Big, Ray was down there working on beats. Small in stature but with a Zen-like focus on crafting tracks, Ray quickly earned the nickname "Yoda"—the Dungeon's own Jedi master beat maker—from Outkast. "The first day, Ray was teaching me stuff already," Andre recalls. "He showed me every record Dr. Dre got his samples from, all the records Das EFX got their songs from. He was breaking it down for me and showing me how it was done."

Big similarly fell under Ray's tutelage. "Ray taught me how to rap," he says. "He'd just tell me how you had to say things like you mean it. I was a writer, and he taught me how to be an MC."

At first, Dre and Big came with a rhyme style very much borrowed from the new breed of rappers—Tribe and Das EFX from New York, and Souls of Mischief from the Bay Area. But Organized Noize heard in them raw talent and energy, and figured the duo's still-evolving voice could be molded to suit their own stylistic explorations. Because, while Organized had dutifully turned out New York–style beats for P.A., as Pebbles requested, they were now looking to try something new—as Ray describes it, "clashing the East and the West and the South to make something."

One thing that did carry over from Organized's work with P.A. and Pebbles: original music. "Pebbles told us we couldn't sample, period," Ray explains. "'Don't bring me no music with samples in it, I'm not clearing no samples.'" Pebbles' request was likely motivated by the cost of samples, but it presented an opportunity: a chance for Organized Noize to find its own musical voice.

As OutKast integrated itself into the Dungeon, Dre and Big began spending nearly all their time at Rico's house. That they were still in high school—and expected by their families to stay in high school—presented a challenge. For Big Boi, quitting school meant having to go back to Savannah, so he kept trips to the Dungeon limited to after school. He'd sleep over at Rico's with the rest of the crew, but when morning came, Rico's mom made sure he was up and off to school. "My momma was like a grand-momma, where she treated everyone like her kid," Rico says.

Dre, on the other hand, had already basically dropped out, and once he fell in with the Dungeon, going to McLaren became even less a priority. Though Dre lived with his dad at the time, when his mother began hearing about his long hours at a place called the Dungeon, she wanted some answers. "[Big's aunt] Renee loved me, so I could keep Big Boi out late, it wasn't any problem," Rico says. "Then all of a sudden, Andre's momma was just so concerned, like, 'What the fuck is going on?' That's when she started making crazy comments, calling my momma and asking me some really disrespectful shit, like, 'What, you gay or something? Why they want to be around you?'"

By then, though, Andre's direction was largely beyond his mother's control. And eventually, the tension abated. "She turned around later and became the most important person in his career," Rico says of Sharon Benjamin. "She's real, too, so I don't fault her for nothing."

While the Dungeon brought a critical group of Atlanta hip-hop artists together, there were limits to how much actual music could be created there. Besides some drum machines and samplers, the Dungeon lacked the equipment required to actually record songs. Working with P.A., Organized Noize had already logged time in a professional recording space—Bobby Brown's Bosstown Studios. If OutKast was ever going to be more than an after-school hobby, they were going to have to get out of the Dungeon and into a real studio.

THE ROAD TO *SOUTHERNPLAYALISTICADILLACMUZIK*

With the success of TLC's 1992 debut album, LaFace moved full-steam ahead. A Jermaine Jackson record didn't generate much excitement, but LaFace's soundtrack to the Eddie Murphy film *Boomerang* gave the label its second huge hit and introduced its next megastar, Toni Braxton, who'd score her own multiplatinum debut in 1993. The soundtrack also solidified Dallas Austin's role as an architect of LaFace's decade-defining R&B sound (though L.A. and Babyface were themselves behind the record's biggest hit, Boyz II Men's record-breaking chart-topper "End of the Road").

Austin returned again in the summer of '92 with the album *1746DCGA30035* by Atlanta quartet the Highland Place Mobsters, of which Austin was a member. By the following year, Austin found himself head of a new Arista-affiliated label, Rowdy Records, which L.A. Reid helped to orchestrate as a hip-hop-oriented LaFace spin-off. Among Rowdy's first releases: Illegal, yet another teen rap group, and the Atlanta hip-hop foursome Y'All So Stupid, whose sole Rowdy release, 1993's *Van Full of Pakistans*, offered a less political, more fun-loving take on the upwardly mobile alt-rap being created by Arrested Development.

Meanwhile, with LaFace's fortunes rising, Babyface took the opportunity to step away. After a few years in Atlanta growing the company, he found he preferred being on the creative side—as a producer, songwriter, and solo artist. In 1993, Babyface gave up his position at LaFace and moved back to California. As Reid assumed control of the label, the pair ended their writing and production partnership as well.

As LaFace grew quickly in 1992 and '93, the label opened up to possibility of discovering young, unproven producers and artists. That, in part, is why Pebbles—acknowledging Rico Wade's role in TLC's creation and Organized Noize's production work on P.A.'s debut—introduced Rico to her husband, L.A. Reid. With Dallas already in the LaFace fold, and Jermaine Dupri finding success elsewhere, Reid and Pebbles began to wonder whether Organized Noize was Atlanta's next hit maker.

Impressed by what Organized was doing with P.A.'s still-unreleased debut, Reid and Pebbles asked the trio to do a remix of TLC's single "What About Your Friends." The producers then invited their newest protégés, OutKast, to drop verses on the track. It turned out to be a fairly obscure remix—and OutKast comes on nearly four minutes into the six-minute track, with Das EFX–style stuttering and Dre's miscalculation that "underground is where I'm staying." But this inauspicious recording debut was a debut nonetheless—and a tool to earn the notice of LaFace Records.

L.A. was not exactly bowled over by the remix, but he heard enough promise in OutKast to pay for studio time to cut some demos. The tracks they came up with—including "On and On" and "Benz or a Beamer," both songs that would show up later in different forms—proved inconclusive, only increasing L.A.'s doubts about whether OutKast would ever be stars. Admittedly, hip-hop was not L.A.'s strength—he came from the live R&B/funk band era and didn't quite jibe with the aesthetics of rap. So Organized Noize pressed its case, and L.A. agreed to take OutKast up to the LaFace offices to perform live for the staff.

"We went to the office with DAT tapes of tracks we'd been working on," recalls Andre, who along with Big Boi had grown his hair back in and dyed it blond. "L.A. called in the entire staff of LaFace and said, 'Go.' I was nervous, but Rico put in the DAT and we started rapping. I don't think L.A. got it, but he's a businessman and understood hip-hop was about to go off."

Then Reid asked OutKast to perform at an industry showcase, to gauge how much excitement Dre and Big generated from an audience. This time, L.A. came back with a more definitive assessment: no go. "'I don't think they're stars,'" Rico recalls L.A. telling him.

Returning to the Dungeon dejected, Andre decided to bow out of rap. "I was upset because I thought we were really good, so at that point I decided I didn't want to do it anymore."

Rico began to second-guess his initial feeling about OutKast, and consider whether it was irresponsible of him to string Dre and Big along any further. "Those boys were seventeen about to be eighteen and I really cared about them," he says. "They were thinking about college, and so if I felt like it wasn't going to happen, I was going to tell them. You come out of high school, your parents are on your ass—you're going to college, you're going to the military, you're doing something: 'What do you mean you rap? What's that?' If you're black and you're seventeen, you get the hell out this house.'"

But Big Boi remained undeterred and convinced Dre to keep at it. "He was always hypercritical," Big says of Dre. "But I always said if we do what we do, we'd be all right."

Ultimately, what got OutKast moving forward was the threat of a little competition for LaFace. While L.A. took his time deciding if the duo was worth signing, A&R scouts from Polygram Records began expressing interest. That motivated L.A. "His whole thing was nurturing Atlanta into his moneybag," says KP. "He figured he was going to come set up Motown. So he was like, 'I can't let some shit get out of Atlanta and not be involved.'"

Still, L.A. wanted to take baby steps. Instead of a full album deal, he offered OutKast the opportunity to record a song for a 1993 LaFace Christmas album—a prospect that didn't exactly thrill Andre and Big Boi. When you grow up poor in the 'hood, the kind of jolly, merry Christmas associated with holiday music is just some white bullshit that doesn't apply.

But it was a chance to record, so Rico advised them to just write what they wanted to write, without worrying if the song would be Christmasy enough. That was also Organized Noize's approach in creating the track. The idea was to do Christmas, but on their own terms. Their first try was a track called "Socks and Drawers," which complained about the gifts you tended to get in the 'hood. They scrapped it, though, and Organized Noize reused the music for TLC's entry on the compilation, "All I Want for Christmas." At the last moment, Organized had come up with something else that would change the sound of OutKast, and eventually, of hip-hop itself.

Ray and Sleepy were working in the studio on tracks for the Christmas album. Sleepy, by then, had gotten in well with L.A. and Pebbles and was doing his own work for them while Ray and Rico focused on the P.A. album. Sleepy was more of an R&B guy, less interested in making hip-hop, so he found himself somewhat ambivalent about being part of Organized Noize. But OutKast's involvement with TLC and LaFace's Christmas project brought the trio together as a unit. As Sleepy recalls, "We were working on a track for OutKast, and Ray had a beat I thought was incredible. He said, 'It would be fly if we could find somebody to sing it kind of like Curtis [Mayfield].' I was like, 'I can do that.' It was like five in the morning, and I just went in there and did it."

The concept was simple, and only indirectly connected to Christmas. It was a party, but laid-back and funky, the way they do it down South: "All the player's came from far and wide," Sleepy sang in a soulful falsetto croon, imitating Mayfield, "Wearing Afros and braids, kicking them gangsta rides." The song was more directly tied to African American oral tradition than to most hip-hop; toasts about the gatherings of street hustlers go back generations, up through Lightnin' Rod's 1973 album-length toast, *Hustler's Convention*. Sleepy had found his musical voice, and in doing so had given some identity to Organized Noize's production style and OutKast's music.

Once Dre and Big added their verses to "Player's Ball," everyone involved knew they'd hit on something. The lyrics supported the chorus both thematically and musically, with a singsong style that rushed right into the hook. Beginning with the line, "It's beginning to look a lot like what?" Dre launches his no-bullshit take on the holiday season, arriving at the conclusion that, "I made it through another year can't ask for nothing much more." Big sets the scene of "getting tipsy off the nog and high as hell off the contact smoke," but never keeps his mind far from business; when his pager beeps, it reminds him that "a junky is a junky 365/ It's just another day of work to me, the spirit just ain't in me."

It was a synthesis of hip-hop styles, meeting at the Atlanta crossroads: the mellow '70s funk that defined Dr. Dre's West Coast flavor, mixed with the rapid-fire lyricism of Native Tongues MCs, delivered with the slur and slang of a Southerner. It was an audacious blend, and Ray worried the song was too weird—and too melodic—to win over hip-hop fans. But what did L.A. think?

One night just before the Christmas album's release, Big Boi remembers OutKast doing a show at the Masquerade club on North Avenue. He hadn't yet heard the final mix of "Player's Ball" until a limo pulled up blasting it out the window. "It was L.A. sitting there ecstatic, bumpin' to it," Sleepy recalls. "From that point I knew we might have something going on."

Keeping Christmas sentiment out of "Player's Ball" not only preserved OutKast's street credibility, it also improved the single's chances for success. It soon became apparent that "Player's Ball" could be much more than a holiday novelty—with just slight tweaking, it was hard to tell the song had anything to do with Christmas. As the holiday passed and 1994 jumped off, OutKast found its single climbing the rap charts.

To help it along, L.A. brought in an up-and-coming hip-hop flavor man named Sean "Puff Daddy" Combs, who was just starting to make his own connections with Arista Records (LaFace's parent company) for his Bad Boy label. Puffy didn't have any connection to OutKast, nor did he know anything about directing, but Arista believed in his sense of taste, so the label sent him to Atlanta to make a video for "Player's Ball." He worked with Rico to depict Atlanta's down-home vibe—its neighborhoods, its trees, the barbershops and pool halls where the player's hang. It also sparked a rivalry, at least in Rico's mind, between himself and Puffy—both asserting themselves as a hot young hip-hop guy on the rise at Arista. When Puffy took some Atlanta flavor back with him to New York—revived Kangol hats and slang like "playa"—to use in shaping the image of his new act, the Notorious B.I.G., the Dungeon Family considered it an affront.

But things never got nasty—Biggie himself professed nothing but love for the ATL, and his adoption of Atlanta style was more about admiration than theft (before his death, Biggie planned to get a house in Atlanta, like so many Northern hip-hop stars). The intermingling of Bad Boy and Dungeon camps deepened when Andre entered a two-year romantic relationship with Keisha Spivey of the trio Total. And it was Puffy who took Andre and Big Boi out of Georgia for the first time, to open for B.I.G. at Howard University. As Big Boi recalls, "That was my first ride on an airplane, and I was terrified, but I knew if this was my career I had to get used to it. We weren't even old enough to be drinkin' the edge off, but we was drinkin'. We came out and performed and they clapped when we came off. It was happening. It was first blood, first taste of performing in front of an audience."

L.A. Reid was convinced OutKast could be stars, after all. Now he wanted a full album.

In late 1993, within weeks of the release of "Player's Ball," Savvy Records put out the first Dungeon Family–related album, P.A.'s *Ghetto Street Funk*. Given its self-conscious attempt to sound like something it wasn't (current hit makers Naughty by Nature), it was no surprise that the record went nowhere. Ray, Rico, and Sleepy had already moved on to more promising musical adventures, and P.A.'s failure only reinforced their belief that finding success required developing their own voice. P.A.'s leader KP knew that as well, and he tried to impart what he'd learned to his "little brothers" in OutKast. Eventually, providing musical direction to others became more important to him than pushing his own group; while P.A. put out two more albums—1998's excellent but little-heard *Straight No Chase* and 2000's *My Life, Your Entertainment*—KP wound up working for LaFace Records as OutKast's A&R guy.

Meanwhile, the success of "Player's Ball" emboldened Organized Noize. As production on OutKast's first album began at Bosstown, they gave their new hybrid formula another spin with "Crumblin' Erb," a hazy, slow jam again driven by Sleepy's soulful hook. Punctuating Dre and Big's verses of ghetto vice and violence, the chorus turns the act of rolling a joint into an existentialist metaphor:

> *There's only so much time left in this crazy world*
> *I'm just crumblin' herb*
> *Niggas killing niggas, they don't understand*
> *(what is the Master's plan?)*
> *I'm just crumblin' herb.*

Like "Player's Ball," "Crumblin' Erb" blended the grit and machismo expected of post-gangsta hip-hop with something more sophisticated: a philosophical world-weariness, a sense of perspective about street life, and above all, a strong musicality.

"'Crumblin' Erb' was really Sleepy's vision," Ray says. "That gave us an idea about how far we could take shit: 'Don't think of it like rap, or R&B, think of it as music that we are rapping or singing to.' That concept made him be himself."

Musically, Organized Noize had made Pebble's no-sampling directive part of who they were as artists. Egging them along was Dr. Dre's *The Chronic*, which changed the sound of hip-hop by making live instruments a natural part of the mix. But where Dr. Dre's live tracks were often interpolated from '70s funk songs, Organized Noize made it their goal to create entirely new music. "The vibe was to do what had never been done," Ray explains. "Dr. Dre's *Chronic* album was very influential, it was so seamless, and that was the template for us. But we put our own vibe on it."

To help create the sound, Organized Noize enlisted a group of local players who'd appear again and again on Atlanta hip-hop records: bassists

Lemarquis Jefferson and Preston Crump, guitarists Craig Love and Edward Stroud, keyboardist Kenneth Wright, and vocalists including Debra Killings and Peach (aka Peaches). More than just session players, the musicians fleshed out the sounds in the heads of producers who were, for the most part, non-musicians.

The creation of OutKast's first album provided, for many of the rappers hanging around the Dungeon, a first chance to participate in making a record. Though it was another seven years before the Dungeon Family actually released a collective album, the producers and rappers in the crew understood that, in many ways, OutKast's debut was a group effort. "Everybody put a piece of themselves into it," Sleepy says. "It was really like a Dungeon Family album, because back then we moved like a unit."

With so many collaborators, ideas rolled out fast. "Git Up, Git Out," for example, featured a guest verse from Big Gipp, who ended his verse with an owl call, "hootie hoo." "At the time, 'hootie hoo' was a call in the trap," Gipp explains. "The Red Dogs, the drug task force, used to be around in Atlanta real bad. So when they come, we used to say, 'hootie hoo.' And then [Organized Noize] took that little bit and made the song 'Hootie Hoo.' So the whole album was just using everybody's ideas and giving everyone a voice in what was going on."

"Git Up, Git Out," along with "Call of Da Wild," was credited as "featuring the Goodie Mob," four Dungeon rappers who were still coalescing into a single unit. In addition to Gipp, the Goodies included the Lumberjacks—Willie "Khujo" Knighton and Robert "T-Mo" Barnett—and the Dungeon's latest entry, Dre's friend Cee-Lo. Even while consumed with creating what would be OutKast's *Southernplayalisticadillacmuzik*, Organized Noize also set sights on the Dungeon's next project, and increasingly it looked to be the Goodie Mob (complete with new spelling).

There was also the Society of Soul, Sleepy's R&B project, which made its debut on "Funky Ride," a *Southernplaya* track on which Dre and Big don't appear at all. Here, Sleepy forsakes his Curtis Mayfield imitation for something more reminiscent of George Clinton and Sly Stone. On the interlude "True Dat," Big Rube asserts his role as the Dungeon Family's spoken-word poet and political conscience, while the skit, "Flim Flam," features a snippet of a track from P.A.'s *Ghetto Street Funk* (Pebbles never said they couldn't sample their own music).

Even with so many hands in the mix, *Southernplayalistic* manages to be remarkably cohesive. Indeed, the many voices create a sort of tapestry—the record sounds like a true reflection of the Dungeon Family's world, of life in the SWATs, and of, ultimately, what Southern hip-hop should be. The music was consciously Southern—but not in the academic way of Arrested Development, nor in the provincialism of bass music. Rather, this was life in the real South—the New South still trying to break free from the Old, but otherwise not so removed from what it was like in any American ghetto. It depicted a street life familiar to hip-hop, just delivered with a stronger drawl and a little more humidity.

Where Sleepy provided the sophisticated funk music, and Ray created the hip-hop beats, it came down to Rico to conjure the ineffable quality that would live up to the name Southernplayalisticadillacmuzik (a name, incidentally, inspired by Memphis soul legend Isaac Hayes' epic jam, "Hyperbolicsyllabicsesquedalymistic"). "Rico was the extra-Atlanta person, so everything kind of took on his personality a little," KP recalls of the recording sessions. "At that point it was like, 'Man, we gotta go with what we do.' We figured the only way anything would happen was if we were ourselves to the tenth power—to show people outside Atlanta what it's like to be in Atlanta."

The trick—being identifiably Southern, and true to hip-hop, and free of cornpone cliché—is accomplished in the details. It's in the way Peaches introduces the record as "fat like hambone and tight like gnat booty"; the way Dre and Big glide into a chorus singing how it "ain't no thang but a chicken wing"; in the slang-talk of 'Lacs with the Vogue tires and the Quad Knock sound system; in the references to catfish and grits, to Dolemite and Club Nikki's and Maynard Jackson and the Georgia Dome ("which, by the way, still flies the Confederate battle flag"); and of course, by taking hip-hop pride in repping your 'hood: East Point, College Park, the SWATs—"talk bad about the A-Town, I'll bust you in the fucking mouth."

As a counterpoint to this assertion of regional identity, *Southernplayalistic* offered a set of great rap songs that could stand even if stripped of their Southernness. The chorus of "Ain't No Thang" may begin with a country aphorism, but it ends with a sly double-entendre: "It's all about the sense in your chest (It's the joint)." The title track may be peppered with down-South slang, but the saxophonist can't resist slipping in a melody from the opera *Carmen*. "Claimin' True" may be anything but true, with its pimp and gangsta boasting, but Dre still manages to humanize the strippers at Magic City, "shakin' titties just to pay the rent." The working-class aspirations of "Git Up, Git Out" trump any impulse to floss, while the militant stance and weird jazz bassline of "D.E.E.P." match progressive New York hip-hop at its own game.

Southernplayalisticadillacmuzik, which was released the last week of April 1994, set a landmark—the start of an era when Southern hip-hop was not just regional or novelty, but a full partner in the culture. With debts to the East Coast's hip-hop purity and the West Coast's live instruments and smooth melodies, *Southernplaya* defined a third stream that was both an integration of sounds and a reinvention for hip-hop. It represented a coming out for a region that would dominate hip-hop by decade's end, and the start of a group's artistic journey that would be the decade's most compelling adventure in hip-hop—arguably in pop music as a whole.

It didn't take long to catch on. For Freaknik 1994, black college students from throughout the country descended on Atlanta, as in year's past, for the annual spring break free-for-all. An OutKast street team greeted revelers with an album sampler packaged with dice and incense. "We made these packets and passed them out so everyone went back home and had our sounds," Andre says. "So people go home bumpin' to this tape and started asking who it was. That's how OutKast got around the country."

"Player's Ball" was already generating momentum with a six-week run at number one on the rap chart, and with the album's street publicity and uniformly good reviews (including an impressive four-and-a-half out of five mic rating in *The Source*), *Southernplaya* went gold by the summer—platinum before it had been out a year.

Locally, the impact was tremendous. OutKast was the first local act that had clearly come from the streets—and was proud to talk about it. "The first OutKast album was like the whole energy and chi of the South," Big Rube says proudly. "It represented all our asses. You could literally drive around listening to it and find some shit, because motherfuckers were talking street names. Look at Campbellton Road—it was dying down, there wasn't no business. Then OutKast came out big-upping Campbellton Road, talking about Club Illusions, and next thing you know Club Illusions is packed every week, and there's more people coming over to Campbellton Road to get their hair done, get something to eat. Greenbriar Mall is making a comeback. Next thing you know they're widening the road to four lanes. That whole southwest Atlanta area has been built way up since that first OutKast record. I'm not saying it's specifically because of OutKast, but it was a catalyst to make everybody want to be over there."

Rube goes even further to suggest *Southernplayalistic* played a role in diffusing a gang problem that was building in Atlanta in the mid-90s. "At the time OutKast came out, *The Chronic* was the Bible of rap," he explains. "And kids are gonna emulate that style. They were associating the gangbang style with hip-hop. There never was no real gangs down here, but when the gangbanger thing started you'd have West Coast gangs popping up, like

Crips and shit. They were recruiting from Atlanta. But when OutKast came out, the young kids had something to look up to that wasn't necessarily gangsta. It was like putting a fire extinguisher on the fire that was starting."

Still, there was a limit to the impact the record would have nationally. It peaked at number twenty on the pop chart, and number three on the R&B/hip-hop chart. Then, in January of 1995, came OutKast's turn to shine in front of the hip-hop nation at the Source Awards. This was the very same event where Suge Knight dissed Puff Daddy from the stage, setting into motion an East Coast/West Coast conflict that ultimately cost the lives of Tupac Shakur and the Notorious B.I.G.—and underscored that the South was not yet fully part of the equation in hip-hop.

The New York crowd was already riled up. So when it was revealed that OutKast had upset hometown favorite Redman in the Best New Artist category, the crowd erupted in boos. As OutKast strode on stage to collect their statues, Big Boi was able to take the slight in stride—he just went ahead and said thanks.

But Andre couldn't hold back his annoyance. In defiance, Dre leaned into the mic. "It's like this, though. I'm tired of folks . . . closed-minded folks. It's like we got a demo tape and don't nobody want to hear it. But it's like this: The South got something to say, and that's all I got to say."

Folks down South still talk about that garbled statement as if it were a rebel yell.

SERVING UP THE *SOUL FOOD*

As a measure of Organized Noize's growing stature, L.A. Reid hired the production trio to contribute two songs to TLC's second album, *Crazy-SexyCool*, released in late 1994. It put Organized's work side-by-side with proven hitmakers Dallas Austin, Jermaine Dupri, Puff Daddy, and Babyface, on a record designed to weigh more heavily on sophisticated R&B than the girlish hip-hop of TLC's debut. Organized Noize's more promising contribution was "Waterfalls," which competed for attention with the record's other top-notch tracks, Austin's "Creep" and Babyface's "Red Light Special"—not to mention the tabloid drama of Left Eye's 1994 arrest and probation sentencing for burning down the house of her boyfriend, Andre Rison, wide receiver for the Atlanta Falcons. But "Waterfalls" sported soulful horns and wah-wah guitar, plus an unforgettable hook written by former Uboyz member Marqueze Etheridge. Though it wasn't released as a single—the record's third—until May of 1995, "Waterfalls" became TLC's biggest hit ever, spending seven weeks at the top of the chart.

Amazingly, as "Waterfalls" set new records and *CrazySexyCool* climbed toward selling eleven million copies, the members of TLC were declaring bankruptcy—partly because of the bad deal they had with Pebbles and LaFace, and partly because of insurance claims related to Left Eye's arson. But for Organized Noize, "Waterfalls" was an unequivocal triumph—the song was lavished with four MTV Video Music Awards and two Grammy nominations. Combined with the success of *Southernplayalistic*, Organized Noize were as hot as they would ever be. So L.A. Reid was anxious to ask the question: "What do you guys have next?"

Though it was still more of a concept than an actual group, Organized pushed ahead with its next project. They told L.A., "This is what we feel: Goodie Mob."

The Goodie Mob record was conceived at first as a sort of compilation, a vehicle to get on record a bunch of the Dungeon's most promising MCs. Though it would soon become a more defined foursome, until recording commenced on the group's debut album, *Soul Food*, the quartet had never actually recorded any songs together.

Initially, the Goodie Mob name covered an entire crew of people who were down with Khujo and T-Mo. "Goodie" referred to the "goodie bags" Khujo and T-Mo had taken to carrying around. "Me and T-Mo started fucking with them Crown Royal liquor bags, the purple and gold bags," Khujo explains. "We used to strap them on our belts and have goodies in them. We'd have weed in there, a couple dollars, it was just a little bag we used to walk around with that would swing on the side."

Before the Dungeon, Khujo and T-Mo had recorded some demos—including one called "It's a Goodie Mob Thang"—as the Lumberjacks. They took their music over to Ray, whom they knew from Mays High School. Once they were part of Organized Noize's crew, they fell in with Gipp, another Mays classmate.

Cee-Lo had also gone to Mays prior to dropping out, but he was three years younger than Khujo, T-Mo, and Gipp and only distant acquaintances. Cee-Lo grew up one street away from T-Mo, he'd met Gipp because his cousin was friendly with Gipp's brother, and he remembers that his older sister had a crush on Khujo. But then he met Khujo at a cookout, where they took turns spitting rhymes and formed a friendship. They ran into each other again at a studio, where both were cutting demos, and they bonded afterward by shoplifting some merchandise from Kmart.

That was around the time Dre and Big Boi were falling in with the Dungeon, and so Dre told Cee-Lo about Organized Noize. But despite Cee-Lo's connections with both Khujo and Dre, neither led him directly to the

Dungeon. Instead, one day in Greenbriar Mall, a mutual friend introduced Cee-Lo to Marqueze Etheridge, one of the original Uboyz who remained part of the Dungeon Family. Cee-Lo sang and rapped for him and, impressed, Marqueze invited Cee-Lo back to the Dungeon.

"Dre was telling me about these new guys Organized Noize that had a studio called the Dungeon," Cee-Lo says. "So it was all familiar, but I didn't connect it at that moment." When Cee-Lo arrived at the Dungeon with Marqueze, Sleepy and some other guys were hanging out. So Cee-Lo performed for them and Sleepy was also impressed. He invited Cee-Lo to stay and meet Rico, who'd gone off to get a bite to eat.

Soon, Rico returned to the Dungeon with Dre and Big Boi. Spotting his friend, Dre got excited, "That's my homeboy I was telling you about!" he told Rico. Cee-Lo showed Rico what he could do, and that sealed the deal; Cee-Lo was welcomed as part of the Dungeon Family. OutKast was putting together material for *Southernplaya*, so Dre told him, "You're going to put a track on this album."

When Cee-Lo returned to the Dungeon a second time, he found more familiar faces. "Dre and them were there," Cee-Lo recalls, "and next thing you know, Khujo and T-Mo walk in. I was like, 'What y'all doing over here?' Then Gipp pulls up. He was at cosmetology school, with the white robe on. When I saw their familiar faces, I was immediately comfortable."

As part of "Goodie Mob," Cee-Lo appeared on two *Southernplayalistic* tracks—with Khujo and T-Mo on "Call of Da Wild," and with Gipp on "Git Up, Get Out." After the album's success, Rico got the idea to put the four together as a unit. "We were all cool, all friends, all coming up together sleeping on the floor," Gipp says. "So it was the way to get us all in."

They signed to LaFace based on their *Southernplayalistic* appearances alone, and on L.A.'s faith in Organized Noize. The group's signing advance: twenty thousand dollars split four ways. "I remember all of us spent that shit in a week," Gipp recalls. "So it was still grind time, we were still doing what we had to to survive, and at the same time trying to focus on the music."

With Organized Noize's success, Rico's family was able to leave the Lakewood house. He moved into a modest mansion off Cascade Road, in a middle-class section of southwest Atlanta. The basement had plenty of room for a new Dungeon, but setting up a full-service studio there took time. Meanwhile, Organized Noize and Goodie Mob convened at Curtis Mayfield's home studio, Curtom, as well as at L.A. and Pebbles' home studio, LaCoCo, and at Bosstown.

Despite the temptation to fashion Goodie Mob's debut as a sort of follow-up to *Southernplayalistic*, the quartet was prepared to present something that was, while complementary to what OutKast had created, also entirely unique. Ray Murray characterizes it this way: "Goodie Mob was a more direct approach. OutKast said a lot of shit on their first album, but most cats would look at the album and think it was a playeristic thing. So when Goodie Mob came with *Soul Food*, it was like we were talking to your soul. We're giving nourishment for your spirit, that was the vibe."

Where OutKast's record featured the entire Dungeon Family, *Soul Food* was more limited to the foursome of rappers. That's partly because Andre and Big Boi were off touring and promoting their own music (though they each showed up on one track). Also, there was no need for Sleepy's distinct singing, because Goodie Mob had its own crooner—Cee-Lo, whose raspy vocals provided a gritty, melodic soul. And with verses that needed to accommodate four voices instead of two, it made sense to create leaner backing tracks and an understated production style that emphasized mood—as in the dub reggae-ish beat on the single, "Cell Therapy"—over flowing hooks.

Above all, Goodie Mob had its own lyrical vision. Where OutKast portrayed the Southern streets, Goodie Mob aimed to capture the entire existential struggle of the black man trying to get by on the land where his ancestors had been enslaved. There was a sociopolitical element to Goodie Mob: It was not quite the polemic that Public Enemy had introduced to hip-hop—though flashes could be seen when the group addressed public housing ("Cell Therapy") or prison overpopulation ("Live at the O.M.N.I.")—but nor was it the wholesome Atlanta-style protest that was the legacy of Martin Luther King Jr. There's a palpable weight bearing down on *Soul Food*—a simmering anger and yearning to break out of the trap. It was, in a way that hip-hop had never been before, part blues and part gospel—from Cee-Lo's pained wails in the opening "Free" ("Lord it's so hard, living this life/A constant struggle each and every day") to his rousing deliverance in the closing "The Day After" ("I'm so happy we made it/I knew one day we would").

Where OutKast talked about the South, Goodie Mob *felt* like the South. It was "soul food," an African American cuisine you can find everywhere, but that always signifies the region. The funereal "I Didn't Ask to Come" and the churchy "Serenity Prayer" feel gothic; there's a down-home familial vibe to "Guess Who," Goodie Mob's momma song, and "Soul Food," the laid-back anthem to black barbecues and Sunday dinners that group members believe inspired the Babyface-produced film two years later (and subsequent TV series).

But *Soul Food*'s greatest gift to Southern hip-hop was the track "Dirty South," which was adopted by rappers from Texas to North Carolina as shorthand for the region's rap flavor. Its title and theme were the creation of Gipp's former rhyme partner Cool Breeze, who appears prominently on the track, along with Big Boi and Gipp. While the song is atypical of Goodie Mob's introspective style, its sense of place ("Life's a bitch then you figure out/Why you really got dropped in the Dirty South/See in the third grade this is what you told/You was bought, you was sold . . . "), mixed with hard-core posturing, encapsulates the tone of the rowdier Southern hip-hop that was to come. While Cool Breeze's own solo work never reached a mass audience, his influence is felt each time a Southern rapper invokes "da Dirty."

While all four members distinguished themselves on *Soul Food*, Cee-Lo stood out with his evocative singing and intelligent, sharply delivered raps. Though the youngest of the group, Cee-Lo's voice, unusual Buddha-like looks, and outspokenness put him at the group's front and center. "As far as what Goodie Mob does, how they're presented and perceived, that's my thing," Cee-Lo says. "The 'Soul Food' [concept] was my idea. And I think that set the pace of how our relationship started to go. I apologized to the guys once, saying, 'I hope I didn't obligate y'all to be something you might not want to be.' This pro-black, political, socially conscious thing, that's my thing. Khujo, T, and Gipp, ultimately, had a lot of the same interests. Everyone was equally instrumental in making Goodie Mob what it was, but I was more of the big-picture, conceptual thinker."

Cee-Lo, not one to hold back out of modesty, believes this imbalance was ultimately a fatal flaw in the group. "I've been singled out from day one," he says. "I did feel guilty at one point. I don't know how I'd feel to stand shoulder to shoulder with someone and an admirer comes up and says, 'Hey, I like the whole group, but you, you're the one.'"

Shortly before *Soul Food*'s release in November 1995, a more immediate complication shook the group's foundations. Cee-Lo's mother—who'd already been paralyzed in a car accident—passed away. But Cee-Lo's extended family—the Dungeon—provided the comfort he needed to push through. "It came at a very awkward time, and I consider it to be the greatest trial of my life," Cee-Lo says of his mother's death. "I overcame it by the grace of God and it gave me focus. I was determined because of it. It was a blessing in that sense."

Ultimately, while *Soul Food* was every bit the artistic triumph that *Southernplayalistic* had been, something in the record's alchemy—its hooks, its messages, its promotion, the group's image and presentation—didn't click with audiences the way OutKast's record had. "Cell Therapy" briefly topped the rap charts, and the subsequent singles "Dirty South" and "Soul Food" both reached the top ten. But none did much to create a crossover to the pop charts, and the album was unable to generate enough steam to get further than gold (half-million copies sold).

Still, a gold record—while it meant virtually no royalty income when split four ways—was a promising start, and with the glowing reviews *Soul Food* received, there was plenty of reason to be optimistic about the group's future. It also kept Organized Noize in good enough standing with LaFace to bring out a third Dungeon Family act just six months later. Building on the R&B success of "Waterfalls," Organized Noize developed more material in that vein, centered around Sleepy's singing and Big Rube's spoken poetry. This was Society of Soul, a group officially consisting of Rico, Ray, Sleepy, Rube, and a female vocalist named Esperanza, but also featuring songwriting by former Uboyz members Marqueze Etheridge and Brandon "Shug" Bennett, and appearances by Goodie Mob, T-Boz, and Sleepy's dad Jimmy Brown.

The group recorded its album *Brainchild* concurrently with *Soul Food*, also at Curtis Mayfield's Curtom Studio. It arrived in April of 1996 only to sink almost immediately into obscurity after peaking at number ninety-six on the R&B chart. Society of Soul looked great on paper—a retro-soul act with smooth grooves and conscious lyrics, aiming to repeat the success of "Waterfalls"—but the result was less than the sum of its parts. Without standout songs, *Brainchild* sounded nice as background music but left no strong impression. Why L.A. Reid—a shrewd hound for R&B hits—saw fit to release the album is puzzling.

But the next time Organized Noize tried an R&B project, it would not be with LaFace. The self-titled debut album by the vocal quartet Mista, released on Elektra/EastWest in July of '96, signaled the first break in Organized Noize's alliance with LaFace. Mista found some success with the minor R&B hit "Blackberry Molasses," but the album didn't make much more impact than Society of Soul had. Still, Organized remained tied to LaFace as long as OutKast and Goodie Mob were signed there. And by the summer of '96, OutKast was ready for its follow-up.

SECOND ACTS: THE *ATLIENS* ARE *STILL STANDING*

When Andre and Big Boi returned from a year of touring, they were now twenty-year-old rap stars, noticeably changed from the enthusiastic teens that had first entered the Dungeon. "You could tell they had been on the road," Big Rube recalls, "their whole demeanor was a lot more confident. They started understanding the power they had in their music. They started showing a swagger that certain artists have—the ones that are stars."

Part of the change was just the normal process of growing up. In 1995, Big Boi's girlfriend, Sherlita, gave birth to their first child, a girl they named Jordan. And his aunt Renee, who'd been like a mother since Big moved to Atlanta, died. Andre's girlfriend, Total's Keisha Spivey, ended their two-year relationship, and he set his mind to finally graduating from high school. They'd been on their own for the first time, traveling the country, experiencing things they'd only dreamed about—and things they hadn't imagined. Dre and Big now confronted the task of a second album with horizons much expanded, and anxious to explore new territory.

Both had grown personally and artistically, but Andre showed the more obvious signs of change. After indulging in *Southernplayalistic*'s taste for weed and liquor, by 1995 he'd given up both and become a vegetarian. He also grew dreadlocks and, while waiting for his hair to grow natty, had taken to wearing a turban. People took this as a sign of increased spirituality, or increased eccentricity—or both. The effect was that Dre began to stand out as an individual; to some extent, it served to distance him from the Dungeon crew.

"Dre went through a metamorphosis," says Ray Murray. "I don't know if it was the introduction to celebrity, or just wanting to have more control of his life. He took a different direction than from where we were. He became more introverted, more expressionist. After the first record, Dre stopped doing a whole lot of shit that we were all doing, which made him be on some whole other shit."

Along with Andre and Big Boi's personal maturation came significant musical growth. Empowered by their success, they decided to pursue making their own music, apart from Organized Noize. Dre took some of the money he'd earned and bought state-of-the-art hip-hop machinery: the MPC3000 sampler, SP1200 drum machine, ASR–10 synthesizer, a Tascam mixing board, and turntables with piles of old records found at local shops. Big Boi also sprung for a set of gear, though he was distracted with his new baby and slower to take it up.

Having watched Ray, Dre didn't approach beat making as an absolute beginner. Still, it's a measure of the musical gifts of both Dre and Big Boi (who wrote the hook) that their first creation was a song as clever and inventive as "Elevators (Me & You)." As the first single from *ATLiens*, the song became OutKast's second number-one rap hit, and the group's biggest pop charting to that point.

As much a slice of Southern hip-hop progressivism "Southernplayalisticadillacmuzik" had been, "Elevators" builds thick atmosphere around humming organ, dubby bass, echoing rim shots, and lonely "wrong-number" phone tones, gliding gently into a chorus cooly sung by Big and others: "Me and you, your momma and your cousin too/Rollin' down the strip on Vogues, comin' up slammin' Cadillac doors." It was classic down-South signfiying: extended families, 'Lacs with high-end tires, car culture. The verses, meanwhile, reflect the group's turning point by taking account of where they'd been—retelling the meeting with Rico at Lamonte's—and where they were going: "We done come a long way like them Slim-ass cigarettes from Virginia, this ain't gon' stop so we just gon' continue."

"Elevators" convinced OutKast they could take more control of their music. "I can remember when I wrote the hook," Big Boi relates. "I said to Dre, 'I might be trippin', but this shit sounds fonky!' And he was like, 'That shit jammin'.' So after that we had another avenue."

Organized Noize did not resist OutKast's inclination to pull away. "Ray and them, they never hated, they never shunned what I was doing," Dre says. "They'd say it was pretty cool or tell me it would be good if I'd just [improve] one thing."

While Organized Noize produced ten of *ATLiens'* fifteen tracks, including great songs like "Two Dope Boyz (in a Cadillac)" and "Jazzy Belle," conceptually, Dre and Big's five productions—particularly the title track and "E.T. (Extraterrestrial)," an unusual drum-less rap song—set the album's tone. Their tracks were statements of individuality, with imagery—aliens, extraterrestrials—that reinforced OutKast's uniqueness. Where *Southernplayalistic* asserted the group's separateness from hip-hop's East Coast/West Coast divide, *ATLiens* took it one step further: OutKast represented Atlanta, but was also set apart from other Southern rap. As the conflated title suggests, OutKast would not be tethered simply by region; it had one foot in outer space.

ATLiens' Afro-futurist imagery—the CD booklet featured a sci-fi comic adventure starring Dre and Big, written by Big Rube—was not entirely new to hip-hop: Afrika Bambaataa had long dressed like a *Battlestar Galactica* refugee, and the music created on P-Funk's Mothership was prime source material. But OutKast's bid for otherworldliness stood out in a post-gangsta climate that had codified hip-hop as needing to be hard, street, and real.

ATLiens also brought a deeper sophistication to the group's words and music. The chorus of "ATLiens" gave classic hip-hop a Southern twist—as so much of *Southernplayalistic* had: "Now throw your hands in the ai-yer (air) and wave them like you just don't ca-yer (care)/And if you like fish and grits and all that pimp shit everybody let me hear you say 'oh yay-yer'." But the verses find Dre paraphrasing Shakespeare and challenging hip-hop cliches: "No drugs or alcohol so I can get the signal clear as day/Put my glock away, I got a stronger weapon that never runs out of ammunition."

Similarly, "Wheelz of Steel" features furious turntable scratching from OutKast's DJ David Sheats—aka Mr. DJ, Rico's cousin and a Dungeon regular—and a final verse where Dre plays old-school MC dropped in the SWATs ("One time for my guhls [girls] doing queen thangs/Dead fresh to the teeth eatin' chicken wings/Three times for my guhls in the beauty shop/Four times OutKast and it don't stop"). Along the way, he drops some unexpected SAT words like *clandestine* and *soliloquy*, and an out-of-the-blue reference to new-wave pop act Tears for Fears.

Not all of Organized Noize's contributions work—notably, there's a slow stretch that includes "Babylon," "Wailin'," and the Goodie Mob-featured "Mainstream." But their "Decatur Psalm"—a crime tale prominently featuring Cool Breeze and the awesome refrain, "It won't be over till that big girl from Decatur sing"—is thrilling, even as it goes against the album's grain. Generally, though, ON beats serve well as tableaux for OutKast's explorations: "Millennium" gets spacey and spotlights Dre's singing, while "Jazzy Belle" voices the group's increasingly enlightened view of women (Dre: "Went from yellin' . . . bitches and hoes to queen thangs"; Big Boi: "I gotta be feedin' my daughter, teach her to be that natural woman").

With the album's nearly eight-minute closer, "13th Floor/Growing Old," Organized Noize and OutKast lay a foundation for structurally unconventional epics to come: There's an opening spoken-word rant from Rube, a melancholic soul refrain sung by Debra Killings, sound-bite scratching, water bubbling, and verses that philosophize on getting old and assert Southern hip-hop's worth (Dre: "While mind-closed niggas laugh at the Southern slang . . . /I grew up on booty shake, we did not know no better thang/So go 'head and dis it, while real hop-hippers listen").

Released in late August of 1996, *ATLiens* found greater short-term success than its predecessor by hitting number one on the R&B/hip-hop album chart, and number two on the pop chart. But, perhaps because of its relative lack of hooks, its moodiness, or its still-tentative experimentation, the record has become OutKast's least-revered work. But if *ATLiens* was transitional, it certainly qualified as a major step in the group's evolution—and left plenty of reason to expect a thrilling ride still to come.

In the two and a half years it took Goodie Mob to return with *Still Standing*, its follow-up to *Soul Food*, Organized Noize had split from LaFace and inked a label deal with Interscope Records. They remained Goodie Mob's primary producers, though, and were executive producers (with L.A. and Babyface) on *Still Standing*. Just as OutKast had done on *ATLiens*, *Still Standing* let Goodie Mob branch out with other producers, including Mr. DJ, Dungeon-affiliated musicians Carlos Glover and David Whild, and Goodie's own T-Mo and Cee-Lo.

As Ray explains, "At first, everybody was signed through Organized Noize for their first album—Society of Soul, OutKast, and Goodie Mob—because we had the relationship with L.A. Once he saw that the acts were viable, we didn't need to be in the middle of the situation. It's just the natural thing, so each artist got more power. There was friction between us and LaFace, and that was turning into friction between us and the artists. Once we alleviated that, we didn't have a deal with LaFace anymore. We all had an understanding, there wasn't no backhanded shit at all."

During Goodie Mob's time away from recording, the group established itself as a premier live act in hip-hop, touring constantly to self-promote and earn money. Time on the road bonded the group, who'd initially been thrown together artificially, into a tight unit. And their dedicated following convinced them they were on the right track in their music.

"With *Still Standing*, we knew we had something," Gipp says. "Our first tour we went out with the Roots and the Fugees. And I think that was one of the greatest shows on the road, three live bands back to back, all three really breaking ground from where they were from. After that tour, we knew we could do things other hip-hop artists couldn't do. We knew we had a voice."

They were also extending beyond the South, spending time on the West Coast collaborating with DJ Muggs of Cypress Hill (who produced *Still Standing*'s "Inshallah") and preparing to work with Tupac Shakur just before he was killed in late 1996. Tupac's death, along with the following year's murder of Notorious B.I.G.—whom Goodie Mob also knew—cast a pall over the recording. "It's a dark album, that was the vibe," Ray says. "It was a dark time. All these cats had died. That's why we called the record *Still Standing*."

Because *Soul Food* started as more of a compilation, *Still Standing* was, in effect, Goodie Mob's first group effort. To encourage thematic cohesiveness, the foursome rented a cabin in the north Georgia mountains and spent a few days writing together and discussing album concepts. By the time they entered the Dungeon—now a full studio in the basement of Rico's new home—the group had a full set of lyrics.

Cee-Lo, in particular, brought an impressive set of material and, once again, dominated the recording. He gets the floor to himself for the opener, a fiery Last Poets–style discourse on the complex semantics of the term *nigger* that stands as one of the group's most focused rants:

> *And a nigger done read history but yet his eyes didn't see*
> *The only reason you a nigger is because somebody else wants you to be*
> *Well a nigger uneducated, integrated, singin' "We Shall Overcome"*
> *A nigger trying to be white is what a nigger seem like have become*
> *And when they call me a nigger to my face,*
> *can't do nothin' but walk away*
> *But here it is niggers call other niggers niggers each and every day. . . .*
> *So many black men out here trying to be niggers*
> *Keeping it real to the point that they dying to be niggers*
> *When in actuality the fact is you ain't a nigger because you black*
> *You a nigger 'cause of how you act.*

Cee-Lo's prominence stems partly from his unique voice (Gipp and Khujo, by contrast, have similarly husky deliveries) but even more from his clarity as a communicator. His group mates' verses are often difficult to follow, or contain only thought fragments—and one of the few times Khujo's lyrics cohere is on "Fly Away," where he self-righteously condemns homosexuality in the most vicious terms. Cee-Lo, meanwhile, ends that song on a high note, standing up for his region: "Well, I'm from the dirty, filthy nasty dirty South/Some of you niggas still think we soft/And I swore I wouldn't never write no rhyme like this/But now you're startin to piss me off."

Many of *Still Standing*'s high points belong to Cee-Lo: His storytelling verse and soaring chorus on the pro–black woman anthem, "Beautiful Skin" (Gipp's verse about his wife, the singer Joi, is also effective); his sung verse in "They Don't Dance No Mo'"; his sense-talking on "Gutta Butta"; his production on the hard-rocking "Ghetto-ology"; his breakdown of street economics on "I Refuse Limitation"; and the album-encapsulating title track's mournful but defiant chorus: "Still Standing, unscathed, 'cause pain is something for soldiers to feel/MCs are running out of things to say/Radio stations are running out of songs to play."

The notable exception to Cee-Lo's dominance is "Black Ice," the album's first and only single, a psychedelic blues produced by Mr. DJ and featuring Dre and Big Boi with Gipp (Dre also plays bass on the track). That it was chosen as a single, despite it having only one group member, suggests LaFace's slipping confidence in Goodie Mob's ability to score hits—and its increasing confidence in OutKast's star power.

Still Standing became Goodie Mob's highest charting album—its only one to break pop's top ten. But by its April 1998 release, other acts had picked up the Southern hip-hop revolution heralded by the Dungeon Family. Due to its passion, its intelligence, its musicality, *Still Standing* is a great album in ways that other, more popular, Southern hip-hop albums of the late '90s could never be. But it was too dark, too heavy, too mired in the reality of Southern black life to provide what listeners really needed: escape. It put Goodie Mob in the difficult position of being the group everyone loved and respected, but too few wanted to actually hear. And the group's attempt to overcome this fate would be its undoing.

chapter 6

VIRGINIA— TRANSMISSIONS FROM THE EDGE

WELCOME TO THE BLANK SLATE

Atlanta may be the crossroads of Southern mythology, recast in post–New South America as a bustling intersection of major highways. But there's a flip side to that bit of folklore: The crossroads were not merely a meeting of two roads, but perhaps more significantly, a dark, desolate landscape where only devils and starving artists dare tread. It's on this side that you find Virginia Beach, the no-man's-land so far on the outskirts of the South that it's sometimes hard to discern Southernness in its music. And yet, it's not quite the North, or anywhere else, either.

Just one highway leads in and out of Virginia Beach. Interstate 264 heads east toward the coast and suddenly ends, dropping you onto a grid of streets that lines the older part of town. But the new part of town makes up most of Virginia Beach—particularly the parts where the black folks live. The faceless stretch of suburbia was molded together with the original beach town forty years ago to create a city boasting a population near a half million. With the beach catering to tourists, the heart of Virginia Beach for locals is this drab, centerless accumulation of avenues. How do you know Virginia Beach when you get there? You don't—because "there's no *there* there."

Take the entire semimetropolitan area together and you have an even starker sense of disorientation. There's no official name to this waterlogged network of land masses separated by rivers and harbors, connected by bridges and dotted with majestic ships from the area's many military bases.

Some call it Tidewater, some Hampton Roads, and others call it Seven Cities because the area has doomed itself to being a conglomeration of small burgs: Norfolk, Portsmouth, Chesapeake, Suffolk, Newport News, and Hampton, in addition to Virginia Beach. Why doomed? Ever try to get seven city governments to agree on the kind of large-scale projects—urban development, mass transit, sports franchises—that might improve and unite an area's civic life? Norfolk is most urban, Virginia Beach is most quaint, but they've all condemned one another to being generally uninspiring.

You'd have to go back three or four centuries to find a time when the area was truly noteworthy. It's here, for instance, that you find Cape Henry, on the northern tip of Virginia Beach—within a mile or so of Pharrell Williams' bay-front bachelor mansion—where in 1607 the first permanent English settlers touched ground in North America. And nearby Jamestown was the first permanent European settlement in what would become the United States—the place where, in 1619, the first African "servants" were brought to this country (it would be a couple of decades before they started calling it slavery). And there's Yorktown, the site of the American Revolution's climactic battle, where the British surrendered to George Washington.

Today, Virginia Beach's position at the end of the highway makes it a true backwater. You don't pass through on your way—it's a place you have to seek out to end up. It's the dark countryside of Southern music lore, the idle lands that are the devil's playground.

In music, it was never much of a hotbed, though a trio of wonderful singers from the blues and jazz era—Ella Fitzgerald, Pearl Bailey, and Ruth Brown—came from this area. In hip-hop terms, Virginia Beach was a forgotten outpost of an entire lost region. While every corner of the country with a sizable black population had developed a local flavor by the late '90s, the stretch from Maryland down to the Carolinas—roughly the mid-Atlantic, though some area hip-hop kids have named it the Middle East—remained largely a blank slate. But where circumstance leaves a vacuum the imagination eventually fills in. In place of any identifiable tradition, and largely untouched by the crosswinds of influence blowing in from other places, a few possessed Virginians conjured a sonic world made entirely from false memory and limitless possibility.

A small group of talents—performers, but more significantly, producers—brought an entirely new sound from the place where the highway ends. The music of Timbaland and Missy Elliott, and of the Neptunes' Pharrell Williams and Chad Hugo, brewed in secret, behind-the-scenes in a place no one would find, then—with no regional ties limiting its appeal—it got exported and turned into hits for just about anyone and everyone in American pop. Compositions that carved out beautifully contoured funk in asymmetrical little chunks, from bits of Indian bling and Chinese twang, Appalachian wail and Miami swing—stuff that wrestled cohesive, catchy slabs of gold from the most free-roaming isotopes.

"We've always created our own world to escape to," Hugo says of his fellow Tidewater artists. "I wouldn't say there's a lot going on in Virginia—it really doesn't have an identity. It's still considered the South, the top of the Bible belt; it's a little conservative. And it's got the military base, which makes it sort of [a] melting pot. It's influenced by a lot of different things. You have a lot of different kinds of kids. So it is what you make of it."

UNTAPPED MARKET: TEDDY RILEY COMES TO TOWN

When superstar producer Teddy Riley moved to Virginia Beach in 1990, the most prominent musician in the area was David "Pic" Conley, leader of the R&B group Surface, who'd scored a series of slow-jam R&B hits in the late '80s that peaked with the chart-topper "The Last Time." So Riley immediately became the most successful local artist from the moment he set foot in town. And that's part of what attracted him to Virginia. He liked the lifestyle, and he believed the area was ripe to discover new artists. "I did my research and was like, 'Dag, I could come down here and I could do some special things,'" he says. "I knew there was talent here, because there's talent everywhere. It's just that nobody came here to build up the market."

Riley himself grew up in a place drenched with artistic achievement: Harlem, New York. As a young kid in the '70s, Teddy's pastor at the Little Flower Baptist Church recognized his musical aptitude and had him playing an assortment of instruments: drums at three, guitar by five, piano by eight. Riley drew the notice of Royal Bayyan, a producer and songwriter who worked with Kool and the Gang, and Bayyan helped develop Riley's interest in creating music while still in his early teens. Then, while hanging around the park near the St. Nicholas Projects, where he lived, Riley met Gene Griffin, a Georgia native whose Sound of New York label had scored a hit in 1983 with "Last Night a DJ Saved My Life." Griffin took Riley under his wing and formed a production/songwriting partnership, GR Productions. By twenty-one, Riley had established himself as a major hit maker—as a producer of like-minded artists such as Keith Sweat and Bobby

Brown, with his own singing group, Guy, and as figurehead of a musical movement that integrated contemporary R&B with the emerging sounds of hip-hop. A writer from the *Village Voice* coined it "new jack swing," and Riley was its king.

Riley's success put him in a circle of Harlem's biggest players, including the notorious team of young drug kingpins, Rich Porter, Alpo, and AZ (whose rise and fall was fictionalized in the 2002 movie *Paid in Full*). In late summer 1988, Riley and his hustler friends chartered several buses from New York to bring a huge convoy down to Virginia Beach. That's because a black college gathering in town known as Greekfest—a start-of-the-school-year equivalent to Atlanta's spring break, Freaknik—had exploded the year before from a small gathering of several thousand fraternity and sorority members to an anarchic event attracting tens of thousands of students and fun-seekers over Labor Day weekend. Riley had such a good time in Virginia Beach that a few years later—after Guy had relocated to suburban Atlanta with Gene Griffin, then broken from Griffin and returned to New York—Riley decided to move to there.

By the time Riley had resettled in Virginia Beach, Greekfest had imploded. In 1989, crowds swelled to what authorities estimated was 100,000 visitors. Police felt overwhelmed by the huge numbers of black kids cruising in cars or walking the beach strip, while visitors resented being made to feel like criminals for simply coming to town on vacation. Whatever the catalyst—some say it was protest, some say lawlessness—rioting and looting broke out, resulting in many arrests and claims of police brutality.

The incident made the national news and wound up on the "black CNN"—Chuck D referred to the incident in Public Enemy's 1990 song "Welcome to the Terrordome": "Places with the racist faces/Just an example of one of many cases/The Greek weekend speech I speak/From a lesson learned in Virginia." By then, Greekfest was dead. So when Riley arrived, young Tidewater blacks were ready for a new shot of excitement.

For a quiet place like the Seven Cities, the appearance of a major artist—a producer who'd bring Michael Jackson and Whitney Houston to record in town—was huge. Aspiring rapper Gene Thornton, better known as Malice, of the group the Clipse, was in high school at the time. "I remember people talking in school that they had seen Teddy Riley here and he was parking sideways in firelanes and stuff," he recalls. "It was a big deal, a lot of gossip when he came to town."

Melvin Barcliff, the rapper known as Magoo, was also in high school. "Teddy Riley made the biggest impact I've ever seen in this area, hands down," he says. "Nobody ever moved to this area and affected it in a positive manner the way he did."

But Riley did not enter a complete void. Missy Elliott, for instance, had been writing down lyrics from the time she fell in love with Run-D.M.C. Born in Portsmouth, Elliott moved around some because her father was in the military, but she and her mom decided to stay when her parents split up in the mid-80s. As a high school junior, Missy and her friend Damy formed a rap duo called 2 Hype M.D.'s. At a talent show in 1990, the 2 Hype M.D.'s won for the best rap, while a trio of local girls won in the singing category. When Damy got pregnant, Missy teamed up with the vocal trio to form the R&B/hip-hop hybrid, Fayze. By the time Riley arrived, Fayze had already put out a record called *First Move*. Still, Riley's arrival made an impression on Elliott. "It made it seem like what we were trying to do wasn't impossible to achieve," she says.

In fact, the Virginia Coast at the time was surprisingly crowded with major producers in training. Though he didn't hit big until a decade after Riley's breakthrough, Tim Mosely would far surpass Riley's success in the end. Like Riley, the man who would become known as Timbaland showed his musical flair as a mere toddler—his mother recalls him writing music at age three. Tim's father sang as part of a successful local gospel group, and Tim himself joined his church choir as a kid.

By the time he was about eleven, Tim had found his true calling. He began listening to early Kid Capri mix tapes that made their way down from New York and quickly understood the craft involved in creating them. Armed with his family turntable and a tiny Casio keyboard, Mosely began mixing records and making tracks. And he never stopped: By middle school, Tim was the go-to guy for beats. The Clipse's Malice recalls being part of a crew of under-fifteen rappers revolving around DJ Timmy Tim's early musical creations. The rappers paired off into duos, and Tim supplied the beats for all of the groups. Collectively, they were known as Def Dual Productions.

Tim's reputation as a party DJ blossomed in high school, but he remained interested in creating original music. That's when a mutual friend introduced Tim to Melvin Barcliff, a fifteen-year-old break-dancer from Chesapeake. The two quickly became close friends and, as Barcliff took up rapping and named himself Magoo, they became musical collaborators as well.

Magoo's life had been a nightmare up until then. Abused by his drug-addicted mother, he was taken away from her and raised as part of his aunt's family—a stable home, but one where he never felt like he belonged. While

Tim grew up in a lower-middle-class two-parent home, violence eventually touched him as well. At sixteen, Tim took a job at Red Lobster, where after work one night, a coworker brandished a gun and accidentally shot Tim in the neck. His right arm became paralyzed.

"Through all of that he was determined to pursue his career as a music producer," says Tim's mom, Leatrice Pierre. "He was in pain sometimes, and I would work with him, give him the medicine and massage his arm, and he'd still go in the room every single day, messing with that turntable and writing down lyrics. He said he was not going to let that injury stop him because he knew one day God was going to heal him."

Pierre credits her family's church, the New Jerusalem Church of God in Christ, with providing strength that encouraged Tim's recovery. The megachurch's "prayer warriors"—including Mother Carrie Williams, who had a grandson named Pharrell—kept Tim in their prayers. And within nine months of the accident, Tim had regained full use of his arm.

While Tim Mosely was running things in the Salem High School hip-hop world, across town at Princess Anne High, Pharrell Williams was making his name as a hotshot drum major in the marching band. At fifteen, Williams spent his summer at band camp—an improvisational workshop for gifted and talented school-band musicians. Though the program was otherwise destined to be completely irrelevant in the course of modern American music, it turned out that the camp introduced Williams to a saxophonist from Kempsville High School, a Filipino American navy brat named Chad Hugo.

Because their love of music went beyond marching band—Hugo recalls arranging school-band versions of "Bonita Applebom" and "Jungle Boogie"—Chad and Pharrell became friends and decided to form a band. They liked the way Earth, Wind & Fire used natural elements in their imagery and music. Being from the waterlogged Virginia Beach area, Chad and Pharrell decided on a water theme: They'd call their group the Neptunes. (For many years, there was also a diner on the beach strip called Neptunes Restaurant, as well as a maritime celebration in town called the Neptune Festival. And being children of the '70s, it's also possible they were familiar with the cartoon *Jabberjaws*, whose title character—a shark—played in a band called the Neptunes.)

"We were trying to do an alternative type of band, and we just wanted a name that stood out," Hugo recalls. "When we started out a lot of our shit had to do with water. Being on the beach tied that in. And the body is made out of 75 percent water, the earth is covered with three-fourths water—all that type of shit."

But Pharrell's musical ambition kept him involved in several projects at once. When he heard about the group formed by the hotshot DJ Timmy Tim, he also joined up with him. The group—featuring Tim, Magoo, their friend Larry Live, and Pharrell—called itself SBI, or Surrounded by Idiots.

The Neptunes and SBI ran concurrently beginning around 1990, the time most of the members graduated from high school. There was no live hip-hop scene in the Tidewater area, so groups mostly just messed around at home. When Pharrell heard Princess Anne was having a talent show, he jumped at this rare opportunity to perform. Even though he'd already graduated from Princess Anne by 1991, he arranged to have the Neptunes play as a noncompeting special guest.

Soon after Teddy Riley arrived, he set up his Famous Recording studio in a building just off Virginia Beach Boulevard. He also actively embraced the local community—a gesture both of altruism and enterprise. He got involved in Little League, gave away Thanksgiving turkeys, and held talent shows at area schools. The first school he approached was practially next door to Famous studio, Princess Anne.

The Neptunes were, at that point, a four-piece band with three vocalists—including future N.E.R.D. member Shay (Sheldon Haley)—and Chad on keyboards. They did jazz-inflected hip-hop, a style inspired by Native Tongues acts like A Tribe Called Quest, with some R&B singing added in. Riley's assistant attended the talent show and reported back: The winner was the group that wasn't competing. Riley invited the Neptunes over to the studio to play, and he liked what he heard.

Riley, however, was in transition between his success with Guy and his re-emergence with a second group, Blackstreet. He stayed busy producing artists, including Michael Jackson, but Riley's Famous Records label didn't have a distribution deal to get new acts released, so he wasn't much help to the Neptunes. Chad and Pharrell, however, wanted to learn their way around a studio, so Riley let them hang around and develop their production skills.

Chad and Pharrell's presence at Famous paid off right away. They spent their time writing and laying down demos—including songs like "U Don't Have to Call," which sat on the shelf for nearly a decade before becoming a huge hit for Usher in 2001. The pair also helped out Riley on his productions, where they made their first recording appearances. Hugo played saxophone and cowrote the song "Tonight's the Night," from Blackstreet's self-titled debut. Pharrell, meanwhile, contributed a rap to female R&B group SWV's Riley-produced 1992 hit, "Right Here." The same year, he wrote Teddy Riley's guest rap verse in the song "Rump Shaker," a big hit for

Wreckx-N-Effect, the group fronted by Teddy's brother, Markell Riley. Pharrell even appeared in the background of the "Rump Shaker" video, the first of many clips in which he'd pop up over the years. Where the Neptunes as a band hit a dead end, the Neptunes as a production/songwriting team took off.

WHEN TIMMY MET MISSY

While Tim and Magoo worked on SBI and other projects, they got word of a local group called Fayze. As Magoo recalls, "Me, Tim, and Larry [Live] were in a record store together. I picked up the twelve-inch by Fayze. They were the only [local] group I knew of that put a record out at the time. I was like, 'Yo, we gotta meet these girls.'"

Magoo soon discovered that a local producer named Emmanuel Perry, whom he'd been recording with, had also been working with Fayze. "So I come by his crib and I'll be damned if Fayze were all sitting there in the car. So I said to Emmanuel, 'Why don't we drive over to Tim's house so Tim can meet them?' We go over there and Missy heard Tim's beats, and it's a wrap. You couldn't break them two apart."

Missy recalls the meeting as well. "Tim had this little Casio keyboard, and he has big hands. So it was hilarious to see him play on that Casio. But he had a way of making a record sound like something I hadn't heard before."

Missy, who was Fayze's main songwriter, immediately started collaborating with Tim. Both were nothing short of obsessed, Tim's mother recalls. "Missy, Melvin, and Larry, they used to come over to my house, every weekend, and sometimes in the evenings—diligently, they were faithful in working on their music. It drove me a little crazy, but I allowed them to do it. Tim used to say he was going to be a famous producer and Missy used to say to me, 'I'm going to be rich and famous. We're going to keep working on it until we get to the very top.'"

Through her connection with Tim, Missy met Pharrell, who passed Fayze's music on to Teddy Riley. He expressed some interest, but never moved forward with any plans for the group. In the meantime, another new-jack producer stepped in to provide Tim and Missy with their big break.

One of Fayze's vocalists, Chonita Coleman, had met the manager of Jodeci, a male vocal quartet from Charlotte, North Carolina, whose hip-hop-influenced bad-boy R&B was breaking huge in 1991. The members of Fayze were big fans—the women even wore matching leather outfits like Jodeci. So when they got word that Jodeci would be performing at the

Hampton Coliseum, Chonita got the group on the guest list for the after party.

First they met Jodeci's Dalvin Degrate, who invited the group up to the VIP area. When Dalvin heard them sing, he called over his brother, Donald "Devante Swing" Degrate. Devante had written and produced Jodeci's debut, *Forever My Lady,* and was looking to build on his success by cultivating acts for his own label. Devante liked Fayze and invited the group to his new home in New Jersey to work on music. One of the first changes he made was to rename the group Sista.

Missy's family had misgivings about her going to stay with an R&B singer they knew so little about, but Missy told them plainly, "This is my ticket out." In New Jersey, Devante had concocted an ambitious plan, far beyond simply working with Sista. He'd invited a dozen or more music makers and created the kind of aspiring-artist colony that, had it been ten years later, would've no doubt been a reality TV show (in the next decade, both P. Diddy, who visited the collective, and Missy herself borrowed from the idea in creating their own reality shows). Devante set up Sista in a Hackensack apartment, while others lived with Devante in his sprawling Teaneck mansion. R&B singer Ginuwine and vocal group Playa were among the acts Devante convened in his Da Bassment project.

Early on, Missy told Devante about Tim's role as Sista's collaborator. Impressed by the production of the group's demos, he invited Tim to join the Bassment crew—and it's here that Tim took on his familiar nickname, Timbaland. He also liked the tracks Tim had created with local rappers, and he invited a crew of Virginia MCs to audition as well. While others didn't make the cut, Magoo was asked to stay. Uncomfortable with the prospect of being a solo artist, he asked Timbaland—who dabbled in rapping—to join him in a duo.

Devante created a performer's boot camp designed to shape raw talent into seasoned artists with polished records that he could release on his Swing Mob label. He invented competitions—for instance, who could write the fastest song—to build creative stamina. Missy quickly asserted herself as Devante's biggest challenger, the Bassment crew's most formidable creative force.

Unlike army boot camp, there was also plenty of free time for hanging out, getting high, and partying in New York City. To limit the distractions, Devante moved his Bassment crew to Rochester, in upstate New York (there, Devante recruited the group Sugah, which featured future Missy protégé, Tweet). He also tried to keep everyone from soaking up too much of what they heard on radio and TV. "We were isolated from any musical influences," Missy recalls, "and I think it forced us to come up with our own sound. You can't imitate something you've never heard."

Missy's skills and hustle earned her a spot rapping on a track ("Sweaty") from Jodeci's second album, 1993's *Diary of a Mad Band*. Timbaland made uncredited production contributions to the record as well (the siren on "Sweaty" grinds sound like Timbaland's work). It inauspiciously marked the start of Timbaland's and Missy's recording careers.

Meanwhile, tensions between Devante and Missy were rising. Missy felt frustrated by the lack of work getting done in the Bassment, and sensed that Devante resented her the more she asserted herself as the crew's creative leader. By then, Sista had signed with Elektra and Missy had enough contacts to break away. Before Missy left Devante, she contributed a standout dance-hall-style rap to "That's What Little Girls Are Made Of," from the debut album by seven-year-old *Cosby Show* alum Raven-Symoné. By 1994, Missy had split from the Bassment, and soon the project fell apart.

Going it alone would not be a smooth road for Missy and Timbaland. Sista's debut album, *4 All the Sistas Around da World*, featured a set of Timbaland/Devante coproductions completed before the break from Devante. Its blend of female R&B with hip-hop earned acclaim from critics who heard the record, but few potential fans ever got a chance. After a single, "Brand New," failed to take off in 1994, the label shelved the record. Defeated, Sista returned to Virginia and broke up.

Then Missy got a second piece of bad news: While Raven-Symoné's "Little Girls" track became a single, Missy was not invited to appear in the video. Instead, the label had hired a slimmer, more videogenic stand-in to lip-sync her verse. "Damn, do I look *that* bad?" Missy wondered. More than simply a stab at Missy's ego, the move suggested a more serious impediment to Missy's ambitions: Would her lack of videogenic beauty keep record companies from ever giving her a chance?

Rather than performing as a solo artist, Missy focused on developing her career as a songwriter. She and Timbaland spent much of 1994 and '95 back in Virginia trying to get another shot at making records. Because they both had impressed A&R people through their work with Devante, opportunities started trickling in.

Among the first came Motown, where Michael Bivins (of New Edition/Bell Biv DeVoe) had signed a Las Vegas R&B trio called 702 to his Biv Ten imprint. She and another Bassment veteran, Chad Elliott (no relation), were invited to write tracks for 702's 1996 debut, *No Doubt*. Of

Missy's two contributions, her and Chad's song "Steelo"—which featured a guest rap by Missy—became 702's first single. When it shot up to number twelve on the R&B chart, Missy scored her first big success.

Timbaland, meanwhile, had developed a contact with Atlantic Records who needed a new producer to work on the follow-up to teen R&B star Aaliyah's 1994 platinum debut, *Age Ain't Nothing But a Number*. That album had been largely written and produced by R&B star R. Kelly, but in making that record, the twenty-five-year-old Kelly had romanced the fifteen-year-old Aaliyah and quietly married her (the marriage was soon annulled). The resulting controversy exiled Kelly from Aaliyah's career and paved the way for Timbaland's rise.

Atlantic agreed to give Timbaland and his writing partner, Missy Elliott, a shot. Their first effort produced "If Your Girl Only Knew," a well-crafted, if otherwise ordinary, bit of R&B funk (featuring Timbaland on background vocals). The label asked for more, and they delivered "One in a Million," a slow-jam with the kind of tricky percussion that would become a Timbaland trademark. In all, Timbaland and Missy wrote seven tracks on *One in a Million*, and both of their first two creations earned Aaliyah top-ten hits (including an R&B number one for "If Your Girl"). Missy and Timbaland suddenly came into focus as one of 1996's hottest new production teams.

Meanwhile, Missy continued getting work as a rapper. With producer Puff Daddy, Missy appeared on "The Things that You Do," a moderate hit for R&B singer Gina Thompson. Missy's cameo, full of the "hee-hee-yows" and vocal effects that would define her style, marked a tipping point for her as a performer. With the notice Missy earned backing Aaliyah and Thompson, labels awakened to Missy's rapping and writing talents, in hip-hop and R&B. Her solo career was soon the object of a bidding war. When the dust settled, she found herself back on Sista's label, Elektra.

Empowered by their successes, Timbaland and Missy stretched out. As they worked on Missy's solo debut, the pair—along with Magoo—found time to write and produce the first album by former Bassment colleague Ginuwine. Of all their work on *Ginuwine . . . The Bachelor*, one of the album's oddest tracks became its biggest hit—and an important creative breakthrough for Timbaland. With "Pony," Timbaland offered something truly unique: The track, with its main riff built on heavily synthesized vocals ("yeah yow yeah") and sound effects (tape rewind squiggles, car screeches), rose to number one on the R&B/hip-hop singles chart. A great song made remarkable by its weird sonics—the sexy sound of a robot regurgitating—it validated Timbaland's notion that funk could be extracted from everyday objects, or from otherwordly sounds we'd never heard before. Like life in the Tidewater, it was all about making the most out of being nowhere at all.

Another key track Missy and Timbaland created for female R&B trio SWV introduced another favorite Timbaland production trick. Either out of expedience or because he was unable to create the sounds he conjured in his head with conventional instruments, Timbaland took to sampling his own vocals and embedding them in songs in a way that disguised them as voice but captured his desired musical effect. For SWV's third album, Timbaland and Missy created the song "Can We," which chugged along on percussion built around voice sounds: Tim imitating a chicken with hiccups, and a yawning dog. Underlying this largely faceless group and an otherwise conventional song, Tim created a collage that was, essentially, an avant-garde composition.

The same summer of '97 that "Can We" appeared, Missy unveiled her first album, *Supa Dupa Fly*. By then, Missy and Tim's reputation had grown considerably—even multiplatinum diva Mariah Carey was flying to Virginia Beach to write with them. Missy's highly anticipated debut was heavily promoted by Elektra and shot up to number three its first week on the charts. The timing was critical: Coming within a year of the deaths of Tupac and Notorious B.I.G., *Supa Dupa Fly* found hip-hop at a crossroads, ready to take a step back from the domination of gangsta sounds.

Missy, indeed, offered something very different. The first single, "The Rain," took the hook from Ann Peebles' 1973 hit, "I Can't Stand the Rain," and overlayed a hazy slice of funk that drizzled down moodiness where so much hip-hop had plodded ruggedly. Though it wasn't catchy enough to ignite the pop charts, "The Rain" and its popular video—which had Missy dancing around in what appeared to be inflated plastic garbage bags—served as the shock troops of Missy and Timbaland's entry into the hip-hop and pop mainstream. Where once the cold reality of the streets reigned, Elliott now presented the Technicolor surrealism of the no-man's-land. Subsequent videos were equally dazzling, earning Missy a reputation as MTV royalty.

With the success of its second single, "Sock It to Me" (number four R&B/hip-hop), *Supa Dupa Fly* easily went platinum, and the following year Missy earned three Grammy nominations and a slot on the largely hip-hop-free, female-centric Lilith Fair. Meanwhile, Timbaland returned in late '97 with the debut by Timbaland and Magoo, *Welcome to Our World*, released on Blackground, the label run by Aaliyah's uncle, entertainment lawyer/manager Barry Hankerson.

Welcome nominally showcased Magoo as a rapper, but by this point Timbaland was fairly well known for his production; Magoo, a competent but often awkward rapper, lacked the presence to shine above the beats. Still, the record delivered two respectable hits: "Up Jumps Da Boogie" and "Clock Strikes" (featuring its interpolation of "Mack the Knife"). And between the Missy and Magoo albums, by the end of 1997 Timbaland's music was firmly established as the most potent new sound in hip-hop.

While Timbaland grew up in the South, by 1998—when he appeared on Aaliyah's "Are You That Somebody" rapping, "Dirty South can y'all really feel me, East Coast feel me, West Coast feel me"—he was clearly an interregional citizen of hip-hop, and spending little time in Virginia. In addition to following up with Aaliyah and Ginuwine, Tim introduced another Bassment alum—R&B group Playa—and manned the boards for top acts in both R&B (Destiny's Child, Total) and rap (Busta Rhymes, Nas, and most notably, Jay-Z), with Missy (as on Nicole's "Make It Hot") or without. He also put together a star-studded solo album, *Tim's Bio*, which featured his usual "Superfriends" crew—Missy, Magoo, Ginuwine, Aaliyah—and guests such as Jay-Z, Ludacris, and Twista. Also appearing was MC Mad Skillz, a highly respected Richmond-based rapper whose 1995 debut, *From Where???*, was the first Virginia hip-hop record to get national release (Skillz, a gifted freestyler, was always stylistically oriented toward the New York underground, though his flow had a strong influence on Virginia Beach rappers).

As Missy and Tim reconvened to create *Supa Dupa Fly*'s follow-up, it culminated a two-year whirlwind where Tim hadn't stopped churning out tracks for the top acts in music and Missy had emerged as a major star on the way to becoming the biggest female artist in hip-hop history. Her life had entered that bizarre zone of mega-celebrity: In early 1999, a teenage boy in Norfolk was caught impersonating Missy and making harassing phone calls. And in the summer, Missy unveiled her first cosmetic product, Misdemeanor lipstick, with proceeds going to Break the Cycle, a group combating domestic violence.

Whether Missy and Tim didn't think enough about the record—or thought too much about the wrong things—*Da Real World* was a decent record that didn't live up to its promise. It wasn't quite a sophomore slump—the record went platinum, and its biggest hit, "Hot Boyz," set a record for most consecutive weeks as number-one rap single. But *Da Real World* suffered from too much conventional R&B and not enough of the knock-your-socks-off productions that Timbaland had been creating elsewhere. Missy and Tim seemed to have consciously opted for something that might have broad appeal (even the guest spot from rising star Eminem sounds out of place). But while playing it safe often works with pop music, Tim and Missy have always confounded the rule: They've hit biggest when they're at their most adventurous.

GOOD OL' VIRGINIA: THE MASTERS OF URBAN POP

Pharrell Williams and Chad Hugo, meanwhile, were slowly gaining momentum as producers. Where Timbaland asserted his revolutionary sound from the start, the Neptunes played it cool with tasteful but fairly conservative tracks for acts like SWV. But things started heating up in 1996: "When Boy Meets Girl," a delicious retro-soul single for female R&B act Total, made it to number twenty on the R&B chart. The following year, the Neptunes scored a number-one rap single with Mase's "Lookin' at Me." By 1998, when the rapper Noreaga reached the top spot with his Neptunes-produced "Superthug," the track's helicopter effects and off-kilter beat suggested Williams and Hugo were beginning to take cues from Timbaland.

These successes empowered the Neptunes to assert more control. In 1999, Williams and Hugo got behind a little-known singer from Harlem named Kelis, the duo's first stab at developing a new artist. As a lead-up to her own album, Kelis sang the chorus on the Neptunes-produced Old Dirty Bastard hit "Got Your Money," a song so lyrically eccentric it benefited from the balance of the Neptunes' straightforward production. It was their most unique track up to that point and marked Williams and Hugo as producers who were able to handle a variety of artist styles and temperaments.

The song's catchy chorus also brought attention to Kelis, who'd soon released her debut, *Kaleidoscope*—the Neptunes' first full album production. Kelis' first single, "Caught Out There," shined largely thanks to her ferocious vocal performance—particularly the chorus, with her outraged yell of "I HATE YOU SO MUCH RIGHT NOW!" But the song's production—a perfect blend of hooks, funky musical dressing, and arrangement surprises—helped make it both a commercial success and a truly provocative piece of music.

But if 1999's twin successes of "Got Your Money" and "Caught Out There" established the Neptunes' reputation, 2000 was the year they became true stars. The breakthrough resulted not only from a string of singles—four top-twenty hits, including two urban number ones—but also because, for the first time, Pharrell himself appeared as a vocalist. On Jay-Z's "I Just Wanna Love U" and Mystikal's "Shake Ya Ass," Pharrell borrowed from the playbook of Organized Noize's Sleepy Brown by adopting a Curtis

Mayfield–like falsetto. Undeniably thin, but charming and comfortable in its lack of polish, Pharrell's croon was a key factor in these songs' successes.

Pharrell also stepped forward as a physical presence—something unusual for a producer who was not also a label head or recording artist in his own right. In the clip of "Shake Ya Ass"—or the clean version, "Shake It Fast"— Pharrell appears in his familiar trucker hat, gyrating with the video vixens. With Pharrell's growing star power and the duo's production—conventional in its classic-soul/funk, but completely infectious and immaculately rendered—the Neptunes, particularly Pharrell, were becoming household names in pop.

Undeniable slices of pop perfection, "I Just Wanna Love U" and "Shake Ya Ass" were enduring signposts of the millennial pop era—not utterly unique in the way that Timbaland's tracks were, but remarkable in their buoyancy and propulsive spirit. The Neptunes hit again in 2000 with Mystikal's "Danger," and Ludacris' "Southern Hospitality"—the latter an early example of the hip-hop deconstruction that would define the Neptunes' later production. Where Luda's brash invitation to get wild (to "throw them 'bows") draws the listener, the bare track—an insistent bass drum pulse accented by panpipe synth—proves equally alluring.

On a roll, Pharrell and Chad wanted to see how far their reach could extend into pop music. During 2001 and 2002, while they continued to work with top rappers—including self-proclaimed "king of the South" T.I. and Houston gangsta Scarface—they also embraced opportunities to produce the princess and prince of '90s teen pop, Britney Spears and Justin Timberlake. The goal was to turn the former *Mickey Mouse Club* stars into viable adult artists.

The Neptunes succeeded in providing Spears with two meaty tracks, "Boys" and "I'm a Slave 4 U," that count among her best. The latter's video-game effects and dense digital soundscapes provide a prime example of the Neptunes' more adventurous direction. With Timberlake (who also enlisted Timbaland for his solo debut, *Justified*), the transition was less severe. Unlike his ex-girlfriend, Justin possessed legitimate singing chops. But as a measure of the Neptunes' cachet, Timberlake saw fit to have Pharrell introduce him to the world of urban pop. Pharrell is the first voice we hear, handing Justin a ghetto pass: "Ladies and gentlemen, it's my pleasure to introduce to you. . . . He's a friend of mine, and he goes by the name Justin, all the way from Memphis, Tennessee. . . . "

For artists outside urban music, the Neptunes' comfort with pop was part of their appeal. Like Missy and Tim, the Neptunes never swore allegiance to hip-hop. Like other outlying areas, Virginia discovered hip-hop fully formed, as a form of pop music more than as a culture, as New York–centrics often describe it. They felt comfortable with hip-hop because it was the sound of the times, but at heart, the Neptunes were always pop classicists. Many of their most irresistible tracks—Beyoncé's "Work it Out," Foxy Brown's "Candy," Common's "I Got a Right Ta"—succeed on a combination of classic soul, blues, and pop bundled with twenty-first-century digital mayhem.

Coming from a place that was largely a clean slate, the Virginians became convenient conduits: For street rappers like Jay-Z, they offered the pop charts; for pop acts like Britney and Justin, they provided urban cred. And for a rock act like No Doubt, who hired the Neptunes for their 2001 hit, "Hella Good," the adaptable producers provided a way out of the formula that had confined the band.

With Missy Elliott's 2001 return, *Miss E . . . So Addictive*, Missy and Tim sounded determined not to repeat *Da Real World*'s mistakes. The introductory title track cops a mock-syrupy R&B style before Missy interrupts, "Man, bump this ballad shit," and launches into a record full of the tightly sculpted hip-hop that defines Missy and Tim's best work.

The album's showcase was its advance single, already climbing the charts when *So Addictive* reached stores. "Get Ur Freak On" was a quantum leap for Timbaland as a producer, and for the sound of commercial pop: Driven by Indian tabla percussion and a brain-rattling riff on a stringed instrument that sounds like a Japanese koto, the song seemed to come from some satellite cross-transmission—or as souvenirs brought to Virginia ports on navy ships from exotic lands. It drew freely from global music styles and created a flawless funk with little heed to funk convention. Timbaland had begun experimenting with world-music elements on earlier hits like Jay-Z's "Big Pimpin'," The Lox's "Ride or Die Bitch," and Aaliyah's "Try Again"; the trick reached full fruition with "Get Ur Freak On." It is one of the weirdest pop songs ever put to record, and one of the decade's most irresistible pop moments—as well as one of Missy's biggest hits.

Nearly every one of *So Addictive*'s tracks offers something inventive, from the electro-funk of "One Minute Man" (the record's second hit), to the house beats and electronic goat sounds of "4 My People," to the frantic reggae bubbling of "Whatcha Gon' Do." But the summer of 2001 was not just about *So Addictive*'s creative breakthrough. Missy also bolstered her reputation as the queen of modern pop when she served as producer for the chart-topping remake of "Lady Marmalade," featuring Christina Aguilera, Mya,

Pink, and Lil' Kim, from the *Moulin Rouge* soundtrack (Timbaland also contributed an unlikely pairing to the film, his recording of Beck covering David Bowie's "Diamond Dogs").

Tim and Missy also contributed tracks to Aaliyah's self-titled album, which arrived in July. The Timbaland-produced single, "We Need a Resolution," was running its course on the charts when, in late August, Aaliyah died in a plane crash. The death shook Tim and Missy profoundly; they'd been her closest musical collaborators for five years, and owed their initial success to her. "She was like blood, and I lost blood," Timbaland told MTV at the time. "Me and her together had this chemistry. I kinda lost half of my creativity to her. . . . Beyond the music, she was a brilliant person, the [most special] person I ever met."

Within weeks, 9/11 eclipsed Aaliyah's tragedy, and while the catastrophe rocked the music industry along with society as a whole, Timbaland pushed forward. In an attempt to take more ownership over his music, Tim made a deal with major label Interscope to create his own record label, Beat Club. The first fruits of his venture arrived in October of 2001: an album by Bubba Sparxxx, a white rapper from rural Georgia. With Sparxxx's lead single, "Ugly," Tim revisited the Eastern sounds of "Get Ur Freak On" (to acknowledge the similarity, Tim cut a snippet of "Freak" into "Ugly").

A month later, Timbaland played prominently on another rap debut from the previously uncharted South. Gravelly voiced North Carolina rapper Petey Pablo's *Diary of a Sinner: 1st Entry* featured three Timbaland tracks, the album's most notable. On "I," Tim trades verses and offers humorous insights such as, "Momma never saw that a star was born/Momma said, 'Star go mow that lawn.'" "Raise Up," meanwhile, posits itself as a North Carolina (and mid-Atlantic) anthem. Indeed, Virginia locals had started mumblings about the mid-Atlantic being its own hip-hop region, distinct from the Northeast or the South. They were calling it the Middle East, though the region's major artists didn't pay much heed. "Virginia is just Virginia," Timbaland has said in his characteristic plainspoken way. "I don't see it as the Middle East, I just see it as good ol' Virginia."

Pablo also made extensive appearances on Timbaland and Magoo's second album, *Indecent Proposal,* also out in November of 2001. The record featured some of Magoo's best performances, but the appearance of Pablo—and Timbaland buddies like Jay-Z, Skillz, and Beat Club rapper Ms. Jade—served to undercut Magoo's status as lead vocalist. As another collection of Timbaland alchemy—dislocated Eastern snippets, unconventional hip-hop constructions, bubbling and dripping effects, postmodern funk, and a posthumous Aaliyah vocal—*Indecent Proposal* had much to offer. For Magoo, though, the album further suggested it was not his destiny to become a star like his friends. This imbalance between Timbaland and Magoo provided plenty of opportunity for strife. But the friendship has endured—they even put out a third, virtually ignored, Timbaland and Magoo album in late 2003.

Magoo says of his life as Timbaland's nominal partner:

> We just have to be strong within the unit. Both believing in God, we don't believe God makes mistakes. So we just take it how it comes. We just don't let it affect the friendship. I got in a group with Tim because I was his friend, and we try to always make that the focus. His success is his success, mine is mine. But we leave that at the job. It makes him a little uncomfortable, too, when he's supposed to be promoting what we're doing and [journalists] want to ask him about things other than that. But it's nothing that we can't handle. I still have the greatest job in the world. Somebody who's my friend is also a great producer. My life ain't so bad. It's like being on a team with Michael Jordan.

While his friends spent more of their time in places like Miami, New York, and Los Angeles, Magoo remained in Virginia and became the first of the group to make overt claim as a Southerner. On *Indecent Proposal*'s "Baby Bubba," he raps, "Stay in the French Quarter and listen to Juvenile/I like that South shit, all my niggas is wild/ . . . South boys ain't fuckin' playing . . . /We got OutKast and No Limit and Eightball/Scarface, Ludacris and Goodie Mob/We do it country cause we proud of this shit. . . . "

In reality, after Timbaland and Missy's experience in New Jersey with Devante, neither returned to Virginia for long. Both maintain houses there, but you're more likely to spot them in Miami. "I like to be away, I just vibe better," he says. "There's no opportunity in Virginia, no jobs, no big buildings. I represent Virginia, but I don't gotta live there to speak on it."

Just as Timbaland made his Beat Club deal with Interscope, Pharrell Williams and Chad Hugo hooked up with Arista Records to create their label Star Trak. Their first signing was the Clipse, a duo of Virginia Beach brothers they'd known for years. The older brother, Gene Thornton, aka Malice, had been friendly with Pharrell since they ran into each other at the barbershop as teens. Malice and his brother Terrence, aka Pusha T, were born in the Bronx but moved as children to Virginia, where their mother's family lived. Around 1996 they started hanging around at Teddy Riley's Famous Recording Studio and talking to Teddy's brother Markell (of Wreckx-N-Effect) about signing to his production company. Instead, they signed to Elektra Records in 1997, only to have their finished album permanently shelved.

After four years of looking for another chance, the Clipse finally released an album, the Neptunes-produced *Lord Willin'*, in August of 2002. The record highlighted a grittier side of the Seven Cities, as the duo raps in "Virginia": "I'm from Virginia, where ain't shit to do but cook/Pack it up, sell it triple price, fuck the books" and "I reside in VA, ride in VA, most likely when I die, I'm gonna die in VA/Virginia is for lovers but trust there's hate here, for out of towners who think they gonna move weight here/Ironic, the same place I'm making figures at, that there's the same land they used to hang niggas at."

Ironically, while the Clipse exhibited a willingness to represent its 'hood, the music sounded no more authentic to the Tidewater than the rootless music created by Missy and Timbaland or the Neptunes. In fact, Pusha and Malice always considered themselves East Coast–style rappers—something that became apparent in 2005, when they joined with two Philadelphia MCs to form the Re-Up Gang, which consciously revived the spirit of classic street rap made by Kool G Rap and Big Daddy Kane.

"I was raised here, but Virginia isn't what I know as Southern," Pusha says. "There's no way I could call this the Dirty South. This is the middle ground before you start going Deep South. This is the mixing pot of everything; it's dead smack in the middle." For the Clipse, Virginia felt closer to Queensbridge than Liberty City.

Lord Willin' sent the Neptunes into another league—past mere superstar producers and into the realm of entrepreneurs and music-industry power brokers. The record also featured some of the team's most adventurous creations—most notably the standout hit, "Grindin'," a top-ten rap single where the Neptunes began to fully embrace their hip-hop deconstruction. It was, in a way, the opposite to Timbaland's kitchen-sink approach, but the result was similarly weird: "Grindin'" jettisoned any kind of conventional arrangement—no keyboards, no guitar, no bassline. In its place was simply a drum pattern: hand claps, finger snaps, bass thumps, and instead of a snare, an industrial crash so grand and booming it nearly fills the song's entire sonic space.

The Neptunes went minimalist on at least two other 2002 tracks: Noreaga's "Head Bussa" and Sean Paul's "Bubble." But that wasn't all the duo had cooking that year. They also scored their biggest hit with Nelly's can't-escape-it summer hit "Hot in Herre," which spent seven weeks as *Bill-board*'s number-one pop single. And Williams and Hugo made their debut as recording artists, releasing the album *In Search Of . . .* as two-thirds of a trio (which also featured Shay, from the original Neptunes band) called N.E.R.D.

The group actually finished *In Search Of . . .* a year earlier, and released it in Europe in July of 2001. But, last minute, they pulled it back in the United States to rework the songs. "We wanted to step out of that so-called in-the-pocket hip-hop sound and just do something totally different," Hugo told MTV News at the time. Where the original featured a sound more familiar to Neptunes fans, the new version—rerecorded with the help of Spymob, a rock band signed to Star Trak—featured live instruments and a harder funk-rock sound.

When the revised *In Search Of . . .* finally hit the stores in March of 2002, many Neptunes fans who'd heard the original expressed their preference for the first version. For whatever reason—the lack of momentum due to the delays, or because N.E.R.D.'s fusion didn't fit on rock or urban radio—*In Search Of . . .* failed to match the Neptunes' production success. But the record garnered its share of praise, and in October, N.E.R.D. received 2002's Shortlist of Music Award, an honor given by fellow musicians and tastemakers for the best album that had not yet reached a mass audience (sold less than a half-million copies).

Between the Clipse, N.E.R.D., and the Neptunes' string of hit productions, many considered 2002 to be their year. And so it sparked controversy when the duo was shut out of the producer of the year Grammy nominations in January of 2003. "Nobody thought to put us on the ballot," Williams told MTV angrily. "It's usually CEOs that do it. And for whatever reason, none of them motherfuckers, as much money as we made for all those guys this year, none of them put us on the ballot to be voted for. I'm pretty sure we would have gotten some votes."

They'd fallen through the cracks: Because artists are put up for nomination by their record label, and the Neptunes operated as free agents—producing for artists on any label—no one record company had taken it upon itself to nominate the Neptunes. (That gaffe was corrected the following year when Pharrell or the Neptunes received six Grammy nominations, including a win for producer of the year.)

By 2003, the Neptunes had so thoroughly set the standard for state-of-the-art pop that when icons wanted to update their sound—as when Ice

Cube reprised old N.W.A. lyrics on "In the Late Night Hour" and the Rolling Stones remixed "Sympathy for the Devil"—they inevitably turned to the Virginia twosome. The Neptunes brand was strong enough to drive a Star Trak compilation—*The Neptunes Present . . . Clones*—to a number-one debut in August. In addition to highlighting Star Trak's roster—a diverse cast that included Norfolk rapper Fam-Lay and N.E.R.D. backing band Spymob—the record yielded a hit that literally flipped the script: Where it was no surprise to hear Pharrell sing the chorus between Jay-Z's verses on "Frontin'," for the first time this collaboration was credited to Pharrell, featuring Jay-Z, and not the other way around.

Clones furthered the Neptunes' taste for deconstruction by including a Snoop Dogg track driven by a toy piano, and one by rapper Rosco P. Coldchain that punctuates a lone snare beat by using a snatch of tape hum (or was it white noise?) as percussion.

Like Timbaland, the Neptunes discovered that, having already established a reputation, they could create more and more outlandish productions with no negative impact. A trio of hits between 2003 and 2005 coupled an off-kilter structure and minimalism with an immediately catchy singsong hook: Kelis' "Milkshake," with its detuned heavy-fuzz bassline (number-three pop hit); Snoop Dogg's "Drop It Like It's Hot," with its tongue-click percussion and ultra-low bass booms (number one); and Gwen Stefani's "Hollaback Girl," with its spare marching-band boom (number one).

Pharrell and Chad also borrowed a trick or two from Timbaland: the Indian vocals and tabla on Nas' "Nas Angels . . . The Flyest," or the lap slapping found percussion on Slim Thug's "I Ain't Heard of That." But by 2005 the Neptunes had largely eclipsed Timbaland as both a hit maker and creator of the most wonderfully strange, fun, and forward-looking pop music of the era. And Pharrell, who released his debut solo album, *In My Mind*, in mid-2006, had become a major pop celebrity as well.

While the Neptunes rose to dominate pop music from 2000 to 2005, Timbaland and Missy's music retained its quality without evolving much. In early 2002, Missy's star power and writing skills (plus Timbaland's production) gave a big push to Tweet, an old friend from their Bassment Crew days, who hit with the single "Oops (Oh My)" and the full-length *Southern Hummingbird*, released on Missy's Elektra-distributed imprint, Goldmind. By the late 2002 release of her fourth album, *Under Construction*, Missy had become a veteran hit maker with longevity rare among pop artists. And her dramatic weight loss—reportedly seventy pounds in all—made Missy celebrity tabloid fodder.

But the album's advance single, "Work It," generated the most attention—and earned Missy her biggest hit yet. Another classic space-funk digital transmission by Timbaland, the song exudes sex and a bravura that seems to say: We can make a hit out of just about anything. In this case, the hook in "Work It" is a line from the chorus repeated backward to make it unintelligible and unrepeatable: "Is it worth it, let me work it/I put my thing down flip it and reverse it," and then what sounds something like, "yurf eminifins wen yet" (which seems to be "flip it and reverse it" played backward).

When *Under Construction* wasn't busy talking nonsense (as it does again on the album's second hit, "Gossip Folks"), Missy sounds determined to say something meaningful. In the "Intro," she admits that, "*Under Construction* simply states that I'm a work in progress, I'm working on myself. You know, ever since Aaliyah passed, I view life in a more valuable way. . . . From the World Trade families, to the Left Eye family . . . to the hip-hop family, we're all under construction trying to rebuild ourselves."

Missy's rebuilding efforts manifest in various ways. "Nothing Out There" and "Ain't That Funny" give voice to the female experience in hip-hop—a segment underserved by female rappers who've presented themselves more as sex objects than women with desires of their own. She also attempts to revive an old-school hip-hop spirit of fun on "Back in the Day" and "Funky Fresh Dressed." And Missy also spends verses paying tribute to those who still haunt her—Aaliyah, and hip-hop casualties Left Eye, Tupac, B.I.G., and Big Pun. For *Under Construction*'s closer, she teamed with TLC's T-Boz and Chilli for "Can You Hear Me?" a song that calls out to those lost: "Aaliyah, can you hear me?" Missy sings, "I hope that you're proud of me/Me and Tim been doing our thing, but it's never been the same since you had to go."

A year later, Missy returned with *This Is Not a Test*, which offered more of the same but failed to generate at least one big single. "Pass the Dutch," a retro-futurist jam driven by handclaps and bass throbs, peaked at number twenty-seven. The album reached number thirteen—Missy's lowest chart showing—and suddenly it became a question whether Missy's seven-year jaunt as a consistent hit maker had run its course.

The same could be said of Timbaland, who by early 2004 had hit a relative dry spell. He continued to score with Missy and Jay-Z ("Dirt Off Your Shoulder"), but his Beat Club offerings (Ms. Jade's debut and Bubba Sparxxx's second album) and the third Timbaland and Magoo record failed to make much noise commercially. Sparxxx's *Deliverance*, however, broke new ground for Timbaland as he embraced Southern sounds, including blues harmonica and wailing fiddle. This, combined with his work on Cee-Lo's "I'll Be Around" single—on which Tim raps, "Here comes Timbaland, I'm also from the South/I like them girls with big butts and gold in their mouth"—suggested the producer had finally embraced his Southernness.

Timbaland's productions, however, began sounding predictable; tracks like Brandy's "Turn It Up," Ludacris' "The Potion," and The Game's "Put You on the Game" all used instrumental hooks created by human voice, an overused trick that suggested he simply couldn't be bothered to hire musicians. As early as 2003, Timbaland talked about retiring from music; then in late 2004, Tim—an already husky guy who'd ballooned up to a reported 331 pounds—became obsessed with weight training. As the *Miami New Times* reported, Tim shed more than 100 pounds in six months on an intensive diet and exercise regimen, and considered entering a Miami bodybuilding contest.

For someone who'd been as relentlessly inventive as Timbaland, it's easy to see how a lack of new ideas could lead to boredom and distraction. In 2005, Tim's most notable release was a "mobile album"—a collection of seven original ring tones for sale online—that seemed a suitable (if limited) application for his digital sculptures. New albums by Missy Elliott and Bubba Sparxxx contained only token Timbaland contributions. But in mid-2006, Timbaland returned in a big way—as the primary collaborator on two major chart-topping releases: *Loose*, by Canadian pop star Nelly Furtado, and *FutureSex/LoveSounds* by Justin Timberlake. Timbaland cowrote and produced most of both albums, and his appearances on Furtado's "Promiscuous Girl"—which found Tim rapping, singing, and flashing his enormous biceps in the video—and Timberlake's "Sexyback" became two of the year's biggest hits. Next, Timbaland plans to release a compilation of his tracks fronted by an eclectic cast of superstars—including Elton John, Dr. Dre, Fall Out Boy, and 50 Cent—called *Timbaland Presents Shock Value*.

Missy, meanwhile, traded on her celebrity to create her own reality television show, "The Road to Stardom," on the UPN network in early 2005 (she also dipped her hands in a second reality show by producing tracks for *American Idol* winner Fantasia's debut album). Later that year, she returned with a new album called *The Cookbook*. It was her first record not produced predominantly by Timbaland; that it succeeded artistically and commercially testified to her position as an important and enduring pop artist. The record's hit single, "Lose Control," worked as a sequel to "Pass that Dutch"; it was similarly driven by an '80s electro spirit (and a prominent sample from techno pioneer Juan Atkins). But *Cookbook*'s most unusual track was "On and On," where Missy teamed for the first time with the Neptunes—a full decade and a half after she met Pharrell. The Neptunes' most extreme effort in digital pop deconstruction, "On and On" pings around a bed made entirely of cartoon sound effects. Virginia, once again, had produced something unlike anything we'd heard before.

In the beginning, there was Luther Campbell.

Houston's Geto Boys, still rowdy three decades later.

UGK's Pimp C, with plenty of time to think behind bars.

Memphis godfathers Eightball and MJG.

No Limit's general, Master P.

David Banner (left) and Jazze Pha revisit their roots in front of
Memphis' famed Stax Records.

OutKast's Andre 3000 and
Big Boi take the stage side
by side.

Jermaine Dupri steps up to the mic.

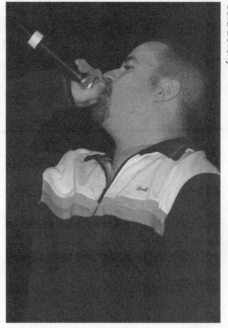

Bubba Sparxxx guzzles down his mic.

Virginia's international hip-hop queen, Missy Elliott.

Timbaland (left) with his Virginia rhyme partner Magoo.

Goodie Mob's Khujo, Big Gipp, and T-Mo,
moving on without Cee-Lo.

Pharrell Williams (front) greets fans with his Neptunes partner Chad Hugo (back, in white jacket).

Rollin' with Ludacris.

T.I. entertains the fans.

David Banner welcomes you to Mississippi.

Kentucky collective Nappy Roots pile in.

Last Hot Boy standing: Lil' Wayne.

Like father, like son: Lil' Wayne (left) with Baby.

Cash Money reunion: Juvenile (left) with Mannie Fresh.

Southern rap love connection: New Orleans' Lil' Wayne with Miami's Trina.

Three 6 Mafia as a quartet (from left): Juicy J, Crunchy Black, DJ Paul, and Lord Infamous.

Lil Jon & the East Side Boyz crunked to the max.

The Ying Yang Twins: D-Roc (left) and Kaine.

A mellower Lil Jon behind the studio board.

Ciara, the Queen of Crunk&B, with Lil Jon, the King of Crunk.

Trick Daddy (left) reps for Miami with Slip-N-Slide's Ted Lucas.

Houston's Paul Wall flashes his grill while dapper Miami rapper
Pitbull takes a sip.

Houston's Mike Jones serves as a
walking billboard for himself.

Julia Beverly

Paul Wall wears his "Free Pimp C" T-shirt proudly.

Julia Beverly

Master and his disciples: Houston's Bun B (center) with Paul Wall (left) and Slim Thug.

Three generations of crunk (from left): Eightball, Lil Jon, and Bonecrusher.

UGK's Bun B helps keep the memory of DJ Screw alive.

**OutKast's Big Boi stays true
to the Atlanta streets.**

**OutKast's Andre Benjamin
keeps his fans guessing.**

chapter 7

ATLANTA AS THE NEW MOTOWN

THE DUNGEON FAMILY MOVES TO THE FRONT OF THE BUS

In the two years and one month between the release of OutKast's second album, *ATLiens*, and third album, *Aquemini*, hip-hop changed dramatically. Just weeks after *ATLiens* hit the charts, iconic West Coast rapper Tupac Shakur was shot and killed in Las Vegas. And five months later, his New York rival, Notorious B.I.G., died by gunfire as well. The simmering East Coast/West Coast hip-hop feud exploded into the mainstream consciousness, while, simultaneously, the rap industry acknowledged that the tough talk and criminal flirtations had gotten way out of hand. As Death Row Records fell apart and its head, Suge Knight, went off to jail, the era of West Coast rap was over.

The East Coast was also showing signs of fatigue. After its multiplatinum 1996 album, *The Score*, the Fugees retreated into semiretirement. Having lost Biggie, Puff Daddy's Bad Boy label ushered in an era of flavorless, substance-free rap, while the venerable Def Jam scored hits with the fairly tired New York flexing of Method Man, Redman, and DMX. The most promising New Yorker to rise during this period was Jay-Z, and part of his enduring success came from a willingness to work with outsiders, particularly Southerners. Surely, he noticed as the South began to rise from both ends—on the pop side with Missy Elliott's *Supa Dupa Fly*, and on the street level with Master P's first chart-topper, *Ghetto D*.

But Southern hip-hop did not yet have its masterpiece—a work that both defined and transcended the genre—until the fall of 1998, when OutKast returned with *Aquemini*. If *ATLiens* had been the group's transitional record, Andre and Big Boi most certainly arrived somewhere with *Aquemini*. The record made clear that OutKast was different—a special kind of group rarely seen in pop music, and even less in hip-hop: a group that scored hits but also followed an artistic vision into new territory.

With *ATLiens*, fans noticed a new look for the group, particularly Andre. Building on the album's Funkadelic-inspired Afro-spaceman imagery, Andre began dressing flamboyantly in performances—wearing blond wigs, freaky glasses, marching band uniforms. No doubt these stabs at exploring new identities were encouraged by his budding relationship with Dallas soul singer Erykah Badu, herself part of an up-and-coming crop of so-called alternative urban artists whose vibe was more bohemian than ghetto. The relationship deepened quickly and, in November of 1997, Badu gave birth to Andre's son, Seven Sirius Benjamin. Seven's birth coincided with a new era of artistry for Andre, and some OutKast fans began to wonder what happened to the smooth hustler from *Southernplayalistic*.

OutKast lampooned fan attitudes on a pair of *Aquemini* skits: A record store customer is offered the new OutKast record, but he declines. "At first they were some pimps, man, but then they some aliens, or some genies or some shit. . . . Man, whatever. I ain't fuckin' with that no mo'." He leaves with a record by the fictional PimpTrickGangstaClick, but soon returns, disappointed by all the rap clichés.

After the album's ethereal opening, "Hold On, Be Strong," *Aquemini* presents some bold answers to fans' doubts. "Return of the 'G'," an introductory manifesto with a lush Organized Noize beat, orchestral arrangement, and Giorgio Moroder interpolation, sets the tone for the whole record. Using "gangsta" to mean someone uncompromising, Dre rhymed, "It's the return of the gangsta, thanks ta' them niggas that get the wrong impression of expression/Then they questioning Big Boi, 'What's up with Andre? Is he in a cult? Is he on drugs? Is he gay? When y'all gon' break up? When y'all gon' wake up?'/Nigga I'm feelin' better than ever, what's wrong with you?/Get down!"

With that, Dre spread the word that, for OutKast to continue growing, there would be no limitations on what they could do. Rather than rapping about "bitches and switches, and hoes and clothes and weed," Dre says, "let's talk about time travelin', rhyme javelin, something mind unravelin', get down!" And while Big Boi didn't abandon his hip-hop wear, he was down with the program: "Stickin' together like flour and water to make that slow dough/We worked for everything we have and gon' stick up for each other like we brothers from another mother."

While the stylistic divisions were becoming increasingly apparent in the lyrics and styles of the twosome—with Andre the more eccentric, arty rhymer, and Big Boi the down-home street MC—OutKast aimed to blend the sensibilities seamlessly. The record's title combined the astrological signs of both—Aquarius (Big Boi) and Gemini (Andre)—as a declaration of solidarity: "Nothing is for sure, nothing is for certain, nothing lasts forever/But until they close the curtain, it's him and I, Aquemini."

Statements of purpose appear throughout *Aquemini*—"Skew It on the Bar-B," for instance, talks about how "they done changed the rules." But *Aquemini*'s most striking declaration came with its climax, "Liberation," a six-minute epic of jazz, blues, gospel, world music, singing, and spoken-word poetry, but no rapping at all. Musically and lyrically, it was OutKast's most profound expression yet. Over an elegant grand-piano arpeggio and the intricate percussion flurry of Jamaican rimshots and African congas, the vocalists testify: "Can't worry 'bout what another nigga think, now that's liberation and baby I want it," Andre asserts; "To have a choice to be who you want to be, is left up to me," Big Boi affirms; "Lord, I'm so tired, my feet feel like I walked most of the road on my own. . . . Is there anything I can say to help you find your way, touch your soul, make you whole," Cee-Lo busts in a powerful verse that culminates in an exultation by Dungeon Family friends Joi, Peaches, and David Whild—a repeated refrain of "Shake that load off" that's as deep in soulful melody and improvisational harmony as a chain gang of angels. Erykah Badu then picks up the song, singing about the chains of stardom—"All you want to do is give the world your heart, record labels try to make you compromise your art"—and Big Rube closes with poetry heavy in down-South imagery, about the chains of exploitation: "It's a hard row to hoe, if your ass don't move and the rain don't fall/And the ground is dry but the roots are strong, so some survive to your surprise."

"Liberation" is gorgeous, soul-lifting stuff rarely heard in hip-hop. As *Aquemini* proved here and elsewhere, OutKast's Southernness didn't lessen its sophistication—rather, it made the music deeper. You can hear it in the way Big Boi recites deliciously evocative lines on "SpottieOttieDopalicious"— "The way she moved reminded me of a brown stallion hoss with skates on/Smooth like a hot comb on nappy ass hair/ . . . Her neck was smellin' sweeter than a plate of yams with extra syrup"—over a track that blends woozy dub reggae with Afro-pop horns. Or the way Dre and Big frame "Da Art of Storytelling (Part 1)" in community, a laid-back Southern afternoon hanging with the boys: "It's like that, now . . . 'bout four, five cats off in my 'Lac now/Just shoot game in the form of story raps now."

But *Aquemini*'s biggest success at blending Southern iconography and music with urban pop came on its first single, "Rosa Parks." The track starts with a juxtaposition of turntable scratching with a back-country equivalent—a voice hiccuping "kakalakalakala." Then an acoustic guitar strum kicks in with funk chords and the chorus: "Ah ha, hush that fuss, everybody move to the back of the bus/Do you wanna bump and slump with us?/We the type of people make the club get crunk," all delivered with proud Jawja drawl ("hush that fuhhs" "back of the buhhs"). The song peaks with a foot-stomping country-blues harmonica breakdown, courtesy of Andre's stepdad, Pastor Robert Hodo. It manages to be hip-hop, country, and pop at the same time. Because of the way it straddled genres, perhaps, the single only reached number fifty-five on the pop chart.

Lyrically, the song took on its own life. The words are fairly oblique, though one could reasonably interpret "Rosa Parks" as a song about the music industry and Southern hip-hop's place in it. That is, Southern rap has been discriminated against—sent to the back of the bus—and OutKast sees itself as Rosa Parks (who's not mentioned in the lyrics), a group that will refuse the discrimination. Or perhaps Parks' name was conjured simply in free association, and OutKast likes to be in the back of the bus—that's where the fun is. Or maybe neither interpretation matches the intent, if there was any intent at all.

It's unlikely that Rosa Parks—or those handling the affairs of the then-eighty-seven-year-old icon—quite understood the song, either. But they took offense to the lyrics and filed a lawsuit against OutKast for trademark infringement—for profiting from Parks' name. Though the suit never had a strong legal standing, Parks' lawyers pursued it for six years, pitting an aging icon against a group that was, ironically, among hip-hop's more positive-minded acts (and who were embarrassed to clash with someone they considered a hero). By 2005, when lawyers dropped the suit in exchange for OutKast's promise to work with Parks' organization on educational programs, Parks was in the last months of her life and her age-related dementia made it clear someone else had been making decisions in her name. Out-Kast finally put the bizarre and unfortunate episode behind them.

While "Rosa Parks" had the longest life beyond *Aquemini*, it was the record's closing track, "Chonkyfire," that most pointed to the future. Driven by a fuzzed-out guitar lead and what sounds like Theremin wave signals, Dre plays pied piper, calling all the freaks to join him on a journey to blaze a new trail in music: "Do you know what brings rats, mice, snakes up out their

hole?/Chonkyfire, spliced with rock 'n' roll/Indubitably, piper-pied."
Then, to remind listeners of Dre's earlier pledge, the track winds down with
a sound bite from the 1995 Source Awards, with Dre's memorable "the
South got something to say" line. And there it was: *Aquemini*, the fruition
of OutKast's promise.

OutKast knew *Aquemini* was special, destined to rank among the greatest
hip-hop records of all time. In "Skew it on the Bar-B," Big Boi refers to how
the group's debut fell just short of a perfect score in what was then hip-
hop's most influential publication: "I gotta hit *The Source*, I need my other
half mic, because that *Southernplayalisticadillacmuzik* was a classic, right."
While the free promotion certainly helped ingratiate OutKast to *The Source*,
Aquemini didn't need extra help to earn the rare, king-making "five-mic"
rating. Within a year, *Aquemini* had sold more than two million copies—
and OutKast entered the upper levels of pop stardom.

Any question as to whether fans would accept OutKast's expanding
sound palette and eccentric appearance could finally be put to rest. If they'd
lost any early fans that wanted to see the "Southern playas," they'd gained
millions more with *Aquemini*'s ambitious sounds. Dre was encouraged to
go even further with it.

"The first time Dre started dressing that way, we were doing the 'Skew it
on the Bar-B' video at [Atlanta venue] the Tabernacle," Sleepy Brown recalls. "I was backstage and he came out in that white feather suit. He had
the white wig on, the shades. I was standing there like, 'Wow, either the
crowd's going to laugh at you, or they gonna be with you.' Dre wasn't nervous, but I was. He jumped up on stage and the crowd went bananas. I was
so happy that they understood."

With OutKast's huge success, ties between the group and the rest of the
Dungeon Family became less central. *Aquemini* was about "him and I"—
named for Andre's and Big Boi's zodiac signs—not the entire crew. Organized Noize produced just four tracks on the record, plus three more by the
Organized-affiliated David "Mr. DJ" Sheats. "By *Aquemini*, it was running
on its own," says Ray Murray. "You don't have to keep fucking with the
wheels—you may have to run alongside it to keep up. Where we might have
been worried [about Dre's direction on *ATLiens*], that died down with
Aquemini. We understood a lot better what he was doing, it wasn't as scary
as it was at first. I could see clearly that it wasn't so much a change, it was
more of a growth."

As OutKast, Goodie Mob, and newer Dungeon Family acts began spending lots of time on the road, doing music separately, and establishing families of their own, relations naturally became more entwined with business—there just wasn't time for hanging around. "There's no way we can go back to everybody sleeping on the floor," Sleepy Brown says. "But of course you miss it, because that's when you're growing up and learning about each other. Everybody's just in tune with each other, all there for one purpose."

As Organized Noize stepped back from defining the sound of OutKast and Goodie Mob, the trio's focus turned to other projects. Through Interscope Records, the producers founded Organized Noize Records and used the advance from the deal to install a full-scale studio—also named the Dungeon—in the basement of Rico's Cascade-area home. Things got off to a rough start, however, with the label's first release, a comeback record from early '90s Atlanta bass artist Kilo. Interscope hoped the producers would discover another OutKast, and were disappointed to get a record by a past-his-prime niche artist. "Kilo wasn't Dungeon Family," says Big Rube. "Everybody knew who he was because he had records out when we were in high school. But Kilo wasn't going to blow up nationally, it was regional booty-shake. I think it put a damper on the Interscope deal. They probably were like, 'What is this shit?' I would attribute a lot of their noninvolvement afterward on the waste of time with Kilo."

A second Organized Noize release, *. . . A S.W.A.T. Healin' Ritual* by Dungeon regular Witchdoctor, delivered a more promising DF style. But Witchdoctor's lyrics and delivery were inconsistent; he was alternately sharp and awkward. The record quickly disappeared, as did a third act—Lil' Will, who dropped a single, "Looking for Nikki." With three failures and the label's most promising signing, rapper Cool Breeze, long overdue on delivering his record, Interscope seems to have written Organized Noize off as a label that could succeed.

"I think they started getting the idea that we weren't really about business," Big Rube says. "I think Organized Noize got the reputation for just being fuck-offs that had talent but weren't on top of their game as far as business. People like Puffy and Master P made us look worse, because Puffy was dropping a single every two weeks. Master P was putting out shit that didn't sound half as good. We didn't want to rush music out. But at the same time, you don't want to miss your windows of opportunity."

Finally, at the end of 1998—with *Aquemini* still high on the charts—Organized Noize dropped an introductory Cool Breeze single that was so dazzling, so undeniable, that Interscope couldn't help but get behind it.

"Watch for the Hook" delivered more of what had been working for Organized Noize—that is, OutKast and Goodie Mob. A blistering posse cut and one of Organized Noize's most unusual, addictive tracks, the song put the entire weight of the Dungeon Family behind Cool Breeze.

The frenetically paced single marched out the members of OutKast and Goodie Mob as well as Witchdoctor (the album version adds a ninth vocalist, Big Rube) to each deliver a short, rapid-fire verse full of passion, humor, and a competitive spirit that made everyone come stringer: "Never has every member in one crew been so diverse," Dre starts. "Tryin to outdo the last verse that I birthed, that is my curse/ . . . Somebody let me a hold a No. 2 pencil 'cause they testin'." By the time T-Mo rounds out the crew, he's breathlessly spitting raw fire. Then, finally, Cool Breeze appears—two-and-a-half minutes into the four-minute track—to remind us why we're all here: "The C stands for Cool Breeze who's known as the champ/Freddy Calhoun, the coolest cutta at camp/My ones and my twos got your whole town shook/You betta listen to your corner, and watch for the hook." Indeed, Cool Breeze's corner was so crowded, it was easy to forget the song was his; but he manages to establish authority and take his place among distinguished friends.

The backing track for "Watch for the Hook" matched its lyrical virtuosity. The music is built almost entirely from a 1971 recording by New Orleans–born gospel-soul singer Merry Clayton. It's her cover of Neil Young's 1970 classic, "Southern Man," a song that bemoaned the racist South (and so offended Southern rockers Lynyrd Skynyrd that they recorded a Neil Young diss, "Sweet Home Alabama"). Essentially, Clayton took Young's finger-pointing condemnation by an outsider and reimagined it as a more personal indictment from a Southern black woman. Then Organized Noize completely flipped it into an anthem of Southern pride, sampling just Clayton's call: "Southern man!" As Neil Young had discounted in his sweeping generalization, black males also counted as Southern Men (see Big Bill Broonzy's 1935 blues, "I'm a Southern Man"). The Dungeon Family reclaimed it.

Further, the sample on "Watch for the Hook" isn't drawn from the main riff on "Southern Man," but rather from its bridge, the transitional section that connects parts of the song together. Using a bridge for a hook—and repeating it over and over—creates an odd imbalance in "Watch for the Hook," and also generates an incredibly effective, and quite innovative, forward momentum. The recontextualization of lyrical and musical source material makes "Watch for the Hook" an awesome specimen of postmodern art, and a glimpse into everything that great hip-hop aspired to be. It caught the

Dungeon Family at the peak of their powers, creating an anthem for the kind of sophisticated, effusively funky Southern hip-hop the crew aimed to make.

"Watch for the Hook" spent three weeks at number one in February 1999 on the rap singles chart. But even with that incredible push, Cool Breeze's debut album, *East Point's Greatest Hit*, peaked at only thirty-eight and disappeared without even going gold (half-million copies). The album's failure was the last straw for Organized Noize Records; Interscope severed the deal before it had produced any lasting stars.

LAFACE'S GOLDEN ERA

While LaFace Records continued to hold dear to its contracts with OutKast and Goodie Mob, now well established as two of Atlanta's most important acts, hip-hop was never really L.A. Reid's game. His magic touch stretched mostly to R&B, where LaFace scored big with TLC and Toni Braxton, then broke the talented neo-soul singer Tony Rich. The former LaFace staff songwriter emerged with a 1995 debut, *Words*, which featured the hit "Nobody Knows" and earned a Grammy for best R&B album.

A year earlier, LaFace had put out the debut album by a fifteen-year-old R&B vocalist named Usher. Despite his age, the Tennessee native was no beginner. When he was just eleven, Usher and his group, New Beginning, had signed with the seminal south Florida bass-music label 4 Sight. Usher left the group, though, and moved to Atlanta with his mother/manager to pursue bigger opportunities. While auditioning locally to appear on the TV show *Star Search*, a LaFace rep heard him and brought Usher to sing for L.A. Reid. Reid signed the young singer and put his favorite deputy, Sean "Puff Daddy" Combs, in charge of Usher's debut. Despite production work from hit makers like Devante Swing (along with Swing's right-hand man, a young Tim "Timbaland" Mosely), Usher's self-titled debut was only a modest success.

When Usher returned, however, as an eighteen-year-old lady-killer on 1997's *My Way*, Jermaine Dupri was now steering the ship and providing a more hip-hop-influenced sound. Increased sex appeal and hipper tracks helped Usher shoot to the top of the charts, where he has remained ever since, with two more huge albums and a dozen or so hit singles.

LaFace scored more short-lived success with vocalists such as Donell Jones and, later, Pink (its first white signing), but as the '90s neared a close, the label's biggest success, TLC, had yet to follow up the tremendous success of 1994's *CrazySexyCool*. The torturous process of getting a new record out involved overcoming management problems (breaking away from

Pebbles), money woes (declaring bankruptcy), legal issues (Lisa Lopes' arson), family priorities (the birth of Chilli and Dallas Austin's son, Tron), outside projects (acting careers, solo projects, and new artist development), health concerns (T-Boz's sickle cell anemia), and inner-group battles (Austin's demands for higher fees and greater control).

Despite it all, when *FanMail* finally arrived in 1999, it spent a month at number one and eventually sold six million copies, while two singles—"No Scrubs" and "Unpretty"—also topped the chart. Still, the group continued to squabble publicly and seemed ready to disband at any moment. TLC stuck it out, though, until 2002, when Lisa Lopes' car ran off a mountain road in Honduras and killed her. T-Boz and Chilli finished and released *3-D*—the album the group had started recording with Lopes, which featured production from Organized Noize, Timbaland and Missy, and the Neptunes, as well as Austin. Finally, TLC called it quits as a working group.

The late '90s was a golden era for many at LaFace: Successes came one after another, but the company was still small enough to be responsive to artists and employees. In this environment, for instance, LaFace A&R guy Tony Mercedes (who'd brought Georgia bass music to the pop charts with "Dazzey Duks") was able to find a Southern bass novelty like B-Rock's "My Baby Daddy" and—without any support from LaFace's New York–based parent company Arista—score a top-ten pop hit. Mercedes claims that Arista head Clive Davis called to congratulate him for the song's success, and noted that no one in New York even knew the song was on the label.

"It was the best shit in the world," says KP (Kawan Prather), the leader of original Dungeon act P.A., who came aboard LaFace in 1996 as the A&R director overseeing OutKast and Goodie Mob. "All the artists knew each other, it was like a family. Everybody did every job—you didn't have a choice. You could go to L.A. [Reid] and play records. If it was dope, he'd tell you why. He'd educate you on making records. If he didn't like it, he'd tell you why and you'd go home and go, 'Man, fuck L.A., he don't know.' But you'd go change it. And he'd be like, 'OK, now that's right.' And he'd put it out and it would work."

In 1999, while still rolling high from the success of *Aquemini*, Reid agreed to give street hip-hop a try at LaFace. He gave KP his own imprint, Ghetto Vision, to pursue a different side of Atlanta hip-hop than OutKast and Goodie Mob represented. "At the Dungeon Family, we were more high brow. We were Southern, but trying to be a little more than country," KP says. "At the same time, there were people who were actually happy with being in the mindframe of the ghetto shit of Atlanta. And I was like, 'OK, that shit is hot, too.' So that was the point of Ghetto Vision."

For his first signing, KP found the Youngbloodz. The Atlanta duo was part of the Attic Crew, a posse of rappers and producers who were admirers and country cousins to the Dungeon Family. As the Dungeon had formed around Organized Noize in a dungeon-like basement, the Attic Crew centered around producers Kenyatta "Pretty Ken" Stokes, Harold "Mark Twain" Willis, and Kevin "Big Floaty" Burton, who were based in a College Park attic (or, at least, an upstairs apartment so hot it felt like an attic). Ties between the Dungeon and the Attic ran fairly deep: Cee-Lo was Big Floaty's cousin, and he actually lived briefly in the "attic" that Floaty and Pretty Ken shared; and P.A. had already featured the Youngbloodz's Sean Paul on its 1998 album, *Straight No Chase*.

The Youngbloodz's Sean Paul Joseph and Jeffrey "J-Bo" Grigsby met in school and got their names because (like OutKast) they were the junior members of their crew. The duo's Ghetto Vision debut, *Against Da Grain*, arrived a week apart from the debut of the Attic's other marquee group, Jim Crow, whose *Crow's Next* was released by Epic Records via local label Noontime. Both albums featured production work from P.A. and Organized Noize, as well as Emperor Searcy and Rob McDowell from Lil Jon's BME camp.

Jim Crow, a trio formed from guys hanging around the Attic, got early radio support for its single, "That Drama (Baby Mama)," but not enough to gain traction for the album. Meanwhile, the Youngbloodz hit big with "U-Way (How We Do It)," a club banger celebrating the Atlanta street salutation, "You way!" A second single, "85," also offered a slice of local color with the appearance of Big Boi and a lyrical shout-out to the interstate running through the SWATs. With the help of a tour supporting OutKast and Goodie Mob, Youngbloodz established themselves as a rising ATL talent.

Ghetto Vision had less success with its second signing, though the rapper—self-proclaimed "king of the South" T.I.—later emerged as a huge artist. KP met Clifford Harris Jr., the Bankhead street hustler and aspiring MC known as Tip, one night in early 1999 at Patchwerk Studios, a popular Westside facility owned by former Atlanta Falcons tackle Bob Whitfield. P.A.'s Reese was there laying down tracks, and a New York native named Jason Geter worked as the studio's night receptionist. Geter's mother was a Georgia native who'd moved north before his birth and recently returned to the South; Geter joined her in Atlanta to get involved in the music industry and was developing a management company called Grand Hustle. That night, Geter brought his artist Tip to the studio and introduced him around. After Tip blew Reese away with his raps, Reese called KP: "You need to come meet this dude in the studio."

"I thought he was incredible," KP says of the unknown lyricist. "He was saying intelligent shit, and it was all street shit."

Tip, in fact, had already recorded an unreleased full album with his group Pimp $quad Click. After one member got killed and another was sent away on an unrelated murder conviction, the group fell apart and Tip began pursuing his rap dreams as a soloist. His cousin was friendly with DJ Toomp—an Atlanta hip-hop veteran who'd recorded with Raheem the Dream, MC Shy-D, and 2 Live Crew in the '80s—and Toomp agreed to produce the teenager. While Toomp was recording tracks at Patchwerk for Jim Crow's album, he met Geter and introduced Geter to Tip.

After hearing Tip in the studio that night, KP knew he wanted to sign him. KP wooed the young rapper by inviting him on a trip to Los Angeles. "Watch for the Hook" was hot at the time, and the Dungeon Family was going out to perform the song at the Source Awards. As OutKast's and Goodie Mob's A&R guy, KP tagged along and brought Tip with him onto the Dungeon Family's backstage bus.

"There was a cipher going in the back of the bus," KP recalls. "Pretty much everybody in the Dungeon Family was there. And T.I. was sitting in the middle of the circle. When T.I. started rhyming, the whole crew just stopped and was like, 'Oh shit, who's this young guy?' He was like nineteen, just a skinny light-skinned dude. That week I signed him to Ghetto Vision."

BOMBS OVER THE DUNGEON FAMILY

For Goodie Mob, the glory of being involved with "Watch for the Hook" didn't last long. Though their first two albums had each gone gold, selling a half million records was barely enough to support an artist—much less four artists with families to feed. The group made ends meet by touring constantly, and had developed a reputation as a great live act. But the grind of the road was wearing them down, and they needed a big hit like their "little brothers" in OutKast had gotten.

"We had been through the ropes," Gipp says. "People were starting to get tired. We had been out on the road so long, it was hard to come back home and really know what was going on. You really couldn't vibe the same, the same streets and the same people. Everybody was changing."

By 1999, members of Goodie Mob could see lots of younger Southern acts selling lots more records—groups that didn't have the "conscious" tag they'd been saddled with. "We made good music, but we didn't make good singles," Cee-Lo says. "We felt like we had a bigger purpose. But with the surfacing of

Cash Money and No Limit and other guys from the South, they couldn't help have some our influence. We started this South shit."

Gipp was first to express his frustration with the group's direction. According to Cee-Lo, Gipp told him, "Damn, we doing this goodie-two-shoes shit. We on every panel, every college discussion, we at children's schools, we taking all the righteous steps, but we ain't reaping the same benefits."

Cee-Lo, who felt responsible for the group's socially conscious stance, decided to step back and let Gipp steer Goodie Mob in a direction that might pay off for them all. LaFace, anxious for the group to reach new popularity with their next album, welcomed more commercial material. "The label was rooting for that album," Cee-Lo says of the record that became *World Party*. "Everything was set up, the energy was dope."

But Cee-Lo had his reservations. He told his group mates, "We're going to disappoint a lot of people on this album."

As a concept, *World Party* sounded great: Just in time for the new millennium, the album would let loose and celebrate by reaching outward to people across the globe—a high-minded, internationalist party worthy of Goodie Mob's social outlook. But the album cover, which depicted the foursome dressed in traditional garb from Africa, India, Japan, and Arabia, had almost nothing to do with the music. After a Spanish introduction, the record doesn't acknowledge internationalism at all. It does, however, indulge in the more lightweight fare they hoped would lead to mainstream success. At times, the attempt is brazenly self-conscious—"Well, I don't know about you," Cee-Lo sings in the title track, "But we all tryin'a play dumb/But don't you worry 'bout me/I promise you we gonna get free/Just party." The goal, as the title to *World Party*'s single makes plain: "Get Rich to This."

World Party, in the end, was not a bad record. Tracks like the majestic "Chain Swang" (with New York–based producer Deric "D-Dot" Angelettie), the T-Mo-produced arabesque dance track "The Dip," and "Rebuilding," the lone song expressing a social conscience (produced by D-Dot and his protégé, an up-and-comer named Kanye West), are all worth hearing. Even the somewhat awkward collaboration with TLC on the Dallas Austin–produced "What It Ain't (Ghetto Enuf)" had some terrific moments. But the album ultimately failed, not because Goodie Mob had no right to let loose, but because it felt forced. The new approach, it turned out, wasn't as freewheeling as the group wanted, and was too lightweight for fans' tastes.

World Party sold about the same number as the group's previous records, and had even less of an impact on the charts. It took a devastating toll on the group's morale, however. Blame began to fly and, as always, Cee-Lo was most vocal. "I was morally disappointed in *World Party*, because I believe I have a responsibility with my music," Cee-Lo says. "I plead temporary insanity, because of what we went through, being the ones who helped kick down the door and [have] not reaped the same benefits as the rest of Southern music and culture. It was as if we were ahead of our time and turned our space ship around to come back to earth to simply fit in. The market was congested with bling-bling, so people were waiting on Goodie Mob to be their last ray of hope. 'If anybody's going to keep it real, I know Goodie Mob will.' And we didn't, we failed the people."

For lack of a better alternative, Goodie Mob hit the road, touring internationally—particularly in Japan, one of their strongest markets—to promote the album and generate income. Cee-Lo, however, opted out—inviting the others to go without him. "I was ready for the album to be over with," Cee-Lo says. "I didn't believe in it, so I wasn't going to encourage anybody to fuck with it."

In addition to his musical reasons, Cee-Lo wanted to stay home with his pregnant wife. And, unlike the others, he no longer had a financial need to tour. Through his friendship with Lauryn Hill—whom he'd met when Goodie Mob toured with the Fugees—Cee-Lo was brought along to appear with Hill on "Do You Like the Way," from Santana's 1999 album, *Supernatural*. By early 2000, *Supernatural* was on its way to becoming one of the biggest-selling records of all time—more than twenty million copies worldwide—and even Cee-Lo's very minor role generated substantial royalties.

It also boosted his confidence as a performer who could stand apart from Goodie Mob. According to Gipp, "After he came back from doing the Santana thing, I knew there was no turning back—because of the acceptance that he got from being part of such a great album."

As Gipp, T-Mo, and Khujo headed off for Japan without Cee-Lo, Goodie Mob's future was in serious doubt.

As Goodie Mob splintered, OutKast continued to rise. Between *Aquemini* and the follow-up, *Stankonia*, OutKast evolved into a virtual industry. Dre and Big secured a deal with Elektra Records for their newly founded Aquemini Records, which released Slimm Calhoun's *The Skinny* in late 2000. Slimm was part of the Calhoun crew named for a street in East Point—a Dungeon offshoot anchored by Freddie Calhoun, aka Cool Breeze. *The Skinny* likely suffered from being released just a week apart from *Stankonia*, with Dre and Big unable to promote their protégé as strongly as they might have during an OutKast down time. But Slim did score a number-one rap hit with "It's OK," and OutKast's and Mr. DJ's colorful production helped the record garner some good reviews.

The Elektra deal helped the group buy its own recording studio, which they named Stankonia. The studio was, in fact, already familiar—it was one of the first they'd ever been in: Bobby Brown's Bosstown Studios.

"We had a concert in Tennessee and Bobby Brown came to the show," Big Boi relates. "He was drunk as hell and we were just kicking it. He was telling us the studio was for sale. And he was like, 'Really, y'all can have the studio. I'd rather y'all have it than someone else get it.' We were thinking he gave it to us! So we told our manager and it came up that it *was* for sale—but the IRS had it for sale. So we bought it from them and revamped it. There's a lot of good vibes in there—it brought back a lot of memories from when we were seventeen, first writing songs like 'Claimin' True' and 'Crumblin' Erb.' We wrote them right there in that building."

Along with their new studio and label, Big and Dre got more serious about being producers. They'd already made tracks for *ATLiens* and *Aquemini*—the latter under the name Earthtone—but beginning with *Stankonia* and Aquemini Records, they invited Mr. DJ to join into a three-man production company, Earthtone III. Dre also worked to expand his musical knowledge and abilities—he took up learning to play the guitar. About the only thing not moving forward for the members of OutKast was Dre's relationship with Erykah Badu; sometime in 1999, they separated and agreed to share custody of Seven.

Having their own studio—as well as smaller setups at home, and another private facility for use at Rico's Dungeon—provided the time and space for greater experimentation. "For *Stankonia*, me and Big were partying a lot and just trying new stuff," Mr. DJ says. "At that point, they'd been accepted and had a fan base, they just wanted to do something different. But I don't think they ever had to think about it—everything they do is natural."

But if Dre and Big were on the same page creatively, they found inspiration in very different ways. Dre, who usually worked alone on demos, claimed he was "dating his guitar." Meanwhile, Big and Mr. DJ often worked together at Big's house south of Atlanta in Fayetteville. They'd break up the night with a trip to the strip club—until Big figured out a way to streamline the process: He installed a stripper's pole in his playroom—dubbed his Boom Boom Room—and had the entertainment come to him.

It's unlikely, however, that even the most acrobatic of erotic dancers could have inspired *Stankonia*'s jaw-dropping first single. Months before the record actually arrived, the track—called "B.O.B.," or "Bombs Over Baghdad"—began making the rounds on hip-hop stations, where it stood out as nothing else on the playlists had.

It began with a placid keyboard pattern and a countdown—"1, 2, 1, 2, 3, yeah!"—that quickly exploded with a booming, overdriven bass beat and the frantic rush of Dre's dense verse: "Inslumnational underground, thunder pounds when I stomp the ground (Whoo!)/Like a million elephants, silverback orangutan, you can't stop the train/Who want some don't come unprepared/I'll be there, but when I leave there, better be a household name. . . . " The pounding beat, slap-funk bass, hand claps, and rapid-fire rhymes ramped into a drum 'n' bass fill, then a wah-wah guitar–punctuated singsong hook—"Don't pull the thang out unless you plan to bang (bombs over Baghdad)/Don't even bang unless you plan to hit something (bombs over Baghdad)." Then came Big Boi's frenetic tag-team flow—"Uno, dos, tres, it's on/Did you ever think a pimp rock a microphone/Like that there boy and we still stay street/Big things happen every time we meet/Like a track team, crack fiend, dying to geek/OutKast bumpin' up and down the street/Slant back Cadillac 'bout five niggas deep/Seventy-five MCs freestylin' to the beat . . . "—set to kettle organ, popcorn synth, and that relentless, supercharged beat. Into the chorus again, then a screaming guitar solo sliced through furious turntable scratching, a breakdown of fuzz-guitar riffing that built into the exultation of a gospel chorus: "power, music, electric revival." And the beat churned on, unbowed, until the fade.

"B.O.B." was an absolute original that combined rap, metal, drum 'n' bass, electro-funk, gospel, bass music, and pop into a remarkably exciting twenty-first-century musical vision. Ultimately the track sounded way too alien to fit into hip-hop, rock, or pop radio formats. It disappeared from radio soon after it arrived, but not before OutKast had proven it had the biggest balls in the biz by even attempting to drop a single like that.

"We knew it was going to be the first single," Andre says. "We just wanted to be in the business of blowing people's minds. The title was symbolism—from when [in the late '90s], the U.S. was bombing Baghdad, but we weren't really hitting anything, just little warning missiles on the outskirts to get them to change their mind about something. Well, we were trying to say, 'We're not playing around at all. We're gonna hit you straight-forward.' Doing songs like that is like saying, 'Fuck it, let's put our neck on the line.' The record company was like, 'I don't know if radio's going to play it.' They actually told us to take the guitar out. But we knew that even if they didn't play it, it would be an eye-opener. They would be like, 'OK, I gotta see what the fuck they're trying to do with this album.'"

With "B.O.B.," Big Boi and Dre (who, postmillennium, started calling himself Andre 3000) had, to borrow their own description, pulled their thang out, slang it in the face of the hip-hop nation, and banged out something completely new, completely awesome. The message had been delivered: *Stankonia* was on its way and would not comply with anyone's notion of what Southern hip-hop—and hip-hop in general—should, could, or would sound like.

"Hip-hop is at its most commercial point," Andre said at the time. "And most music, when it gets to its most commercial point, it's not as cool no more. So I feel like hip-hop has got to change some kind of way. We just knew we had to do something."

After a delay to tweak the album in an attempt to combat piracy, *Stankonia* finally arrived on Halloween 2000. With it came a second single—no less unusual than "B.O.B.," but far more easily digestible. In some ways, "Ms. Jackson" was the inverse of its predecessor: melodious and laid-back, where "B.O.B." had been discordant and frenetic. Built around a strummed chord progression and a pleading soul melody reminiscent of the Brothers Johnson's 1977 hit, "Strawberry Letter 23," "Ms. Jackson" showcased Andre as a guitar-playing songwriter.

Like the music, the lyrics diverged from hip-hop orthodoxy. Addressed to "all the baby's mama's mamas"—and, specifically, to Erykah Badu's mother—"Ms. Jackson" expressed regret over the failure of a relationship, and pledged to uphold the responsibilities of fatherhood. "I'm sorry Ms. Jackson, I am for real/Never meant to make your daughter cry, I apologize a trillion times," Dre sings in the chorus. Big Boi's verse took a more indignant perspective on baby mama drama: "Let her know her grandchild is a baby and not a paycheck/Private school, daycare, shit, medical bills, I pay that/ . . . She never got a chance to hear my side of the story, we was divided/She had fish fries and cookouts for my child's birthday, I ain't invited. . . . " Despite their emotional inconsistencies, the words suggested the possibility of broader, more mature subject matter in hip-hop. And audiences responded favorably by sending "Ms. Jackson" to the top of pop, R&B/hip-hop, and rap charts in early 2001.

Stankonia was full of moments that put it at odds with everything in hip-hop at the time. "I'll Call Before I Come" offered a grown-up perspective on lovemaking and, like "Ms. Jackson," found Andre singing far more than rapping. And in "Red Velvet," Big Boi wondered why rappers were so anxious to brag about their heavy bankroll, but not "how you bought your kids some tennis shoes . . . that your mama, she got her house too . . . that your sister wouldn't have finished college without you."

"Gasoline Dreams," meanwhile, raged against bling-bling fantasy to present a sober adult vision of a world turned upside-down: "I hear that Mother Nature's now on birth control/The coldest pimp be lookin' for somebody to hold," Dre rapped over a juiced-up electric guitar lead. "The highway up to heaven got a crook on the toll/Youth full of fire ain't got nowhere to go." In "Humble Mumble" Big offered motivation in the face of growing up and having to "re-route my dreams." He rapped: "Life is like a great big roller coaster, everything in life don't always happen like it's supposed to/ . . . Fuck wishing, you're missing the ambition on your mission," and ended with a quote from the Bible: "No weapon formed against me prospers, 54:17 from Isaiah." Dre pointed toward a new approach to progress in black America: "The game changes every day, so obsolete is the fist and marches/Speeches only reaches those who already know about it, this is how we go about it. . . . " Then Erykah Badu (post-breakup, still friends) appeared with a soaring metaphysical gospel verse that celebrated the circle of life.

Like "B.O.B." and "Speedballin'" (an ambitious Fela-meets-Photek track that appeared on 2001's *Lara Croft: Tomb Raider* soundtrack), the accelerated tempo and intricate beats in "Humble Mumble" revealed an influence of electronica—particularly British drum 'n' bass. "Hip-hop beats were getting redundant," Dre admits. "Just listening to U.K. music, I was like, 'Man, they're killing us on the beats.' So I was like, 'We need to find a way to make it harder, but American style.'"

Not all of *Stankonia* was revolutionary. It's third single, "So Fresh, So Clean," was a smooth conventional track produced by Organized Noize and featuring Sleepy Brown on the hook. "Spaghetti Junction," an Organized-produced *ATLiens* outtake, "Xplosion," and "We Luv Deez Hoez" also fit comfortably within hip-hop's confines. And while "Gangsta Shit" used "gangsta" in a more figurative sense—Dre boasted about "bitches suckin' on my nouns and I'm eatin' their verbs"—the track brought Dungeon rappers together on an otherwise straightforward posse cut.

But *Stankonia*'s final stretch—"Toilet Tisha," a Prince-like track about a botched abortion, as well as "Slum Beautiful" and "Stankonia (Stanklove)," two psychedelic soul odes to ghetto amour—barely contain rapping at all. Combined with all the other experimentation, it left a question: The album was brilliant and forward-looking, musically sophisticated, and lyrically sharp, but was it still hip-hop? OutKast had moved so far away from its starting point, the group now seemed headed toward something new entirely, something post–hip-hop?

Stankonia certainly put the group far outside the main thrust of Southern hip-hop. While not totally without local color—"Spaghetti Junction" was named after an intertwining of Atlanta highways, "Red Velvet" referred to a favorite Southern dessert—mostly OutKast had transcended regional boundaries and created a genre all its own.

If there were some measure of cultural importance that combined sales figures, industry respect, and critical adoration, *Stankonia* would have made OutKast the biggest group in the world. But even as the album went on to sell five million copies, earn two rap Grammies (for "Ms. Jackson" and best album), and enjoy a sweep of critics' polls, Andre was itching to get out. Feeling uninspired and limited by hip-hop, he began to see a time when he would outgrow the music. He even talked of enrolling in Juilliard to study music formally.

"I don't really see me rapping forever," he said at age twenty-five. "Hip-hop is really about the streets and the youth. Once you get older, don't nobody really want to hear that."

JD WELCOMES YOU TO ATLANTA

Across town, another leader in Atlanta's urban-music ascent had no misgivings about getting older. By 1998, Jermaine Dupri had been going strong for ten years. That September, Dupri rented out part of the Woodruff Arts Center in Midtown for his twenty-sixth birthday party. Mariah Carey and part-time Atlantan Elton John attended, wearing what the invitation requested would be "jiggy attire only." The following year, Dupri outdid himself with a weekend-long, million-dollar, multi-venue twenty-seventh-birthday bash, which he called "Can I Live."

In addition to personal ego gratification, Dupri noted that these events were designed to show off Atlanta's successes to the world. "People already say I'm the flashiest guy in Atlanta," he told the *Atlanta Journal-Constitution* about the "Can I Live" events. "They see the cars I drive, the jewels I rock, and all that. People know me. This weekend's about people knowing and respecting my city. I want more people to come to Atlanta and see how everybody is living here, from the celebrities in music, to the superstars we have in basketball and football, to the hard-working 9-to-5ers with the big houses and Benzes in southwest Atlanta. I'm trying to be the city's mascot."

If Atlanta had become the new Motown, as often claimed, then Dupri was happy to assume the role of a young Berry Gordy. Inspired by the sign Gordy had once erected in Detroit reading, "Welcome to Motor City,

Home of Hitsville U.S.A.," Dupri has for many years rented a prominent billboard on the northbound side of the I-75/I-85 connector heading from the airport to downtown, that says, "Atlanta: Home of So So Def Recordings."

Certainly, Dupri had earned a right to assert himself as one of the city's new cultural leaders. Following the success of his breakthrough act Kris Kross, Columbia Records offered Dupri a deal that turned his So So Def production company into his own imprint. So So Def's first release, Xscape's 1993 platinum debut, *Hummin' Comin' at Cha*, proved Columbia had made a good bet with Dupri, and So So Def was made a full-fledged label. Dupri set up offices in Buckhead and hired a full staff—promotions, publicity, A&R—to build his company.

So So Def's second release was *Funkdafied*, the 1994 debut by twenty-year-old female rapper Da Brat. While on tour in 1992, Kris Kross had met Chicago-native Shawntae Harris, aka Da Brat, after a show. She impressed them with her raps, and they gave her Dupri's number. Given the relative difficulty female MCs had scoring hits, JD wasn't convinced it was something he wanted to pursue. But, on the phone, he invited Brat to come see him if she ever got down to Atlanta.

Soon after, Dupri got another call. It was Da Brat again, waiting to be picked up at the airport. "She called me and said, 'Come get me,'" JD recalls. "Brat was talking like she knew me. She's like, 'I'm in Atlanta. I came to see you.' So I came and got her. Her whole mentality was really pushy, and that's what made me sign her. She had really put herself out to be part of my crew."

Funkdafied was neither particularly unique nor anything that would be considered Southern. Rather, its primary influence was the Dr. Dre/Snoop Dogg sound dominating hip-hop at the time. *Funkdafied*, however, contained a bunch of memorable, catchy songs—notably the title track, with its Isley Brothers–sung chorus—and showcased Da Brat's tough-girl, razor-sharp rapping. With "Funkdafied" spending months atop the rap singles chart and two other tracks hitting the top ten, the album hit number one and went platinum—a first by a female rapper.

The Atlanta transplant continued her winning streak with 1996's *Anuthatantrum* and the somewhat more mature vibe of 2000's *Unrestricted*. Dupri kept the hits coming as well. In addition to Da Brat and Xscape, So So Def scored with local R&B quartet Jagged Edge, which debuted in 1997, and with Dupri's own star-studded solo album, 1998's *Life in 1492*. And, in Dupri's first embrace of an overtly Southern sound, the label released three volumes of the booty-shake compilation, *So So Def Bass Allstars*—a series compiled by So So Def A&R man Jonathan "Lil Jon" Smith. Before So So

Def ended its long and prosperous association with Sony (Columbia's parent company), Dupri delivered one more big star—and one more teenage rapper: Lil' Bow Wow.

Dupri also found huge success as a songwriter and producer, working with a list of artists that extended far beyond his label roster—Lil' Kim, Mase, Destiny's Child, Monica, Jay-Z, Master P, DMX, Alicia Keyes, and many others. He worked particularly closely with two artists that have proved among the most enduringly popular in R&B: Mariah Carey and Usher. Dupri's work with Carey goes back to her 1996 number one, "Always Be My Baby," through her 2005 comeback hits "It's Like That," "Shake It Off," and "We Belong Together." And Dupri helped make Usher a star with his 1997 album, *My Way*, and has remained involved as the singer jumped to superstardom in 2004, with the JD cowritten and coproduced number-one hits "Burn" and "Confessions Pt. 2."

In 1998, Dupri became the first producer with three different records in the number-one spot on three different charts—pop, rap, and R&B. For his songwriting, Dupri has netted a reported seventeen million dollars in publishing deals, plus millions more on the production and songwriting fees he charges directly to artists. In 1999, he launched So So Def's film division and a short-lived sports agency. He's also tried his hand at clothing and alcohol companies, TV production, and in 2005, he launched his first Café Dupri restaurant in Buckhead.

JD's effort to represent Atlanta through music reached its pinnacle in late 2001, when his second solo album, *Instructions*, yielded a track called "Welcome to Atlanta." An instant smash in JD's hometown, the track earned enough spins nationally to reach number three on the rap chart.

"Every city has a theme song," Dupri says. "Frank Sinatra has 'New York, New York,' L.A.'s got 'I Love L.A.' There's 'South Bronx Style' by KRS One, 'Compton' by Eazy E. How can you be a popular city like Atlanta and not have a theme record? I personally wrote that song for Atlantans. They should play that song at Braves games, Falcons games, Hawks games, because it's welcoming people to our city."

As a Southern hip-hop anthem, "Welcome to Atlanta" rides on a memorable hook and party lyrics. But if Dupri wanted an ATL equivalent to "New York, New York," he fell short. It's unlikely that mainstream institutions like professional sports teams would embrace JD's chorus: "Welcome to Atlanta where the playas play, and we ride on them things like every day/Big beats, hit streets, see gangstas roamin', and parties don't stop till eight in the mornin'." And Dupri's verse—which outlines his weekly club-hopping itinerary—is way too specific and easily dated to endure as a theme song.

At the same time, the specificity of "Welcome to Atlanta" is part of what made it so awesome. He shouts out everything from the old days when MC Shy-D ruled ATL rap to latter-day radio personality Frank Ski, to hotspots of the moment such as the strip club Strokers, and hangouts like 112, Kaya, and the Velvet Room. Most of the clubs he names are now gone, but hearing the song in 2001 and 2002 was like getting a tour from the hip-hop mayor himself.

Even more fun was the "Welcome to Atlanta (Remix)," where Dupri came with a new and improved verse: "Remix it had to go down, I got somethin' else to tell you 'bout the new Motown/Where people don't visit, they move out here, and ain't no tellin who you might see up in Lenox Square/I don't know about you but I miss the Freaknik, 'cause that's when my city use to be real sick/People from other cities use to drive from miles, just to come to get a taste of this ATL style." While still name-dropping clubs, he's revised his social schedule a bit: "Strokers, I don't go no more, 'cause they don't know how to treat you when you come through the door."

It was just the kind of immediate and detailed communication that made hip-hop so vital—if not quite the "black CNN" than at least a player's *Entertainment Tonight*. "Remix" went further by inviting other cities to the party: P. Diddy jumps in to represent New York, then Murphy Lee for St. Louis, then Snoop Dogg for Long Beach. And it inspired others to create their own bootleg remixes, including Pitbull's "Welcome to Miami." Here was an example of the whole country buying into Atlanta hip-hop's infectious spirit—and the South setting the tone for an intercity rap dialogue.

LUDACRIS DISTURBS THE PEACE

"Welcome to Atlanta" solidified Jermaine Dupri's position as the guy repping his city the hardest circa 2001, but it also helped elevate another local who was establishing himself as the city's most popular rapper. Ludacris, who appears on both versions of the song, emerged nationally in 2000 as the leader of Atlanta hip-hop's new generation. While "Welcome" helped define Ludacris as the city's go-to rapper, it was just one of the seemingly endless string of singles and guest appearances that made the College Park rapper ubiquitous starting in 2000 and barely diminishing over the handful of years after that. By 2003, Ludacris was the biggest solo rapper to have emerged from the South.

Born Chris Bridges in Champagne, Illinois, where his parents were going to school, he was performing for his folks' college friends from the time he started walking. He started rapping at age nine and, at twelve, he moved to Atlanta to live with his father. "I knew Atlanta was *the* place," Ludacris says. "I was like, man, I need to move to Atlanta because that seems like the place to get put on."

With his first group, the Loudmouth Hooligans, a teenage Bridges started making the rounds at talent competitions and showcases. In school at College Park's Banneker High, Chris was known as that kid who was always rapping in the hallways, the lunch hall, the playground. He starting calling his crew Disturbing Tha Peace.

Bridges graduated in 1995 and enrolled in Georgia State to study music. When he heard Atlanta was about to get its first all-hip-hop radio station, WHTA Hot 97.5, he quickly signed on as an intern and started helping out with the station's morning show—while taking classes during the day and working at night at Pizza Hut.

But it was never Chris' ambition to work in radio. He just figured it was the quickest route to getting himself *on* the radio, as a rapper. The station let Bridges—who became known as Chris Luva Luva—record promos that featured his raps; he made one for every DJ at the station. Soon he was one of the most recognized voices at Hot 97.5. For Freaknik, the black-college spring break, Chris recorded the extended promo "Two Miles an Hour," his tribute to the standstill traffic the event brought to Atlanta each year (later reworked on his *Red Light District* album).

By 1998, Chris Luva Luva was cohosting WHTA's night show, "Future Flavors," and learning about voice control, enunciation, and music industry politics. And his rap career was building steam. As he'd intended, the radio opened him to all sorts of opportunities. There he met Chaka Zulu, a station coworker who became his manager and business partner. He also met many of the artists—Scarface to Organized Noize to Lil Jon—he'd later work with as a rapper. As early as 1996, Timbaland visited the station, heard Chris rapping on promos, and invited Chris to appear on his guest-filled solo album, 1998's *Tim's Bio*. When the song "Fat Rabbit" began raising eyebrows for its outrageously lewd content, people started asking about Ludichris, the track's guest rapper. After he settled on the spelling Ludacris, Jermaine Dupri approached him to rap on the theme for the *John Madden 2000* PlayStation football game.

Slowly, Ludacris was getting his name out as a rapper, but the transition from radio DJ was proving difficult. "People knew me as this personality on the radio, so it took a long time for people in Atlanta to take me seriously," Ludacris says. "They were like, 'Oh, that's Chris Luva Luva.' They didn't take me serious until a good six months to a year, to where I was on BET, doing interviews, then they had to take me seriously. Then they could see how serious I was."

Meanwhile, Chris' Disturbing Tha Peace crew was growing. Early on, Chris shared an apartment with DTP members I-20 (Bobby Sandimanie, an Atlantan of Liberian parentage) and Lil' Fate (Arbie Wilson). And in 1999, he met the Chicago rapper Shawnna when she came through Hot 97.5 on a promotional stop. Rashawnna Guy, the daughter of blues legend Buddy Guy, had just released an album as part of the duo Infamous Syndicate. When her group fell apart, Shawnna fell in with DTP.

While Chris had been trying to score a major-label record deal, Lil' Fate was taking a cue from Southern independents like Master P and putting out his own CD. Seeing how lucrative the independent route could be, Ludacris decided to put out his own record as well. He worked mainly with DTP's in-house producer Shondrae, and also enlisted the help of Jermaine Dupri and Pastor Troy (who both appear on "Get Off Me"), as well as Organized Noize ("Game Got Switched"). After securing a deal with Southern Music, Atlanta's primary distributor of independent hip-hop, Ludacris dropped his debut album, *Incognegro*, in May of 2000.

Even without a large label behind it, *Incognegro* quickly became a regional hit, and its single, "What's Your Fantasy," got airplay—not just on Hot 97.5, but all over the South. The song perfectly established the basic ingredients Ludacris would use throughout his career: dirty jokes, brash delivery, and rapid-fire, well-enunciated rhymes. After teaming with Shawnna on the chorus, 'Cris bursts into a litany of situations he'd like to explore with his girl: "I wanna get you in the Georgia Dome on the 50-yard line, while the Dirty Birds kick for t'ree/And if you like [it] in the club we can do it in the DJ booth or in the back of the V.I.P."

While "Fantasy" contained references to 2 Live Crew and TLC, there wasn't much overtly Southern about Ludacris' music—his hyper-animated, loudmouth delivery recalled, if anything, the spastic flows of Busta Rhymes. But like JD, regional solidarity came through in lyrics stocked with local color. More subtly, Ludacris seemed to hark back to an older Southern-rooted tradition of declarative, eloquently delivered, nasty rhymes: the toasting of Dolemite and his generation of black comedians (Richard Pryor, Redd Foxx).

It's likely Ludacris' ability to appeal regionally while not sounding overly regional helped major labels take note. But more than anything, record execs noticed how *Incognegro* was outselling many national releases in the South—up to thirty-thousand copies within the first few months. By summer's end, Ludacris was the focus of a major bidding war. And because he'd already proven himself independently, he had the bargaining power to command an attractive arrangement for himself.

Just about every label with a presence in hip-hop wanted to sign Ludacris, but one seemed uniquely qualified: Def Jam South. After more than fifteen years as a force in New York hip-hop, Def Jam recognized the opportunities it was missing down South. So in February of 2000, Island Def Jam Group invested about one million dollars to set up Def Jam South in downtown Atlanta, to compete with the So So Defs and Rap-A-Lots thriving in the region. To head the operation, Def Jam tapped one of Southern hip-hop's most legendary figures: Brad Jordan, aka the Geto Boys' Scarface.

Though Scarface might have seemed a surprising choice, choosing him helped establish Def Jam's Southern credibility. Scarface was, after all, the South's first great lyricist, and remained a viable rap star—in fact, Def Jam also signed him as an artist, and he delivered one of his best solo records with 2002's *The Fix*. Scarface soon proved himself a capable A&R man when, within months of opening, Def Jam South had signed Ludacris.

Scarface first met 'Cris back in '96, when the Houston kingpin brought his Face Mob side group to Hot 97.5. Over the years, they'd continue crossing paths. "We used to see each other all the time, going in and out of spots," Scarface told *Vibe*. "When I heard that Ludy's shit was blowing up, I was like, that boy's playing his own shit [on the radio], that's why it's blowing up. But a couple of weeks later, I found out that the station that this cat's working at ain't even the station that's playing the fuckin' record. . . . I was like, Goddamn, Ludy, we've been seeing each other all this time, and you had a hit motherfucking record and you didn't tell me."

Def Jam South moved quickly and, just five months after *Incognegro*'s release, Ludacris made his major-label debut with *Back for the First Time*. It was mostly the same record as *Incognegro*, with three additional key tracks: the previously released Timbaland track, slightly retitled "Phat Rabbit"; "Stick 'Em Up," featuring Southern rap heroes UGK; and the Neptunes-produced "Southern Hospitality," which followed "What's Your Fantasy" to become the record's second top-ten R&B/hip-hop single.

Though Luda's in-your-face delivery could be grating and/or exhausting, *Back for the First Time* soared to immediate success on the basis of its terrific singles; it sold a quarter-million records in the first two weeks and eventually passed the three million mark. "Southern Hospitality" was particularly appealing, with its scorching minimalist beat and lyrics that introduced a reckless dance-floor move described as "throw dem 'bows"—a slice of Southern club culture somewhere in the neighborhood of Memphis' gangsta walk, 2 Live's "Throw the D," and the Bankhead Bounce.

Over the next two years, Ludacris secured his place as one of hip-hop's biggest stars by appearing everywhere—guesting on records by regional favorites (Eightball, Three 6 Mafia), East Coast (Fat Joe) and West (Nate Dogg); hitting the pop charts with tracks from soundtracks ("Area Codes") and compilations ("Fatty Girl"); appearing on hits by Missy Elliott ("One Minute Man"), Mariah Carey ("Loverboy"), and Dupri's "Welcome to Atlanta." And, just over a year after *Back for the First Time*, he returned with a second album, *Word of Mouf*.

Mouf offered a lot more of the same—potty-mouthed humor, an even more impressive lineup of the top (mostly Southern) producers, and an even larger number of irresistible singles: Timbaland's hooky "Rollout (My Business)"; the Medicine Men's crunked up "Move Bitch" (featuring Mystikal); Organized Noize's jiggy anthem, "Saturday (Oooh! Oooh!)" (which, along with OutKast's "So Fresh, So Clean," helped break the production trio's dry spell); and the previously released "Area Codes," featuring Jazze Pha's pimping chorus and Nate Dogg's smooth vocals.

Through it all, Ludacris surely set a record for the number of times a rapper used the word "ho." The pun-filled skit "Howhere," for example, suggests a true obsessive with the word: "Where you at?/Shit, over here at the Texa-hoe filling up ... /You still got that girl Stacy's number from Vallehoe? ... You can't check your Hoe-ledex or something? / ... Oh hey, man, congratulations ... didn't your sister graduate today? Oh yeah ... valedicwhorian and all." The track leads into "Area Codes," with its chorus—"I got hoes, in different area codes"—and more puns in the verses.

Few would argue that the context in which Ludacris uses words like *hoes*—with humor and creative wordplay, in a tradition descended from the profane toasts of generations past—is as ugly and offensive as when *ho* gets deployed in misogynistic fury by some gangsta rappers. "People just really need to understand where I'm coming from," Ludacris says. "If they really listened to the first song I had out called 'Ho' [from *Back for the First Time*], they would understand I wasn't trying to degrade women. I was desexualizing the word. I call myself a ho in the damn song. So if it can go for men and women, then what is anyone upset about? These are just words."

Still, with *Word of Mouf* heading toward triple platinum, Ludacris' combination of massive popularity and use of derogatory language made him an open target in the culture wars. So in August of 2002, Bill O'Reilly, the conservative host of Fox News Channel's *The O'Reilly Factor*, took aim at Pepsi, the company that had recently signed Ludacris to appear in an ad campaign. On his show, O'Reilly slammed Pepsi for employing a "thug rapper": "I'm calling for all responsible Americans to fight back and punish Pepsi for using a man who degrades women, who encourages substance abuse, and does all the things that hurt particularly the poor in our society," O'Reilly said. "*I'm calling for all Americans to say, Hey, Pepsi, I'm not drinking your stuff.* You want to hang around with Ludacris, you do that; I'm not hanging around with you."

Pepsi, in an inept attempt at damage control, quickly capitulated to O'Reilly's threatened boycott and dropped Ludacris as a pitchman. It then signed on with Ozzy Osbourne—hardly a paragon of family values—and the racial double standard enraged the black community. Russell Simmons and his Hip-Hop Summit Action Network threatened a boycott of their own: Reinstate Ludacris and donate five million dollars to the philanthropic Ludacris Foundation, or else face lots of bad publicity among hip-hop fans. Pepsi, recognizing a no-win situation, negotiated with Simmons to call off the boycott: They wouldn't rehire Ludacris, but would donate several million dollars to the Ludacris Foundation, a fund used to generate and sponsor community and educational programs.

While Pepsi was forced to swallow yet another expensive PR blunder, Ludacris was barely stung at all by bad publicity—in fact, the ordeal merely proved he'd reached a level of infiltration into the popular culture that even wealthy, middle-aged white conservatives were taking note. 'Cris grabbed the opportunity to grow his empire and released a Disturbing Tha Peace posse album, *Golden Grain*—a springboard to launch Shawnna, Lil' Fate, I–20, and Tity Boi into solo careers. While posse records are always a tough sell, padding the album with tracks from *Word of Mouf* ("Growing Pains," "Move Bitch") didn't help, and high-profile guests (Too Short, Twista, Scarface) only further crowded the record.

DTP's affiliated management company, Chaka Zulu's Ebony Son, also expanded by signing St. Louis production team Trak Starz. They, in turn, introduced their artist, Chingy—a soundalike of fellow St. Louisian, superstar rapper Nelly—who became the first outsider to sign with Ludacris' new Disturbing Tha Peace Records. By the summer of 2003, Chingy's "Right Thurr" topped the rap singles chart.

Ludacris branched out in one more direction: acting. Ludacris shot a small role in the 2003 action film, *2 Fast 2 Furious*. It wasn't until 2005, when he appeared in two concurrent films—holding his own next to Matt Dillon, Don Cheadle, and other acclaimed actors in the racially charged *Crash*; and providing the antagonist foil to Terrence Howard's star-making turn in the Memphis hip-hop drama *Hustle & Flow*—that Chris Bridges' acting talents fully shone.

Between DTP projects and acting, Ludacris dropped his fourth album in three years—2003's *Chicken-N-Beer*—and, for the first time, topped the pop album charts. The Kanye West–produced "Stand Up"—with its dance-floor invitation, "When I move, you move, just like that"—also earned Luda his first number-one single. Besides a few barbs directed at Bill O'Reilly, it offered more of what Ludacris had been dishing out from the start. Its title suggested something vaguely Southern, but only in the least nutritious sense—just chicken and beer, that is, not *Soul Food*.

But there was a sense that, ever so slightly, Ludacris was evolving. By *Chicken-N-Beer*, he was so big that his rapping at times seemed to challenge rap's dominant personality, Eminem, at his own game of clever insult and fast-flying delivery (see "Hip Hop Quotables"). The opener, "Southern Fried Intro," melds gospel and rock elements with breakneck rapping, but that new sonic territory doesn't really pan out. But both "Hard Times" and "Diamond in the Back"—which draw on the credibility of guest Memphians, Eightball & MJG on the first, and producers DJ Paul and Juicy J on the second—pause from the boasting and sexing to reflect on the struggle out of the 'hood. The closing track, "Eyebrows Down," also indulges in some autobiography suggesting Ludacris had arrived at a place where he felt comfortable looking back at leaner years.

While Ludacris remained a top Southern hip-hop celebrity, there were indications his popularity may have peaked. Solo debuts by DTP crew members Shawnna and I-20 failed to garner much attention, and the label's biggest success, Chingy, left after a falling out in 2004. Ludacris' own December 2004 release, *The Red Light District*, may have tested the public's ability to stick with him through four albums that show only the slightest evolution. Still, *Red Light* topped the pop charts and featured the hits "Get Back" (produced by the Medicine Men) and "Pimpin' All Over the World"—the latter introducing DTP's first R&B signing, Bobby Valentino (formerly of the Organized Noize–produced Mista).

But Ludacris' Achilles' heel remained the sense that, as clever as his one-liners could be, his music ultimately lacked the depth and conviction to make fans really love him. In late 2006, Ludacris attempted to address that shortcoming with *Release Therapy*, an album that promised a newfound depth and seriousness from the rapper—though that was nowhere to be found on the lead single, "Money Maker" (featuring Pharrell Williams). It remains to be seen whether issues-oriented tracks like "Slap" and "Runaway Love" will resonate with listeners and signal a new phase in the rapper's career.

As it turned out, Atlanta's next great solo MC would create a cult of personality that exceeded Ludacris' core fan base, despite selling far fewer records. Unlike Ludacris, T.I. succeeded by conveying a persona that was at times disarmingly self-confident, at times humanly self-reflective, but all heart.

LAFACE'S LEGACY

In early 2000, right around the time Def Jam set up shop in Atlanta, the city's largest major-label-affiliated operation was getting uprooted. LaFace Records became a victim of its own success when Bertelsmann Music Group, the parent company of Arista Records (which was the parent of LaFace), identified L.A. Reid as the person they wanted to bring to New York to succeed Arista's retiring founder, the legendary record executive Clive Davis.

Preparations had been gaining steam for years. In 1998, BMG had Reid attend Harvard to get his MBA—the kind of thing that might separate the self-made execs of urban music from the disciplined number crunchers at the majors. And in early 2000, BMG bought the half of LaFace Records it didn't already own, paying Reid and Babyface one hundred million dollars to cash out—and freeing Reid of his ties to the label. The German-based media conglomerate then cited the company's mandatory retirement policy that required executives to step down at age sixty (Davis was said to be sixty-seven at the time), and announced that Davis was out and Reid was in.

Davis, however, was not ready or willing to retire—in fact, he was enjoying record-breaking success with Santana's *Supernatural* album. The whiff of age discrimination turned BMG's move into a public relations nightmare, with L.A. in the uncomfortable position of forcibly replacing his former mentor. Worse, some in the industry grumbled that Reid was not qualified for such a major role. It was a charge, perhaps, laced with racism, but it also had basis in fact. Reid's LaFace had, after all, seen two of its biggest acts—TLC and Toni Braxton—declare bankruptcy after hugely successful albums. Despite his record of success—and his good reputation among artists—Reid had developed a reputation for overspending on record promotion. It didn't help L.A.'s image that, just a few months earlier, he'd thrown a lavish, three-day wedding for himself and his new wife in Capri, Italy.

By the time the dust settled, the BMG executives who'd orchestrated Davis' forced retirement were gone, the company had given Davis $150 million to start a new BMG-affiliated label and, with the coast clear, Reid was installed as Arista's new president. For the first time, a product of Atlanta's urban music explosion was running a major label—another sign of the South's rise at all levels of the music business.

But Reid faced challenges at Arista, both from marquee artists that had expressed solidarity with Davis to the employees he'd inherited from Davis. He soon brought in many of his LaFace employees, including the marketing exec Shanti Das, to fill key roles at Arista. At LaFace, meanwhile, the initial plan was to leave a skeleton staff in Atlanta to serve as a field A&R team. Reid left KP in charge, but soon it became clear LaFace would never be anything more than a name slapped on the back of some records. Both KP and Das eventually wound up at Sony.

With all the upheaval, it's a measure of the faith that LaFace staffers' had in Atlanta rapper Tip's potential that he ever got a record out at all. When LaFace stopped functioning separately from Arista, established LaFace acts like OutKast, Usher, and TLC moved to Arista (though some still carried the LaFace imprint), while others were simply dropped. Though LaFace's Ghetto Vision imprint fell by the wayside, its signings, the Youngbloodz and Tip, landed on Arista. But as Tip readied his debut, *I'm Serious*, he was asked to make one major change: his name. Arista had signed former A Tribe Called Quest MC Q-Tip, and so there was not room on the label for another Tip. Reluctantly, Tip agreed to clip his moniker; he was already calling himself T.I.P., so he shortened it to become T.I.

By the time *I'm Serious* dropped in late 2001, L.A. was focused entirely on making his new role at Arista a success—and part of that involved proving himself capable of breaking acts outside his urban-music comfort zone. As he introduced Avril Lavigne and shepherded Pink's shift to a more rock-oriented sound, T.I.'s record was made a low priority.

For anyone listening, however, *I'm Serious* revealed a charismatic MC and able storyteller. In the record's first minute, T.I. identified himself as "a young arrogant nigga from Atlanta who calls himself the king of the South." He was a king without a kingdom as yet, but one who sounded like he never doubted one would arise. The Neptunes-produced title track further lays out T.I.'s boundless ambition: "Picture me as one of the greatest that'll ever be/Compare me to Tupac, B.I.G., and Jay-Z," he raps.

Some were turned off by the premature coronation—in fact, the "king of the South" claim played a role in both of T.I.'s early beefs: with Houston's Lil' Flip and Ludacris' DTP crew. But something about T.I. suggested real substance. Though his down-home partner DJ Toomp produced most of *I'm Serious*, T.I. was not shy about using guests like Jazze Pha, Beenie Man, and Too Short to draw attention to himself. And while some of *I'm Serious'* best material is thoroughly thugged-out, such as the drug-dealer shout-out "Dope Boyz," T.I. was not afraid to lay down some vulnerabilities—his guilt for fallen friends, his regret at disappointing his mother. And yet, despite his growing reputation as the South's answer to Jay-Z, *I'm Serious* got little support from Arista and sold an abysmal one hundred thousand copies.

T.I. knew his relationship with Arista was over. "There was just an understanding of what I expected from a label, and what they had to offer," T.I. says. "And the two just didn't match. They didn't come from where I came from, so they didn't understand it at the time." Despite L.A.'s reluctance to release T.I., Reid understood the rapper would be dissatisfied at Arista, and so he let T.I. buy himself out of his contract.

LaFace's retreat from Atlanta in 2000 was not a catastrophic loss—over the label's decade in the city, Atlanta had developed a huge urban music-industry infrastructure that included not only popular acts but also hit-making songwriters and music publishing companies, star producers, and nationally renowned recording studios, as well as other labels anxious to become LaFace's successor.

While Jermaine Dupri remained Atlanta's biggest music figure, Dallas Austin also continued to find great success. Though his Rowdy Records venture with Arista didn't pan out—nor have Austin's other label start-ups—he stayed in the charts working with many of the era's biggest pop acts. Most notably, he wrote and produced much of Madonna's 1994 album, *Bedtime Stories*—including the hits "Secret" and "Human Nature"—and also contributed a pair of songs to Michael Jackson's 1995 *HIStory* album. In addition, he executive produced teen R&B star Monica, Miami hip-hop veteran JT Money, and TLC's triumphant return, *FanMail*, while also cowriting and coproducing four songs on Pink's hugely successful *M!ssundazstood* album.

In his third decade as a hit maker, Austin has worked with everyone from Janet Jackson to Gwen Stefani to Duran Duran, while also branching out into film. In 2002, Austin served as executive producer of the film *Drum-line*, a story set in an Atlanta black college that echoes Austin's own experience playing drums in his high school marching band. In 2006, Austin coproduced *ATL*, which featured the acting debuts of T.I. and OutKast's Big Boi, and was based on Austin's own experiences in the late '80s at the SWATs skate rink Jellybeans. He stayed in the news, as well, when Austin—traveling to the Arab emirate of Dubai to attend model Naomi Campbell's birthday party—was arrested and jailed for drug possession. Some high-level diplomacy resulted in his eventual release.

Behind Dupri and Austin, an entire new generation of behind-the-scenes players emerged around LaFace—writer/producers including Anthony

Dent (who produced Destiny's Child's hit "Survivor"), Sean "Sep" Hall (Pink, Xscape), Christopher "Tricky" Stewart (Mya, Tyrese, Britney Spears), and the Platinum Brothers (Jamie Foxx, Keyshia Cole). But Reid cast the largest shadow over Kevin "She'kspere" Briggs, a songwriter signed to Reid's Hitco Music publishing company. When Briggs scored big with two of 1999's best and biggest hits, TLC's "No Scrubs" and Destiny's Child's "Bills, Bills, Bills," he became a star in his own right. Reid rewarded him with his own Arista-distributed label, Spere Records, though the label never really got off the ground.

The most consistent set of urban hit makers to operate within the world created by Atlanta's pioneers (Reid, Dupri, Austin, Organized Noize) came from a company called Noontime. In 1997, four childhood friends from Richmond, California—Ryan Glover, Henry "Noonie" Lee, Chris Hicks, and Terry Ross—reconvened in Atlanta and set up Noontime as a full-service music publisher: They signed songwriters, provided them with a studio, managed their careers, and helped get their songs into the right hands (later, they also formed a label). By 1999, Noontime was rolling with its biggest songwriters: Brian-Michael Cox, who wrote and produced number-one hits for Usher, Jagged Edge, Bow Wow (formerly Lil' Bow Wow), and Toni Braxton; and Teddy Bishop, who wrote and produced for Braxton, Whitney Houston, and Aaliyah, and penned the Montell Jordan/Master P number one, "Let's Ride." Donnie Scantz and Kevin Hicks added to the success, while Johnta Austin went on to sign with So So Def as an artist.

But the Noontime writer/producer to gain the most success, and celebrity, has been Phalon Alexander, the scion of Memphis music royalty who called himself Jazze Pha. Perhaps more than anyone except Jermaine Dupri and Pharrell Williams, Pha has come to represent the Southern hip-hop producer who's as much a star as the artists with which he works. Phalon was born in Memphis, but grew up in L.A. with his mother, the R&B and gospel singer Deniece Williams. "My life was music," Pha says. "The O'Jays, Patti Labelle, Gladys Knight. People like that came to my house all the time, cooking, kicking back and being comfortable."

Phalon would spend his summers with his dad, bassist James Alexander of Stax soul great the Bar-Kays. On the road with the Bar-Kays, he'd help out as part of the crew and hobnob with tour mates like Rick James; Earth, Wind & Fire; or Cameo. Phalli's dad also let him sit in during studio sessions, and by the time he finished high school he was bitten with the urge to record.

Phalon signed a solo deal with Elektra and, in 1990, released his debut album, *Rising to the Top*. Though Memphis' hard-core street-rap sound had kicked off by then, Pha's record leaned more toward new-jack R&B with touches of positive hip-hop. "I wasn't really a part of the gansta walk whole thing," Pha says. "I was more into R&B and commercial rap. I was cool with it, and I met those guys, but I didn't really grow up the same way they did. My daddy was rich, so we had a different thing."

When the solo deal fizzled, Pha fell into producing. He worked with his father to form a rap act called the Funkahawlikz, for which Jazze served as resident producer. Two years before the group released its one album, 1995's *Futuristic Ghetto Sicknezz*, Pha traveled to Atlanta with the Funkahawlikz to do some shows. There, the group's manager hooked Pha up with MC Breed, a Michigan rapper who'd settled in Atlanta to record with Ichiban. Breed was then at his peak with "Gotta Get Mine," a top-ten rap single featuring Tupac, and he bought a bunch of Pha's tracks. Pha decided to stick around in Atlanta and stayed at Breed's suburban Kennesaw home on and off over the next year.

From Breed, Pha got work producing a bunch of Ichiban projects, including a female duo from Memphis called UNLV (Unfortunately No Longer Virgins, not to be confused with the male duo UNLV from New Orleans), Kool Ace, and MC Brainz. Pha's big break came in 1996, when he reunited with his Memphis pal Tela, a rapper signed to Houston's Suave House. Pha produced two tracks on his debut, *Piece of Mind*, including the top-ten rap hit "Sho Nuff," a Southern pimpin' classic with Pha singing the chorus and rapping by Tela's fellow Memphis-expatriate labelmates, Eightball & MJG. From then on, Pha says, "Everybody started calling."

Pha could play and write music, sing and rap; his rare blend of talents made him sharp with both R&B and hip-hop. His creations were also reliably catchy, with deep soul roots that helped his songs stick to your bones. "When I was a young cat, we always listened to gangsta rap—NWA, Triple Six," Pha explains. "But me growing up in the Bar-Kays family, I was around real music at all times. So I had the best of both worlds."

Or, as he told Atlanta's *Creative Loafing*, "People come to me because they want that fish and grits, that real South. It's authentic, it's real, it's in me. They're not just looking for songs or beats, they're looking for a vibe."

Pha's career took off when he signed with Noontime in 1998: He worked with Dave Hollister, Lil Jon, E-40, Too Short, the D.O.C., Youngbloodz, Juelz Santana, Murphy Lee, Twista, Nelly, Pastor Troy, Slim Thug, Trina, Bun B, David Banner, and OutKast, among many others. He cut tracks for Noontime's Epic-distributed label, and scored hits for Slick Rick ("Street Talkin'"), Ludacris ("Area Codes"), Trick Daddy featuring Cee-Lo and Big

Boi ("In Da Wind"), Aaliyah ("I Don't Wanna," "Come Over"), Field Mob ("Sick of Being Lonely"), T.I. ("Let's Get Away"), and Ciara ("1, 2 Step").

When radio DJ Greg Street hooked Jazze up with Baby, head of New Orleans' Cash Money label, for a track on Street's *6 O'Clock* mix CD, he impressed Baby with the speed at which he created quality work. Baby offered Pha a deal to create fifty beats for Cash Money and, starting in 2002, his tracks began showing up on records by Lil' Wayne, Baby (aka Birdman), and the Big Tymers.

As Jazze's successes piled up, his celebrity grew. He started doing a radio show on Atlanta's Hot 107.9 (Ludacris' Hot 97.5 had switched frequencies). Attempts to restart his recording career stalled—a solo record for Atlantic went unreleased, and collaborations with Mannie Fresh (as Big Luv) and Cee-Lo (as Happy Hour) have yet to materialize. But Pha had better luck when he formed Sho'Nuff Records with Noonie Lee and Russell "Block" Spencer: The label put out Ciara's multiplatinum debut, *Goodies*, through Arista; it also signed rapper Jody Breeze and put together Breeze's group Boyz N Da Hood (which also featured breakout star Young Jeezy).

TO CAMELOT LIKE CAMPBELLTON

The Dungeon Family had long talked about doing a collective album, but it never happened. Then in 2001—with Goodie Mob falling apart, failed albums by Society of Soul, Withdoctor, Cool Breeze, Slimm Calhoun, and Backbone (who dropped his debut, *Concrete Law*, in June of the same year), and OutKast's massive popularity overshadowing the larger crew—suddenly a Dungeon Family album was on the table.

"I'm not certain the world was sleepless waiting on the DF album after all that time," Cee-Lo joked. But the Family had the support of L.A. Reid—who, after *Stankonia*'s success was happy to indulge OutKast's pet projects. And the success of 1999's DF posse cut "Watch for the Hook" suggested great potential. So why not?

But no sooner had the deal been made that divisions began to appear. "We're in a meeting at the Dungeon," Big Rube recalls. "L.A. is on speakerphone. The whole DF is there. Everything's sounding great, like it always does in those initial meetings. Everybody's going to get an equal split of the money that we get from the budget. But then Arista was like, 'We're going to pay our artists [OutKast, Goodie Mob] more.' Which completely negates the whole thing. DF was supposed to come before what label you're on. The whole point was to try to bring up some of the guys who were in a slump, just bring some life into this whole thing. So then you got one guy who might get five thousand dollars. Then another might get ten thousand dollars. But then the motherfuckers that were already basically rich getting fifty to one hundred thousand dollars."

Still, the recording process proved as democratic as could be expected. All ten core DF rappers appeared on a roughly equal number of tracks, with production handled by Organized Noize on about two-thirds of the album, and Earthtone III on the rest. Rappers teamed up in all manner of combinations—sometimes chosen specifically to evoke a desired sound, often compiled at random. Only the record's single, "Trans DF Express," made sure to feature the DF's best-known MCs: Andre, Big Boi, Cee-Lo, and Gipp (all signed individually to Arista). "It felt like everybody was going to have a say, the real family aspect of how we call it the Dungeon Family," Rube says. "And it felt like it was about to be on point again."

Far from the days when the DF all slept on the same floor, it was now a challenge to get them in the same place at the same time. Where once the album may have come together more organically, now it needed to be compiled piecemeal. Still, *Even in Darkness* managed to sound cohesive. In part, that was due to a conceptual strand that united the look and sound of the album.

Since early on, the Dungeon Family viewed itself as a pillar of the SWATs community—the crew that put the area on hip-hop's map and continued to represent it. They imagined themselves as a sort of Knights of the Round Table, with the Southwest Atlanta/East Point/College Park area their kingdom. As Big Boi raps in "Trans DF Express," referring to a key local road: "Dungeon Family got my sword and shield/To Campbellton like Camelot, let's smoke a joint and chill."

Of course, the Round Table metaphor was overblown and pretentious. But if they were more delusional dons Quixote than actual knights, they at least had a sense of mission—like Quixote, they understood that the quest is the thing. And it was possible to imagine some members fitting certain roles: Rico Wade as King Arthur; Ray Murray as the wizard Merlin; OutKast as the standout knight, Sir Lancelot.

While tracks like the funky "Crooked Booty," the crunked-out "Emergency," the poetic "What is Rap?," or the old-school vibing "Six Minutes (Dungeon Family It's On)" are all memorable, the best songs are the ones that most stir the spirit. In particular, "Follow the Light" begins with Rube saying, "People don't use our music to get high, they use our music to get by," and then follows Sleepy, Big Boi, Gipp, and Cee-Lo through terrific inspirational verses and a repeated promise in the church-like chorus, "follow the lights, they lead to something. . . . "

Even more rousing is "Excalibur," the album's climax and centerpiece. Full of cinematic orchestral arrangements of horn, percussion, and choir, the song builds from Gipp's claim of status ("Forever we pillars in this stature/In this ASCAP rapture") and Rube's pledge of integrity ("Prepared to defend the next us/Didn't get in for no Lexus/Didn't get on through connections/Or to get off my erection") up to a rousing group chorus: "We are few! We are strong! We are proud holders of the Excalibur!"

It was an ecstatic culmination of a decade of work, an over-extension of the DF's influence so full of heart and good intentions that, despite its corniness, it was easy to be moved by it. To celebrate the album's release, the Dungeon Family rented out a Turner Field parking lot and held a free carnival—rides, treats, personal appearances, the works. Mobbed by young autograph seekers, Rico Wade proudly took on his dream role as the unofficial mayor of southside Atlanta.

But there's another way the Dungeon Family's story echoes the Knights of the Round Table. In most versions of the Arthurian legends, Sir Lancelot—the knight with the most star quality and skills—becomes a rival to King Arthur, almost by accident, doomed by circumstance. Arthur's wife, Guinevere, falls for Lancelot and the trouble that ensues leaves Arthur mortally wounded and the Round Table destroyed. As the hip-hop world fell in love with OutKast above all other Dungeon members, the duo's power unavoidably created an imbalance ripe for conflict. It's never been something that escalated into an acknowledged beef—particularly not one aired publicly—but the ever-increasing disparity inside the DF caused difficulty.

As fate would have it, Arista decided to release an OutKast best-of anthology—*Big Boi & Dre Present . . . OutKast*—just four weeks after *Even in Darkness* came out. As "Trans DF Express" floundered at the bottom of the R&B/Hip-Hop chart, *Big Boi & Dre*'s "The Whole World" shot into the pop top twenty. Faced with whether to spend resources promoting a one-off project featuring many artists not signed to Arista, or OutKast's anthology, the label's choice was clear. "As soon as the OutKast album dropped, you don't hear shit about the Dungeon Family record," Ray Murray says. "Nothing. I'm not going to blame OutKast for that, I'm going to blame Arista."

While *Even in Darkness* faded before the crew had a chance to mount any kind of full-scale tour, early on they made a few promotional stops. "We were on the road, we had Dungeon Family posters," Big Rube recalls. "But they'd have even bigger OutKast posters. You could kind of tell that Big Boi was losing interest because he was on the phone, he was mad at the numbers on a weekly basis. 'Kast wasn't used to splitting their money ten ways. So after that promo tour, we never did go on tour again."

Though he nominally reunited with the rest of Goodie Mob to record *Even in Darkness*, Cee-Lo remained committed to exploring his own path after the *World Party* debacle. In March 2002, Arista released his solo debut, *Cee-Lo Green and His Perfect Imperfections*. Its cover depicted Cee-Lo as a wizard in a magician's top hat and flowing wig, which suggested this would not be a typical rap album. Like his elementary school friend Andre, the Dungeon's other eccentric, Cee-Lo had long indulged a taste for the flamboyant and an instinct to push his music beyond the boundaries of hip-hop.

In fact, much of *Perfect Imperfections* didn't contain any rap at all. As Cee-Lo proved with Goodie Mob—and on OutKast and Santana albums—he was a natural soul singer. Here, he not only rapped and sang, he wrote, produced, and arranged sixteen songs that span from churchy gospel to bossa-nova, from Motown sweet to tripped-out psychedelic to amped-up rock. He even updated the *Animal House* ditty "Shama Lama Ding Dong" in the course of his sprawling album.

Perfect Imperfections suggested that, even if *World Party* never happened, Cee-Lo would've needed to break away from Goodie Mob. The album was all Cee-Lo—no Organized Noize tracks, no Dungeon Family guest verses. "The situation I chose to address didn't call for any random gunfire. I got a whole other shape and form of music that had nothing to do with Goodie Mob," Cee-Lo says.

Perfect Imperfections was the swollen floodgates of Cee-Lo's creativity bursting open. He shows a naughty side on the funky "Bad Mutha" and "Closet Freak," but *Perfect Imperfections* is mostly committed to relaying social themes like monogamous love and staking out individuality. The record also reveals Cee-Lo's strong pop instincts, whether reaching back to doo wop ("Great Pretender," "Awful Thing"), embracing regional flavors ("Country Love") or going straight piano-man on the closer, ("Young Man").

But a lyrical unity ties together the musical eclecticism. The words are personal—more like singer/songwriter fare than typical hip-hop. At times confessional, at times cautionary, Cee-Lo sounds thankful for what's been and hopeful of what's to come. For him, *Perfect Imperfections* was everything *World Party* was not. "I consider my album to be a race toward redemption," he says. "And I'll spend the rest of my life redeeming my acts of disgrace."

Still, Cee-Lo had not officially left Goodie Mob. Arista wanted to get the group back in the studio, though Cee-Lo preferred to wait as the other three developed a strong resentment toward their missing group mate. In the meantime, the others started putting together solo records—T-Mo, in fact, had quietly released an independent record, *2 the Fullest*, back in 2000. Khujo was also putting together an independent release, while Gipp worked on a record for Arista.

One night in late June of 2002, Khujo stayed late recording at the Dungeon. Driving home around four a.m., he apparently fell asleep at the wheel and ran off the road at full speed. After a flurry of rumors about his death, reports the next day confirmed that Khujo was alive and in critical condition—and he'd lost the bottom half of his right leg. Members of the Dungeon Family circled around their friend: Andre flew back from L.A., where OutKast was about to receive a BET Award for Best Group. Big Boi stayed behind and dedicated the award to Khujo; Andre brought him a bass guitar to keep him active during recovery.

Along with the rest of the Dungeon Family, Cee-Lo came by the hospital to visit Khujo. The accident, however, only served to increase divisions between Cee-Lo and the rest of Goodie Mob. Gipp even appeared to blame Cee-Lo for Khujo's misfortunes. "Me, 'Jo, and T are older than Cee-Lo," Gipps says. "When this shit started, Cee-Lo was seventeen—he never had a car, never stayed on his own, we damn near raised this kid. When our album first came out, Cee-Lo's momma died and we were the only ones he had to turn to. So to a certain degree, it's about respect. Somebody pulled that man to the side and said, 'You the star, we're going to make it happen for you.' That's all good, but you sacrificed the people that looked out for you all those years. Something as tragic as a car accident happened to a man that was out here trying to feed his family, because his brother decided he didn't want to do anything anymore."

Fitted with a prosthetic leg, Khujo rebounded quickly; by November he'd released his solo debut, *The Man Not the Dawg*. Gipp's *Mutant Mindframe* arrived in March of 2003. By then, Goodie Mob was no longer tied to Arista. L.A. Reid claims the group asked to be released, while Khujo says he read in a magazine that Arista had dropped the group. Gipp's record, initially slated for Arista, wound up becoming the first release on Goodie Mob Records. Soon, Goodie Mob was back in the studio, recording as a trio. Though Cee-Lo had intended his absence to be temporary, the split was looking more like permanent.

Released just a few months apart in early 2004, Cee-Lo's second solo album, *Cee-Lo Green . . . Is the Soul Machine* and Goodie Mob's first trio record—the pointedly titled *One Monkey Don't Stop No Show*—provided ample evidence the two parties were heading in different directions. Unlike

Perfect Imperfections, *Soul Machine* was a more conspicuously commercial effort, full of high-profile guests (Ludacris, T.I.) and the top Southern producers: the Neptunes, Timbaland, and Jazze Pha, as well as Organized Noize. The record's two singles—the Tim-produced "I'll Be Around" and the Jazze-produced "The One"—are catchy, joyous, dance-friendly, and idiomatically regional; magnificent examples of the irresistible appeal of commercial Southern hip-hop circa 2004.

In contrast to Cee-Lo's urban pop, Goodie Mob's *One Monkey* sounds comfortable keeping it rough and underground. While tracks come from a few known producers, including Three 6 Mafia's DJ Paul and Miami team Cool & Dre, mostly Goodie sticks with Organized's Ray Murray and less established locals such as Mark Twayne (Attic Crew) and Speedy. The record is surprisingly soulful and melodic in parts, though *One Monkey* at times suggests the group was trying to fit in with more current crunk styles. Crunk is even more prevalent on 2005's *Livin' Life as Lumberjacks*, a Khujo/T-Mo duo album that brought Goodie Mob back to its original formation.

While Cee-Lo struggled to find mainstream success as a solo artist, he developed a reputation as a talented vocalist, writer, and producer. His song "Don't Cha"—originally recorded by his protégé Tori Alamaze, then rerecorded by the neo-burlesque cabaret-turned-pop act, the Pussycat Dolls—reached number two on the pop singles chart.

After recording a collaborative album with producer Jazze Pha that got shelved (perhaps temporarily), Cee-Lo embarked on another collaboration with a celebrated producer—Brian Burton, aka Danger Mouse. Burton had spent his teens in the Atlanta area and started making records while at the University of Georgia in Athens. But major success didn't hit until 2004, when he created an album-length bootleg mash-up of music from the Beatles' *White Album* and lyrics from Jay-Z's *The Black Album*, which he called *The Grey Album*. Though he could not sell the album because of its unauthorized samples, its massive popularity as a download catapulted Danger Mouse to fame and led to him producing the double-platinum 2005 album *Demon Days*, by the animated electronic group Gorillaz. The same year, Burton teamed with acclaimed underground rapper MF Doom (Daniel Dumile)—a New Yorker transplanted to suburban Atlanta, and performing in a Dr. Doom metallic mask—for an album called *The Mouse and the Mask*, which sampled prominently from the Atlanta-based Cartoon Network's "Adult Swim" programs.

A chance meeting with Cee-Lo sparked the 2006 album the duo recorded as Gnarls Barkley, called *St. Elsewhere*. In Burton, Cee-Lo found the perfect comrade for his mix of eccentric playfulness, hip-hop iconoclasm, and pop instincts. With Cee-Lo as frontman, they scored a top-ten single, "Crazy"—a bigger hit than Cee-Lo had ever scored, solo or with Goodie Mob. Unexpectedly, Gnarls Barkley—Cee-Lo's third try at a star-making creative outlet—proved to be the charm.

By the end of 2006, Gnarls had outpaced its kindred spirits in OutKast as *St. Elsewhere* achieved platinum sales and five Grammy nominations—including one for album of the year.

While a Gnarls Barkley follow-up is inevitable, talk also continues to build of Goodie Mob returning as a foursome—plans are said to be in the works, in fact—but bridges have been burned. "These are slanderous remarks about me," Cee-Lo says about being the "monkey" of Goodie Mob's album title. "I've been depicted as some cutthroat individual who left the guys out to dry, when in fact it was an agreed upon separation. None of us are getting any younger. We were selling a decent amount, but just breaking even, really. So it was about attaining stability—I had a son on the way and a mortgage and a wife and a whole family. It just started to change. But we do have a magic when we're all together. I can't honestly say that one monkey won't stop the show."

KINGS OF THE SOUTH

With LaFace out of the picture, L.A. Reid wanted to bring another label aboard to maintain the company's Atlanta hip-hop presence. His interest coincided perfectly with Jermaine Dupri's own needs. Dupri wanted a position at or near the top of a major label, and was frustrated by a lack of opportunity for growth at Sony, So So Def's longtime home. After more than a decade, Dupri broke from Sony in early 2002 and sought a new distribution deal for So So Def. In January of 2003, Arista announced it would bring So So Def on board, uniting Reid and Dupri, two main architects of Atlanta's "new Motown." L.A. made Dupri Arista's senior vice president of urban music, which gave Dupri the major-label position he wanted. And Dupri brought So So Def to Arista, which put Reid back in the Atlanta urban music game.

The deal came just in time for Dupri, who had found himself with some embarrassing financial problems after years of gloating on record about his fabulous material possessions and lavish lifestyle. In December 2002, the IRS (with news cameras following) came to collect a bill of $2.5 million Dupri owed in back taxes from 1998. The government seized Dupri's cars, furniture, and computers from his home. When the Arista deal brought twenty million dollars, the IRS got its cut and Dupri put the episode behind him.

So So Def and Arista quickly conjugated their partnership with "Never Scared," the advance single from Bone Crusher (a former member of Lil Jon's BMG crew). "Never Scared" was, in some ways, the song that proved most emblematic of Atlanta hip-hop's new generation. It adopted the city's new sound (crunk), introduced the new L.A./Jermaine partnership, and featured Atlanta's most promising up-and-comers—Bone Crusher, along with OutKast protégé Killer Mike and the new "king of the South," T.I.

Meanwhile, T.I.'s Ghetto Vision label mate, the Youngbloodz, survived LaFace's demise at Arista and got passed over to So So Def. In September of 2003, the Youngbloodz's second album, *Drankin' Patnaz*, debuted at number five on the pop chart, as its Lil Jon–produced single, "Damn," climbed to number four.

Reid appeared to be succeeding quite well at Arista: He'd pushed career acts like OutKast and Usher to new levels of popularity, and broke younger acts like Avril Lavigne. But the bottom line was not adding up. Reid had spent so much in the effort that Arista had posted a net loss despite its apparent successes. While no one questioned Reid's ability to spot talent, BMG was a multinational corporation and not an arts organization. So by January of 2004, Reid was out. As BMG prepared to merge with fellow major label Sony, Arista was put under the umbrella of BMG's RCA label—run by Clive Davis. After four years away, Davis was again in charge of the label he created.

Reid quickly landed on his feet. In February, he was named chairman of the Island Def Jam Music Group, which put Reid in charge of the Scarface-run Def Jam South, among many other labels. By then, though, Scarface was through. Def Jam South had not produced much beyond Ludacris, and Scarface felt he'd missed out on some key Southern artists (Lil' Flip, David Banner) because he lacked support from New York. When Reid came aboard, Scarface requested his release and, reluctantly, L.A. let him go.

The artists and labels L.A. left behind at Arista were moved over to BMG's Jive Records, a label best known in recent years for releasing the likes of Britney Spears and NSync. Arista's major pop acts, including Usher and OutKast, had no reason to worry about the switch, but smaller groups like the Virginia duo The Clipse wound up in limbo—officially signed to Jive but low on the label's priority list. Meanwhile, two Southern hip-hop power players that had label deals with Arista—the Neptunes (Star Trak) and Jermaine Dupri (So So Def)—won their release from Jive, at the cost of leaving some of their marquee artists behind. The Neptunes landed at Interscope to join the company's stable of successful artist-run labels, including Eminem's Shady Records and 50 Cent's G-Unit. Dupri, meanwhile, took So So Def over to Virgin Records, where he was named president of urban music. Among the operations under his authority was Big Boi's Purple Ribbon label (a successor to Aquemini Records), which had already linked with Virgin.

The alliance was short-lived. After the failure of *20 Y.O.*, the presumed comeback album by Dupri's girlfriend Janet Jackson—an album he executive produced—Dupri stepped down from Virgin in late 2006. Within months, he'd rejoined L.A. Reid and become president of urban music for Island Records. As Southerners stepped into all levels of the national music industry, the lines between what was Southern music and just plain mainstream urban nearly vanished.

After his Arista deal ended, T.I. was determined not to go back to the life of drug dealing he'd left behind as a teenager. "I just don't want to go to jail, I been too many times," T.I. said, sounding like a world-weary hustler, though he was still in his early twenties ("a young man with an old soul," to quote his own lyrics). "Part of becoming a man, you have to look at what really benefits you and your family. If I'm dead or locked up, I can't support my mom, my daughters, my sons, my loved ones. So the dope game is out. The music thing didn't pop off the way I wanted to at first, so I got to do something else to get some money. Construction. But I have to wait two or three months to flip a house, so I'm selling cars. If cars don't get me the money as soon as I need it, I'm opening a barbershop. Whatever I need to do, I'm keeping my wheels turning. It's the mentality of a hustler, but straight up and down."

T.I. remained focused on music, though, and in 2002 he and Jason Geter turned Grand Hustle management into a record label. With his Pimp $quad Click, T.I. released two volumes of a mix tape, *In Da Streets*, each of which sold more than twenty thousand copies. With his reputation growing in the underground, major labels were soon courting Grand Hustle Records for a label deal. And by the summer of 2003, T.I. was back—on Atlantic Records now—with a second album called *Trap Muzik*.

Because he was a young Atlanta rapper who appeared on a hit with Bone Crusher, T.I. was at first lumped in as a crunk artist, but he made no claim to it and his music didn't contain crunk's telltale elements. Rather, T.I. seemed to be making his own Atlanta hip-hop movement—one that retained regional flavors while attempting to compete with the street lyricism most associated with New York rappers like Nas and Jay-Z.

He called this new Southern flavor trap music. It wasn't a term T.I. invented, but rather a word he made his own. Specifically, *trap* was the ghetto slang for a drug house—a run-down, boarded-up rattrap where humans go in and don't always come out. More generally, it was a street life centered on dead-end hustles and other fast tracks to jail or the morgue. Trap music was the soundtrack to this grim world—and, in glimmers of hope, a buried map showing the way out.

Trap Muzik proved T.I.'s ideal vehicle—a blend of hard-core lyricism, trademark bravado, radio-friendly jams, and enough nuance to back the rapper's own claim of being among the top rappers out there. He talked sense—whether addressing U.S. involvement in Iraq ("No More Talk") or explaining the perspectives of drug dealers ("Doin' My Job"). He embraced his Dirty South heritage—whether the car culture ("24's") or his rap predecessors ("Bezzle," featuring Eightball & MJG and UGK's Bun B). He was happy to make hook-heavy music that moved the crowd ("Rubber Band Man," "Let's Get Away"), but he also injected high-concept into some tracks. "T.I. vs. T.I.P.," for instance, featured the rapper double-tracked—in the guise of the polished star (T.I.) and the street kid (T.I.P.)—and passing the mic back and forth to himself.

Even more interesting was "I Still Luv You," which divided itself into three verses that get more devastating as they go: the first an apology to an ex-girlfriend he failed to appreciate; the second an assurance to his dead father that he accepts him, despite his father's parental failings; and third, a plea for forgiveness to his young daughter whom he once denied fathering ("I ain't ashamed of you, I'm more ashamed of me/It's not at all your fault, you'd be better off blamin' me/But now I realize where the problem lies/Forgive me babygirl, I apologize").

What made *Trap Muzik* worthy of a place alongside the best works of Southern hard-core rap by Scarface, Eightball & MJG, and UGK was T.I.'s passion. He may have alienated rivals with his claims to greatness, but there was never a doubt T.I. believed his hype. In that way, he was every bit the "Jay-Z of the South," as *Vibe* reported Pharrell Williams labeled him. Like Jay-Z, his swagger and self-confidence were infectious. Enough fans caught on to make *Trap Muzik* go platinum, and put three singles into rap's top fifteen. After a false start, T.I. had finally arrived.

Unfortunately, the rapper's troubled past had not yet receded far enough to keep him immune from trouble. Picked up for parole violations stemming from a 1998 drug charge, T.I. was sentenced to jail in suburban Cobb County in 2004. After six months, he was let out on work release and quickly made two notable appearances. At the first—the annual Birthday Bash festival thrown by Hot 107.9—T.I. publicly dissed Houston rapper Lil' Flip, who was also on the bill, because he'd heard Flip was questioning his "king of the South" claim.

T.I.'s second stop was Atlanta's Fulton County Jail, which had given the OK for the rapper to shoot a video on location there. When the media reported that an inmate had escaped from the jail during the shoot, and that Fulton Sheriff Jackie Barrett—who's in charge of the jail—had been unaware of the shoot, it became a national story that exposed large-scale mismanagement in Atlanta's correctional system and cost top officials (including, indirectly, Barrett) their jobs.

Given the fulfilled ambitions represented by *Trap Muzik*, T.I.'s late 2004 follow-up, *Urban Legend*, seems like a disappointment. It's actually a stronger record musically—with great tracks by star producers, including Swizz Beatz, Jazzy Pha, Mannie Fresh, the Neptunes, Scott Storch, and David Banner—but lyrically gets mired in flexing and preening that even T.I. cannot keep from getting tiresome over a full album. But the record's cast of interregional guests—including Nelly, Lil' Kim, and West Coaster Daz Dillinger—suggests T.I. had transcended his qualifiers (king . . . of the South; Jay-Z . . . of the South) to become, simply, one of the nation's most respected rappers.

Meanwhile, T.I.—who seems to be slowly reverting back to Tip—continued to grow Grand Hustle Records, not only releasing an album by his own Pimp $quad Click, but also putting out the soundtrack to *Hustle & Flow*. In the summer of 2006, Grand Hustle hit the top of the charts with "Shoulder Lean," a hugely successful first single by Tip's old Bankhead buddy Young Dro (Dro's debut album, *Best Thang Smokin'*, also scored big). And in the same week in March, T.I. released his fourth album, *King*—which entered at number one on the pop chart—and made his feature film debut in the Dallas Austin–produced *ATL*. While *King* mostly delivered more of the same styles T.I. has offered since the beginning, the single "What You Know" became his biggest hit yet. With stature as an MC, a budding film star, and a successful label head at the age of twenty-six, it's entirely possible T.I. could assume the type of leadership role in hip-hop that Jay-Z has long held.

THE BEATLES OF HIP-HOP

As OutKast reached the decade mark as a recording act—a point few popular rap groups have ever reached—they had, amazingly, still not reached the peak of their success. Dre and Big Boi's empire continued to expand: In late 2001, the group launched its own clothing line—a near-mandatory step for top hip-hop acts at the time. Big Boi's Pitfall Kennels, which breeds and sells champion bloodline pit bull terriers, blossomed into a respected dog breeder with a list of celebrity clients. In March of 2003, Aquemini Records released *Monster*, the debut by Killer Mike, the Atlanta rapper who appeared on OutKast's 2001 hit, "The Whole World."

Meanwhile, OutKast's production arm, Earthtone III, splintered into three companies: Big Boi's Boom Boom Room Productions, Andre's Slumdrum, and Mr. DJ's Dungeon Ratz Productions. The split came, in part, because Andre and Big Boi were so rarely working together. Itching to expand creatively, Andre was living in Los Angeles and pursuing an acting career. In 2003, he landed a minor role in the Harrison Ford dud *Hollywood Homicide* and shot an episode of the cop series "The Shield." He also signed on for his first substantial role, as a dim gangsta rapper in the John Travolta/Uma Thurman film *Get Shorty*.

While out on his own, Andre also followed through on plans to record a solo album. Feeling burned-out by hip-hop, Dre found himself writing pop songs, funk songs, jazz-flavored songs—music that involved singing and playing instruments, with little or no rapping. Hearing a thematic strand in the songs—the search for true love, the impossibility of finding it, and thus, a committed post-Erykah bachelorhood—Andre considered building a music-based movie around the tunes. He'd call it *The Love Below*.

"Four or five songs in, I told Big Boi about these plans, and he was cool with the idea but didn't know if it was the right time," Dre says. "We had just won Grammys and Big Boi and my manager thought the record company would be expecting to cash in on the next OutKast album. I had to put the movie on hold and we decided to make the [OutKast] double album."

Both Dre and Big Boi had recorded individually, so they needed to decide which tracks could go on the OutKast album, and which they'd hold for solo albums. "But then we realized both our [solo] records are OutKast records, so we'd just give them two sides of it," Big Boi says. In the compromise, OutKast had come up with a novel, potentially disastrous idea: The next release would be a double OutKast album *and* a set of solo albums. Andre's *The Love Below* would be paired with Big Boi's *Speakerboxxx* to create a two-disc OutKast album.

Speakerboxxx/The Love Below stuck to a "separate-but-equal" spirit, so when the album arrived in September 2003, rather than having to pick between Andre and Big Boi for whose song would be the first single, Arista simply dropped two tracks simultaneously: Big Boi's "The Way You Move" and Andre's "Hey Ya!" There was no fear of confusing audiences—the two songs could not have been more different.

For "The Way You Move," Big Boi recruited Atlanta producer Carl Mo—best known for his latter-day bass and crunk tracks for Raheem, Pastor Troy, and Ying Yang Twins—to craft a paean to Atlanta's bass music legacy. Over a rumbling 808 beat full of low-end and hand claps, Big charms with rhymes about the state of OutKast ("Not clashin', not at all, but see my nigga went to do a little actin'"), the visceral joys of car audio bass ("Trunk rattlin', like two midgets in the back seat wrasslin'/Speakerbox vibrate the tag, make it sound like aluminum cans in a bag"), and life as an equal-opportunity stud ("I was looking at them, there on the dance floor/Now they got me in middle feelin' like a man-whore/Especially the big girls, big girls need love, too, no discrimination here, squirrel"). Intercut with Sleepy Brown's catchy hook, it's a nostalgic party track that imagines how "adult contemporary hip-hop" might sound.

"Hey Ya!" overlaps with "The Way You Move" only in its sense of fun and use of hand claps—and in the way it carves out a space in the pop landscape all its own. Counted off "1, 2, 3, uh!," the song dives right into its driving rock beat, acoustic-guitar strum, and Dre's full-on singing—all performed in a style closer to power pop or Beatles rock than anything resembling hip-hop. While the exuberant music inspires Andre to assert, "Y'all don't want to hear me, y'all just want to dance," in fact the lyrics are rather sober: "If what they say is 'nothing is forever,' then what makes love the exception?/So why oh why are we so in denial when we know we're not happy here?" The message gets easily missed because the second half of the song is all ad-lib and break-down, full of immortal pronouncements like "I wanna see y'all on y'all's baddest behavior/Lend me some sugar, I am your neighbor!" and the endorsement-ready "Shake it, shake it like a Polaroid picture."

The dueling singles were a microcosm for the double album, whose structure offered a fractured view of the duo's aesthetic: *Speakerboxxx* dropped cutting-edge hip-hop that was at turns freaky and socially aware; *The Love Below* eschewed hip-hop almost entirely with a set of jazzy pop funk steeped in the eclectic influence of Prince. But *S/TLB* actually made the case that the duo had been arguing at least as far back as *Aquemini*: Creatively, the two were not really so far apart. Both records, after all, challenged the urban music status quo.

On its own, *Speakerboxxx* had extraordinary range—domestic issues ("Unhappy," "The Rooster"), politics ("War," "Knowing"), philosophy and religion ("Church," "Reset")—and a wider emotional terrain than Big Boi had attempted, from melancholy to outrage to exasperation. With production split between Big, Dre, Mr. DJ, and Carl Mo, and guests including Jazzy Pha, Ludacris, Lil Jon, Jay-Z, and various Dungeon Family cohorts and protégés—including his little brother, James Patton, and a pairing of estranged Goodie Mobbers Khujo and Cee-Lo—*Speakerboxxx* was the more diverse of the two records. But the tracks featuring both Dre and Big—"Ghetto Musick," "Church," "Knowing"—were among the most powerful on either disc.

The Love Below, meanwhile, was startlingly intimate. The few outsiders in-volved were all women—actor Rosario Dawson, ATL soul divas Joi and Peaches, singers Kelis and Norah Jones, Dre's mother—and the themes in-volved women as well: finding love ("Prototype"), exploring lust ("Spread"), hating love ("Love Hater"), fearing love ("Dracula's Wed-ding"), self-love ("Vibrate"), and selfless love ("She's Alive"). Music ranged from lounge jazz to hard bop, live funk to electro-acoustic drum 'n' bass, orchestral arrangements to spare acoustic picking. Dre's raw singing and in-ventive melodies unified the record.

While all of *The Love Below* reflected Andre's personal experience, twice he put his real life out for public entertainment. The closing track, "A Day in the Life of Benjamin Andre (Incomplete)," had the record's only full-song rap, which told his life story from his early days with Big Boi through his relation-ship with Erykah Badu. A second track, "She's Alive," features voice record-ings of Dre's mother, Sharon Benjamin, talking about how she raised Andre without any help from his father. But Dre's father was never fully absent from his son's life—in fact, Dre lived with him during high school—and so he took deep offense at the song. Given the plague of kids growing up without know-ing their fathers, the criticism may have been overstated.

Certainly, mixed in with many flashes of brilliance are moments Dre and Big will likely regret—and perhaps enough nonessential material they could have trimmed away in creating an ultra-lean single album. But releasing such as oddly structured, sprawling, and ambitious work showed audacity and vi-sion. *Speakerboxxx/The Love Below* furthered the group's artistic narrative, a story that grows more involved and compelling as it moves from *Southern-playalisticadillacmuzik* through *ATLiens*, *Aquemini*, and *Stankonia*, before arriving at this bloated masterwork—OutKast's very own *White Album*, its *Sandinista!*, its *Sign O' the Times*.

The huge success of its tandem singles launched *Speakerboxxx/The Love Below* into music history. "The Way You Move" had an easier time fitting into a radio format, so it hit the charts first. But "Hey Ya!" gained momen-tum due in part to an immensely popular video (it won four MTV Video Music Awards in 2004, including Video of the Year) that, thanks to the wonders of digital imaging, depicted Andre as the lead singer, the band members and backup singers of a group appearing in front of rabid fans on an "Ed Sullivan"-style live television show. With his various roles—the high-energy singer, the geeky keyboardist, the cool guitarist (Johnny Vulture), the oddly gesticulating equestrian-clad backup singers—it was clear to any-one watching that Andre was a big star, one of the few truly entertaining, multitalented pop stars still around.

Soon "Hey Ya!" had overtaken "The Way You Move" and landed at number one on the *Billboard* Hot 100 on December 13, 2003. A week later, "The Way You Move" crept up to number two, and the two singles stayed lodged in the top positions for eight weeks (making OutKast only the fourth act in history to have the top two songs). In an unprecedented crossover, "Hey Ya!" also made the top twenty on the R&B/hip-hop, Modern Rock, Hot Digital Tracks, and Adult Top 40 charts—and hit number thirty-four on the Latin Pop Airplay chart. Meanwhile, "The Way You Move" became the number-one rap single (making OutKast the first group with two singles simultaneously atop two different charts). And, in mid-February, "Hey Ya!" made way for "The Way You Move" to spend a week atop the pop chart as well.

That same month, *Speakerboxxx/The Love Below* won three Grammy awards, including one for Best Rap Album and Album of the Year—the first record ever to win both. The group swept the *Village Voice*'s annual Pazz & Jop poll of the nation's music critics, winning top album and single ("Hey Ya!"), and *Rolling Stone*'s critics also picked the album and single as the year's best, adding OutKast as its Artist of the Year. After spending seven weeks as the country's top-selling album, *Speakerboxxx* went on to sell more than five million copies—which, for a double album, made it ten-times platinum.

The accolades lasted through 2004: an NAACP Image Award, two Soul Train Music Awards, two BET Awards, two Nickelodeon Kids' Choice Awards, three American Music Awards, and three World Music Awards. Oprah invited them on her show, and *Esquire* named Andre the "world's best dressed man." OutKast was even the recipient of an elaborate prank on MTV's popular show *Punk'd*. (The episode included an obscure Southern hip-hop reference: In the course of the prank, when a fake police officer asks Andre his name, he responds, "Bill Bixby," quoting MJG's rap in the song "Sho Nuff"—"so I told the ho my name Bill Bixby.")

OutKast became a true cultural force. In the presidential election of 2004, General Wesley Clark—an early favorite among the Democratic nominees—invoked the group in a campaign ad designed to attract young people. "Well, to answer your questions," Clark says to a group of college students, "No, I would not have voted for the Iraq war. I am pro-choice and I am a strong believer in Affirmative Action. And I don't care what the other candidates say, I don't think OutKast is really breaking up. Andre 3000 and Big Boi just cut solo records, that's all."

As the race heated up, veteran television producer Norman Lear approached Andre about getting involved with voter registration. Dre had never voted before, and had even disparaged it on OutKast's first album:

"Y'all tellin' me that I need to get out and vote, huh. Why? Ain't nobody black runnin' but crackers, so why I got to register?" But Lear convinced him he was the perfect person to attract other young people who'd never voted, so Andre took up the challenge. He made personal appearances at registration drives, attended both party conventions, and hosted a documentary about the political process for HBO. No longer a rapper, Andre had become a celebrity icon.

OutKast had so fully moved beyond the world of Southern hip-hop that it had done so much to define. By 2004, OutKast was part of Southern hip-hop only in the way the Beatles were part of the British Invasion: They were rooted in it, but had so far transcended it that the group could no longer define itself next to regional peers.

The Beatles analogy is apt in another way. To find a precedent for Out-Kast's rare combination of immense commercial success and critical adulation, one would have to go back to the Fab Four. Certainly, OutKast has not scored nearly as many lasting hits, nor has it exerted a comparable influence on the larger culture. But in fairness, OutKast operates in a pop-cultural landscape far more crowded, with audiences far more distracted. Just look at the way OutKast has grown its popularity and critical approval over a decade, how the group evolved artistically far beyond what might have been expected, and how the duo has expanded the possibilities of its genre—and of pop music as a whole. Indeed, OutKast had become the Beatles of hip-hop.

Despite an assumption that *Speakerboxxx/The Love Below* was a trial separation between Big and Dre that would inevitably become permanent, no breakup has yet materialized. Andre continues to build steam, and good reviews, as an actor, while Big Boi pursued his own label, Purple Ribbon—a successor to Aquemini, which folded when Andre bowed out. In addition to a *Purple Ribbon All-Stars* compilation, which yielded the hit "Kryptonite (I'm on It)," the label also released *Mr. Brown*, the solo debut by Organized Noize's Sleepy Brown.

In the summer of 2006, after lengthy delays, Andre and Big Boi returned with their feature film, *Idlewild*, and an OutKast album of the same name. Written and directed by Bryan Barber, who shot many of OutKast's best videos (including "Hey Ya!"), *Idlewild* cast Andre and Big Boi as childhood friends on different paths in a Prohibition-era Georgia town. With a supporting cast that includes Terrence Howard, Ben Vereen, and Cicely Tyson, and a stylized cinematic vision that was both contemporary and echoed an earlier age of all-black musicals, *Idlewild* proved far more substantial than a mere rappers' "star vehicle." And its music, which at times blended hip-hop with early jazz flavors—such as on the album's lead single, the Cab Calloway–inspired "The Mighty O"—provided a new direction when it appeared OutKast had pushed hip-hop as far out as it could go: backward. With its era-spanning fusion, OutKast again kept audiences surprised as it carved its own path across the pop landscape.

It remains to be seen what impact *Idlewild*, and any future OutKast records, will have on the culture at large. The early indication is that OutKast may, in fact, have its first commercial disappointment with *Idlewild*, which does not bode well for the group's future. Certainly, after *Speakerboxxx/The Love Below*, sustaining the group's growth may be impossible. "I'm willing to accept that no matter what I do next, it may not be as big as 'Hey Ya!' or OutKast," Andre told *Rolling Stone* in 2004. "But it's a growth thing. Paul McCartney and John Lennon never did anything as big as the Beatles. But they still did some cool shit on their own."

chapter 8

HIP-HOP'S RURALIZATION

THE TWICE-MARGINALIZED RURAL SOUTH

When we talk about the Great Black Migration that, during the middle decades of the twentieth century, moved millions of African Americans from their homes in the rural South, we usually refer to those who wound up in Northern cities like Chicago, Detroit, and New York, or in California. But the migration wasn't simply regional; it was just as much a shift from rural to urban living. In other words, many of the black migrants who left the rural South merely moved to Southern cities—Atlanta, Miami, Houston, Memphis, and so on.

According to census figures, in 1910, 89 percent of the black population lived in the South, and just 16 percent of them were urban. By 1960, only 60 percent of American blacks lived in the South, and they were 33 percent urban. So the move to the cities, no matter what region, was even more dramatic than the shift out of the South.

While transplanted Northern blacks transformed the fabric of African American life, the South's urban blacks—for instance, the leaders of the civil rights movement—also had a profound impact on black history. In that sense, the population of black rural Southerners that stayed behind became twice marginalized—as Southerners and as rural in a modern landscape that had relocated the heart of black cultural life to the cities.

But while rural blacks had become a minority even among Southerners, their cultural influence remained strong—many urban blacks were only a generation (or less) removed from the country. So black country talk, food, and music became familiar sights from 125th St. in Harlem to Crenshaw Blvd. in L.A., to Auburn Ave. in Atlanta.

Despite the reality that city life today in Houston or Memphis probably has more in common with that in Chicago or Detroit than with the black towns that still dot the South, the image of the entire South as being "country" endures. It's no surprise, then, that the hip-hop most enthusiastically identifying itself as Southern has emerged from areas outside the main population centers. Country rap, blues rap, hick-hop—though they often descend into cliché, at their best rural (and semi-urban) acts present Southern hip-hop at its most distinct.

HIP-HOP SINGS THE BLUES

The blues, the Southern-born black music that developed early in the last century out of sharecropper work songs and distant memories of African tonality, has every right to claim its place as a precursor to hip-hop. From the blues, hip-hop inherited its raw delivery, its declarative vocals, its romance with the outlaw, its position as the voice of the underclass. Still, while hip-hop is built entirely on borrowings from the past (in turntable loops or digital sampling), blues remains oddly underused as source material.

From the start, hip-hop drew mainly from '70s funk, soul, and R&B—the music hip-hop kids heard growing up. By the late '80s, groups like A Tribe Called Quest and Gang Starr were mining jazz records for samples and inspiration, and jazz-based hip-hop quickly evolved from novelty to cliché. It seemed natural, at that point, that producers would turn their focus toward that other megalith of twentieth-century black music: the blues. But, it never happened in any significant way. In 1992, Arrested Development offered the blueprint of a blues/rap fusion with "Mama's Always on Stage"—a song that married turntable cutting with harmonica and a basic blues-guitar figure—from the group's hugely successful *3 Years, 5 Months and 2 Days in the Life of* . . . album. But core hip-hop audiences never fully embraced the group, and it quickly receded from prominence.

When the blues/hip-hop fusion was attempted, it tended to come from blues artists. In 1995, the Louisiana blues guitarist Chris Thomas King released *21st Century Blues . . . From Da 'Hood*, an album that embraces hip-hop syntax ("KKKrossroads," "Anotherdeadhomie") as well as beats and rapping, but in the awkward manner of an outsider—not one likely to attract hip-hop fans. Thomas King reprised this fusion with 2002's *Dirty South Hip-Hop Blues*.

When the blues finally meshed with modern beat-oriented music in a way that garnered mainstream attention, it was at the hands of non-hip-hop (and white) producers. In 1996, a one-man studio project called Primitive Radio Gods hit with a trip-hop song, "Standing Outside a Broken Phone Booth With Money in My Hand," that featured a prominent B.B. King sample in the chorus. Two years later, Beck's producer Tom Rothrock remixed tracks for Mississippi blues elder R.L. Burnside's *Come On In* album. And in 1999, techo/pop crossover Moby found massive success with *Play*, an album featuring prominent blues samples.

But the young African Americans who were constantly digging through bins in used record stores, looking for new sounds to mine—why had they avoided the blues? It could be simply that, by the '80s, blues music was beyond the experience of young hip-hop producers. Or perhaps the blues' meter—stiff when compared to jazz's fluid rhythms—did not lend itself to the elastic nature of rap vocals.

But there's something else. To many young African Americans, the blues evokes the Jim Crow days of downtrodden blacks that were always on the losing end of things. By contrast, funk and soul evoke the power and uplift of civil rights, while jazz has gained more elegant, intellectual associations over the decades. What's more, it's easy to observe that, today, the blues is almost entirely the province of middle-aged white people—from musicians like Eric Clapton to the crowds at blues clubs. It's possible the blues have simply not been seen as something particularly hip to draw upon.

In 2000, the blues/hip-hop marriage got its best chance to flower with *New Beats From the Delta*, a compilation by Mississippi-based blues label Fat Possum. Using the label's roster as source material—artists such as T-Model Ford and Junior Kimbrough—a group of hip-hop producers, including Organized Noize's Ray Murray, crafted hip-hop tracks out of the blues. While these hybrids were generally successful in creating credible hip-hop using blues elements, it failed to make an impact on the larger hip-hop landscape. Integrating blues into hip-hop's sonic language proved to be, once again, a dead end.

And yet, the blues have crept into Southern hip-hop through osmosis. On albums such as their 1995 classic, *On Top of the World*, Memphis duo Eightball & MJG offered a street rap so full of hard luck and yearning it could only be described as hip-hop blues. OutKast evoked the blues throughout its 1998 masterpiece, *Aquemini*—from the harmonica breakdown of "Rosa Parks" to the elegant field holler of "Liberation." And there's more: UGK's "country rap," Scarface's bad-man tales, Three 6 Mafia's hellhound music—it was all, in subtle and impressionistic ways, haunted by a blues spirit.

"The blues is primal, that's why you're going to always come back to it," Ray Murray says. "Everything else is wall covering. Blues is the fucking frame of the house. [The Dungeon Family] has always made blues. Hip-hop is the amalgamation of everything, and eventually even hip-hop is going to get back to where it's just somebody beating on a table and saying whatever they feel. And that's blues."

MISSISSIPPI BURNING

It took almost two decades for hip-hop to send an official dispatch from Mississippi, the birthplace of the blues and—in the eyes of many—the picture of Southern rural backwardness. In the mid-90s, groups such as Wildlife Society made some tentative bids representing the state capital of Jackson. But it wasn't until 1999, when the duo Crooked Lettaz released the album *Grey Skies* on Tommy Boy–affiliated Penalty Records, that the home of the blues got a foothold in national hip-hop.

The name itself spelled Mississippi—literally, it referenced the children's rhyme, "M, I, crooked letter, crooked letter, I, crooked letter, crooked letter, I, humpback, humpback, I." Like other Southern rappers, Crooked Lettaz's blues connection was more spiritual than explicit, but the way they associated themselves so integrally with their home state tied the group to all the assumptions about Mississippi. While *Grey Skies* confounded some stereotypes—particularly the notion of Mississippians being ignorant—the record also freely embraced Deep South culture.

Crooked Lettaz's leader was a 6'3", 240-pound college student named Lavell Crump, who adopted as his *nom de rap* the moniker of the Incredible Hulk's alter ego, David Banner. Banner grew up in a neighborhood of Jackson called Queens—tough enough in parts to have earned the nickname "Killer Queens," but otherwise a middle-class section of town. The Crumps were not struggling tenant farmers, but rather, Mississippians who'd taken advantage of the region's many black colleges. Banner's father had been fire chief of Jackson, and his mother and grandmother had earned college degrees; before becoming a rap star, Banner himself earned his bachelor's and entered a master's program.

As a kid, a family member who worked as a DJ gave Banner a collection of rap records, and by age twelve, he was figuring out how to use a drum machine. At Hardy Middle School and Northwest High School, Banner developed his battle-rapping chops. In the early '90s, as Banner began his college stint at Southern University, he made the trek so many black college kids took—to Atlanta for the Freaknik spring break celebrations. At one Freaknik-related concert, Banner got backstage and found himself freestyle rapping in a cipher with members of Souls of Mischief, A Tribe Called Quest, and Wu Tang Clan. As he related on the DVD documentary, *Dirty States*, he impressed onlookers with his lyrical skills. They wanted to know where he was from. "I told them I was from Mississippi," Banner said. "And everybody laughed."

Undeterred, Banner hit the local talent show circuit and met a hip-hop duo from Jackson State University. Though he attended college in Baton Rouge, Banner came home weekends to perform with rapper Kamikaze (Brad Franklin) and DJ Phingaprint as the group Crooked Lettaz. It was an impressive juggling act: As Banner was elected student government president at Southern University, Crooked Lettaz earned a spot in *The Source* magazine's "Unsigned Hype" column. By the time Banner graduated, the group had signed with a Los Angeles label called Correct. Correct soon folded, but its publicist wound up at New York's Penalty Records, which snatched the group.

Though Crooked Lettaz completed its debut album, *Grey Skies*, in 1997, it sat on the shelf for two years until the label finally released it—Banner told *XXL* magazine that he moved to New York "with $300 and a pistol" and lived in his van to get himself directly in the faces of Penalty executives so they'd put it out. But Penalty folded soon after *Grey Skies'* release, and though its parent company, Tommy Boy Records, took over the album, not much happened. When Tommy Boy dropped Crooked Lettaz, *Grey Skies* had sold only eighteen thousand copies.

The few who actually heard *Grey Skies* had no complaints. As a statement of what Mississippi hip-hop should sound like, the record was suitably deft in its balance of countryisms, hip-hop deference, and progressive black consciousness. An intro set the down-home vibe—on the phone, grandma instructed the group to "show these white folks you can do sumthin' sumthin'" over a bass-heavy 808 beat. Then, the first of the record's two minor regional hits, "Get Crunk," presented an ingenious conceit: It borrowed the hook from Run-D.M.C.'s seminal hit "Rock Box," but smoothed out the original's rough edge until it moved with a distinctly Southern glide, and included a guest spot by UGK's Pimp C. The message: It's a new beginning for hip-hop, and this time we're doing it Southern style.

"Fire Water" similarly juxtaposed New York–centric hip-hop with Mississippi flavor, with the chorus—"y'all want that fire water, we got that water"—being the backwoods moonshine-evoking metaphor for the group's rhymes, and label mate Noreaga providing a guest verse to remind doubters that Jackson's Queens and New York's Queens were not so far apart: "We both from the ghetto so we kick it the same," he raps.

In places, *Grey Skies* displays a remarkably expansive worldview—"Straight Outta Africa" features Congolese rapper Aliou Diallo (rhyming in French), while "Pimp Shit" uses Japanese koto. Even with "South's on My Mind," Banner emphasizes the Southern heritage that extends to a majority of African Americans: "Why y'all frontin' on the South, come and get some/Ask your scared-ass parents where you from."

While "Caught in the Game" drops blues-guitar stabs in the background, *Grey Skies* doesn't so much adopt the blues' musical language as it occasionally evokes the pain and pathos of living in Mississippi in a way that's reminiscent of the blues. But while Banner's later music mined agony even more intensely, Crooked Lettaz sounds too collegiate and politically engaged to draw obvious connections with the country blues.

Brimming with potential, *Grey Skies* was no Mississippi hip-hop masterpiece—the music wasn't strong enough to convince coastal hip-hop fans. But it deserved more attention than it received. With Banner's later success, perhaps *Grey Skies* will be rediscovered someday as a lost "classic" of Southern hip-hop.

Meanwhile, without a deal for Crooked Lettaz, David Banner turned to working as a producer, at first in New York and then after returning to Jackson. He also put together an album credited to David Banner & Crooked Lettaz, released on his own b.i.G. f.a.c.e. Entertainment (believe in God for all comes eventually). *Them Firewater Boyz, Vol. 1* became an independent hit in the South, and Banner built on its success with a string of notable production work—most notably for Lil' Flip and Trick Daddy. By early 2003, he'd become "the dirty South's best-kept secret," in the words of *XXL* (which commissioned a major feature on Banner, unprecedented for a still-unsigned artist).

By the time *XXL*'s article ran, Banner had signed a deal with Steve Rifkin, the New York hip-hop entrepreneur who'd founded Loud Records, to be the flagship artist of Rifkin's new Universal-distributed label SRC. The deal's much-publicized price tag was an impressive ten million dollars—a sum Banner did not collect in full, but rather represented some calculation of how much the rapper stood to earn over his five-album deal. The effect, however, was to hype Banner as an important new artist destined for massive popularity. For Banner, throwing around the ten-million-dollar figure also provided a burst of self-esteem for Mississippi—a symbol that his state could produce first-rate hip-hop.

Banner had lots of material stored up, so within a year of signing with SRC he'd already released two full albums—*Mississippi: The Album* and *MTA2: Baptized in Dirty Water*. Though the records embraced the crunk sound—the unrefined, inarticulate style that was fast rising in the South—Banner distinguished himself as the soul and conscience of the otherwise vapid movement.

Mississippi established Banner's bona fides early on, with straight hardcore crunk tracks featuring Lil Jon ("Might Getcha"), Pastor Troy ("Fuck 'Em"), and No Limit producer KLC ("What It Do"), as well as the club hit "Like a Pimp," which sampled UGK in the chorus and "Drag Rap (Triggerman)" on the track. By design, David Banner's solo stuff did not wear its consciousness as conspicuously as *Grey Skies* had. Banner had decided in signing with SRC that he was in it not only for the cause—to represent Mississippi, to present hip-hop in the context of its historical roots—but also to earn as much fortune and fame as the next guy. Banner reasoned the cause and the fame went hand in hand: If his music wasn't being heard by enough people to make him rich and famous, he wasn't going to have the resources or forum to support any cause at all.

But rather than remove all social critique from his music, Banner buried it deep within the grooves. Banner inferred—perhaps subconsciously—a spiritual connection between the pent-up aggression and latent pain of crunk music and the cathartic Mississippi blues. In drawing that connection, Banner found a place within crunk to channel his vision of Mississippi hip-hop.

With *Mississippi*'s "Intro," Banner entered growling from that sinister snarl he wore in nearly all his photos (including the *Mississippi* album cover): "This album right here is dedicated to that muthafuckin' state y'all don't scream on your muthafuckin' songs, the place your grandparents scared to come if they ain't already here, the place your mama ran from, Mississippi," he speaks. ". . . Feel the pain of slavery, discrimination; my grandparents watched your grandparens run, while brothers and sisters died, great aunts, great uncles/ . . . This is what came out of all that pain." Then, to marry Mississippi's grim history with gangsta rap payback, Banner's spiel boiled over into a hail of gunfire: "Fuck you suck a dick die bitch!" he concludes. Nearly a century in the making, here it was: the crunk blues.

"The blues is the way people express the pain," Banner says. "That's what crunk music is to me. It's just that loud 'Fuck!' when you slam your hand in the door. Or that 'God please help us!'—that release of energy. Even though [crunk] is party music, you're only partying to get away from the pain. So if I can have a song talking about busting a motherfucker up, just so you don't have to, I take that responsibility wholeheartedly. I know Tupac kept me from doing a lot of things to a lot of people."

But in one way, Banner's concerns were far more middle class than any pain his Mississippi forebears experienced: His songs addressed the tension between the spiritual and the material, between art and commerce. In the music, it manifested as a tango between the organic and synthetic; in the lyrics, it was a tug-of-war between impulses to critique hip-hop's pathologies and engage in them. Banner intermingled these competing impulses to generate tension, and also perhaps in the hope that he wouldn't have to choose between them.

It was most notable on "Cadillacs on 22s," a song driven by the 808's electro beats and an earthy, Southern-rock acoustic-guitar strum. On the surface, it was yet another Southern rap track that celebrates cars and rims; but deeper, it was a prayer to God that freely melded the sacred and the profane—"Cadillacs on 22s, I ain't did nothing in my life but stay true/Pimp my voice and mack these beats, and pray to the Lord for these Mississippi streets." Banner cried out for guidance away from (or else permission to partake in) all the material distractions that tempt him: "God I know that we pimp, God I know that we wrong, God I know I should talk about more in all of my songs/I know these kids are listening, I know I'm here for a mission, but it's so hard to get 'em when twenty-two rims are glistening."

Mississippi's title track similarly blended acoustic guitar with drum-machine beats. Describing his home state, Banner offered a series of endings to the repeated phrase, "We from a place . . . ," including: ". . . where [civil-rights leader] Medgar Evers lived and Medgar Evers died . . . where we chokin' on sticky green to get high," and ". . . where your grandmama still showin' you love, and we still eatin' chicken in the club." The chorus flaunted ghetto fabulousness and centuries-old existential pain: "We from a place: Where them boys still pimpin' them hoes . . . where Cadillacs still riding on Vogues . . . and my soul still don't feel free, where a flag means more than me."

Released just seven months after *Mississippi: The Album*, its sequel *MTA2: Baptized in Dirty Water* drew mostly from the same recordings Banner had made prior to signing with SRC. Though arguably second-string material, *MTA2* was in most ways comparable to its predecessor—and completely compatible in style. There was, perhaps, a more explicit embrace of Bible-belt religious imagery—though, as the album title suggests, a similar impulse to juxtapose the exalted with the lowly. "Eternal," "My Lord," "We Ride Them Caddies," and "The Christmas Song" all involved pleas to God, resistance to the devil, and struggles to maintain spirituality surrounded by bleak reality.

In the spoken-title track, Banner explained the album's name. "Seeing all the people that was doing real fucked up shit in the hood, most of the people are really good people at heart . . . but they were just put in a situation where they had to survive. Baptized means a full change, but just imagine . . . if you were getting baptized in dirty water. It don't really matter what your intent was, if everything around you is negative you gonna become a product of that. And that's basically what happened to most of my niggas—baptized in dirty water."

Banner packaged five random copies of *MTA2* with tokens that could be redeemed for ten-thousand-dollar college scholarships—a remarkable gesture compared to a similar marketing scheme offered around the same time by 50 Cent's G-Unit, which promised winners a twelve-thousand-dollar diamond-encrusted medallion. But despite promised payoffs to buyers, Banner's growing stature as a hip-hop producer, and widespread respect for Banner as an artist and activist, neither of his first two records sold anywhere near what SRC had hoped. Long after their release, neither had even sold the five hundred thousand copies to make them gold records—a baseline considered only a modest success by major-label standards (*Mississippi: The Album* later went gold).

Two years later, after scoring a major production success with T.I.'s hit "Rubber Band Man" and developing a reputation for his sweaty, Confederate flag-burning live show, Banner returned with a third album, *Certified*. Determined to shake the rep that increasingly saddled him—as more Southern-rap spokesman than an actual hit-making star—Banner took special care to make *Certified* a commercial success: He copied the Ying Yang Twins' successful whispered rap hit "Wait" by enlisting their producer Mr. Collipark and recording a remarkably similar song, "Play." He embraced sex and love as never before with "Fucking" and "Thinking of You." He enlisted R&B hit makers Jagged Edge and producer Jazze Pha to craft slicker, more melodic tracks. And he courted fans outside his base through his West Coast tribute, "Westside," and his use of rock music.

But none of *Certified*'s overtures made much difference—the record's sales were comparable to Banner's first two. *Certified* stuck to Banner's familiar juxtapositions—blending rock guitars with 808 beats; seeking salvation from the Lord while deep into thug life. Banner's interest in rock music seems more the result of growing up middle class and suburban—raised on MTV—than of any connection between rock and Mississippi blues riffing.

But the blues is there, both consciously—in *Certified*'s closer "Crossroads"—and unconsciously, in the existential pain at the base of Banner's music.

"You can't help but live the blues in Mississippi," Banner says. "Like how people say hip-hop is a lifestyle, the blues is the only common ground that all people have. No matter how much power and influence you have, somebody close to you is going to die. So everybody can say that they have some form of pain, or some form of blues."

HOLLERS FROM THE COTTON FIELDS

Though ironic, it's also somehow appropriate that the idea of introducing notions of "country"—that is, rural, rustic, unsophisticated, Southern—into hip-hop's identity politics emerged from Atlanta, the big city whose modern-day civic life has less connection with Southern heritage than just about anyplace in the region. Moreover, it came out of the Atlanta Art Institute in the upscale Buckhead district, and from the imagination of Todd Thomas—aka Speech of the group Arrested Development—who grew up mostly in Wisconsin. Appropriate, because, after all, the very idea of being country is, in part, an artifice—an affectation informed by received notions of what it means to be rural and Southern.

To be fair, Speech's concept of a group enmeshed in black Southernness was partly informed by real experiences he had spending summers with his grandmother in rural Tennessee. But it's reasonable to attribute Arrested Development's lack of staying power—its massive initial success, almost as a novelty, then its quick retreat from the mainstream—to its self-conscious artsiness. It didn't ring true to the experience of most real Southern blacks, much less to African Americans elsewhere.

Country hip-hop—that is, not just Southern, but Southern and rural—did not die with Arrested Development, though it has never recaptured the mainstream success of A.D.'s 1992 debut. OutKast flirted with country flavors on its 1998 hit "Rosa Parks," but neither OutKast nor the larger Dungeon Family—a group of Atlanta city kids—ever made being country a central part of its identity. Still, starting around 2000, three otherwise unrelated acts emerged in the shadow of the Dungeon to present a more authentic expression of the rural South—more authentic if only because they actually came from the country.

One couldn't find too many places more emblematic of the Old South and its agricultural plantation society—a place still living, to a large extent, in a postbellum world—than south Georgia and its central city, Albany. This was the real "way down South in the land of cotton" that Daniel Decatur Emmett (an Ohioan) imagined in conjuring his famous minstrel-show song "Dixie." In the prosperous years before the Civil War, cotton from the entire region poured into Albany, where it was loaded onto steamboats and shipped to textile mills in the Northern states and Europe.

In his famous 1903 work, *The Souls of Black Folk*, W.E.B. DuBois describes the land and people of Albany and the surrounding Dougherty County—the heart of south Georgia's Black Belt, what they once called "the Egypt of the Confederacy." "By 1860 there had risen in West Dougherty perhaps the richest slave kingdom the modern world ever knew," DuBois wrote. "A hundred and fifty barons commanded the labor of nearly six thousand Negroes, held sway over farms with ninety thousand acres of tilled land, valued even in times of cheap soil at three millions of dollars."

During Reconstruction, things improved for the freed slaves that made up a majority of the population around Albany, but that was short-lived. By the early twentieth century Jim Crow was firmly entrenched and the land—once boasting some of the country's richest soil—began paying the price for years of over-cultivation. The cost of cotton fell, the yield was down, and most blacks discovered they had traded slavery for other forms of servitude: the permanent debt of tenant farming or the bondage of a prison term often justified only by the state's need for inexpensive laborers.

New crops like pecans and peanuts helped defray the loss from King Cotton's demise, and later, military bases attracted people to the area. Ray Charles was born there, but he left for Florida as a child. And in 1961, Albany became an early battleground in the struggle to desegregate the South—a lost battle that taught Martin Luther King Jr. valuable lessons when he moved on to Birmingham and other cities. Eventually, the tides of change caught up with Albany, but neither desegregation nor anything else has made Albany more than an impoverished outpost of Southern black life.

Albany is the kind of place William Faulkner had in mind when he wrote, "In the South, the past is not dead. It isn't even past." Take, for example, the Albany neighborhood known as the Field. It's called the Field because its development is relatively sparse, but there's also an implication that its residents live on the very same cotton fields where their slave forebears once worked. And there's a larger sense that Albany's black community is itself the modern-day manifestation of the "field slave"—more rural and less polished than the "house slaves" whose spiritual descendants might be found in a place like Atlanta.

In this context, the decision of Albany rappers Shawn Johnson (Shawn Jay) and Darion Crawford (Smoke) to name themselves Field Mob is rich in meaning. Applied to hip-hop, as Shawn and Smoke have suggested, the idea of the field slave can refer to the entire South, as the region given less respect, possessing fewer resources, and having a harder struggle. In Field Mob, hip-hop found its first major-label act from the Black Belt's small-town South.

Shawn and Smoke, who initially rapped under the names Kalage and Boondox Blax, respectively, came together in the late '90s after battling each other in the school yard. They signed with a local label called Southern House and put out a single called "Hey Shawty." A second track earned the attention of MCA Records, which signed Field Mob as the label's first Southern rap act. The song was "Project Dreamz," which became the lead-off single to the group's 2000 debut, *613: Ashy to Classy*.

If for no other reason, the refrain in "Project Dreamz" refrain—"If you ever been broke, put your hands up"—made the song instantly remarkable, a welcome break at the height of the bling-bling era. It was an anthem, delivered without shame, for which far more of hip-hop's core audience—Southern or otherwise—could relate, from the opening line ("Rent thirty days late, gotta be gone by Saturday") to the mic-passing reminiscences at the end:

> *(Boondox): Now put your hands up if your broke folks weren't able,*
> *you ate free lunch and you never had cable*
> *(Kalage): Put ya hands up, if you feel my hurt, have you ever bathed*
> *with soap the size of a Cert?*
> *(Boondox): Don't disguise dirt did, 'cause we all know rocks is the*
> *real reason furniture goes to the pawnshop*
> *(Kalage): 'Cause ya crackhead cuz smokin' the car antennas*
> *(Boondox): Understand see . . .*
> *(Kalage): There's a junkie in every family.*
> *(Boondox): Them my hand-me-down tight pants, lookin' slim in 'em,*
> *if they too big . . .*
> *(Kalage): What you do?*
> *(Boondox): Put a hem in 'em.*
> *(Kalage): 'Member talkin' over the loud sounds when the wind*
> *blows, 'cause the trash bag's replacin' your car window?*

But the chorus in "Project Dreamz" was also a classic slice of good ol' American aspiration: "I'ma have me a big nice Caddy, house on the hill for my ma and my pappy/Live life happy, hair still nappy, makin' legal money, no Feds tryin'a trap me." Its sentiment was unselfconsciously provincial—alien to city slickers either too jaded to hope for anything at all, or else already well familiar with the reality of "mo' money mo' problems." A courageous, terrific track, "Project Dreamz" earned significant airplay regionally, but only enough to reach number ninety-one on the national R&B/hip-hop chart.

While "Project Dreamz" suggested what real "country rap" could be—honest, unguarded, full of homespun humor—*Ashy to Classy* also shucked plenty of self-conscious cornpone, from Kalage's overstated, minstrel-like delivery, to lines describing home as a place "where watermelon, pecans and peaches be growin' at," to the tortured wail of the backwoods cuckold: "I *luv'ded* you!" Like the blues, Field Mob's debut included an uncommonly large amount of rapping about being cheated on (in hard-core hip-hop, it's generally the rapper who's doing the cheating).

As David Banner would later do, Field Mob also introduced the idea of the South as the secret home to all American blacks—a place from where Northerners and Westerners fled but can never truly escape. On the spoken opening track, Boondox says, "People be scared to be country . . . they ashamed of it. We ain't scared, we fittin' to bring it out there as our style. . . . The South is where everything originated from. The slaves came from the South and migrated to the North. . . . So we tryin' to let everyone know, Hey, don't forget where you from. The South created the West Coast and the East Coast."

Field Mob returned in 2002 with *From Tha Roota to Tha Toota*, a second album that reprised many of *Ashy to Classy*'s themes, but with A-list production from Jazze Pha and OutKast's ET3 team to help bump up sales from the debut's very modest 140,000 copies sold. The strategy worked with "Sick of Being Lonely," a mellow R&B-driven Jazze Pha track that reached into the top twenty on the *Billboard* pop chart, and up to number five on the rap chart. Perhaps by design, there wasn't much to distinguish "Lonely" as country rap aside from the pig in the song's video and occasional lines—like one describing a lady as looking "mo' gooder than a plate of neck bones."

Elsewhere, though, the country molasses was poured on thick. The album title was a bit of local color describing the parts of the pig available for consumption by rural black Southerners: everything, that is, from the tail to the snout. Field Mob revisited the sad-sack Southern characters that are pathetically poor, hopelessly uncouth, unlucky in love, and ultimately devoted to church (*Toota*'s second single, "All I Know," is a gospel rap featuring Cee-Lo). In "K.A.N.," Shawn Jay raps, "I'm a kuntry ass nigga, Shawn show no shame/Barefoot on your block selling rock cocaine/Georgia boy from the South, spit when I talk/Smack when I eat, from the Field, pimp when I walk."

As with Field Mob's debut, *Toota* contained moments of surprising depth and emotion. "Nothing 2 Lose," an ET3 track featuring Sleepy Brown vocals and a Slimm Calhoun verse, found the rappers rhyming in the guise of slave. While Sleepy crooned "I want to be free!" Curtis Mayfield–style, Shawn rapped, "Master say being born colored was the first disease/And we the worst to breed, worse than fleas/As long as I work for he, I work for free/ . . . If it's pride or die I'm choosin' respect, I saw my daddy hung dead with a noose on his neck/ . . . But one day, things gon' change for better, Lord knows it can't rain forever/That's what I told my momma/Two days later master sold my momma."

"It's Hell" cut even closer to the bone. It began, like "Project Dreamz," by giving struggles a comedic airing: "Why we had a house and couldn't keep it?/Why we evicted, why we get more pink slips than Victoria's Secret?/ . . . Why I ain't graduate?/Why through high school I didn't have a date?/Why I had to masturbate?" But as Kalage and Boondox dug deeper into their characters' plight, layers of regret, and confusion turned the song into the dark sequel to "Project Dreamz"—the tale of how dreams get smothered.

One verse horrifically detailed the emotional disorientation of domestic violence: "He put his hands on my momma again/Family ties, this is where the drama begins/Talkin' 'bout my momma on the floor, 'Bitch this' and 'Bitch that'/Locked in my room prayin' to God, 'Please make him get back.'" Kalage indicts hip-hop itself—specifically a seminal Southern artist— as contributing to the problem: "Eleven years old, and I don't need to be seein' this shit/But in my tape deck, Eightball talkin' about beatin' a bitch/It got me confused, but damn, you shouldn't pop her that hard/And when them folks come, her stupid ass be droppin' the charge."

Surrounded by humor, the group's social commentary got overlooked. But subversiveness was part of the plan. "Don't muthafuckin' approach me and say, 'Y'all funny,'" Shawn told *XXL*. "Nah, my nigga, I'm *smarter* than yo' ass. I'm tightrope walkin', doin' somethin' that ain't many people doin'. . . . Niggas ain't clowns. If you really listenin' to shit we sayin', we givin' it to niggas straight up and they sleepin' on it."

But bold material was the least of Field Mob's problems. A few months before the album's release, Smoke (Boondox) got hit with a cocaine possession charge. Then, before *Toota* could catch on, Universal Music folded MCA Records into Geffen, which effectively put Field Mob in limbo. Despite a hit single, sales of *Toota* stalled before they even reached gold. While Smoke signed a solo deal with Trick Daddy's Miami-based Dunk Rider label, Shawn Jay faced his own legal troubles—including a charge leveled by his baby's mother for kidnapping the infant daughter he'd raised since birth (charges were later dropped and Shawn got joint custody).

When it looked like Geffen was not anxious to make another Field Mob record, Shawn considered quitting rap entirely. Before he did, though, fellow Georgia rapper Ludacris, a fan and friend of the group, offered Field Mob a deal with his Disturbing Tha Peace label. DTP worked out a joint venture with Geffen and started putting together a third Field Mob album, *Light Poles and Pine Trees*, which arrived in the summer of 2006 and quickly rose into the top ten based on their hit single, "So What," featuring Atlanta vocalist Ciara. Ludacris also featured Smoke and Shawn Jay on his 2005 compilation *Ludacris Presents Disturbing Tha Peace*, which featured a Smoke solo track and a Field Mob collaboration with Luda.

The latter, a Peach State anthem called "Georgia," landed the group back in the Top 40. Punctuated by a sample of Jamie Foxx impersonating Ray Charles, Ludacris crafted wordplays about shooting intruders in their "Georgia Dome" with his "Georgia Tech." Smoke and Shawn, meanwhile, colored the landscape with country cooking ("I'm from the home of the neck bones, black eyed peas, turnip and collard greens/We the children on the corn dirtier than Bob Marley's pee pee"), culture ("Where Gladys Knight's got the Midnight Train/The birthplace of Martin Luther King"), and club hopping ("Now you might come for vacation, leave on probation/Home of the strip club, known for the thick gulz"). But by the end, Shawn had invoked the past that still isn't past in his home state: "When you see them Confederate flags you know what it is, your folks picked cotton here that's why we call it the Field."

PORTRAIT OF A WHITE BOY

If the fields of Albany were where the descendants of slaves faced the hardships of freedom, then the cotton-mill town of LaGrange—130 miles northwest, near the Alabama line—was a place where the sons of former slave owners inherited handsome antebellum mansions and the privilege to build the South into what it is today. LaGrange was among Georgia's wealthiest communities before the Civil War, and though the city suffered extensively at the hands of Union troops, it bounced back in the late nineteenth century as a center for cotton manufacturing.

Among LaGrange's most prominent families are the Callaways. In the 1890s, Fuller Earle Callaway built a textile empire from scratch, and his son Cason Jewell Callaway expanded the family holdings in the 1920s and '30s. After retiring, Cason opened a large tract of his family's real estate to the public as Callaway Gardens, a resort and nature preserve that is today one of Middle Georgia's biggest tourist attractions.

By the early '50s, with Cason's health in decline, his son Howard "Bo" Callaway took a lead role in developing the Gardens. Bo, however, had a passion for politics and traded on his family name to win a seat in the U.S. House of Representatives in 1964. This was no ordinary election, however, but the start of a political revolution. Breaking from a century of anti-Republican feeling (it was, after all, the party of Abe Lincoln), Callaway—disenchanted with the leftward swing of Northern Democrats—ran for Congress as a Republican, and became the first Republican congressman from Georgia since Reconstruction. Two years later, Callaway ran for governor and, despite winning the most votes in the general election, lost to segregationist Democrat Lester Maddox through a technicality. But the tide had turned; within a generation, the entire white South would be reliably Republican—so essential to the party, in fact, that it would largely set party policy and leadership.

LaGrange, then, could be called ground zero of Southern Republicanism, the quintessential white-majority small town that remade itself from being a center of slave-owner wealth in the nineteenth century to become the beating heart of today's political conservatism. But it's not all country clubs and mega-churches. There's also a sizable population of lower-middle-class whites and a large minority of blacks in the area. And this is the world in which Andy Mathis—better known as the rapper Bubba Sparxxx—grew up.

The son of a bus driver and grocery clerk, Bubba was born in LaGrange and raised in a small house on a dead-end road outside of town. Football was his main passion—he made All-Region as a linebacker in high school—but when it didn't work out for him to play in college, he turned his focus to rapping. He'd been a fan since he was a kid—a black neighbor turned him on to tapes he was getting from New York—and when 2 Live Crew corrupted the South, the preteen Mathis was there to take it in. After discovering West Coast gangsta rap, Bubba discovered the sound that would impact him most: the Georgia hip-hop of OutKast and the Dungeon Family.

Still, Bubba's career choice was unusual for a white linebacker from Middle Georgia. As he told *XXL*, "To tell people I was gonna be a rapper, I might as well have been telling them I was gonna be an astronaut."

After graduating in '96 and trying community college, Bubba went to stay with his former Troop Valley High teammate Steven Herndon in Athens, where Herndon was now playing football at the University of Georgia (Herndon would go on to an NFL career with the Atlanta Falcons, among other teams). In Athens, Bubba found a manager who introduced him to So So Def staff producer Shannon Houchins. Houchins paired Bubba with another rapper in a group called One Card Shi, but when those demos didn't yield much excitement, Houchins started working on Bubba solo tracks. In 1999, these recordings yielded an independent release, *Dark Days, Bright Nights*, which got some regional airplay and sold about 1,500 copies. Word of the record spread to Fred Durst, the Limp Bizkit leader who was starting to do A&R work for his band's label, Interscope. Durst brought Bubba to the attention of Interscope head Jimmy Iovine, who in 2000 gave Bubba a record deal.

The appearance of a rapper whose identity rested largely on being white and Southern raised eyebrows, given long-held assumptions that "white South" and "hip-hop culture" were incompatible. But Bubba Sparxxx's 2001 debut was entirely inevitable, given hip-hop's ever-expanding cultural umbrella, given the exploding popularity of Southern hip-hop, and given the rise of hip-hop's white superstar, Eminem.

In fact, Bubba's "hick-hop" shtick was not actually a new idea. Beginning in 1998, Detroit-based Kid Rock found success marrying rap music with a white-trash aesthetic and Southern-rock flavor. The same year, House of Pain's "Irish" rapper, the L.A.-based Everlast, returned as an acoustic guitar–strumming rapper, rhyming about the struggles of the white poor on his hit album *Whitey Ford Sings the Blues*. And the following year, Sony Music scored moderate success with *Southern Discomfort*, an album by a white rap/rock duo from Georgia called Rehab. Led by Brooks Buford, a rapper/singer who'd later find semi-fame as host of MTV's *Trailer Fabulous* reality show, Rehab landed a hit on modern-rock radio— the format that embraced white rappers most enthusiastically. Though Rehab's music wasn't particularly Southern, its primary theme of substance abuse (the duo met during a stint in rehab) played on stereotypes of the rural South as the land of whiskey binges and crystal meth labs.

Another Georgia-based pale-skin rap act, Po' White Trash & the Trailer Park Symphony, put out an independent album—featuring production from Organized Noize and Lil Jon—the same month that Bubba Sparxxx's debut arrived. But Bubba's clearest precursor came from Nashville, where as far back as 1998 a rapper named Haystak was part of the city's small hip-hop scene.

Like Bubba—and unlike the rock hybrids of Kid Rock, Everlast, or Rehab—Haystak was straight hip-hop. He also shared with Bubba the body build of a redneck raised on football and fried food, and an image focused on being a Southern white boy. Haystak named his 2000 album *Car Fulla White Boys*, and his 2002 breakthrough, *The Natural*, featured a song called "White

Boy": "I'm that white boy, cracker . . . *huero*, damned old evil blue-eyed devil, paleface, and I'm proud to be that dude, make some more shit to mean 'white boy,' I'll be that too." By 2004, the idea of a white-trash rapper was so commonplace that Haystak created another track, on his *Portrait of a White Boy* album, called "First White Boy": "I was the first white boy claiming white boy/When these white boys wasn't white boys, I was a white boy."

While not completely novel, Bubba Sparxxx's arrival was still significant. Here was the complete package: A real Southern white boy, making straight hip-hop, and signed to a major label with the backing of hip-hop's biggest producers. In fact, Bubba's model wasn't Haystack, it was Eminem. Interscope's Iovine, after all, had been the record executive behind Marshall Mathers' rise, and it was clear the goal for Bubba was to become the Southern Eminem.

Iovine modeled Bubba's development plan on Eminem's: Like Slim Shady, who gained a shield of credibility by coming up as a protégé of Dr. Dre, Bubba needed to pair with his own super-producer. Bubba was anxious to work with Organized Noize, who'd been his local heroes for years. Iovine, however, had given the Atlanta producers a deal already with their short-lived Organized Noize Records, and it had yielded little fruit. He wanted someone at the peak of his powers. He turned to Virginia studio wizard Timbaland, who signed Bubba up as the first artist on his newly formed, Interscope-affiliated imprint, Beat Club Records.

Bubba also got his wish to work with Organized Noize on two tracks, while Timbaland provided seven. They added those nine to seven tracks drawn from the original independent version of *Dark Days, Bright Nights* (mostly produced by Houchins), plus two more new ones, and in September of 2001, Bubba Sparxxx made his national debut with a revamped *Dark Days*. The record debuted at number three.

The record's first single, "Ugly," found immediate success as a sort of sequel to a Timbaland-produced top-ten hit from earlier in the year, Missy Elliott's "Get Ur Freak On." Like Missy's smash, "Ugly" featured a tightly wound, Far East–sounding instrumental loop paired with a boot-slapping beat (to further draw the connection, "Ugly" also contained a sample from "Get Ur Freak On"). While the music signified Timbaland, the lyrics set out to define Bubba's unique persona. He explained his "Bubba talk" ("I call my girlfriends Bettys and my shits Grumpies") and his rowdy redneck pride ("go 'head throw them 'bows, fuck it, break a bottle/Let's be honest, none of us will ever date a model"), and embraced of the term "New South" as a code for his (a Southern white guy's) embrace of hip-hop: "This that New South, take a picture of me/'Cuz I'm a fuckin' legend and this is getting ugly."

To drive the point home, Bubba had "New South" tattooed up his forearms. As he told the Allhiphop.com Web site, "Basically the New South is just to dispel all of the negative stereotypes associated with the Old South, with the understanding that those stereotypes still exist. That can refer to rural backwardness, race relations, poor education, you know just everything, just trying to show that the South still has a long way to go in all those departments, but we've also come a long way."

While the odd mix of ultramodern beats and plainspoken rhymes on "Ugly" offered something fresh, its video played into redneck clichés: scary-looking hillbillies, a woman shaving her mustache, kids racing tractors, boys in overalls riding hogs in a muddy pen. Other tracks indulged in similar country hokiness—farm animal sounds, backwoods skits—that came across as being forced.

But *Dark Days* also offered some New South reconstruction: A vision of black and white getting together. On the Organized Noize–produced "All the Same," Sleepy Brown sings while Bubba interjects: "A fifth of Beam when you celebrate (that's white things)/ . . . Sipping Hen, swervin' wood grain (that's black things)/But to me it's just all the same (all the same)." And on the title track, Bubba takes his plea for racial harmony further: "I also get praise from the other side of the tracks/You the dark days part of town where intentionally they hide the blacks/Ain't got no reply to that, except I'm sorry if I'm to blame/I try like hell to soothe your soul by planting facts inside your brain/I never once lied to gain the acceptance of not one black dude/It's just Bubba that country fucker, smoking schwag, and eating snack foods."

Dark Days went gold, which was respectable but something of a disappointment after all the Eminem comparisons. While promoting the album, Bubba had a chance to reflect on just how much a redneck caricature he wanted his image to be. So when Bubba and Tim reconvened in Miami to make a follow-up, they set two goals: first, to make a record that would push Bubba into platinum sales, and second, to craft a richer representation of what it means to be a white Southern hip-hop artist.

"I feel like people were interested and wanted to know more about what Bubba Sparxxx was about," Bubba told the hip-hop Web site BallerStatus.net. "And I'm thinking the first time I didn't really do a good job of telling my story—because, you know, it really is an interesting story. I really have experienced a lot of things in my life that are unique, especially as far as scenery goes to what most hip-hop artists experience. Even though it may be the same pain and same struggle. My struggle was kinda unique in detail because I did grown up in a rural area, as compared to their stories. So we just went back and focused on telling that story this time."

Deliverance threatens to commit the same error as its predecessor. Its title refers to the 1972 cult film of the same name—a movie that elevated gross caricatures of rural Southerners (as antisocial deviants and worse) into the stuff of horror flicks. But any kinship the record might have shared with the movie is quickly dispelled. In fact, the title seems ironic—it suggest a "deliverance" from the stereotypes of *Deliverance*—or else simply literal: This was Bubba's artistic arrival and (hoped for) commercial salvation.

That the record succeeds in reconciling hip-hop and Southern white experience is a credit not only to Bubba's lyrics but also to Timbaland's music. Where *Dark Days* relied mainly on Tim's signature kitchen-sink sound, for *Deliverance* the producer stepped out of his comfort zone to craft music uniquely suited to Bubba. From the dueling harmonica lines of "Jimmy Mathis" to the wailing fiddle and sampled yodel-sing of "Comin' Around," to the bluegrass banjo of "She Tried," the music succeeds in fusing traditional Southern (and often white) music with Tim's futuristic hip-hop bump. It made perfect sense: Bubba's very existence suggested at least some working-class Southern whites were finding a connection to hip-hop they might have once had to country music.

Where *Dark Days* signified its countryness through lyrics and skits, *Deliverance* marked its Southernness through music. That gave Bubba space to imbue his lyrics with further depth of emotion and storytelling. There's room for family pride, regret, an earnest yearning to succeed, and above all, a journey toward self-discovery. "I've been traveling for some time," Tim sings on the title track's chorus, ". . . cause I gotta find a way, to find my way." (The song's video, incidentally, did not send up the movie *Deliverance*, but rather a more recent film stereotype: *O Brother, Where Art Thou?*)

A central track thematically is "Nowhere," which takes the form of a journey through dark backwoods, with a wise old voice instructing, "You must travel, a long, desolate road/This road that you shall travel, will seem like nowhere/That nowhere will turn into somewhere/Keep your head up, Bubba." Bubba then recounts the struggles of growing up poor and draws comparisons between the experiences of the black and white underclass: "Let these cats amuse you with comical depictions/But where I'm from being broke is no honorable affliction/Love some Jimmy Carter, but we never even voted/But slum is still slum, so you best believe we toted."

After a chorus noting, "I know what it's like to be nowhere," Bubba's final verse turns toward his deliverance. "It all comes down to this, one last chance to advance," he rhymes, "beyond the second round of the big dance/All my plans of being viewed as something special, more than just the other one, will vanish in the vapors of the plague the South has suffered from." He's struggling to define himself as more than "the other one"—the other white rapper, besides Eminem—and break from the Southern stereotypes that limit him.

While Timbaland largely defines the sound of *Deliverance*, Organized Noize play a significant secondary role on four tracks. Bubba's increasing ties to the producers made him an official Dungeon Family member, a banner (or tattoo, as the case may be) he wore with pride. Organized's tracks pushed Bubba toward OutKast's eclectic-funk territory on the anthemic "New South" and "Like It or Not," with its Afropop horns and slick Sleepy Brown vocals. And with the superfast, power-chord-driven "Back in the Mud," Rico Wade crafted a single that provided *Deliverance*'s statement of purpose: "Bubba K, hey, what's that they say?/Hick-hop, redneck, that's a safe place/Say what makes you comfortable with me cuz I like it here/How about a rural dwelling urban music pioneer?/ . . . Now I'm on the brink of something truly inconceivable/Bubba's international, but still I kept it regional."

Despite critical acclaim, *Deliverance* failed to register in the highly stratified world of commercial radio and fell short of even gold sales this time. Disappointed, Bubba parted ways with Interscope, and his close collaboration with Timbaland, while not ended entirely, loosened considerably. "I can honestly say me and Tim put everything we had into that record," Bubba told *XXL*. "I can't even listen to it. I mean, I'm not bitter, but it does sting a little bit. No matter what nobody says about that album . . . it didn't succeed."

Solidifying his Dungeon ties, Bubba found a new home at Purple Ribbon, Big Boi's Virgin-affiliated label. With his third effort, 2006's optimistically titled *The Charm*, Bubba tried a new road to stardom by forsaking much of the overt regionalism and racial-identity politics. Instead, Bubba played it straight Dirty South—his single, "Ms. New Booty," wallowed in the guilty pleasures of a Mr. Collipark beat and Ying Yang Twins backup—and scored his first-ever top-ten pop hit. Hick-hop, meanwhile, has been put up on cinderblocks in the backyard.

OUTKAST'S NAPPY CHILDREN

Bubba Sparxxx and Field Mob emerged directly out of the Dungeon Family's long shadow—by virtue of being Georgians, and later by working with Organized Noize. But the rise of Kentucky sextet Nappy Roots in 2002 suggests that OutKast's take on Southern hip-hop influenced rappers beyond state lines and found a home on Southern college campuses. Not surprising, since OutKast had, early on, sought audiences on campus: Freaknik, Atlanta's black college spring break, was an important avenue for getting the word out, and long after the group had a national audience, OutKast commonly featured step dancing—that black fraternity ritual—as part of its stage act.

Like Bubba and Field Mob, Nappy Roots came from outside the South's urban centers—the small city of Bowling Green, Kentucky. But Nappy Roots was hardly country. Bowling Green was, in fact, the home of Western Kentucky University, a major regional college with about eighteen thousand students. And four of the group's six members had come to Bowling Green from Louisville, one of the South's biggest cities (and, right across the Ohio River from Indiana, just barely in the South). Still, the group capitalized on Kentucky being uncharted hip-hop territory to craft an image as country as anything hip-hop had seen. Like Arrested Development, they were a large group that echoed the extended family units of Southern black life, and like A.D., they were upwardly mobile collegians whose depiction of the South was as much affectation as true identity.

Though both born and raised in Louisville, Skinny DeVille (William Hughes) and Ron Clutch (Ronald Wilson) didn't meet until they came to Bowling Green in 1993 to attend WKU. Big V (Vito Tisdale) was a Bowling Green local who'd left town to play football at Eastern Kentucky University, but returned home after an injury and hooked up with Skinny and Ron around 1995. Around the same time, Fish Scales (Melvin Adams)—a 6'6" All-American power forward from Milledgeville, Georgia, on scholarship to WKU—also fell in with the crew. The name Nappy Roots came up one day when Skinny commented on Clutch's hair.

R. Prophet (Kenneth Anthony) came to Bowling Green in 1996. Though born in Oakland, when he was eight his family moved to Louisville—where his dad had grown up—in search of "a better place to raise family," he says. He enrolled in Louisville's performing arts high school to study theater, and preferred his hip-hop hard-core—either Bay Area acts like Too Short and E-40 or Texans like the Geto Boys and UGK. He wanted to rap, but was told, "You can't be no rapper, you in Kentucky."

At college, Prophet started getting into OutKast and Goodie Mob, and through WKU's Louisville clique, he met the guys from Nappy Roots. After hearing him freestyle on the college radio station, Skinny invited Prophet to join. B. Stille (Brian Scott) started at WKU the next year and became the group's sixth member. Stille was also from Louisville, and though he was a few years younger than the rest, he was the group's most seasoned member—he'd been MCing at talent shows since he was eleven.

Nappy Roots quickly became Bowling Green's biggest rap group—members had connections to the school's various cliques: basketball fans, the

Louisville crowd, Bowling Green locals. Besides, there wasn't much competition. By 1997, some of the group's older members had graduated. They
pooled their money together from savings and family loans and bought a
house. On one side they built a record store, and on the other a recording
studio. They called it ET's Music (Everything's Tight) and, from that base,
they began selling mix tapes and T-shirts. "We were trying to be like Master
P, we seen him doing it independently," Prophet says.

Forming their own label, Deep Rooted Records, the Nappy Roots put out
a debut CD in early 1998, called *Country Fried Cess*. It was a low-budget
collective effort; friends chipped in to do the photos, graphics, and videos.
At the end of the school year, the group pressed up hundreds of copies of
the CD and got them into the hands of departing students any way they
could—selling them at deep discounts, giving them away, whatever. The
word spread, and by July they got a call from Atlantic Records, which signed
Nappy Roots to a national deal.

But the major label debut didn't arrive for more than three years. The
group recorded, but the label wasn't happy with what they were producing.
"They was on more of a stereotypical view of folks from Kentucky," Clutch
told *Rolling Stone*. "They wanted us to . . . well, to me, it felt like buffoon-
ery. And that's not what we was about."

While waiting for Atlantic to come around, the group released a second
independent album, 1999's *No Comb, No Brush, No Fade, No Perm*. Then,
in early 2002, Atlantic finally released *Watermelon, Chicken & Gritz*. The
record's calling card was "Awnaw," a musically rich track that featured Jazze
Pha on vocals, with two interwoven hooks both evoking the South: one
rapped ("Awnaw, hell naw, boy! Y'all done up and done it") and one sung
("them country boys on the rise . . . "). The track's popular video pulled out
all the stops: Six black males with hair in varying states of nappiness, dressed
in overalls, straw hats, and cowboy Stetsons, standing amidst sprawling
fields, dilapidated shacks, and barnhouses—with the obligatory pig as a prop
(see both Field Mob and Bubba Sparxxx videos). The song peaked at number eight on the rap chart in May, which helped push *Watermelon* to number three on the R&B/hip-hop album chart, and to platinum sales.

With the benefit of their six voices, varying perspectives, and assorted
musical talents, the Nappy Roots created a dynamic, highly accessible record
well stocked with memorable tracks. By 2002, the signifiers in their lyrics—
country cooking, Cadillacs and grills, being poor, regional slang ("Awnaw,"
"Sholiz"), and local color ("Kentucky Mud")—were well established in
Southern hip-hop, but Nappy Roots managed to be more than the sum of
those parts. Indeed, the group's six-member setup and fairly nonaggressive

stance evoked old-school hip-hop's more playful, group-oriented approach. Perhaps it was a sign of Southern hip-hop's success that, by 2002, a group could be both unabashedly Southern and identifiably steeped in classic rap.

But more than any other association, *Watermelon* was reminiscent of OutKast and the Dungeon Family—stylistically, spiritually (the large, close-knit unit), and vocally. Skinny's voice bore resemblance to Andre's, while Prophet's throaty toasting recalled Cee-Lo's eccentric flow. The album's opening track, "Hustla"—with Skinny's ad libs, turntable cuts, and deep funk track—sounded like it was pulled straight from the Dungeon's playbook.

In fact, just over a year later, when Nappy Roots quickly returned with a second album, *Wooden Leather*, the lead single, "Roun' the Globe," seemed exactly the kind of world-wise and down-home sentiment Goodie Mob was shooting for with *World Party*, but largely failed to achieve. "Been all around the globe from Monday to Sunday/Y'all the same folk we see in Kentucky," the Nappy track's chorus goes. "It must mean: The whole damn world is country."

By then, Nappy Roots' massive sales and radio success had, in fact, taken the group around the world. Within a year of *Watermelon*'s breakthrough, the group had gone on a USO tour to Kuwait and Iraq, and then returned home to celebrate Nappy Roots Day, mandated by Kentucky's governor for September 16. But *Wooden Leather*, despite some excellent material—notably, the deeply soulful "Sick and Tired," featuring North Carolina crooner Anthony Hamilton—failed to have the impact its predecessor had, and Nappy Roots retreated from the mainstream scene after just two albums.

SWEET HOME CACKALACKY

By the time the Nappy Roots broke nationally, major labels were well aware of the potential for mining the South for new hip-hop. Atlanta, New Orleans, Houston, and Miami were well covered by smaller labels and production companies that snatched up new talent and fed the most promising acts up to the majors—for a price. So enterprising major-label A&R reps looked to pan for gold in the few places that had not yet been scoured. By the end of 2002, Universal, MCA, and Jive had released debuts by artists from three Southern states that had not yet made an impact on the national rap scene: Alabama, South Carolina, and North Carolina. Of the three, however, only Jive's Tarheel discovery—Petey Pablo—became a star. (Pablo was not actually the first North Carolina rap act with a major release; Raleigh trio Yaggfu

Front put out *Action Packed Adventure* in 1994 on Mercury Records to lit-tle mainstream notice.)

The relative lack of success majors had in breaking acts unaffiliated with the South's grassroots labels and personalities suggested the tremendous power established indies—whether Houston's Rap-A-Lot or Atlanta's Big Oomp—had to make or break new acts.

When MCA released *Pain*, the 2002 debut album by Charleston, South Carolina, rapper Infinity tha Ghetto Child, it seemed to come out of nowhere—and very promptly retreated back into obscurity. Though an early independent single called "Carolina Love" apparently generated some heat locally, Charleston is a fairly isolated coastal city, so Infinity's reach was lim-ited. Given his lack of grassroots popularity and MCA's difficulty scoring with Southern hip-hop (see Field Mob), the record was ignored and South Carolinians missed out on having their own rap hero any time soon.

Montgomery, Alabama, duo Dirty enjoyed a somewhat larger under-ground following when it signed with Universal in 2000. First cousins Daniel "Big Pimp" Thomas and Tavares "Mr. G Stacka the Gangsta" Web-ster had already released two albums on the local Nfinity label, and the re-gional success of the singles "Rollin' Vogues" and "Hit Da Floe" secured their place as Alabama's top rap act. Likely attracted by Dirty's stylistic kin-ship with the OutKast/Goodie Mob sound, Universal signed the duo and revamped its second album, *The Pimp and the Gangsta*, for national release. The record, though plagued with the same old pimp, gangsta, and riding clichés, had its charms—including a smooth, down-South flow and a sense of the oral tradition. "Bending Corners" even summons the spirit of Petey Wheatstraw: "Now ask yo' self: Am I the slickest pimp you eva saw?/They call me Peter Wheatstraw, the devil's son-in-law."

However, neither that record nor its follow-up, *Keep It Pimp and Gangsta*—which included guests Mannie Fresh, Pastor Troy, and R&B group Silk—registered on the hip-hop radar. Dirty returned South and hooked up with Houston's Rap-A-Lot, which has released two Dirty albums so far—including 2005's *Hood Stories*, featuring the home-state anthem "Al-abama." Meanwhile, a second Alabama act, Mobile-based solo rapper Rich Boy, was poised for a national debut in 2007.

Given the difficulty breaking acts from the South's quieter corners, Greenville, North Carolina, native Petey Pablo's sudden success in 2001 was particularly surprising. For one, eastern North Carolina hadn't produced a black rhymer since Durham's chitlin' circuit comedian Pigmeat Markham had a proto-rap novelty hit with "Here Comes the Judge" in 1968. What's more, Pablo had spent much of his young adult life in jail and had no local following. For him, breaking into rap meant leaving North Carolina.

Born Moses Barrett, Petey Pablo grew up in a middle-class household of women in Greenville, a city of about sixty thousand near North Carolina's coast. He left home at thirteen to stay with family in Baltimore, where he began getting into trouble. When he returned to North Carolina a few years later, Pablo was busted for armed robbery in Raleigh. He spent five years, from age twenty to twenty-five, behind bars. Without the distraction of criminal pursuits, Pablo turned his focus to music, something he'd been involved with growing up in church and school. When he was released in 1998, Pablo decided to pursue music full-time.

Pablo moved up to New York and, after some false starts, fell in with a crowd of New York hip-hop veterans, including Eric Sermon and Busta Rhymes. His connection to Busta led him to Bad Boy Records rapper Black Rob, who put Pablo on a 2000 remix of his hit single, "Whoa!" While hanging out with Rob, the story goes, a Jive Records A&R rep overheard Pablo rapping in a bathroom. Jive signed him, and then set him up to appear on his fellow Southerner Mystikal's late 2000 release, *Let's Get Ready.*

Around the same time, Pablo met Missy Elliott, who introduced him to her production partner Timbaland. Tim had been impressed with Pablo since hearing the "Whoa!" remix, and he further embraced the rapper as a fresh voice from his own neck of the woods (Greenville being a short drive from Virginia Beach). So Tim recruited Pablo to appear on five tracks on the second Timbaland & Magoo album, *Indecent Proposal.* While the guest spots were designed to raise the rapper's profile in anticipation of his solo debut, delays in *Indecent Proposal*'s release meant those tracks did not appear until late 2001. By that time, Jive had pulled together Pablo's first album, *Diary of a Sinner: 1st Entry,* and dropped a smash leadoff single, the Timbaland-produced "Raise Up." In little more than a year, Pablo had progressed from North Carolina novice to one of the country's most promising new artists.

Embraced almost immediately by pop and hip-hop audiences, "Raise Up" reached number one on the *Billboard* rap singles chart. The track's dramatic swells gave Pablo an attractive bed on which to lay his impassioned hook and verses. The song's anthemic quality connected with listeners— and, perhaps, so did the novelty that "Raise Up" heralded something new: North Carolina hip-hop.

After the voice of a mock broadcaster reports that Petey Pablo and Timbaland are on "a quest to redeem the title and bring North Carolina, and Virginia, to the front of the line," Pablo dives into his crunked-out chorus:

"This one's for North Carolina! C'mon and raise up/Take your shirt off, twist it 'round your head, spin it like a helicopter!" Noting that he and half of "Carolina niggas done time together," Pablo says he's "Puttin' it down for my niggas in the south side/North Carolina, South Carolina, and all my little bitty overlooked hick towns." Right off the bat, Pablo takes ownership of the slice of hip-hop geography known by a term—of uncertain origin, probably dating back several decades—as Cackalacky.

Though Timbaland only produced three of *Diary of a Sinner*'s seventeen tracks, they were the record's three singles. Neither "I" nor "I Told Y'All" replicated the chart success of "Raise Up," but they were otherwise among the album's catchiest and most adventurous tracks. They were also the songs that dealt most explicitly with Pablo's regional identity: In "I," he raps, "I'm the quicker picker-upper, crazy soda-can crusher/River, rock path, mobile home, country muthafucka/ . . . Like the smell in the pasture, I'm the Cackalacky shit"; while "I Told Ya'll" features Pablo listing North Carolina towns with the boast, "Please don't get me started, I can call 'em out till tomorrow/Carolina list alone is sixteen bars."

But there's an interesting symmetry to *Diary of a Sinner* that adds richness to Pablo's surprisingly diverse and accomplished album. The Timbaland-produced, overtly Southern material appears early on, but the record ends with a stretch of songs that are more organic, less radio-friendly, and more subtly Southern. There's the doo-wop shuffle and the bluesman's lament of "Fool For Love" and the deep soul talk-sing and religious overtones of "Test of My Faith"; plus the gospel-tinged confessions in the "Truth About Me"; the cry for salvation in "Diary of a Sinner"'; and finally revelation and redemption in "My Testimony."

Pablo's debut fulfilled the apocryphal tale told by a fictional sibling in the album's "Intro": "[My brother] used to have this book he carried around with him all the time. He used to call it a diary. . . . One day he took it to church when we went to Sunday school, and the pastor asked him, 'Boy, what's that you got in your hand?' And he said, 'This is my diary.' And the pastor told him that sinners couldn't have no diary. My brother said he was lying. And my brother said if he couldn't have a diary and he was a sinner, he would just call it a Diary of a Sinner."

Pablo had created a work immersed in African American and Southern traditions—where the Bible was not merely a prayer book or history but a steel shackle to be dragged up the hill by every man, where God and the devil battle it out in the hearts of each person, and where deliverance is always in sight but just beyond reach. Plus, *Diary of a Sinner* was a thoroughly contemporary bit of popular hip-hop fun.

If Pablo seemed poised for greatness in 2001, by the summer of 2004 there was reason to doubt he would live up to his potential. While Jive had planned to release Pablo's second album fast on the heels of the debut, chronic delays dragged the sequel—titled *Still Writing in My Diary: 2nd Entry*—on for nearly three years. And when *2nd Entry* finally arrived, its lead single traded the *esprit de Cackalack* and Timbaland's gourmet mix in "Raise Up" for strip-club luridness and Lil Jon's fast-food production. Though "Freek-A-Leek" wound up an even bigger hit than "Raise Up" (reaching into the pop top ten), it undoubtedly hurt Pablo's credibility. The song was both groundbreaking and controversial in that it featured an actual paid advertisement within the lyrics: "Now I got to give a shout out to Seagram's Gin," Pablo noted during a break. "Cause I'm drinkin' it and they payin' me for it."

Pablo's album *2nd Entry* contained glimpses of the artistry that made its predecessor notable—the Kayne West–produced "I Swear," for instance, showcased Pablo's ability to cut between raw-throated singing and breakneck rapping, and "He Spoke To Me" revisited gospel elements. But high-profile guests (including Southern notables Baby, Mannie Fresh, Bubba Sparxxx, Young Buck, and Missy Elliott) undercut the intimacy that *Diary of a Sinner* had, and forays into hard-core clichés ("Stick 'Em Up") suggested Pablo was pandering to mainstream expectations.

With Pablo breaking from Jive and reportedly signing with troubled West Coast gangsta label Death Row, it's unclear how soon Pablo will return for a third record. In the meantime, Pablo reteamed with Lil Jon on the Jon-produced number-one pop hit "Goodies," which introduced "crunk & B" diva Ciara in 2004.

BLACK COWBOYS IN NASHVILLE

Twelve years after Arrested Development's "Tennessee," and one year after Bubba Sparxxx and Timbaland's Appalachian adventure on *Deliverance*, Nashville's country-music establishment finally took notice of hip-hop. By 2004, though, Southern hip-hop was preeminent in pop music, and rappers had long since adopted country words and sounds as a key part of their music. So the arrival of a black rapper named Cowboy Troy onto the mainstream Nashville scene seemed less like an innovation for hip-hop than a sign of just how out of touch country music had become.

But Cowboy Troy's arrival was notable in one way: While hip-hop long ago adopted country elements into its vocabulary, this was the first time country music had allowed hip-hop into its world. Though it was likely more of an isolated novelty than a trend, the breakthrough was, at least, of symbolic importance.

Troy Coleman grew up in Dallas, where it was not unlikely to have had exposure to both country music and hip-hop in the '80s. In 1993, Troy, an aspiring local musician, befriended another rising star, John Rich. Rich was a member of the group Texassee, a Nashville-based country quartet of Texas transplants. Renamed Lonestar, the group became a top country act, and in the late '90s, Rich left to pursue something more adventurous.

In 1998, Rich teamed with fellow Nashville songwriter Ken "Big Kenny" Alphin to create a live showcase they called Muzik Mafia. Here, Rich and Alphin began to formulate the eclectic and inclusive sensibility that would later make them revolutionary country-music stars. Troy, who'd come to Nashville to drum up interest for his rapping country music, fell into the Muzik Mafia's mix. When Rich and Alphin's group Big & Rich released its 2004 breakthrough, *Horse of a Different Color*, they featured Troy on the track "Rollin' (The Ballad of Big & Rich)," a song that perfectly captured the group's weird, witty, and worldly perspective: "Brothers and sisters, we're here for one reason and one reason alone: to share our love of music," goes the song's opening. "I present to you: country music without prejudice."

"When the party is crunk the girls back it up/We've got the systems in the cars and the 20s on the trucks," Troy raps in his guest verse, over a country-rocking track. "Six-foot-four with a cowboy hat, I don't mess around, yo, what's up with that?/I'm Cowboy Troy, a Texas hick, and I'm rollin' with the brothas, Big & Rich!"

As Big & Rich's fortunes rose, so did Cowboy Troy's, and within a year Warner Bros. Nashville signed Troy to make a full-length of his own. Released in May 2005, *Loco Motive* reached number two on the country chart, fueled by the fiddle- and banjo-driven single, "I Play Chicken with the Train." As hip-hop, the record was barely passable—full of stiff rhymes and funk-deficient grooves. But as Nashville-centric "hick-hop," *Loco Motive* is fascinating, an odd apex to the vistas opened by the introduction of Southern regionalism to hip-hop.

PART THREE
WHAT GOES AROUND

chapter 9

BOUNCE MUSIC— FROM BUCK JUMP TO BLING-BLING

THE SPIRIT OF NEW ORLEANS

In 1997 and 1998, Master P's No Limit label put New Orleans hip-hop on the national radar in a big way—not just by dominating the city, or the South, but by becoming hip-hop's most successful label at the time. But by 1999, with P off chasing hoop dreams and in-house producers Beats By the Pound on the outs, it was clear No Limit had peaked. Right at that time— perhaps by coincidence, or because opportunity shined—a second New Orleans label began showing up on the charts.

Like No Limit, they drew roots back to the dangerous and decrepit Uptown projects. But while No Limit emerged nationally first, Cash Money had been in town longer. While Master P was building his company in California, Cash Money stayed close to the 'hood the entire time. Where No Limit represented New Orleans in the hip-hop world circa 1998, Cash Money *was* New Orleans.

Cash Money was closer to New Orleans' true hip-hop spirit, if for only one reason: The years No Limit spent in California coincided with the most crucial period in the formation of the city's indigenous hip-hop sound— bounce music. And Cash Money was the label that brought bounce music to the nation.

"P was more West Coast, but Cash Money started as a bounce label," says Beats By the Pound producer KLC, who made bounce music before helping to define No Limit's more gangsta-influenced sound. "That's why Cash Money was always more favored, they always had the top bounce artists."

If No Limit proved successful because the ghetto life it depicted looked similar in the inner cities across America, then Cash Money ultimately broke through because it offered something that fans, consciously or not, could recognize as New Orleans: the swaggering march step, the *joie de vivre*, the carnival beats meant to dance away the struggle.

BUCK JUMPIN' IN THE BIG EASY

Bounce music kicked off in the early '90s, but its roots go back to the '80s, when hip-hop first came to New Orleans. DJ crews would set up along Louisiana Parkway, in the yards of the projects, at school dances and talent shows—wherever they could get a crowd. DJs like Slick Leo—who introduced New York–style scratching and broadcasted club mixes live on the radio—and crews such as the Sugar Brown Clowns, the DJ Magicians, and the Fellas DJs (led by Shawn "Lil' Nerve" Temple, with his little brother Jerome "DJ Jubilee" Temple).

Among the earliest rap groups that locals remember was New York Incorporated, led by Big Apple native turned Big Easy transplant Denny D. In addition to featuring future No Limit rapper Mia X, the group had in its ranks Byron Thomas, a young DJ who took on the old-school rap name Mannie Fresh. About fifteen at the time, Mannie had already been DJing professionally for three years. His father was a DJ as well, and Mannie got his first pair of turntables for Christmas.

Though the Thomases didn't have much, they managed to avoid the projects and get a house downtown in the Seventh Ward—on North Miro St., just outside the French Quarter. And Mannie had the advantage of growing up with two married parents and two older sisters—so there was enough love and support around that he didn't really notice how poor they were. "You're not really paying attention to your environment if you got both of your parents there and you have a hobby," Mannie says.

Music was the diversion that kept Mannie out of trouble. Through his dad, he had access to equipment and the latest records. "When hip-hop came along I just fell in love with it, and my dad just gave me the tools for it," Mannie says. "Before New Orleans was even a hip-hop scene, I was knowing about it, because my dad was buying those records, like 'Rapper's Delight.'"

School provided another musically rich environment for Mannie. He attended Joseph S. Clark High, a school in the Tremé neighborhood that was legendary for producing musicians. Though Mannie was a few years younger, he remembers going to school with trumpeter Kermit Ruffins when Ruffins and some friends from Clark formed the Rebirth Brass Band.

"If you have a whole bunch of people around who are interested in music, things are going to happen," Mannie says of his days at Clark. "So we're sitting in band class and everybody's like, 'All right, let's come up with something that's going to be our own.' If we had a second to just do something, that's what we were doing. We had a second line going on."

Mannie played drums and—like his Uptown friend and rival, KLC—his later style of programming hip-hop beats showed the clear influence of the New Orleans marching band, with its sputtering triplets and drumroll breaks. Drumming, however, was never as important to the teenage Mannie as spinning records. When New York Incorporated fell apart, Mannie and another NYI member, DJ Wop, formed a spin-off group, Ya Boy N 'Em.

Before Mannie's groups gained much traction, another act stepped forward to become the first New Orleans rappers to expand beyond the city limits. The Ninja Crew featured two rappers, Sporty T and Gregory D. Like Mannie, rapper/producer Gregory D learned to play marching band–style drums in school. After a stint as part of the Rescue Crew, around 1985 he teamed up with his childhood friend Sporty T to form the Ninja Crew. The duo started out doing talent shows, where they'd dress up in ninja outfits. They wanted to make a record but didn't know where to go, until chance put them in touch with 4 Sight Records, the south Florida bass-music label run by Billy Hines.

"One day Sporty went digging through the record crates," Gregory D recalls. "And he pulled up a record that said 4 Sight. At that time, Shy-D was on 4 Sight and he was popular in New Orleans, so Sporty just dialed the number. He just asked to speak to Mr. Hines. We both got on the phone with him and said, 'Listen, man, we can rap. Just call out a subject.' We'd been freestyling and that's what really tripped Billy out, how we could just go off on a subject."

In 1986, Gregory, Sporty, and their DJ Baby T traveled to Ft. Lauderdale to record a debut single, "We Destroy." Though the Ninja Crew didn't come to Florida planning to create a bass record, the track got an instrumental hook to the tune of "Mary Had a Little Lamb" and a bottom-heavy 808 beat. The record did well among 4 Sight's core audience in Florida and Georgia, and also wound up on AM 940 WYLD in New Orleans. But the Ninja Crew proved short-lived; Gregory and Sporty decided to go solo.

By that time, Mannie Fresh had established himself as one of the most popular DJs in town. So when David Moses, the head of a Los Angeles–based independent rap label called D&D Records, came through town looking for a DJ to scratch on a record, people sent him in Mannie's direction. In the studio, Moses asked if Mannie knew any local rappers he should sign and Mannie suggested Gregory D. They called Gregory down to the studio and, when the chemistry between Greg and Mannie clicked, Moses signed them to D&D.

Over a few twelve-inches and a full-length called *Throw Down*, the duo's D&D tracks were mostly 808-fueled electro-bass novelty rap—the single "Freddie's Back" paid tribute to the *Nightmare on Elm Street* movies, while "Monster Boogie" sang the praises of TV's *The Munsters*. The tracks, though, provided a first look at the eighteen-year-old Mannie Fresh's talents. *Throw Down*'s title track featured an exciting collage of shifting parts, frenetic scratches, and sampled bits from all over the place. On many tracks, Mannie stole the show.

"Freddie's Back" did well in the South in 1987, but when it came time to collect royalties, Gregory D says, "the label shut down and we never heard from them again." So Greg found a new investor, Brian Smith—a friend who'd made some money in "real estate," Greg says. Forming Uzi Records, Gregory went back into the studio with an idea for a track that wasn't simply a Miami bass retread, but rather something distinctly local in flavor. Released it 1989, the single was called "Buck Jump Time."

In New Orleans, "buck jump" was associated with second-line dancers—the crowd of revelers and improvisers that followed a marching band (the first line) during a parade. New Orleanians who lacked instrumental skills could take part in the fun by second lining—and buck jumping was one of the popular dances second-liners performed on the parade route. (The term "buck jump" was also used in the Memphis rap scene, but had an entirely different meaning, connected with that city's gangsta walk tradition.)

"Buck Jump Time" was the first popular New Orleans rap song to engage the city's musical traditions. Its beat, inspired by Gregory and Mannie's days in the marching band, drew directly from second-line rhythms—the ringing cymbals and clanging cowbells dancing around the steady driving snares. Re-created by Mannie on the drum machine, with sampled horn bleats and a springy bassline, the resulting fusion was both credibly hip-hop and fully rooted in New Orleans.

Just as important, the lyrics celebrated New Orleans as no rap song had done before. Known locally as "The Project Rap," it kicks off with a call-out to the housing developments: "That Calliope! Buck jump time! That Melpomene! Buck jump time! Magnolia! . . . " Then Gregory includes shouts-outs to Crescent City neighborhoods, from Gert Town to New Orleans East, and stakes his city's hip-hop claim: "The point behind this whole rap, this city is cold as any other on the map/New York this, California that, forget that talk, this is where it's at/They talkin' 'bout California like it's so dope, let me see Cali walk through the Calliope."

The song became a local smash. "We were moving beaucoup records," Gregory D says. "It turned the whole situation over for New Orleans. We had to take a stand; nobody was representing our own city. I wanted to represent uptown, downtown, every ward and project. Still to this day, when that song comes on, it's over. It's a classic."

Greg and Mannie went to Miami to record a full album, and larger labels started inquiring into signing the twosome. But again, just as the money was about to flow in, things fell apart. Brian Smith, the guy who invested in Uzi Records, died after a run-in with the cops.

"It was a situation where the DEA was claiming he jumped from the twelfth floor of a hotel trying to elude a drug bust," Greg explains. "When the people at different record stores heard they found, from what I hear, four and half pounds of coke—a whole bunch of shit—the record was taken off the shelves. And the Feds seized the bank account, so everything that was made from 'Buck Jump Time' was seized."

With the single's success, though, Greg and Mannie found a manager who put out the duo's CD—1990's *D Rules the Nation*—on his own Yo Records. With the success of the single, "Clap to This," Greg and Mannie scored a deal with RCA Records. In 1992, they released *The Real Deal*—credited to Gregory D only, but just as collaborative as the previous work. New Orleans hip-hop's first major-label release went nowhere, and Greg and Mannie parted ways. By then, a new tide of local rap had taken off, inspired by the local flavor of "Buck Jump Time." Bounce music had arrived.

TRIGGERMAN'S UNLIKELY GETAWAY

While "Buck Jump Time" served as a prototype for New Orleans' bounce music, it was not actually the primary influence on the genre. That distinction goes to a fairly obscure 1986 rap single by a group from Queens, New York. It had been out for years before New Orleans DJs turned it into bounce music's Rosetta stone—and there's no obvious explanation why the makers of bounce assigned such importance to the track—but still the song "Drag Rap" by the Showboys became the source material on which bounce was created.

The Showboys were Orville "Can Can" Hall and Phil "Phil D" Price, a duo from Hollis, Queens. Hall was a friend of Run-D.M.C.'s Jam Master Jay, whom he met in the junior high school band. He and Price formed the Showboys around the same time Run-D.M.C. came together in 1982, and both groups landed on the New York independent label Profile Records. Unlike Run-D.M.C., the Showboys were destined to be a minor group remembered only by old-school rap obsessives. They released just four tracks: a debut single, "The Ten Laws of Rap" backed with "Cold Frontin'" in 1985; 1987's "That's What I Want for Christmas," on the same *Christmas Rap* album that featured Run-D.M.C.'s "Christmas in Hollis." And in 1986, the Showboys put out "Drag Rap," a twelve-inch single with the instrumental on the back.

At the time, TV theme songs were commonly used for rap hooks; after seeing a rerun of the '50s detective series *Dragnet,* Hall decided to borrow its theme. Because the show dealt with gangsters, he got the idea to create gangster personae for himself and Price—as Buggs Can Can and Phil D Triggerman—and they wrote raps in character, as gangsters fighting for control of Hollis. They quickly recorded a demo and performed the song live at a show they had with Kurtis Blow and LL Cool J. The crowd loved it, so they took it to Profile, which gave them $2,500 to professionally rerecord the demo for release.

The result was a six-minute crime caper in the tradition of mid-80s electro-era rap—built around 808 beats and a novelty hook. But the song was more sophisticated than most. For one, it was highly conceptual: To reflect an actual television show, the track featured a break halfway through that quoted Wendy's hamburger slogan "Where's the beef?" and the melody from an Irish Spring soap commercial. And the main part of "Drag Rap" had two distinct musical sections that shifted back and forth: The first featured the hook, a synth interpolation of the *Dragnet* theme, with a hard-hitting Linn drum beat; the second was a refrain built around a three-note arpeggio of what sounds like a xylophone (a synth sound called "bones"), with a milder 808 beat punctuated by the Roland machine's distinctively artificial-sounding cowbell. Both parts were later sampled in bounce music, but the second was far more common and became the "Triggerman" stamp by which bounce could be immediately identified.

The record got a few spins in New York when it came out in '86, but it didn't gain much traction and was soon forgotten. The Showboys continued to perform live sporadically, and left Profile in '98. Eventually, Hall and Price moved on with their lives—Hall started working for Adidas and Price got a job at Bellevue Hospital.

They had no idea anyone even remembered the song—much less had built entire genres of music around it—until 1992, when Orville's brother Cliff Hall, who'd produced "Drap Rap," got a message at his barbershop from a show promoter in Memphis. The guy had been trying to track down the guys that recorded "Triggerman" for four years; he wanted to bring them down to do a show. They weren't sure what he meant by "Triggerman," but it became clear when they called back and heard "Drag Rap" on the promoter's answering machine. It was their first indication the song was alive in another part of the country.

The promoter agreed to pay them $2,500 to do a show at Memphis' Club 380. They were greeted in Memphis with a limo, and soon discovered the radio station had orchestrated extensive promos for "Triggerman Weekend." The night of the show, they heard the radio warning listeners to stay away from Beale St., where a huge crowd had gathered in front of the club. At a restaurant, they told a woman they were the Showboys and, excited, she called her friends down to meet Triggerman. But, she told Hall, she wasn't planning on going to the sold-out show—it was too dangerous. "When they put y'all record on, they get too buck," she said. "They be elbowing, they be fighting."

"We're bugging out, like, what the fuck?" Hall says. "We made the record in '86. We had no idea how big we were." Once word spread that the Showboys were (contrary to rumors) still alive, Hall and Price started doing shows again. Over the next few years, they traveled to Memphis, Houston, New Orleans; all places where "Triggerman"—as the song was popularly known—continued to get played. In New Orleans, where by 1993 bounce music had become well established, they were awarded a key to the city.

When Hall started working with Adidas, his marketing job put him in contact with rappers like Tupac, Scarface, and Too Short, who all told him how big "Triggerman" was in their area. Once Cash Money started getting big nationally, Price went back and counted how many uncredited samples of "Drag Rap" appeared on the label's early releases; he counted thirty-four. It showed up on the 504 Boyz's 2000 hit "Wobble Wobble" and on David Banner's 2003 hit "Like a Pimp," among countless others. Profile told him the record sold only fifteen thousand copies, though its enduring popularity causes him to doubt that figure. And, he says, he and Price have received virtually no royalties from the dozens—likely hundreds—of tracks that have sampled "Drag Rap." Compensation aside, he still calls "Drag Rap" just "one of those perfect songs."

BOUNCE BABY BOUNCE

Given the odd afterlife of "Drag Rap" as the inspiration for Memphis' gangsta walking and the source material for New Orleans' bounce music, the question begs: What did Southerners like so much about "Triggerman"? To some extent, that will remain a mystery forever.

"I don't know why, but a lot of clubs were playing it and a lot of dudes could vibe off it," says DJ Jubilee, an '80s party DJ who became one of bounce music's most prominent artists. "One time we were in the club back in the day, and this DJ must've played the song for two hours straight, just bouncing and scratching."

Given how strongly gangsta rap insinuated itself in the South in the late '80s, it's possible part of the appeal of "Drag Rap" rested in its lyrics. Though it almost never gets credited as such, "Drag Rap" was perhaps the first gangsta rap song. It arrived a year before Schooly D's "P.S.K." or Boogie Down Productions' *Criminal Minded*, and a year before Ice-T and N.W.A. set off the genre on the West Coast. It could also be that, subconsciously, Southerners heard something in that 808 beat—the pimp stride, the menacing arpeggio, the buck-jump shuffle, the booming bass—that reminded them of home. We'll never know for sure.

It wasn't until around 1989 that "Triggerman" asserted itself as an essential track in Southern club sets. Soon, New Orleans DJs began isolating and looping the audience's favorite part—the xylophone refrain—just as early hip-hop DJs had done with funk breaks. They'd then scratch over it and, when people started grabbing the mic and chanting on top, bounce music was born.

According to Jubilee, bounce first took hold in the 17th Ward, on the far west end of Uptown, in a club called Ghost Town. That's where T.T. Tucker started getting noticed for chanting over "Triggerman." He'd shout out commands to get the dance floor moving: "Shake that ass like a saltshaker, just shake that ass like a saltshaker!" At first it was just a soundtrack to "twerking," the term for dancing to the music. Then, in 1991, Tucker teamed with DJ Irv to record what they'd been doing in the clubs.

KLC, later of No Limit's Beats By the Pound production team, claims his early group, the 3–9 Posse, was the first to use a "Triggerman" sample, on the song "Ask Them Hoes." Most, however, credit Tucker and Irv's "Where Dey At?" as the first bounce track. It wasn't much more than a series of chants set to "Triggerman"—Tucker offers non sequiturs like "Fuck David Duke, fuck David Duke!" and "Let me hit it from the back, 'cause I got a jimmy hat!" But it became a local hit, and a favorite of local DJs who no longer had to loop "Triggerman" manually.

Others soon followed with their own take on "Triggerman." Overlapping was inevitable, but New Orleans DJs, rappers, and fans embraced the duplication of ideas as a sort of conversation—exactly in the way the Jamaican dub aesthetic valued the *version* (what an artist did with pre-existing music) rather than the new composition. Indeed, each subsequent bounce track seemed to reference its predecessor and add a new element to it.

After "Where Dey At?" came "Where They At?" by DJ Jimi. A more polished and sophisticated production than Tucker's, it reprised the title phrase and the "shake that ass like a saltshaker" chant, and also added on lines that became bounce standards, including "do it baby stick it baby, stick it baby do it" and the uncharacteristically nasty, "Bitch, stop talking that shit, and suck a nigga's dick for an outfit."

Then a rapper calling himself Everlasting Hitman came up with "Bounce Baby Bounce," which he intro'd by saying, "Everybody's running round town biting Tucker's rap" (while inserting his own references to "Where Dey At?"). But Hitman's innovations were key: He was first to put "bounce" into his "Triggerman" chant, and also first to reprise the spirit of "Buck Jump Time" by calling out New Orleans projects and referring to second-line dancing: "Bounce for the Calliope, bounce for the St. Bernard, bounce baby bounce bounce bounce/I say bounce for the Magnolia, bounce for the St. Thomas, bounce baby bounce bounce bounce/ . . . Say bounce biggety bounce for a bottle of wine, bounce biggety bounce for a second line."

DJ Jimi picked up where "Bounce Baby Bounce" left off, releasing a single that featured the recording debut of a teenage rapper from the Magnolia named Terius Gray. Because he was not yet eighteen, Gray called himself Juvenile. The single, "Bounce (For the Juvenile)" became a huge local hit, and again upped the ante on the developing genre. While expanding Jimi's line from "Where They At?," Juvenile—a Catholic school student—clipped out the profanity and added humor: "Trick, stop talking that 'it, and buy Juvenile his outfit/ I want a sharp Girbaud shirt, Polo socks, Girbaud shorts and a pair of Reeboks." And borrowing from Everlasting Hitman, Juvie rapped, "Bounce for the Juvenile, bounce for the Juvenile, bounce trick bounce bounce bounce."

Juvenile also created a new chant for the projects: "Magnolia projects keep slinging iron, a bunch of Uptown villains who don't mind dying/That

Melpomene projects keep slinging iron. . . . " Juvenile's teenage singsong is barely recognizable as the voice that would later bring "Back That Azz Up" to the top of the national charts; still, "Bounce (For the Juvenile)" is impressive. Displaying tremendous swagger over DJ Jimi's chugging beat and funky guitar line, Juvie rolls lyrics off his tongue like a dance-hall reggae toaster—he even shifts into patois at times. That "Bounce (For the Juvenile)" lacked the "Triggerman" sample suggested there was something more that tied this burgeoning genre together—a New Orleans spirit in the chants, and a growing lexicon of phrases to adopt, adapt, or augment in the effort to get the crowds moving.

More songs popped up locally in this same tradition: "Get It Girl" by Warren Mayes, "Get the Gat" by Lil' Elt & DJ Tee (featuring KLC's production), and Lil' Slim's "Bounce Slide." Because the word *bounce* popped up often in these songs, and because the word described the energetic feel of the music, people started referring to this new sound—chant-driven hip-hop with lots of "Triggerman" samples—as bounce music.

By 1993, a whole slate of local artists—including a disproportionately high number of females—worked within the parameters of bounce: Cheeky Blakk, Partners-N-Crime, Joe Blakk, Silky Slim; even Gregory D's old rhyme partner, Sporty T, released his "Sporty Talkin' Sporty" single. But '93 was a breakthrough year for bounce for two reasons: It marked the arrivals of both DJ Jubilee, the "king of bounce," and Cash Money Records, the label that would bring bounce to the mainstream.

Jerome Temple, aka DJ Jubilee, grew up in the St. Thomas projects and was a teen in the early '80s when he joined the Fellas DJ crew. Through the mid-80s, he and the Fellas were regulars at the city's popular school dances. The primary social outlet for underage kids, these dances were parties that raised funds for schools and drew kids from all over the city to a rotating schedule of auditoriums.

Jubilee left for college in northern Louisiana, at Grambling State, but he returned to New Orleans and witnessed first-hand as his friend T.T. Tucker jump-started bounce music. After graduating, he moved home and became a regular substitute teacher at Walter L. Cohen High in Uptown. When he wasn't teaching, he was DJing the school's dances—large, raucous affairs held in the gym or on the sports fields.

Jubilee embraced bounce wholeheartedly and, in addition to playing early bounce records into his set, he improvised his own bounce music. Over the "Triggerman" loop, he'd call out the names of dance moves—creating, in effect, something like how Simon Says would look on "Soul Train." "Do the beeny weeny," "do the low low," "do the prime time"; "now walk it like a dog," "walk it like a model," "now shake it on a stick," "now do the tiddy bop," "now show the globe," "shake it on a stick"—some were self-explanatory, others required dancers on stage to demonstrate; many Jubilee invented himself, other were inspired (and then named after) friends, fans, or whoever had an interesting move to make.

By 1993, acts like Magnolia Slim (later Soulja Slim) and U.N.L.V. were injecting bounce with gangsta lyrics to create a hybrid known as gangsta bounce. But Jubilee held down a real job at the school where he DJed, so he wasn't about to spout a string of expletives over the mic. Besides, Jubilee had managed to overcome the negative influences around him growing up in the projects, gotten out of the city and graduated from a respected black college. Overcoming the odds wouldn't have been possible without a sense of personal responsibility. So instead of talking about bitches and guns, Jubilee focused on dancing. And that suited his audience just fine.

At one dance in 1992, Jubilee met Earl Mackie, owner of Take Fo' Records. Mackie started the label as an offshoot of a cable-access show he produced called *Positive Black Talk*, and was looking for acts that fit his company's mission. When he heard Jubilee rocking the crowd that night, and found out he was a teacher, he immediately wanted Jubilee to record for Take Fo'.

Jubilee was content to be a schoolteacher, but Mackie finally convinced him and, in 1993, DJ Jubilee debuted with an EP of dance songs led by the local bounce sensation, "Stop Pause (Do the Jubilee All)." The track was full of references to earlier bounce records: "Trick, stop talking that 'it, and buy Jubilee his outfit/I want a white T-shirt, some khaki pants, some All-Stars and some money for the dance"; "Bounce for the Juvenile—that ain't it!—do the Jubilee All, we made that hit"; "twerk baby twerk baby twerk twerk twerk"; "Stop (shake it once and twerk it), pause (slide biggety bounce), now stand up tall—do the Jubilee All." Mostly, the track was a joyous romp through all manner of dance moves: "Do the Eddie Bauer"; "do the K.C."; "do the T. Slim"; "do the Da Sha Ra"; "do the sissy Shannon"; "do the duck"; "do the pork chop"; "do the bus stop"; and so on for nine minutes.

Jubilee continued recording some of the most exciting and ambitious bounce music, including a kids record of cartoon dances ("do the Barney All"; "do the Miss Piggy"). In 1997, the same year he became a full-time special-education teacher at West Jefferson High, Jubilee recorded a track called "Back That Ass Up," which predated Juvenile's mainstream breakthrough, "Back That Azz Up," by several months. It wasn't the first time one bounce song lifted bits from a previous bounce song, but having the later track become a top-ten hit suddenly created a financial incentive for asserting intellectual property rights. Take Fo' sued Cash Money, though ultimately the songs were deemed too different to justify any compensation.

That same year, Jubilee appeared on another bounce classic, "N.O. Block Party," by Partners-N-Crime. Hailing from the 17th Ward, the duo of Walter "Kangol" Williams and Michael "Mr. Meana" Patterson initially signed with Big Boy Records, the original home to rapper Mystikal, but by '97 were recording for a label called Upper Level. For the group's *Watcha Wanna Do?* album, P-N-C collaborated with Jubilee to create a song linking New Orleans hip-hop with the city's musical heritage as no song since "Buck Jump Time."

With a hook sung to the tune of Mardi Gras standard "Iko Iko," and mixing in bits of "Triggerman" and other elements, "N.O. Block Party" captures New Orleans' living musical culture—intergenerational, cumulative, and strong enough to integrate outside elements without losing its character: "My hot girl and your hot girl were sitting by the bayou, my hot girl told your hot girl I got a hot boy that is fire/Talkin' bout hot boy (hot girl!), hot boy (hot girl!), everywhere that we go/Upper Level, Take Fo', now you know I go, representin' down South for sho'."

Years later Partners-N-Crime hooked up with Juvenile and signed to his UTP (Uptown Projects) label. Bounce, meanwhile, has proved enduringly pliable as a genre. A group called 2 Blakk melded "Triggerman" with brass-band horns to create a thrilling bounce track called "Second Line Jump." U.N.L.V. sampled the other section of "Drag Rap," the *Dragnet* theme, in its popular song "Drag 'Em in the River"—a ferocious diss aimed at Mystikal. And Take Fo', which has remained a pre-eminent bounce label, broke new ground by signing Katy Red, a transvestite rapper who called himself (herself) "the Millennium Sissy." Despite mainstream hip-hop's homophobia, "sissy rappers" have flourished in New Orleans' bounce scene. And younger MCs including Choppa, 5th Ward Weebie, and Josephine Johnny have kept bounce alive to the current era. Through it all, "Triggerman" remains the constant.

"It was always 'Triggerman' back then when it first started," Jubilee says. "And right now 'Triggerman' is still going on. They made it different, they speed it up, they slow it down, they add organs to it, horns to it, second-line band to it, everything. So you get a lot of variety of 'Triggerman,' but it's the same old beat."

CASH MONEY GETS ITS ROLL ON

Though Cash Money, the label founded in 1993 by Bryan "Baby" Williams and his older brother Ronald "Slim" Williams, is most associated with the Magnolia projects, the Williams brothers spent their earliest years in the Melpomene. Their father had twenty-five or so children, though they were two of only four born to their mother Gladys. "He was a rolling stone," Ronald says. "He had his own businesses—bars, grocery stores, nightclubs. He didn't have a lot, but he was hood rich—he had more than others."

As kids, Slim and Baby, who is four years younger, hung out at their dad's bar on South Saratoga, near the Melpomene. He named the place Gladys' Bar. "I grew up in a bar room, so there was a lot of blues," Baby recalls. "I was in and out of that shit all day."

Their mom died when they were still young, and the Williams brothers went to live with their dad and stepmom. Eventually, they wound up in the Magnolia. "It's like a war zone, man," Slim says. "It's just hard. Your odds are against you. You ain't got no opportunities. It's you against the world." They saw war casualties up close. An older half-brother named Terrance "Gangsta" Williams got a life sentence for heroin dealing and solicitation to commit murder. And Baby wound up doing a couple years at Louisiana's Washington Correctional Institute. But when he got out, he was ready to move forward, and Slim was with him.

"Our dad always used to tell us, 'Get your own business, be your own boss,'" Slim says. "When Baby came home we got together and said, 'If we're going to do something, we need to do it together.' So we started sitting down and thinking about the things we wanted to do, and we wanted to do music. For us to be successful, it had to be something we enjoy."

With few resources and virtually no experience, the Williams brothers formed Cash Money Records. At first, the label didn't have the basic independent distribution to get records in stores. But selling tapes out of the back of the trunk, they managed to sell a couple thousand copies of their first release, Kilo-G's *The Sleepwalker*. They did a little better with *Legalize Pass tha Weed* by the group PxMxWx (pronounced P.M.W.). By late 1993, when Cash Money dropped *6th & Barrone*, the debut from Uptown trio U.N.L.V., the label secured distribution and things started rolling.

Early Cash Money releases were full of bounce's singsong chants, project shout-outs, and "Triggerman" samples. But the label's acts—soon bolstered with Pimp Daddy, Lil' Slim, Ms. Tee, and Mr. Ivan—were steering bounce away from DJ Jubilee's party-oriented style, toward something that reflected the gritty realities of the New Orleans projects. They called it gangsta bounce.

U.N.L.V.'s *6th & Barrone* was the label's first to prominently feature Mannie Fresh, the DJ who was, by then, well-known as one of New Orleans' most skilled music makers. Mannie was no longer working with Gregory D, but he had a production deal with Greg's label RCA. The deal, however, limited his ability to release anywhere near the volume of music he was creating. "I love doing tracks, I can do them all day," Mannie says. "I can't wait for the label to say, 'I want you to do three tracks a year.' It was kind of holding me down, so I looked at it as a bad deal."

Meanwhile, Mannie went back to DJing in clubs. In addition to playing bounce records in his sets, Mannie augmented his turntable setup with an 808 drum machine and keyboards, so he could create live bounce tracks in the club. This impressed Baby, who met Mannie at the club through a mutual friend. Baby asked him to do some tracks for Cash Money, and Mannie handed over a couple. Baby paid him about a hundred dollars per beat.

"I used to buy beats from him," Baby recalls, "But then we said, 'What if you just did them?'" Baby and Slim made Mannie an offer he couldn't refuse: the chance to serve as Cash Money's in-house producer, a position that allowed him to write, record, and release dozens of songs a year with an entire cast of rappers.

"They had a whole roster of artists but they didn't have no beats," Mannie says. "So I was like, 'Hey, I can do complete albums? If y'all [Cash Money] really want to do this, let's do it.'"

As Mannie took over all of Cash Money's productions, the label's sound evolved. On records like Mr. Ivan's *187 in A Hockey Mask*, Lil' Slim's *Thug'n & Pluggin'*, Ms. Tee's *Having Thing$!!*, and U.N.L.V.'s *Straight From the Gutta* and *Mac Melph Calio*, Cash Money began taking steps away from the bounce sound. The content got increasingly hard-core—even horror-core—and to keep up, Mannie's tracks strayed from bounce's bright and springy beats. But bounce remained the core of Cash Money's more commercial acts—U.N.L.V. and the R&B-ish Ms. Tee.

By 1996, the gangsta rantings of Cash Money's original roster were looking more like prophecy. After Kilo-G released his tribute to the murder capital, *The Bloody City*, he caught a bullet with his own name on it. Not long after, the same fate befell Pimp Daddy. And the next year, U.N.L.V.'s Yella Boy wound up murdered as well.

Perhaps Slim, Baby, and Mannie began questioning Cash Money's hard-core turn—and the real-life tragedies that had followed. It's unclear whether it was a conscious decision, or if the new direction was thrust upon them—because so many of early Cash Money's core acts were gone. The label found itself at a turning point, and a new generation of Cash Money was stepping forward.

Christopher Dorsey was a kid from the 13th Ward, and word got around that he could rap. He'd spend weekends with his dad in the Magnolia, but his dad got killed when Chris was twelve. His mom couldn't control him, and he got into stealing cars and doing drugs while still in junior high. But Chris' barber knew about his rapping, and when some neighborhood guys told him about their label, he arranged for Chris to meet Baby and Slim Williams. They saw potential in him, so by the time he was fifteen, Doogie—as he called himself—started showing up on Cash Money releases.

Not long after Doogie arrived, Baby and Slim met a second little kid who rapped. D'Wayne Carter, two years younger than Chris, was born in St. Thomas but raised in the 17th Ward's Hollygrove neighborhood. Early Cash Money rapper Lil' Slim was also from Hollygrove, so when Wayne was just eleven, he got Lil' Slim to introduce him to Baby and Slim. He started hanging around the Cash Money offices and in 1995, when Wayne was thirteen and Doogie fifteen, Cash Money put them together to form the B.G.'z, or Baby Gangstaz. Wayne became Baby D and Doogie was Gangsta D, set to become the gangsta Kris Kross.

The duo started recording an album, but Wayne's mom pulled him out of the group when his grades started to slip. He wound up on just two of the eight tracks on the B.G.'z debut EP, *True Story*. Meanwhile, Doogie dominated the record so much that fans assumed his name was B.G. The name stuck, and what had been conceived as a teen duo became the solo debut of Cash Money's new star, B.G.

With the deaths of Kilo-G, Pimp Daddy, and Yella Boy, and B.G.'s rise to the forefront of Cash Money's roster, the label found itself transformed. The following year, B.G. released his first full-length album, *Chopper City*, which featured the first appearance by the Big Tymers—Mannie Fresh and Baby. The track "Retaliation" also contained the Cash Money debut of Juvenile, the veteran bounce rapper who was about to start recording for the label. *Chopper City* moved Cash Money further away from bounce, and when the record became a top-seller, it confirmed the label was heading in the right direction.

A second breakthrough came a few months later with *Solja Rags*, Juvenile's Cash Money debut. Here, with the teaming of Juvie with Mannie—arguably bounce's top rapper and producer—the label hit on a sound from which they'd soon mine gold. While *Solja Rags* was certainly far removed from the "Bounce (For the Juvenile)" era, there were enough bounce signifiers—"3rd Ward Solja"'s "Triggerman" sample, Juvenile's self-referential "Pimpinabitch"—to keep it rooted in the style. Here, Mannie developed a signature style that combined the 808 shuffle of "Triggerman" with New Orleans drumline cadences—fluttering hi-hats, popping snare trills—and the propulsive chord progressions that marched his songs forward.

According to Mannie, Cash Money decided to make bounce music more accessible to people outside New Orleans. "The only way we going to get mainstream money was to change the bounce sound, make it more musical," he says. "We'd include bounce with classic music, just do something different the world never heard. *Solja Rags* was a completely different sound than anybody had heard out of New Orleans. It had music, it had flavors, it made sense. The raps were in 16s, it wasn't just no babbling on."

Juvie also found his style, taking the singsong quality of bounce chants and applying it to full rap verses. In his best performances, such as in the title track, Juvenile comes just short of singing: "Is you a paper chaser? You got your block on fire/Remainin' a G, until the moment you expire? You know what it is, to make nothin' outta somethin'?/You handle your biz and don't be cryin' and suffering."

Solja Rags tracks "Hide Out or Ride Out" and "Spittin' Game" also featured combinations of Juvie, B.G., Lil' Wayne, and newcomer Turk, who'd appear collectively at the end of the year as the Hot Boys, Cash Money's own supergroup. After B.G. returned with two volumes of his *It's All on U* record—which further solidified him as Cash Money's street hero—the Hot Boys came together for *Get It How U Live*. Cash Money's reinvention was now complete: The label's releases were now popping up on the *Billboard* R&B/Hip-Hop chart, Juvenile and B.G. were well on their way to becoming national stars, and the two successful rappers helped shine a light on their newcomer group mates.

How U Live was the first release that prominently featured Lil' Wayne, still only fourteen. By the time the record hit, Wayne's stepfather had been murdered and Baby had unofficially adopted Wayne as his own son. B.G., too, had come under the protection and influence of Baby following his father's death years earlier, but B.G. had already developed independence by then. Wayne, on the other hand, took to calling Baby "dad."

The Hot Boys' debut saw Mannie further refining the "post-bounce" sound he'd developed on *Solja Rags*, while the Big Tymers—Mannie's duo with Baby—also stepped up to new prominence on the album's "Neighborhood Superstar." Neither Mannie nor Baby had a particular interest in becoming rap artists—their roles as musical mastermind and label owner, respectively, kept them busy enough. But Mannie started appearing on tracks, particularly album introductions, as DJs often do. And, in the tradition of Rap-A-Lot's J. Prince or Suave House's Tony Draper, Baby occasionally popped onto a track as the voice of the commander-in-chief.

The pairing of the two "amateur" rappers snowballed, and with "Neighborhood Superstar," they arrived at a persona that worked for the Big Tymers. Rather than focus on their roles as rappers, Big Tymers songs used Mannie and Baby as characters who set the tone for the record, if not actually delivering the best lines. Mannie and Baby were the guys behind the scenes—reaping the rewards of the label's success, living lavishly on Cash Money's profits. In "Neighborhood Superstar," Baby raps about, "Takin' flights, be in Las Vegas overnight," while Mannie boasts, "I got a house in Cali and a ranch in Texas, seventeen inches on a brand new Lexus."

The Big Tymers' heavy-flossing image proved so successful, they followed in March of '98 with their own full-length album, *How U Luv That*—its cover a classic Pen & Pixel design featuring Mannie and Baby sitting at a table covered with sparkling champagne, jewelry, money clips, and cell phones, while in the background a Hummer and other vehicles sit parked on a gold-plated driveway. By then, the claims of wealth were no longer ridiculously far-fetched: Cash Money's records were routinely selling 100,000 to 200,000 copies, and earning millions of dollars through independent distribution. But following *How U Luv That*, Universal Records approached the Williams brothers with an offer too good to pass up: a major distribution deal worth thirty million dollars, with Cash Money retaining ownership of its master recordings.

The deal was made, and Universal re-released *How U Luv That* with some adjustments to the track lineup, amending it as *Vol. 2*. "Big Ballin'," the album's single, featured a minimalist synth-string track and included Mannie and Baby rapping both about spinning "Triggerman" in the projects and having a car for each day of the week. The record sold decently, but the Universal deal truly took off at the end of 1998, when Cash Money/Universal released Juvenile's *400 Degreez*.

400 Degreez was the full flowering of everything Mannie had been building toward as a producer. The tracks were fluid, the beats intricate, and the hooks catchy; but more, Mannie's instrumentals had attained a level of sophistication, even elegance—particularly on tracks where the finely orchestrated strings and synth lines created what Mannie called a "classical" feel. "It was bounce music," he says, "but it had some Johann Sebastian Bach chords and strings going on, with these 808 beats. It was just the whole combination, doing something new."

The record's first single, "Ha," turned "Solja Rags"'s best lines ("You a paper chaser . . . ") into a hook and landed at number eleven on the national rap chart—by far the label's biggest hit to that point. Its follow-up, "Back That Azz Up" (or "Back That Thang Up" on commercial radio), reached even higher, into the top five on urban and pop charts. Both offered great slices of Southern flavor—from the New Orleans slang of "Ha" to the country euphemisms of "Back That Thang Up": "You's a big fine woman, won't you back that thang up."

While No Limit was coming off an incredible two-year run of hit albums, it had never scored a mainstream pop hit anywhere near what Juvenile reached. Just three years after a quarter of its roster was gunned down on the streets of Chopper City, Cash Money was now riding high with pop-rap crossover geared for anyone—soccer moms and bat mitzvah guests included—not too prudish to back their thang up on the dance floor. "Back That Azz Up"'s video, a near-constant presence on MTV and BET, showed the Cash Money Clique rolling through the Magnolia (which, by then, was already being torn down). The Uptown projects and bounce music had finally made the big time.

By the end of 1999, *400 Degreez* had gone multiplatinum on its way to selling nearly five million copies. But at the same time as *400 Degreez* was running through the top of the *Billboard* R&B/Hip-Hop album chart, three other Cash Money releases were up there with it. In fact, during the week of November 20, 1999, the label celebrated having four of its albums in the Top 20: *400 Degreez* was hanging steady at number eight (having peaked at two), while B.G.'s third release, *Chopper City in the Ghetto*, was at nineteen (it peaked at two as well); the Hot Boys' second album, *Guerilla Warfare*, trailed behind at twenty (after peaking at number one); and Lil' Wayne's debut, *Tha Block Is Hot*, entered at number one. All would go platinum.

In the final month of the twentieth century, each of those Cash Money albums had also put a single on the chart, including "Back That Azz Up," Lil' Wayne's "The Block Is Hot," and the Hot Boys' "We on Fire." But the track that has endured the longest of any Cash Money single was "Bling-Bling." Included on B.G.'s album, it also featured verses from Baby, Mannie, Wayne, and Juvi, all singing the praises of the shiny things they had on their necks, on their pinky fingers, on the wheels of their cars—and wherever else they could set a stone. It was the ultimate anthem to hip-hop materialism, and as great slang is known to do, "bling-bling" spread—first into the mainstream vernacular of kids nationwide, and then to just everyone else: teachers, television commentators, and eventually, into the dictionary. Within a few years, "bling-bling" had lodged itself into contemporary language—Cash Money's modest contribution to world culture.

For some, the celebration of "bling-bling" was just crass materialism, another terrible message being disseminated through popular culture. For Cash Money, however, it simply made for good marketing. "The whole image of Cash Money is success—that's the American way," Mannie says. "Everybody wants to be successful—you done thought about it, you done dreamed about it. And that's business. Who wants to do business with a company that's not successful? So it's just selling tools."

Living up to the image, Slim and Baby Williams moved to homes in the exclusive English Turn area and bought a house in the New Orleans East country club Eastover as a sort of Cash Money rumpus room, with large screen TV and Playstation, hot tub, a pool table, video games, an indoor pool with a Cash Money dollar-sign waterfall, and, tucked away in one of the small bedrooms upstairs, a recording studio. And with their spare money, Slim and Baby tried a bit of altruism: They approached the city of New Orleans about buying the Magnolia Projects, with plans to fix it up and let people live there rent free. The city, though, declined the offer.

CASH MONEY IN SLOW MOTION

Following Cash Money's late 1999 high point, the label cruised on its spectacular success. The Big Tymers went platinum with 2000's *I Got That Work*, which featured a pair of worthy singles, "Get Your Roll On" and "#1 Stunna." The label followed No Limit into the world of straight-to-video independent movies with *Baller Blockin'*, which featured music and marginal acting by the Cash Money Millionaires (as the label called its roster). Follow-up albums by Juvenile, B.G., and Lil' Wayne were disappointments only in comparison to the successes of the previous year.

Meanwhile, Mystikal—a New Orleans rapper not signed to Cash Money— had his own chart run in 2000, with two top-ten hits produced by the Neptunes: the creeping "Danger (Been So Long)" and up-tempo funky "Shake Ya Ass." After leaving No Limit, the rapper had returned to Jive Records for a trio of albums, including 2000's *Let's Get Ready*. Pairing Mystikal with mainstream producers, Jive brought the rapper's distinctive Louisiana bark— like James Brown as a crazed backwoods Cajun—to the mainstream.

The same year, St. Louis rapper Nelly exploded onto the pop scene with a singsong flow reminiscent of the bounce-inspired Cash Money sound. But Cash Money itself began to crumble starting in 2001. B.G., who'd fallen deeper into a heroin addiction, left the label and formed Chopper City Records. After hitting rock bottom and getting cleaned up in 2003, B.G. filed a lawsuit against Cash Money for unpaid royalties. He told *XXL* that, rather than being a father figure, Baby had taken advantage of him financially—B.G. even suggested Baby and Slim condoned his drug addiction as a means of controlling him. Independently, Chopper City released four more B.G. solo albums.

Following the commercial failure of his only solo album, *Young & Thuggin'*, Hot Boys' fourth man, Turk, exited Cash Money on bad terms as well. Also fighting drug addiction, Turk drifted and, in 2005, was convicted on weapons charges and sent to jail.

Juvenile, who faced his own (far less serious) confrontations with the law, also broke away from Cash Money in 2001 after the release of *Project English*, an album that hit with "Set It Off," another song drawing on "Drag Rap"'s *Dragnet* theme. Meanwhile, Juvenile launched his own UTP (Uptown Projects) label with his brother, Corey Gray, and signed acts including bounce veterans Partners-N-Crime and the duo D-Boyz. He also filed suit against Cash Money for unpaid royalties. When they settled out-of-court in early 2003, Juvenile presumably got paid, and agreed to record one last album for Cash Money.

With most of Cash Money's hit makers gone, the label focused on Lil' Wayne—who at first tried to reclaim Hot Boys' glory by naming his 2002 album *500 Degreez*, but soon found success as he matured into a confident star. For Wayne's 2004 hit, "Go DJ," Mannie reached back more than a decade to a bounce track he made for U.N.L.V. What was once marginalized regional music was now good enough for the pop charts. As a reward for staying loyal to his "dad" Baby, Wayne was made president of Cash Money and given his own affiliated label, Young Money Entertainment. When he wasn't working both sides of the music industry—releasing chart-topping records *The Carter* and *The Carter II*—he also enrolled in the University of Houston to study psychology.

As Cash Money searched for new acts to replace the departed, one strategy was to subdivide: In addition to putting out Big Tymers records, Cash Money released solo albums by Baby (aka The Birdman) and Mannie Fresh, plus a full-length collaboration by Lil' Wayne and Baby called *Like Father, Like Son*. The other strategy was to broaden, which involved signing West Coast gangsta rapper Mack 10 as well as R&B/funk veteran Teena Marie, and bringing in Atlanta producer Jazze Pha to break Mannie's monopoly on production. (Mannie himself would amicably break away from Cash Money in 2005, and explore more outside production.)

In 2004, Juvenile returned to release one last Cash Money album, *Juve the Great*. The cover depicted Juvie close up, and in the background a Dumpster in the yard of the Magnolia projects. For the record's single, Juvenile reunited with an old friend from the 'Nolia, legendary street rapper Soulja Slim. After leaving No Limit in 2002, Slim managed to stay off drugs and out of jail while launching his own Cut Throat Comitty label. He released an album, *Years Later*, which did well enough locally that Koch Records agreed to rerelease it nationally. *Years Later . . . A Few Months After* came out in August of 2003. Slim was also working on a record with his old friend B.G. For Juve's record, Slim wrote and recorded a song called "Slow Motion."

Things were looking brighter than ever for Slim, the much-loved rapper whose career had always been hampered by his inability to stay out of trouble. He'd even bought a house for himself and his mother in the middle-class Gentilly neighborhood. But trouble didn't stray far. In late November 2003, Slim was shot in front of his mom's house, and died a short time later. No one knows, or says they know, why he was murdered. No one was arrested for the crime.

Nine months later, "Slow Motion"—rerecorded by Juvenile but still featuring Slim's verse—became the number-one song in the country, its subtle blues lick and sexy, sweaty vibe helping it become the biggest New Orleans hip-hop track ever.

From the shockingly long list of New Orleans rappers killed by guns, Soulja Slim was the most beloved in the 'hood. "Everyone misses him. That was a little Tupac right there," Juvenile told *Vibe*. Producer KLC, the first to work with Slim, told *Murder Dog*: "Slim had the people so bad, if he would have endorsed somebody for governor and put it on record, that candidate would be whom the people would vote for. He had it like that."

While so much of the city's hip-hop history breaks into No Limit and Cash Money camps, locals considered Souljah Slim—more than Master P or Baby or anyone else—the king of New Orleans rap. On December 6, 2003, Slim's family and friends held him a traditional New Orleans jazz funeral. Three thousand people marched with Slim's casket, held in a horse-drawn carriage, from the mortuary to the Magnolia and back. The Rebirth Brass Band played, and a second-line formed around them. The Lady Buck Jumpers, the marching group in which Slim's mom was a member, joined in as well.

That day, Slim was gone from New Orleans. And less than two years later, so was everyone else—some killed, but most just displaced by a flood that may in the end have succeeded in washing away an entire culture.

"There ain't nothing like New Orleans," Juvenile told *XXL* in Houston, where he set up after Hurricane Katrina. "We got spirit. We the smallest city, the highest in poverty. . . . The school board system was corrupt. Our police system is corrupt. Our judicial system is corrupt. . . . So it's like it was a big minus, but it was a plus. . . . It was open twenty-four hours a day by law. You can walk out the club with your drink in your hand on a Sunday. We didn't have no curfew hours. We had drive-thru liquor places. We had clubs that never closed. We had crawfish, we had gumbo, we had second lines, we had Mardi Gras, we had parades. We had it all! And that's a lot for a person to sit and let go."

While Juvenile has been active, along with other New Orleans rappers, in benefits to aid Katrina victims, he missed an opportunity as the first major artist to release a post-Katrina album—March 2006's *Reality Check*, his Atlantic Records debut. Most of the record makes no reference at all to the disaster, and his single "Get Ya Hustle On" seemed to encourage doing and dealing drugs as a way of coping with the loss: "Everybody need a check from FEMA/So he can go and score him some co-ca-ina."

Lil' Wayne offered something a little bit more pointed a few months later, when he included a song called "Georgia . . . Bush" on the end of his DJ Drama-produced mix tape, *Dedication Pt.2*. The bootleg, which used the music from the Ludacris/Field Mob track "Georgia," points the finger at the president: "Hurricane Katrina, we shoulda called it Hurricane (Georgia) Bush."

As yet, however, no one has truly spoken for the people who lost the most in the storm—the poor folks who endured rundown projects, who created bounce music, who created jazz. It's by no means clear the city, if and when it gets rebuilt, will have a place for them. Surely some developer, some city planner will realize that, without those people, there is no New Orleans. After all, who's going to second-line?

chapter 10

CRUNK GETS CRUNK

BACK IN MEMPHIS, PAUL & JUICY TEAR DA CLUB UP

The departure of Eightball & MJG from Memphis in 1992 left a void for a new act to assert itself as the biggest group in town. With On the Strength's acts either leaving or outgrowing the label, the local scene coalesced around a few key mix-tape DJs. Where Memphis' original hip-hop DJs—guys like Spanish Fly and Soni D—once had a corner on the mix-tape market, by the early '90s, new crews emerged. Because record stores were unwilling to stock unauthorized cassette mixes, these new DJs began taking tapes to car stereo stores.

Each mix-tape DJ amassed his own roster of rappers that he featured on his mixes. Two camps dominated the field. The first was centered on DJ Squeeky, an Orange Mound DJ who got his start spinning at the neighborhood's Club Memphis. Along with his partner, DJ Zirk, Squeeky began getting notice for his tapes around 1991. His early mixes featured national rap stuff, as well as prominent locals—Al Kapone's "Lyrical Drive By," for instance, got a boost on the streets through Squeeky's first mix. Another popular early track, a paean to oral sex called "Lookin' for the Chewin'," featured Eightball & MJG as well as Kingpin Skinny Pimp (later versions added many more rappers). Others in Squeeky's circle included Lil' Syl and Lil' Ced (known as Ruthless Ass Niggas), Kilo G (part of Zirk's Too Thick Family), Criminal Mane, and Tom Skeemask (aka Tom Skee).

Skinny Pimp was the first in Squeeky's camp to rise, thanks to his mix-tape appearances and his own controversial album with 211, *Pimps and Robbers*. He was also among the first to fall out with Squeeky. One night in

1993, Skinny and Squeeky had a confrontation at Club Memphis. According to some, Skinny pistol-whipped Squeeky and, in the melee, a bullet grazed the head of Skinny's partner, 211. In the fallout, Skinny Pimp defected over to Squeeky's main mix-tape rival—the other prominent Memphis mix-tape crew—DJ Paul and Juicy J.

The conflict began playing out on the mixes. Paul and Juicy made a song with Skinny called "Go To War," which savaged Squeeky. The 2 Thick Family fired back with a song about Skinny called "Lock Him in the Trunk." Physical confrontations continued as well. But all the *ana* (to use Memphis slang for "animosity") built interest in the mix tapes—everyone wanted to hear what one rapper had to say about the other.

Eventually, the mix-tape battle died down as Paul and Juicy's path diverged from Squeeky's. Paul and Juicy had been using their mix tapes to showcase their own production skills—unlike Squeeky, who tended to compile tracks created by others. As Paul and Juicy's mix tapes evolved into being, essentially, collections of their own material featuring a core group of rappers, the natural next step was to create a group and make original albums. And thus, the Triple Six Mafia was formed.

Paul Beauregard came from White Haven, which before it was more infamously renamed Black Haven, was known as the South Memphis neighborhood of Elvis Presley's Graceland. By the late '70s, upwardly mobile blacks moved farther south out of Orange Mound and other ghettos to White Haven, while middle-class whites promptly retreated. The Beauregards were among the early black families to take root in the neighborhood. They were a musical and religious family, with Paul's much-older sister becoming a preacher and his uncles forming the successful gospel duo the Bogard Brothers. But there was a dark side to Paul and his nephew Ricky Dunigan, who grew up next door and was more like a brother. They were into metal music, and at Hillcrest High they were known to carry around Chucky dolls. When they formed a rap duo around 1990, they named themselves after a subject of endless fascination: the Serial Killerz.

DJ Paul was born with a stunted arm, and it's possible that the birth defect made him more introverted. After getting into rapping in his early teens, Paul discovered an interest in the studio side of hip-hop. His older siblings helped him get the equipment—a turntable, four-track recorder, keyboards—and he went to work becoming proficient on them. He started making mix tapes as a way of learning the equipment; his first, in tenth grade, featured gangsta rap tracks mixed on one side of a ninety-minute tape. Paul took it to school and sold it for two dollars. "I said if you give me another two dollars I'll bring you the other side," Paul recalls of *DJ Paul Vol. 1.*

It sold, and more volumes followed. With *Vol. 4*, Paul began putting his own songs on the tape; by *Vol. 12*, the mix consisted entirely of Paul's own creations. Paul also started DJing weekend nights at Brown's Barbecue on South 3rd St.—he called it Paul's Playhouse—then graduated to the higher profile Club Memphis. But Paul kept focused on producing. His brother had gone to school with On the Strength Records' Reginald Boyland, and Boyland invited Paul to come by the studio to watch Eightball & MJG record. "I remember MJG told me that if Reg signed me to their label that he would make some beats for me," Paul says. "I was happier than a mu-fucka. But we never got signed. We were wack then."

After *DJ Paul Vol. 16*, Paul joined forces with a popular DJ from the northside, Juicy J. Juicy had put out some mix tapes of his own before they collaborated on *DJ Paul and Juicy J Vol. 1.* Jordan Houston grew up in a two-bedroom apartment in the Evergreen neighborhood, with his brother Pat (the rapper Project Pat), two sisters, his mother and father. His father was a preacher, and when he no longer had a local church to preach in, he hit the road and became a traveling evangelist.

Houston decided he wanted to be a DJ in junior high, after he saw DJ Jazzy Jeff scratching. He practiced on a Fisher Price kids turntable and when the needle wore out, he replaced it with a piece of the metal from a bread wrapper twist-tie. Then he graduated to one of those turntables that came in a case. At Cypress Junior High, Jordan started a group with his friend Vasco and took the name Juicy J.

"I wanted something to go with J, and Jazzy J was too much like Jazzy Jeff," he says. "One day I was sitting with my brother on top of my bunk bed and I saw a Juicy Fruit wrapper on the floor, and I said, 'Juicy J, that sounds kind of good.'"

Vasco ended up going to jail, but Juicy hooked up with an older estab-lished DJ named D Magic, who invited him in to his DJ business. He started spinning at block parties and at the neighborhood Boys Club, and gained a reputation as a scratching DJ. By the time he graduated from high school, Juicy was one of the northside's best-known DJs.

Like Paul, Juicy started hanging around at On the Strength when Eight-ball & MJG were starting to record there. Paul and Juicy did not meet at OTS, but rather through a mutual friend, around 1992. They lived and DJed in separate parts of the city, but they'd run into each other at clubs and connected through music. Through their friendship, they began work-ing on each other's mix tapes; eventually, they decided to join forces. "The chemistry was there," Juicy says. "He was hot on the south side of town, and I was hot in the north, so we just combined it."

In consolidating their mix-tape operations, Paul and Juicy also brought together their crews of rappers. Paul's camp included his nephew Ricky (known initially as Scarecrow, then Lord Infamous) and Crunchy Black, while Juicy brought his brother Project Pat as well as female rapper Le Chat, Lil Glock, and others. The new combined crew, known as the Backyard Posse, swelled to more than a dozen members, including Gangsta Blac, Playa Fly, Skinny Pimp, Gangsta Boo, Koopsta Knicca, Lyrical Dope (aka 38 Slug), and the rock guitarist Eric Gales, who as a teenager rapped as Lil' E.

Melding two of the city's most popular crews made the *DJ Paul & Juicy J* mix tapes immediately the most popular in town. The music had a dark and spooky vibe, with a minimalist low-fi production style that made it sound even creepier than the early horror-core of the Geto Boys. Given Paul's shadowy persona and shriveled arm, he, like Bushwick Bill, seemed ripped from the pages of some urbanized Southern gothic novel. Juicy was not as dark—his idea of naughty was more along the lines of his popular early track "Slob on My Knob." But as a unit, Paul & Juicy's crew were goth rappers all the way. Referencing the number of the beast in Revelation (666), they called themselves the Triple 6 Mafia and released a posse tape, *Smoked Out, Loced Out.*

The popularity of the Triple 6 Mafia peaked in 1995, when they shifted from being an ever-widening cast of rappers on homemade mix tapes to become a static rap group with commercial recordings. To finance the start of their own label, Paul and Juicy hooked up with a young but prodigious Memphis hustler named Nick Jackson—aka Nick Scarfo, or Saint Nick. With Scarfo bankrolling the label and a studio, they formed Prophet Records, and arranged distribution through Select-O-Hits.

As Paul and Juicy streamlined their posse into a cohesive group, they guessed the satanic implications of the Triple 6 name would be too controversial—they figured folks in the Bible belt might ignore gangsta rap's depictions of black violence and depravity, but they'd never stand for a reference to the anti-Christ. So they toned it down to where the reference might go unnoticed and renamed themselves the Three 6 Mafia.

"People say we were devil worshippers, which we weren't," says Juicy, whose preacher father raised an eyebrow over his son's music but always understood it to be an image. "We had to change the name so people wouldn't be scared to pick our CD."

The first product of the newly named group, *Mystic Stylez*, was an immediate success in May of 1995. The single, "Da Summa," got the group onto the radio with a relatively clean and mellow groove—punctuated by a slowed-down Eightball sample in the chorus that rolled as languidly as the Deep South on a summer afternoon. Elsewhere, though, the vibe was dark and dismal—not evoking gangsta rap as much as occult heavy-metal perversity. "Break the Law" chants its title as if it were the mantra of a teenage doomsday cult, while "Now I'm High Pt. 3" (an update of popular mixtape material) finds Lord Infamous boasting of the dangerous combination of hard drugs he consumes. "Sweet Robbery" just strings together violence and hate.

While it was not appreciably more shocking than what had been heard in gangsta rap, Three 6 Mafia stood apart in its embrace of Satanism. Paul and Juicy went to lengths in later years to reassure the public that it was just an image, though *Mystic Stylez* clearly sounds like the expression of rappers who haven't so much made a deal with the devil as spent some time partying with him. Three 6's Gangsta Boo calls herself "the devil's daughter," while Lord Infamous and Koopsta Knicca take it much further. Koopsta raps on the title track: "Mystic styles of the ancient mutilations, torture chambers filled with corpses in my basement/Feel the wrath of the fuckin' devil nation, Three 6 Mafia creation of Satan." In "Now I'm High," Lord Infamous raps: "Your soul is horrified, flesh falling from the sky/The Three 6 anti-Christ, bloody seven seas/The blackness in my eyes, I hear an angel cry/Now I lay down to die, come and burn with me."

Paul and Juicy's production amplified the horror show with tracks that jerk along dyspeptically on muddy basslines, distant chimes, eerie landscapes, and Halloween sound effects, plus a fondness for samples that have been slowed to sound low and ghostly. The result is by turns a clearinghouse of horror-movie clichés and something more artful—what Kelefa Sanneh, writing in the *Village Voice*, called "a thoroughly accidental sort of low-budget Southern trip-hop."

Where most of *Mystic Stylez* is rather charmless, one song goes so far over the top to become comical. "Live By Yo Rep" was a standout track because it took the rap diss to epic proportions. Directed at the Cleveland group Bone Thugs-N-Harmony, who'd recently debuted with a sound the Three 6 camp felt was stolen from them, the song posed the question, "What would you do if someone tried to duplicate your ideas?" Members took turns answering, beginning with Lord Infamous, who would "Take a thousand razor blades and press them in their flesh/Take my pitchfork up outta the fire, soak it down in their chest."

In fact, there was a stylistic resemblance between early Bone Thugs and Three 6. Both created an eerie gothic sound, and the singsong delivery of

Lord and Koopsta sounded something like Bone's rap-croon. An unlikely and unsubstantiated Memphis legend has it that a Three 6 member had passed a copy of the group's demo to N.W.A.'s Eazy E (Bone's label head), who then instructed Bone to imitate the style. In reality, Bone Thugs achieved commercial success because, unlike the Three 6 rappers, they could actually sing—even harmonize—and also create catchy hooks, none of which is in evidence on *Mystic Stylez*.

The album's main claim on posterity stems from the track "Tear Da Club Up," another song that had been updated from a mix-tape appearance. It had been born from a conversation Paul and Lord Infamous had in a White Haven McDonald's one night after the clubs. Paul noted that "niggas be tearing the club up"—true, given incidents like the shootings at Studio G and Club Memphis, and all the getting buck and gangsta walking going on.

So Paul and Lord went home and created a track for Paul's DJ set. "We started making our own little get-buck beats—we called it *get buck*, we didn't use *crunk* in terms of music," Paul says. "Since they didn't have no words in them—it was a beat we made the night before—we would chant stuff over the mic. We'd be doing fight chants, like 'I bet you want to hit a mufucka, hit a mufucka,' or like, 'Tear the club up.' They used to be doing the gangsta walk in a circle, and we just be chanting along."

After landing on a mix tape, "Tear Da Club Up" was bolstered with an additional verse for *Mystic Stylez* (the song showed up in one more version, on 1997's *Chapter 2: World Domination*). Not simply a matter of the group's tendency to recycle their best material, the song's reappearance was also a measure of it having been ahead of its time. "Tear Da Club Up" is pure rowdy energy, splintering frantically along a bass-style 808 beat with Memphis hip-hop's trademark fluttering hi-hats, and building intensity on dueling wheezy synths (the '97 version is even more intense). It significantly upped the ante on Eightball & MJG's pre-crunk club anthem, "Lay It Down," with the sheer ferocity of chanting—"Tear the club up, nigga! Tear the club up!"—that called for destruction as a means to catharsis and even entertainment.

Memphis rap historian J-Dogg refers to the famous song "If I Had My Way," by Texas bluesman Blind Willie Johnson, in pointing out: "There's a blues song that says, 'If I had my way I'd tear this building down.' It's not a far stretch from that to 'Tear Da Club Up' by Three 6 Mafia." In fact, Johnson's song was so controversial, he was reportedly arrested in New Orleans for singing it in front of the Customs House.

Certainly, there's far less a distance between the raucous chanting and buck-wilding of "Tear Da Club Up" and the style Lil Jon would soon "invent" called crunk. The song's success led the group to record more chanting songs, establishing a second, entirely separate style from its gothic trip-hop mode. For a while, the two styles coexisted—after all, there were six group members—but eventually the crunk material asserted itself as Three 6's dominant sound.

GETTE'M CRUNK IN THE CRAB BUCKET

Late 1996's *The End*, Three 6 Mafia's follow-up to *Mystic Stylez*, marked a transition for the group. Production values had improved significantly, making the dark stuff seem less scary, while a number of tracks—in particular, "Gette'm Crunk"—followed in the mold of "Tear Da Club Up." *The End* revealed Paul and Juicy's love for the slowed-down style of Houston's DJ Screw, who was just then beginning to develop a name outside of his home city. Hometown musical heritage also got its due with the uncharacteristically bright and upbeat "Good Stuff," a hip-hop remake of a favorite by Johnnie Taylor, the Memphis soul singer who recorded for Stax in the '60s and '70s.

The same year, Prophet Records also released solo albums by Skinny Pimp and Gangsta Blac. Combined with the success of Three 6's two albums, Prophet had more than proven its ability to sell records. Taking note, major labels began calling. Within months, Three 6 Mafia had an offer from Sony's Relativity Records, which it accepted on one condition: Paul and Juicy could continue putting out projects independently. "They agreed because they know that's the bread and butter right there," Juicy says.

In October of 1997, Relativity released Three 6 Mafia's third album, *Chapt. 2: WorldDomination*, which reprised earlier tracks such as the singles "Late Nite Tip" and "Tear Da Club Up," the latter of which was redone with milder lyrics and a more powerful, multivoiced chant, and retitled "Tear Da Club Up 97."

Here, the crunk style began to assert itself, with the Satanic flirtations of *Mystic Stylez* almost completely gone. Even the spooky singsong that Lord Infamous and Koopsta Knicca had once used was toned down significantly. On "N 2 Deep," another carryover from *The End*, Lord Infamous tells the old story of selling his soul to the devil, but here—as in the blues tradition—there's an implication that this is a bad thing (as opposed to Lord's apparent pro-Satan position on *Mystic Stylez*). And with "Anyone Out There," Lord tells a chilling tale of live burial that actually has some literary quality—recalling Edgar Allan Poe, or at least *Tales from the Crypt*—rather than the mere shock and perversity of *Mystic Stylez*.

There's also some talk about voodoo (Lord had taken to wearing a bone through his nose, witch doctor–style)—particularly on "Spill My Blood," a weird track that suggests Kurt Weill doing dub reggae. But mostly, the record sidesteps demonic evil in favor of more pedestrian gangsta poses. *Chpt. 2*'s "I Ain't Cha Friend" and "Flashes" even quote scripture. Meanwhile, tracks such as "Hit a Muthafucker" and "Are U Ready 4 Us" refine the get-buck chanting style to something unmistakably crunk. At this point, Lil Jon picked up the style and made it his own.

Working with both Relativity and their own Prophet label, Paul and Juicy began flooding the market: a collective album by the Prophet Posse, called *Body Parts*, arrived around the same time as *Chpt. 2*. In 1998, Relativity released *Crazyndalazdayz* by the Tear Da Club Up Thugs (Paul, Juicy, and Lord Infamous) and the solo debut from Three 6's Gangsta Boo. Posse member the Kaze dropped an album on Prophet the same year. Between 1999 and 2000, Paul and Juicy released three volumes of their *Underground* CD series, featuring pre-*Mystic Stylez* tracks, while Sony-affiliated Loud Records released another collective album, this time renamed the Hypnotize Camp Posse.

All told, Paul and Juicy were behind at least a dozen releases from 1996 to 2000. Not all the material was essential—some not even close. But it was stylistically consistent enough to leave an impression on hip-hop—their distinctly Memphis sound became known as the Paul and Juicy sound. And, according to some fellow Memphis hip-hop artists, Paul and Juicy did little to reflect the attention or credit they were getting for their dark, sinister funk onto the rest of the scene. "It got to where a lot of people thought that if you were doing Memphis music that you were sounding like Three 6," Al Kapone says.

Some began to believe they were actively trying to stop other Memphians from following in their footsteps. That, along with a series of public spats with associates, led Paul and Juicy to be simultaneously Memphis' most popular artists and the city's least liked among fellow artists.

With their growing mainstream success, Paul and Juicy now had a motivation for staying out of beefs, cleaning up lyrics, and staying away from shady business dealings. On *Chpt. 2*'s "Motivated," Paul ponders his and Juicy's new position: "Why must some local bustas try to diss me/When they don't even know me/Not knowin' I'll run up on they ass . . . /I'm tryin' to keep my cool/Cause I got plenty to lose/I fucks around be another nigga singin' the blues."

But trouble kept coming, as posse members broke away—usually not amicably. Playa Fly was gone by '96, and Three 6 offered *The End*'s "Gotcha

Shakin'" as a parting kick. Fly hit back with the popular diss track "Triple Bitch Mafia." The same year, veteran Memphis rapper Gangsta Pat, who'd never worked with Paul and Juicy, let out his own diss called "Tear Yo Club Down," he says, in reaction to comments from Three 6 that he perceived to be disrespectful.

Gangsta Blac soon followed Fly out of the Prophet Posse. Then Skinny Pimp broke away, claiming Paul and Juicy had taken advantage of him financially. Another Three 6–affiliated rapper, T-Rock, left and recorded a few songs attacking Paul and Juicy, including the low blow of "My Little Arm." Eventually, Three 6 members Gangsta Boo and Koopsta Knicca would leave as well, armed with their own complaints, downsizing the Mafia to four members.

By 2000, their Prophet Records partner, Nick Scarfo, was also claiming he'd been screwed over by Paul and Juicy. Not long after helping finance Prophet Records, Scarfo was busted in Georgia and sent to federal prison for drug trafficking. By the time he got out eighteen months later, Three 6 Mafia had taken off. Scarfo collected money from his involvement, but he claimed he was owed more. After they fought it out for a few years, Scarfo settled out of court with Paul and Juicy, and walked away with the rights to the Prophet name. Paul and Juicy's label became Hypnotize Minds Records.

But it was hard to argue with success—particularly since no one else in Memphis was having much. When Three 6 Mafia returned in the summer of 2000 with *When the Smoke Clears*, the record debuted at number six on the pop charts and Paul and Juicy were within reason to dub themselves the "kings of Memphis" (though, as it turned out, Eightball & MJG were quietly moving back to town around that time). "They say 'Kings of Memphis,' well business-wise they are," Gangsta Pat says. "You may dislike them personally, but business-wise you have to respect them, because they real CEOs, they got their shit structured."

As *When the Smoke Clears* went platinum, Commission of Shelby County, where Memphis is located, announced it would award Three 6 a key to the county. Eventually, someone bothered to hand the commissioners some of Three 6's lyrics, and with some embarrassment, the award was rescinded.

But while Paul and Juicy were selling plenty of records, Three 6 Mafia was still fairly removed from the mainstream. *When the Smoke Clears* was almost entirely driven by raucous crunk chants: "When I say 'weak ass' you say 'bitch!'"; "There's some cowards in the house, if you see 'em point 'em out"; "Put ya sign in his face, gang sign in his face." In "Fuck Y'All Hoes," Lord Infamous suggested, "We ain't entertainers we warfare trainers." But crunk had yet to go mainstream, and so the music stayed regional. The record's relatively mild single, "Sippin' On Some Syrup"—featuring Texas duo UGK and Project Pat—earned the group its biggest hit to that point, though it peaked at number thirty on the R&B/Hip-Hop chart and did not reach the pop chart at all.

Less than a year later, Hypnotize Minds scored a second hit with Juicy's brother Project Pat, who'd launched a solo career after getting out of jail. His third album, *Mista Don't Play: Everythangs Workin*, featured the comical single "Chickenhead," which reached number twenty-four on the R&B/Hip-Hop chart. Three 6 Mafia returned later that year with a sound-track to *Choices*, an independent film written by and starring Paul and Juicy. Without massive pop stardom, Hypnotize Minds had quietly built a multi-media empire for themselves, with new acts such as Frayser Boy and Lil' Whyte keeping the label's grassroots fan base coming back.

By then, the get-buck/crunk sound had been exported out of Memphis clubs and picked up by Atlanta acts, who'd inject it with more bass-music danceability and market it to the rest of the country in a way Memphis could never do. Why did crunk become an Atlanta sound when it had incubated for so long in Memphis? It could be that the Memphis sound was too dark and menacing to attract the mainstream. But many Memphians say it's more than that: It has to do with the city's "crab bucket" syndrome.

Folks who've spent time on the muddy banks of the Mississippi know that when you catch crabs and put them in a bucket, the crabs will fight to en-sure that none of them are able to climb out. When one tries, the others grab to pull him back down. In Memphis, locals believe, the people act that way, too. "Somebody makes it from here, there ain't a lot reaching back and pulling in those that need to be pulled in," says Gangsta Pat. "We don't have beefs here, we call them grudges. We be hating you and you don't even know about it."

Juicy J concurs. "A lot of Memphis artists don't know how to go about connecting with each other. We're on top and somebody comes out with a song about 'Fuck Three 6 Mafia,' and I'm like, 'Who is this guy?' That's not a good way to introduce yourself. Memphis artists diss each other so much that don't nobody want to work with nobody. Maybe if everybody started approaching each other, 'Hey, you want to jump on my album and I'll jump on your album?,' then everyone will be working together and making this money."

It could be that things are finally starting to change. For one, Three 6 Mafia's 2005 album, *Most Known Unknown*, included a single, "Stay Fly," that features Eightball & MJG and Nashville rapper Young Buck—what Juicy calls the "Tennessee anthem." It was not only the first time they'd reached out to local rappers outside their camp, it also proved to be the group's biggest hit to date (number-three rap; thirteen pop). And just as "Stay Fly" made rounds on the radio, the film *Hustle & Flow* hit theaters nationwide. With its glimpse into Memphis hip-hop, it proved a rallying point for the whole scene.

While the movie played on all of Memphis' negative stereotypes—small-time pimps, aging rappers, and a star who won't lift a finger to help out fellow Memphians—the production itself provided an unprecedented opportunity for building bridges. It was possible, for instance, to spot Juicy J and Al Kapone appearing together in cameos as members of the same posse (Paul appeared briefly in the film as well). And both Kapone and Paul and Juicy (with Frayser Boy) had a hand in ghostwriting the rhymes of the film's main character, aspiring Memphis rapper DJay (played by Terrence Howard).

Says MJG, "I think Memphis artists are trying to see the big picture now. We're trying to get together."

Amazingly, in early 2006 Paul and Juicy found themselves with an Academy Award for best song, after performing *Hustle & Flow*'s "It's Hard Out There for a Pimp" for millions of viewers on the Oscars' live broadcast. With the mainstream attention given Three 6 Mafia (now whittled down to only Paul and Juicy), *Most Known Unknown* reached number one on the R&B/Hip-Hop chart, and number-three pop, while the Hypnotize Minds label entered a major distribution deal with Warner Bros. While Three 6 finishes up a new album, Paul and Juicy have entered the ranks of A-list producers, working with pop celebrities like Justin Timberlake and Paris Hilton. They also have a feature film called *The Streets of Memphis* in the works, and a straight-to-DVD film *Choices III: The Return of Big Pat*. Perhaps that deal with the devil they'd made more than a decade earlier was now paying off handsomely.

THE MAKING OF LIL JON

If Memphis' rap scene was too much of a crab bucket to take its get-buck chanting music to a national audience, at least Atlanta was listening. From the time Eightball & MJG and Three 6 Mafia began, they could rely on Atlanta to be their biggest market—even bigger, perhaps, than Memphis. Perhaps Atlanta embraced hard-core underground hip-hop from Memphis—and also Houston's Geto Boys and New Orleans' Master P—simply because there was a demand not being met locally.

By the mid-90s, the bass music that had once attracted the ghetto-bound segment of Atlanta's African American population was in decline, and the

main thrust of local urban music tended toward more commercial sounds—
from the pop-oriented music of Dallas Austin and Jermaine Dupri to the sophisticated Southern hip-hop of OutKast and Goodie Mob. So Atlantans
with a taste for the grimy gangsta stuff being made on the South's west side
embraced the big hard-core groups: Geto Boys and UGK (both Scarface
and UGK's Pimp C were living part-time in Atlanta by the late '90s), as well
as Master P, Eightball & MJG, and Three 6 Mafia. South Atlanta's mom-
and-pop record stores stocked these regional favorites and brought these
acts in for appearances when they came to town. Clubs noticed how these
acts got crowds pumped up and onto the dance floor. Also taking note was
someone who, as a DJ and So So Def A&R man, couldn't avoid it: Jonathan
"Lil Jon" Smith.

Jon Smith grew up in a middle-class area of southwest Atlanta, where his
mother was a military nurse stationed at nearby Fort MacPherson and his father, a former military man, worked as an engineer at Lockheed (three of
Jon's four siblings served in the military as well). As the oldest child, Jon became a secondary parent for his younger brothers and sister, and in school
he was an avid reader and high achiever with an independent streak. His
mother recalls how Jon refused to do any more schoolwork. "He said, 'I already have an A. If they're going to give me an F, I'll still pass. I work harder
than anyone else,'" she says. "So he wanted to relax that day."

Jon met his best friend Rob "Mac" McDowell in kindergarten at Beecher
Hills Elementary, but they didn't start hanging out until Southwest Middle
School. By eighth grade, Jon and Rob had hooked up with Vince Phillips
and Dewayne "Emperor" Searcy—and the four have remained friends, and
then business partners, ever since.

Jon broke away from his buddies to attend the magnet school at Frederick Douglass High, where he could study computers. But he spent time with
his friends over at Benjamin Mays High, the same school members of
Goodie Mob attended. He and Rob also ventured up to Piedmont Park in
Midtown Atlanta, to hang around at the Skate Escape shop. Both were avid
skateboarders and BMX riders; they'd hang around with the punk kids up
by the park, work on their boards, learn tricks on the park's obstacles, and
listen to skateboarding's music of choice: punk rock.

Jon and Rob listened to Agent Orange and other hard-core punk bands,
and attended punk shows where they got a first-hand taste of slam dancing
and moshing—practices similar in energy to what crunk would later exhibit.
"We were definitely into the slam dancing," Rob says, "back when the Red
Hot Chili Peppers used to come to the Masquerade. Just the aggression of
it, the anarchy."

As a teen, Jon discovered his talent as a party ringleader and gifted promoter. His first venue was his own basement—at around sixteen, he and his friend Searcy, an aspiring DJ, threw regular "Old Eng and Chicken Wing" parties. When they graduated from high school in the late '80s, Searcy went off to the marines and gave his turntables to Jon, who took to them immediately. After earning experience DJing house parties and smaller clubs, around 1991 Jon was hired as a regular DJ at Club Phoenix, the hottest club in downtown Atlanta. He grew out his hair in dreadlocks and got into spinning reggae, as well as hip-hop and house music.

As Jon established himself as a DJ, he and Rob Mac formed Black Market Entertainment to manage Jon's career. Eventually, the company expanded into managing other acts and, later, became a record label. Their friends Vince Phillips—who got his law degree—and Searcy, who became a popular DJ on Atlanta's Hot 97.5 (later Hot 107.9), became partners as well, to aid in legal affairs and radio promotions, respectively.

But Jon never wanted to DJ as a career—he considered enrolling in college at Georgia State, and took some courses at Fort MacPherson through Georgia Military College. But before he could enter college full-time, an old acquaintance made him a job offer he couldn't refuse.

Jon met Jermaine Dupri a few years earlier at Club Phoenix. At the time, Dupri was known for his work with Silk Tymes Leather and had begun developing Kris Kross. "That was the only club I could get into, because I was nineteen," Dupri recalls. "They let me in because of my celebrity." Dupri befriended Jon, whose fun-loving persona made him a social magnet. He told Jon he was starting a label, and when he got it off the ground he'd get Jon to work for him. By 1993, So So Def was fully functional with major label distribution. That's when he offered Jon a job in A&R and promotions.

While it was an odd transition from the mixing booth to an office, Dupri didn't expect Jon to give up on nightlife. In fact, hanging out in clubs was a key part of the job. As a promoter, Jon would position himself outside of clubs and, using a megaphone, hollered out "So So Def!" to announce the label's latest record. The barking skills Jon developed came in handy later, when he became a vocalist in his own right.

Jon's biggest success doing A&R for So So Def came after Tony Mercedes, the entrepreneur who put Georgia bass music on the pop charts with Deuce's hit "Dazzey Duks," approached him with another hot bass record. His artist Playa Poncho had a song called "Whatz Up, Whatz Up" that Jon loved. So So Def licensed the track from Mercedes and decided to build an entire bass compilation around it. The 1996 record *So So Def Bass Allstars* featured Atlanta bass veterans such as DJ Smurf, Raheem the Dream, and

Edward J, as well as lesser-knowns like Triggaman, Ghostown DJs (whose "My Boo" got substantial club play), and Playa Poncho, who contributed three tracks. Though bass music seemed to be in decline, *Bass Allstars* climbed to number nine on the R&B/Hip-Hop chart. As the album's executive producer, Lil Jon put the record together, and served in places as producer, arranger, engineer, and programmer. Its success was a major boon for Jon, already in his third and fourth careers as a record executive and producer (having already been a promoter and DJ) and still in his mid-twenties.

Just as Lil Jon began enjoying success in bass music, he noticed a shift in taste on the Southern streets. A new sound was taking hold: the aggressive, high-energy, hard-core street rap of Master P, Eightball & MJG's and Three 6 Mafia. Nowhere was the shift more apparent than at 559, a club on Atlanta's West End, where Emperor Searcy was DJing and Jon would often lend a hand in the booth.

"We saw the crowd at the 559 go from where they'd want to hear bass the entire night to where they'd want to hear Master P, Mystikal, Eightball & MJG—that rowdy shit," Jon says. "The crunk shit killed the bass game."

Though the word "crunk" was not yet associated with this type of music, the term had been around as a handy bit of Ebonics. At its most basic, *crunk* is just a misconjugated form of the verb *crank*, meaning, "to operate by turning a handle"—that is, *crunk* instead of the correct *cranked*. Over the years, however, to *crank up* something has taken on a connotation of power, intensity, or volume—as in "crank up the stereo." And so, for someone to "get cranked up"—or "get crunk"—means to become more intense, more powerful, more excited, wilder. *Crunk* may have floated around for years as a term no one thought much about. OutKast may have been first to put it on record, when Big Boi used it in the group's 1994 song "Hootie Hoo." But with this new rowdy style of Southern hip-hop coming up, *crunk*'s time in the spotlight was about to arrive.

One night at a club called The Gate, Jon observed the crowd when inspiration struck. "Damn, ain't no records just specifically made to get you crunk," Jon thought. "Eightball and them just made a hot song, they didn't expect necessarily to make you get crunk in the club. We said, 'We're going to do a song that's goal is to make people crunk.'"

That night, or one of the many similar nights around that time, Jon was rolling through the clubs with a large crew. Among the group was Wendell "Lil Bo" Neal and Sam "Big Sam" Norris, two buddies of the rapper Playa Poncho who'd grown up together in Decatur, on Atlanta's east side. Two big guys—Bo had played football at Alabama A&M—they had developed a good rapport with Jon.

"One night in the club, everyone was chanting, 'Who you wit?' It was just being in the club, feeling good," Big Sam recalls of the formation of the East Side Boyz. "We'd be the rowdy crowd in the club. So Lil Jon told [me and Bo], 'We're going to do a song, "Who U Wit."'" It was like, 'OK, we'll do a song and that'll be it.' And a couple weeks later they came back and said, 'We want you guys to do an album.' So we did an album. I don't know why he chose us, I'm just glad he did."

Rob Mac was surprised to hear of Lil Jon's plans, because Jon had never revealed any ambition to be a rapper. And Jon, in fact, had no long-term goal of being a recording artist. He was merely acting as someone in A&R (artist and repertoire) who'd come up with some repertoire and couldn't find an artist to perform it better than himself. Besides, what he had in mind—while certainly within the bounds of hip-hop—did not exactly involve rapping. Jon never considered himself a rapper. Rather, the formula for "Who U Wit" was this: "a hot beat, a hot hook, and something people can chant along with, that's basically it," Jon says.

While inspired by the rowdy club music coming out of Memphis and New Orleans, Jon and many Atlantans were still deep into bass music—Jon, after all, put out three volumes of *So So Def Bass Allstars* at the same time as he was getting Lil Jon & the East Side Boyz off the ground. "Bass is what we grew up on," Jon says. "In the South, we don't want to hear some shit if it ain't got a lot of bass in it. It's about growing up and getting your first sound system in your car. You've got to have more bass in it than anyone else, so somebody can hear your bass as you're driving down the street."

In fact, crunk is best defined as a fusion of Miami bass and Memphis buck—roughneck chants backed with 808 beats and humming bass. Says DJ Smurf, who'd soon make his own transition from bass to crunk, "Lil Jon was able to fuse the energy of bass music with street rap and came up with crunk."

As the world's first official crunk song, Lil Jon & the East Side Boyz's 1996 single "Who U Wit" was a milestone in pop deconstruction. Where hip-hop cut the pop song down to just lyrics and a hook, "Who U Wit" did away with lyrics in the verses and reduced the hook to a series of terse shouted chants—not far from the called-out dance instructions in early New Orleans bounce songs: "Who you wit, get crunk, who you wit!"; "To the floor, let's go"; "get 'em up," "just bounce," "just ride," "grab shorty," "now hump," down to the throat-clearing syllable, "Ey! Ey! Ey! Ey!" "Who U Wit" was designed solely for the clubs, as strictly functional sounds for

DJs to get crowds moving, and it makes no apologies for its lack of sophistication. As Lil Jon guessed, it was a big success in the clubs—leading Jon and
the Boyz back to the studio for a full album.

Get Crunk, Who U Wit: Da Album offered evidence of the extent to
which crunk grew out of bass. The record arrived in October of 1997 on
Dm Records, a label run by multi-instrumentalist/producer Carlos Glover,
who often appeared on Dungeon Family projects. At least half of the
tracks—including the DJ Toomp-produced hit single "Shawty Freak a Lil
Sumtin'" and "Giddy Up Let's Ride"—are full-fledged bass songs, with accelerated beats, R&B hooks, and the sex/party rapping of bass favorites like
Kizzy Rock, Disco Rick, and Playa Poncho. The rest, however, followed the
chant-heavy format of "Who U Wit."

As *Get Crunk, Who U Wit* reached the range of forty thousand copies
sold—strictly regional and grassroots—and "Who U Wit" climbed to number twenty-six on the national rap chart, crunk became a known Southern
hip-hop flavor and Lil Jon & the East Side Boyz wound up an established,
permanent group. Still, Jon had other business to attend to, including his So
So Def job. So it took another three years before Jon retired from Dupri's
company and rejoined the East Side Boyz for another album. In the time
between, acts like Three 6 Mafia and Master P had broken into the mainstream, suggesting tastes were coming around to the music that had shaped
Jon's crunk sound. He released the album through his BME company,
which had evolved into a label, and titled it—in case fans had forgotten—*We
Still Crunk!*

Jon and the boys were still crunk, and they had refined the formula to
new potency. Gone were the overt dips into bass music, though it remained
an important influence. Instead, crunk's chanting and full-voiced hollering
moved much of the record. Circa 2000, *We Still Crunk!*'s relentless coarse-
ness sounded grating, though it soon became the standard in hip-hop as the
mainstream moved toward Jon's sound.

The record yielded one big hit—the number-three rap single, "I Like
Dem Girlz." It was among the record's milder tracks, with its R&B vocals
courtesy of Jazze Pha, its more laid-back pace, and a slightly discernible
melody in the spoken (as opposed to screamed) chants. And the lyrics were
more humorous than aggressive: "I like them girls with them bright colored
wigs/That be them girls with two or more kids/I like them girls that'll help
your boy fight. . . . "

With "I Like Dem Girlz" suggesting crunk could attract a national audience, Jon signed with the large, New York–based independent label TVT
Records. Just nine months after *We Still Crunk!*, TVT released a revamped

version called *Put Yo Hood Up*. Only seven of the sixteen songs were new, but *Put Yo Hood Up* was a major leap. Adding to the already impressive lineup of guests—including Too Short, Khujo of Goodie Mob, and Three 6 Mafia—*Hood Up* brought on board Eightball & MJG, Ludacris, Atlanta bass legend Kilo, and rowdy New York rappers M.O.P. In addition, Jon was developing his own BME Click, including the rappers Bo Hagon and Chyna White, singer Oobie, and rhyme duo the Lyrical Giants (featuring future solo crunkster Bone Crusher). Jon was positioning himself not so much as a group leader, but as the ring leader of a movement unified by his own unique crunk sound.

Hood Up marked the point where Lil Jon stepped forward as a national figure—for example, in the jump from *We Still Crunk!*'s relatively amateurish cover art to the professionally photographed, well-conceived image designed on *Hood Up*. The cover depicts Lil Jon draped in a Confederate battle flag, while other Confederate flags burn in the background. For many in the South, the flag had long symbolized the region's continuing problem with racism. At the start of the civil rights movement in the '50s, the Georgia legislature had inserted the Confederate emblem into the state's own flag design. At the time of *Hood Up*'s release, the debate over the Confederate flag's place in Georgia politics was raging, and in January 2001 the state's Democratic governor, Roy Barnes, had hastily arranged a vote to replace the state flag with one less offensive. The sudden change enraged Confederate flag supporters and led to Barnes' re-election defeat (his successor, Republican Sonny Perdue, diffused the issue by installing a third flag design after a statewide referendum in 2004). The image of Lil Jon draped in the flag and burning it was revealing. Like so many Southern rappers, Jon was both a part of the South and a victim of it; he was simultaneously representing his region and re-creating it. The photo was, perhaps unwittingly, an allusion to the black Southern experience.

CRUNK'S HIDDEN CODES

This paradox depicted on the cover of *Put Yo Hood Up* was part of the story often missed in the discussion of crunk—a complication that belies the apparent simplicity and crudeness of the music. As Lil Jon's crunk music began to reach a national audience, it stirred more than a little revulsion outside and inside the South.

The reaction was felt most intensely in segments of the Northeast, with its legacy of black-pride rap and its self-image as the arbiter of lyrical sophistication in hip-hop. To some, crunk was more than just crude and simplistic.

As Lil Jon began popping up in magazines and on TV baring his gold-fronted grimace and posing as the ever-crunked party machine, some viewed his shtick—and his music—as a twenty-first-century return to minstrelsy, the popular nineteenth-century entertainment form that humiliated blacks by acting out stereotypes of the happy ignorant Negro. To some, Jon was the ghetto gangsta stripped of righteous anger or even danger, a lovable fool grinning with a mouth full of garish dental work and a costume jewelry-encrusted pimp chalice in his hand to keep him drunk. Many viewed Jon's crunk creation as a step back for hip-hop, an embarrassingly gauche expression of Southern provincialism coming just as hip-hop attained a privileged status as a cultural institution.

At the same time, something about crunk connected with people in an almost visceral way. If crunk was hip-hop deconstructed, it was also hip-hop at its most potent, its most enervating. Certainly this power had a lot to do with the vocal intensity—a throat-shredding yell that put it in league with headbanger music from metal to punk to screamo. But the language of crunk itself—a terse and clipped lexicon that placed it on the wrong side of the tracks that has divided the English language for nearly a millennium—also made it a powerful expression of the dispossessed.

To backtrack considerably, the mutt-like language of Modern English was born as a result of the Battle of Hastings in 1066. That's when Norman invaders from France beat the Saxons on their home turf and settled in as rulers of England. The Normans brought with them a Latin-derived French language—ornate, flowing, multisyllabic—and it became the tongue of England's ruling class. Meanwhile, the short, sharp, blunt-speak of the Germanic-rooted Old English that had served the Saxons for centuries—giving English words like *mad* and *fight*, *fuck* and *shit*—became the language of the conquered lower classes.

Over the centuries, the Normans blended with Saxons and embraced the native language as their own. Latin-based words, however, mingled in—giving English words like *incensed* and *quarrel*, *intercourse* and *defecate*—and brought so much French that Modern English became a new language entirely. While Normans and Saxons long ago blended their way out of existence, the language differentiation between dominant and marginalized people has survived. For instance, while the Germans gave us the simple, utilitarian word *house*, its French counterpart, *maison*, transmuted to English as the haughty, sloping *mansion*.

Today, Latin-derived English still tends to be the province of privileged classes, while the terse eloquence of Germanic words spark the language of the underdog. The mere sound of some Germanic words carries an unpolished, almost subversive, edge and lends nicely to hip-hop. For instance, it's less likely rappers will claim they *fail to comprehend the significance of the situation* and more likely they'll say they just *don't give a fuck.*

As a word, *crunk* presents an extreme example of Germanic word power—consider the subgenre's prospects had it been called *enthusiasm* or *rotate* (to use the closest Latin equivalent to *crank*) music. Crunk takes *crank*'s Old English severity up a notch by mutating *cranked* from a weak verb (one with suffix added, as in *dance/danced*) to a strong verb (with an internal vowel change, as in *swim/swum*). That *crunk* rhymes with *drunk* and *funk* makes the word not only severe and strong, but also revelrous and grimy. It's a marvelous specimen of the visceral impact a Germanic-rooted word can have. *Crunk* just sounds nasty.

Lil Jon's lyrics reduce language to primal energy. Take, for example, the single from *Put Yo Hood Up*, "Bia' Bia'." Jon accentuates his hook—the word *bitch*—by stretching it into two syllables: *bee-atch*. But then, the word is not sufficiently pithy to fully realize its crunkness, so it becomes the truncated *bee-ah*. The music is similarly raw, unsubtle, and highly repetitive. It's also aggressive, almost violent—as tailored for the mosh pit (or gangsta walk circle) as hip-hop gets.

Jon's bursts of "yea-ah!" and "okaaay!" and chants like "you scared!" and "get crunk, get buck, and throw your muthafuckin' middle finger up!"—it's all part of a continuum in Southern black music, from James Brown's *yaaow!*s and *hit me!*s to Howling Wolf's growls, and on back. It's the aggravated verse of the marginalized, going back to the foundations of the English language.

CRUNK GETS CRUNK

While *Put Yo Hood Up* only reached number forty-three on the pop chart, it climbed to the top of the independent album chart and made Jon a familiar figure on the national hip-hop scene. By the October 2002 release of a fourth album, *Kings of Crunk*, all signs suggested that Lil Jon & the East Side Boyz were poised for something bigger.

With *Kings of Crunk*, Jon elevated crunk music from a convenient description of his music into a Southern hip-hop movement. Jon, Sam, and Bo were the titular kings of crunk—they were the only group that actively embraced the term. But such was Jon's marketing savvy and larger-than-life persona—Jon, with his expanding network of collaborators, created the illusion of crunk as a force sweeping the nation.

Kings of Crunk neatly divided into an all-out crunk first half—with tracks like "Throw It Up" (featuring Pastor Troy), "I Don't Give a Fuck" (featuring Mystikal and Krazy Bone), and "Push That Nigga, Push That Ho"—and a more sedate and diverse second half that included Houston screw music ("Diamonds" featuring UGK and MJG) and R&B, both slow jam ("Nothin' On") and up-beat ("Nothins Free"). Jon further expanded his cast of guest voices, both Southerners (Bun B, Petey Pablo, Big Gipp, Devin the Dude, Trick Daddy) and beyond (Jadakiss, E–40, Fat Joe). But while *Kings of Crunk* was perhaps Jon's strongest record, it was held together by a few standout tracks. Four albums in, Jon's well-worn themes—threatening people in the club; mocking them for being "scared"; goading people to represent their 'hood—were growing tiresome.

The first three of the album's four singles—"Rep Yo City" in the summer of 2002, "Nothins Free" in the winter, and "I Don't Give a Fuck" in the spring of 2003—only dipped into the upper reaches of the R&B/Hip-Hop chart. Then, almost a year after the album's release, its fourth single, "Get Low," took off. Featuring the Ying Yang Twins, another Atlanta act that had emerged out of bass music, "Get Low" was only moderately crunk—the chants were milder, the hooks catchier, and the beat suggested it belonged more in a strip club than mosh pit. Perhaps because it was a more accessible "crunk lite," "Get Low" soared to number two on the pop chart (number-one rap) and ignited Lil Jon as a national media celebrity. Crunk suddenly became the latest hot trend.

By the time "Get Low" hit, however, crunk was already moving toward the mainstream. Just months earlier, one-time Lil Jon protégé Bone Crusher—born Wayne Hardnett in the tough West Atlanta neighborhood Adamsville—made it to number twenty-six on the pop chart (number-six rap) with a song very much in the crunk mold, "Never Scared."

Bone Crusher was, in fact, an Atlanta rap veteran. Beginning around 1994, he was part of a group called the Lyrical Giants that had hooked up with a popular live band called the Chronicle. Beginning at the Loft in downtown, the Chronicle later moved to Midtown's neo-soul/alt-hip-hop mecca Yin Yang Café (where Bone Crusher also served as chef), Oxygen in Buckhead, and the semi-annual mega-party, the FunkJazzKafe. For these gigs, the Chronicle served as live band—reproducing the latest hip-hop tracks with an acid-jazz vibe—for guest rappers. Singers like Usher and Joi, and rappers from Goodie Mob to Common, sat in with the Chronicle on special nights, but Bone Crusher—who lived with Chronicle keyboardist James "LRoc" Phillips—was a mainstay.

Through these live sessions, the Lyrical Giants came to the attention of Eric Sermon, the famed hip-hop producer (EPMD) who was living in Atlanta, and Sermon signed the group to his Def Squad label. Though that deal went sour, the L.G.s signed with BME, Lil Jon's management company, who got the group a deal with Tommy Boy Records. After the L.G.s appeared on four tracks on Tommy Boy's 1999 compilation, *Get Crunk*, that deal fell through as well.

Then, one night out at the club, Crusher ran into Jermaine Dupri. It's likely Dupri had seen Crusher before, either through their mutual association with Lil Jon and LRoc (who worked as a session keyboardist for Dupri), or at the Yin Yang Café. But on this night Crusher handed Dupri a tape. Dupri's long-standing relationship with Sony was about to end, and in 2003, he linked So So Def with L.A. Reid's Arista Records. As a newly installed senior vice president at Arista (and president of So So Def), Dupri's mission was to bring street-oriented hip-hop to the label. He made Bone Crusher his first signing and, within months, Crusher's debut, *AttenCHUN!*, hit stores.

As larger-than-life and cartoonish as Lil Jon, Crusher—with his linebacker physique and madman hair—played off his looks and so-called "vainglorious" bravado to create a character somewhere between Big Foot, John Belushi, and a WWF bruiser. The video for "Never Scared"—which featured his fellow emerging Atlanta rappers T.I. and Killer Mike, and other ATL luminaries—depicted Crusher as a Godzilla-like giant, stomping through Atlanta and leaving destruction in his wake. It was harmless fun that played the hard-core hip-hop pose for laughs.

While Lil Jon's style was the primary influence on "Never Scared," the song served, conversely, as the shock troops for crunk that helped "Get Low" reach unprecedented heights a few months later. A second hit from the summer of 2003—"Like a Pimp" by Mississippi rapper David Banner—helped as well. Though the track was not chant oriented like Lil Jon's crunk sound, Banner's intense vocal delivery associated his music with the growing critical mass of crunk crossovers.

"When Bonecrusher came through on Arista, it made the music seem more inviting," Lil Jon says. "When we were doing it, it was just like, 'Naw, that's just some regional shit.' So you had Bone come through, Banner come through, they're all getting hella MTV love, BET love, selling some records, getting radio play. It just opened the doors for us to come back through, like, 'OK, I see now.'"

Still, "Get Low" was the tipping point for crunk's emergence as a national phenomenon. In the twelve months following "Get Low," Lil Jon's crunk sound served as the basis for six more top-ten pop hits (two number ones): "Damn" by the Youngbloodz, "Salt Shaker" by Ying Yang Twins, "Freak-A-Leak" by Petey Pablo, and "Let's Go" by Trick Daddy, plus two smash R&B/crunk hybrids—"Yeah!" by Usher and "Goodies" by Ciara. From late 2003 through 2004, it was impossible to listen to pop or urban radio without hearing Jon's signature wheezy synths, 808 bumps, and aggravated barks.

Incredibly prolific, Jon also produced tracks that didn't make the top ten: for the Bravehearts, Young Jeezy, Elephant Man, Yo Gotti, David Banner, Murphy Lee, Nappy Roots, Mobb Deep, Master P, Twista, Young Buck, T.I., and more. Recognizing his moment to shine wouldn't last forever, Jon churned out tracks as fast as he could, often without a clue who would end up using them. The backing track of "Freak-A-Leak," for instance, was originally sent to Jive Records to be used by Mystikal. But Mystikal never showed up for his session, so Jon passed the track on to Usher, who used it to write his mega-hit "Yeah!" But Jive passed the track on to Petey Pablo, who recorded "Freak-A-Leak" without Jon's involvement. When Jon heard "Freak-A-Leak" on the radio, he knew Usher needed a new track, lest Jon become guilty of plagiarizing himself. Two huge singles resulted.

As it became apparent that crunk was a full-scale pop phenomenon, Jon and BME set about milking it. BME acts Chyna White and Oobie got deals through TVT first, then the company entered a venture with Warner Bros. that provided major-label muscle for Lil' Scrappy, Trillville, and Bo Hagon. Lil Jon attached his name to projects like the "Girls Gone Wild"–inspired *Too Crunk For TV* DVD and the Lil Jon & the East Side Boyz *American Sex Series* pornos (with Jon hosting, not performing). Lil Jon reviewed movie scripts, while BME developed a Comedy Central series called *A-Town*. TVT Records, meanwhile, released the inevitable *Crunk Christmas* compilation.

"It's been fucking my head up," Lil Jon admitted at the height of his fame. "Not being able to walk through certain clubs without being bum-rushed. To go to different cities where you never could get a record played and people running up to you."

The newfound demand on Jon to constantly fulfill the role he'd created for himself proved exhausting. He remained gracious to fans and photographers who wanted to see Lil Jon glaring his fronts or holding up his pimp cup, but the real Jonathan Smith remained behind the shades—intelligent and quiet, with big puppy-dog eyes—patiently riding out his moment.

"He's always been a thinker, focused on what he wants to do next," Rob Mac says. "But once you go out he's wild as hell. You gotta keep your eye on him. But if he was crunk all the time, either he'd pass out or be in somebody's prison. So he's blessed that he has some sort of medium in there."

But if no one in American culture has really made it until they've been parodied on a major TV comedy show, then Lil Jon became a true icon once the country's hottest comedian, Dave Chappelle, donned dreadlocks, dark glasses, and gold fronts and began screeching "yea-ah" and "okaaay" on his Comedy Central skit show. "It was real flattering—amazing that he even thought enough to do some skit off me," Lil Jon said at the time, reeling from the attention.

Or, perhaps, a newer mark for a cultural icon involved having your own energy drink. Lil Jon got that, too, in 2004, when he unveiled Crunk Juice, a vitamin- and caffeine-enhanced citrus drink designed to make consumers—what else?—crunk. When Jon and the East Side Boyz returned in 2005 with a new album named *Crunk Juice*, it was likely the first time a record had served as a promotional tie-in for a soft drink.

With the combination of songs produced by Lil Jon, featuring Lil Jon, made by artists affiliated with or imitating Lil Jon, crunk had indeed become a musical movement. Steve Gottlieb, president of TVT Records, broke it down: "Musical movements happen because they're in the water, and then lightening strikes. Jon is lightning striking. And so this scene has been percolating in the South for years, and Jon brings it all together. The production chops, the musical vision and then star quality that turns it into a movement, and all of a sudden he becomes its natural leader."

But for crunk to be an actual movement, it needed to exist beyond the tentacles of Lil Jon's empire. Artists began talking about crunk as an extension of Southern life. "Crunk music is so much more than just one person," David Banner says. "It's more than music—it's a feeling."

To hear Atlantans describe it, crunk is woven into the city's fabric. Consider two of the more impressionistic descriptions of crunk's connection to life in the ATL:

D-Roc of the Ying Yang Twins says, "Crunk is a culture for us, how we live. We talk loud, when something comes on [the radio] we get crunk to it, and if we don't know the words we say our own words. Instead of running down the street to tell you what I had to tell you, I'm fixin' to yell all the way down the street. 'Hey! Thug! You goin' to the store? Bring me back two blunts! And some chips! And a juice!' I ain't gonna run up there and give you the money. I give you the money when you get back. That's Atlanta."

Lil Jon says, "Crunk is part of the culture of Atlanta. We live to get crunk. It's how we grow up. You can be going to the mall on a Saturday and you

see six muthafuckas in an old-school Chevy, bouncing up and down at the
same time, swerving. That's being crunk."

CRUNK'S FELLOW TRAVELERS:
PASTOR TROY, OOMP CAMP

Developing alongside Lil Jon in the years before his breakthrough, a number of Atlanta crunk artists were not so much Lil Jon imitators as they were
under the heavy influence of Master P. In 1999, a rapper named Drama released, "Left, Right, Left," on Raheem the Dream's Tight 2 Def label. The
song featured chanting that imitated marching drills, evoking the military
imagery employed by Master P's No Limit Records. The regional success of
"Left, Right, Left" earned Drama a deal with Atlantic Records, which released his album, *Causin' Drama*, in 2000.

A second group of Atlanta militarists, the 404 Soldiers, emerged around
the same time and scored a local radio hit, "Walk Like a Soldier." They also
got a major-label deal, but quickly faded from the spotlight. And in 2002, a
teenage rapper from College Park named Archie Eversole—born in Ger-
many to parents in the military—landed on MCA Records. His album, *Ride
Wit Me Dirty South Style*, yielded a minor hit with "We Ready," which borrowed the melody of the 1969 hit "Na Na Hey Hey (Kiss Him Goodbye)"
for its crunked-out hook. Eversole was actually young enough to be a generation removed from No Limit: "We Ready" seems to be inspired mostly by
Pastor Troy—the most significant Atlanta rapper to emerge in the Master P
mold—whose 1999 debut album was called *We Ready—I Declare War*.

Micah "Pastor" Troy also had a parent in the military, but while growing
up in Fairburn—a town fifteen minutes outside southwest Atlanta—his father exchanged his rifle for a Bible, becoming the real Pastor Troy after
whom Micah named himself. When Troy graduated Creekside High in
1996, he moved two hours east to attend Paine College in Augusta. Troy
was interested in rapping and saw leaving Atlanta as a strategic move.

"Those years—'96, '97, '98, '99—Outkast and Goodie Mob were at
their peak. LaFace was in Atlanta. So imagine trying to be a rapper, coming
out of Atlanta," Troy says. "That was on lock. My theory was, All right,
I'ma go to another town. We get people behind it, that's people behind it. I
took everything I peeped in Atlanta to Augusta and did it from that city.
'Bout time we were finished, we locked everything down outside Atlanta.
And Atlanta is where I was from the whole time, so it was easy for me to
come here and say, 'Hey, this is your boy.'"

We Ready—I Declare War established Troy as an underground favorite throughout Georgia, turf he marked with frequent claims of being a "D.S.G.B."—Down South Georgia Boy. Interestingly, Troy was a rapper in the Master P mold who, in four separate places, disses P for some unspecified reason (could be he's just angling for a fight; he also says, "Fuck all yall up North muthafuckas . . . fuck Wu-Tang, fuck Puffy . . . "). He begins his single with a skit where he calls No Limit and leaves a message for P: "Tell him that Pastor Troy and them Down South Georgia Boys said, since everybody think they soldiers, then what's up, we'll go to war."

More compelling than his P obsession was Troy's complicated relationship with God. A self-professed "pastor of the streets" in the heart of the Bible belt, Troy repeatedly references the divine and quotes scripture. He's a believer but also a product of the trap, and he struggles to reconcile faith in a just God with the poverty and depravity around him. *We Ready*'s album cover, for instance, depicts Troy in a priest's robe with a garland of bullets. His juxtaposition of the sacred and profane would be offensive to some, oddly spiritual to others: "Me and Jesus wildin' like thugs . . . drinkin' Hennessy/ . . . Picture God fulla marijuana, as I relax and devilish demons disappear/I got the feeling that the nigga's gonna love it here." Other times the juxtaposition is just part of the drama: "Holy Bible, assault rifle/Thou shalt not kill, unless they make you feel/Like they superior, naw bro, who you wit/D.S.G.B. my clique."

The struggle of the fallen preacher—an archetype of Southern literature—played itself out through *We Ready*. Even the title suggests a dual meaning: ready to struggle and fight, and also ready to meet God in death. He cries out "God I'm tired" and is engaged enough in his theology to demand "We Want Some Answers," but by the end he still isn't sure the answers are out there. "Eternal Yard Dash" resigns itself to existentialism—"I'm running for nothing, so I'm gonna kill myself"—but the song's final verse restores moral order: What he thought would lead him to heaven has landed him in hell. When the record ends abruptly—with Troy getting killed at the climax of the bleak crime story, "Ain't No Sunshine"—it feels more like deliverance than damnation.

Troy would carry his scorched-earth vision of God and gangsta to major label Universal for 2001's *Face Off*, but not before shooting off a round of independent projects, including his self-released *I Am D.S.G.B.*; the album *Book I* by Pastor Troy and the Congregation (which featured rappers Eleven Twenty-Nine and T-Mac); a record by his extended posse of Fairburn and Augusta friends, D.S.G.B., called *The Last Supper*; and a compilation called *Pastor Troy For President*. *Face Off* is essentially a compilation as well, with a few new tracks sprinkled in among older favorites, including "Rhonda," his oddly feminist gangsta anthem with a Beach Boys chorus. Aimed at a national audience unfamiliar with the Pastor, *Face Off* provided an adequate sampling, from the crunked-out "Throw Up Your Flags" to the heavenly plea of "Oh Father," and from the R&B-flavored love song "Can You Stand the Game" to the tortured agnosticism of "Move to Mars" ("This is how a nigga do ya/Once ya born, it's like the Lord never knew ya"). Most impressive was the single "Vice Versa," a trippy psychedelic discourse—punctuated by Three 6 Mafia–style church bells—about the disorienting moral landscape of the streets: "What if heaven was hell and vice versa," Troy repeats, struggling to reconcile the evil things good people do.

Face Off made a decent showing on the R&B/Hip-Hop chart, peaking at number thirteen, and 2002's *Universal Soldier* proved more successful, topping off at number two (thirteen on the pop chart) and scoring a minor hit with "Are We Cuttin'." But gone from *Universal Soldier* was everything that made Troy's music compelling. In place of the theological struggle was the strange Christian crunk of "When He Comes" and patriotic crunk of "Bless America." Rather than relying on the raw production that gave the Pastor a storefront church vibe, there were slicked-up songs by A-list producers Timbaland, Jazze Pha, and Lil Jon. It was as if Troy had dealt with the devil, trading fame for his soul. After two more releases—*By Any Means Necessary* and a quickly forgotten major-label D.S.G.B. effort—failed to push Troy higher up the charts, he returned to the indie grind.

Somewhere in Pastor Troy's transition from local Augusta celebrity to major-label artist, he met and signed with Gene Griffin, the music executive and songwriter who'd partnered with a teenage Teddy Riley to create the new jack swing sound. In the early '90s, Griffin had moved back to Georgia, where he was born; after nearly a decade out of the business, he was itching to get back in. He heard about an artist in Augusta who was making crowds go wild. "I knew I needed a [Master] P type sound," Griffin says. "That was a real factor. Troy sounds similar to P."

Though the relationship didn't last, the success he had helping Troy get signed with Universal enabled Griffin to get his label back up and running. His first label had been called Sound of New York, so Griffin named his new label Sound of Atlanta. Through working with Troy, he met a second Augusta rapper, Miracle, who did street promotions for Troy's *We Ready* record. Though Troy and Miracle had a falling out, Miracle found success with his single "Bounce" and signed to Universal as well. After a self-titled debut did well, Miracle took a surprising left turn with 2001's *Keep It Country*. Following through on his claim that, as a kid, he used to help carry equipment for Augusta's favorite son, James Brown, Miracle adopted a sound that, on tracks like "Bad MF" and "Country Stuff," imitates James Brown's proto-crunk rap-sing style. *Keep It Country* was notably more organic and Southern funk-based than hip-hop has been, which was both a mark of distinction and likely a reason the record failed to find its way onto the rap charts.

The other group of Atlantans to significantly impact crunk music has exerted tremendous local influence without ever breaking nationally. The success of entrepreneur Big Oomp (born Korey Roberson) and his Oomp Camp provides a dramatic example of the massive success Southern acts have had on a strictly grassroots and independent level.

Around 1990, Big Oomp—the hulk of a man who could go pound for pound with Eightball—started, like label heads throughout the South, selling mix tapes in a flea market booth. Little more than a decade later, the Big Oomp empire encompassed eight Big Oomp stores, the Big Oomp label, a studio, and music publishing, production, and graphics companies. With his network of operations, Oomp formed a self-contained music industry that loomed large in the 'hoods of Atlanta.

Like Lil Jon, Big Oomp emerged from the bass music world. Through his flea market operation, Oomp hooked up with DJ Jelly, one of Atlanta's most popular club (Magic City), radio (V103), and mix-tape DJs. Jelly and his team—including DJ Montay, MC Assault, and Freddie B—became Oomp's in-house production squad. After years of bootlegs, Big Oomp Records' first official release, Major Bank's *Life After Death*, arrived in 1996. Oomp's big break came two years later, when he signed Atlanta underground legend Hitman Sammy Sam—a veteran of Atlanta's underground who'd never broke beyond the South. Along with his notoriety for live freestyling, Sam's colorful reputation made him a hero among his city's biggest thugs. "Sam is in and out of jail—a lot of people look up to that, that's they role model right there," says D-Roc of the Ying Yang Twins. "Sam is Mr. I-don't-give-a-fuck-who-you-is, if you goddamn disrespect me, I'ma snap. A real 'hood nigga."

Atlanta's hard-core street rappers repped for their zones—one of the six Atlanta Police Department precincts—and Sammy Sam, because he'd been around so long and in so much trouble, was said to be the first rapper to have repped all six zones (Sam recorded a song called "Calling All Zones" with the Ying Yang Twins). He's also credited, in spirit if not strictly in style, to have been Atlanta's first crunk rapper. "Sammy Sam was the first person to get on records talking about getting people ready to fight in a club," DJ

Smurf (Mr. Collipark) says. "You can't talk about this scene without mentioning Sammy Sam. Ain't crunk music without Sammy Sam."

Big Oomp scored a local hit in '98 with Sam's "Ridin' Wit Some Playa's," then he released a full-length, *Last Man Standing*. The following year brought albums from Loko and the duo Intoxicated. Then, in 2000, Oomp introduced a sixteen-year-old rising star named Baby D, who hit with the local favorite "Eastside vs. Westside" and the album, *Off the Chain*. With his youth and local popularity, Baby D soon signed to a lucrative deal with Sony Records, though a major-label debut hasn't materialized.

Meanwhile, in 2003, Sammy Sam wound up with a deal from Universal based on the unlikely success of his comedy novelty, "Step Daddy," in which Sam can be heard telling a chorus of disrespectful stepkids to "shut up" and "go to sleep." And Big Oomp remains one of the South's biggest players, exerting a crucial influence on which records will break through placement in his stores and on his mix tapes.

Though new acts like Crime Mob ("Knuck if You Buck") and Dem Franchize Boyz ("White Tees") continued to be associated with crunk, by 2005 there were signs that the subgenre had run its course, and a new generation of Atlanta hip-hop—led by MCs such as T.I. and Young Jeezy—was emerging as the city's dominant rap sound.

YING YANG IN THE BOOTY CLUBS

Aside from Lil Jon himself, the biggest act associated with crunk music—the Ying Yang Twins—is not really crunk at all. Ying Yang and their producer DJ Smurf emerged from bass music, but where Jon turned bass' energy into a tool aimed at bubbling up the testosterone of young men in clubs—a soundtrack for headbanging, gangsta walking, throwing 'bows—the Ying Yang Twins continued along bass music's booty-oriented path. Their music is at least as much for the ladies, whether dancing on stage or moving in the clubs. In that way, the group's modern-day booty music is the flipside—a counterpart—of crunk. And a large part of the success of "Get Low" rested on its ability to blend Jon's grinding crunk with Ying Yang's dance-friendly sound.

Eric "Kaine" Jackson Jr. and D'Angelo "D-Roc" Holmes went to the same middle school, back when Kaine stayed in downtown's Carver Homes and D-Roc lived in Grant Park's Englewood Apartments. But they didn't become friends until they were sixteen and had become rappers. By then, D-Roc had already seen his first taste of rap stardom come and go. Inspired at age eleven, after going with his mom to see Kris Kross at the Fox

Theatre, D-Roc recalls, "I said, 'I can do the same thing them little boys are doing.' So my mom said, 'Yeah, you can do it, but you've got to do it yourself.' So, I cut grass a whole year, then took my ass into the studio."

At twelve, D formed the Ghetto Funk DJ with his cousin, who also was a member of the Hard Boys, locally popular gangsta rappers that put out an album on Ichiban in 1992. By fifteen, D-Roc scored a breakthrough as the MC on the hit single "Bankhead Bounce" that capitalized on the local dance craze. But the wheels screeched to a halt when the track's producer, Diamond, got arrested on charges of child molestation (he was convicted and sentenced to forty years in prison). By then, D-Roc had also recorded a solo album—1995's *Englewood 4 Life!*, on Ichiban—which, despite being bass music through and through, contained a track called "Get Crunk" (perhaps the first instance of that term being used as a song title). But the record failed to generate much interest and, embittered by sixteen, D-Roc resolved to give up rapping. That's when he ran into Kaine walking down Flat Shoals Avenue in East Atlanta.

Kaine left Carver Homes at around twelve and moved with his mom to East Atlanta, where his parents had grown up. Kaine's grandparents were among the first blacks to move into the neighborhood, which by the '80s had become almost entirely poor and black (in the late '90s, it revived as a hipster arts and nightlife district). D-Roc was visiting his cousin in East Atlanta one day and took a walk to the store. On the way, he passed Kaine, who was in a group with one of the Hard Boys' little brothers. "People had said, 'Y'all would be great together,'" D-Roc says. "So I was searching for him and he was trying to find me, too. We finally met each other walking down the street. He said, 'Shawty, what you doing?' I said, 'I ain't rapping no more.' He said, 'Shit, don't say that. Let's go write.' We went and wrote and I said, 'I can get us an album put out.'"

The album, 1997's *True Dawgs*, was D-Roc's second for Ichiban. Though billed as D-Roc and the 2 Tight Click, it featured Kaine on many tracks. Kaine considered himself a street rapper and was not interested in bass music, so he was apprehensive about appearing with D-Roc. But, according to Kaine, D-Roc tricked him by giving him a No Limit beat to write lyrics over, then later laying the vocals over bass tracks.

D's label mate, DJ Smurf, provided one of the record's beats, and the following year, Smurf asked D to return the favor by appearing on his *Dead Crunk* album. D-Roc brought Kaine with him to the studio and, after both recorded vocals for the song, "One on One," Smurf had an idea. "I like y'all's chemistry, you need to be a group," he said.

Before *Dead Crunk*, Smurf had put out an album called *Collipark Music*—a reference to College Park in the SWATs, where Smurf grew up. He revived the title as the name for his new label, Collipark Music. By then, bass music was being replaced by the harder, proto-crunk sounds of Master P, and Smurf was inspired by the way former bass star Raheem had transitioned to the new style by putting out Drama's "Left, Right, Left" on his Tight 2 Def label. Smurf hoped to follow a similar course, so he signed D-Roc and Kaine—the Ying Yang Twins—to Collipark.

The name Ying Yang Twins had been floating around in D-Roc's head and—despite the misspelling of the Taoist concept of complementary forces, *yin* and *yang*—the name fit. Like OutKast, Kaine and D-Roc had opposing personalities. "I'm a to-myself-type of person," Kaine says. "You know how you're grandparents are, set in their ways? That's me. D-Roc is more energetic—he's the people person. Kaine is the strength of the group, D-Roc is the presence. D-Roc is more of the happy, I'm more of the pain."

At first, there wasn't a whole lot to indicate this internal dichotomy. Indeed, part of what bonded them together was their common struggle: Both had birth defects. Kaine was born with something called spastic dysplasia, a form of cerebral palsy that affected his coordination and muscle control, resulting in a limp. D-Roc was born with a deformed hand, with nubs where his fingers should be.

"It made the growing up in the city another notch harder," Kaine says. "Because kids joke. I'd be lying if I said none of the stuff said to us about our disabilities hurt our feelings. But D-Roc and I had to be thinking, because of the way our fucking lives was. He had a short hand, I got a short leg, it made us kind of be in double jeopardy—growing up black with a handicap."

Still, the Ying Yang Twins never made their disabilities a part of their music. For one, booty-bass music about birth defects would never work. But more, they never wanted to set themselves apart. "By it being what I had to go through, literally, I don't want to put it out as entertainment," Kaine says. "I just ain't comfortable exploiting that."

Perhaps Kaine and D-Roc were overcompensating to cover up their struggles and depth of character, because the Ying Yang Twins established themselves with some of the shallowest, most lightweight music. After a debut track, "True City Thugs," on the third installment of Lil Jon's *So So Def Bass All-Stars*, the Ying Yang Twins began popping up with a track stunning in its insipidity and catchiness. Appearing in late 1999, "Whistle While You Twurk" borrowed the melody of "Whistle While You Work" (from Disney's *Snow White*) and slang from New Orleans bounce culture, and delivered lyrics in a lascivious rasp over 808 beats that transported the innocent princess into the wild world of Atlanta strip clubs. Shouting out the ATL's roster of favored booty clubs—"Now where them ho's that be spittin' that game, I tink they all dance at the Blue Flame/Where them ho's that be hard booty shakin', I think they all dance a the Foxy Lady"—the song entered heavy rotation in all the clubs mentioned, where "twurking" (dancing) was the primary draw. "We got the strip clubs on lock," Kaine says.

The song's popularity in strip clubs translated to spins in dance clubs, which led to heavy rotation on Atlanta radio. Airplay meant record sales for their debut album, *Thug Walkin'*, and soon major labels were taking notice. Universal picked up distribution duties, getting the record out to a wider network of stores. By April of 2000, "Whistle" had climbed to number one on the *Billboard* rap singles chart.

"Whistle" was likely the first song specifically written for strippers—at least since the height of 2 Live Crew—to become a big national hit. The song's ride to the top suggested a new, largely unexplored, path for testing new tracks and launching them on a path to become rap hits.

To understand how groups like Ying Yang Twins turned booty clubs into a proving ground for new hip-hop hits, it's necessary to know the culture of strip clubs in the South. For some reason, many Southern strip clubs have maintained an air of respectability even as they're associated with sleaze and exploitation elsewhere. Perhaps it has to do with the same societal order that made the "old boy's club" such an institution in the South—a patriarchal legacy that made it acceptable, even status enhancing, to gather with other "powerful" men to watch (less powerful) women on display.

Still today, Southern strip clubs are often places for businessmen to network. For instance, the Gold Club—the landmark Atlanta establishment shut down in 2001 when its owner was convicted on federal racketeering charges—was long a popular spot among Buckhead executives for weekday business lunches. In a city that had few significant attractions for visitors, strip clubs did much to sustain Atlanta's convention industry. Many large Atlanta strip clubs offer a full menu, billiards, large-screen TVs for sports, dance floors (for clothed patrons), and other amenities. Not simply for lonely men slobbering in dark corners, upscale Southern strip clubs are more social environments, with a surprising number of women present as well.

No matter the club, music plays a vital role—good music makes for better dancing, which generates the best tips for the dancers. So Atlanta's strip club DJs are among the best DJs in town—people like DJ Jelly, DJ Hershey, D.C. (formerly of Tag Team, of "Whoomp!" fame), and one-time bass star, Playa Poncho. And because a song first heard while watching a woman dance is more likely to stick, strip club DJs have developed a great deal of power to make or break a new song.

Many Southern hip-hop hits—from "Get Low" to Khia's "My Neck, My Back" to Petey Pablo's "Freak-A-Leak"—started with heavy rotation in strip clubs. Producers have noted this development and made booty clubs their first stop for gauging new hits. "That's the first place I'll take records, to test it," Smurf says.

In Atlanta, songs and strip clubs have become deeply entwined: Clubs can make or break a song and, in some cases, songs can make or break a club. The Ying Yang Twins helped many clubs by naming them on record, while Jermaine Dupri damaged the rep of one, Strokers, when he rhymed in his "Welcome to Atlanta" remix, "I don't go no more, 'cause they don't know how to treat you when you come through the door." Strokers, however, bounced back and took a lead role in acknowledging the importance of strips clubs to Atlanta urban music: It instituted an "independent night," where unsigned acts can bring their music to be played in the club.

"That's how you break your music: in the strip clubs," says OutKast protégé Killer Mike, whose single "A.D.I.D.A.S." (all day I dream about sex) bumped first in the clubs. "Music is all about making people move and if you can make naked girls move, you're on to something."

Having first hit from "Whistle While You Twurk," the Ying Yang Twins—more than anyone else—became typecast as rappers who always talk about strippers. While never entirely true, D-Roc, Kaine, and Smurf were fine continuing with what worked. So 2002's *Alley: The Return of the Ying Yang Twins* set as its first single another twurking anthem, "Say I Yi Yi," which climbed to number ten on the rap chart, while "Sound Off" and "Twurkulator" continued the theme. But the opening "I'm Tired," with its bluesy piano and weary singing, suggested something more sophisticated.

The next year, Ying Yang returned with *Me & My Brother*. By the time it started gaining traction, "Get Low" had exploded nationally and the group—now signed to TVT along with Lil Jon—became the crunk movement's second most famous adherents. They were not entirely willing flag-wavers—in interviews, they'd deny they made crunk music—but they were also happy to embrace the notoriety. So *Me & My Brother* dispensed with the bass-oriented style of "Twurk" and, instead, included songs closer to crunk—such as "Georgia Dome," billed as the "Get Low Sequel"; the Lil Jon collab, "Saltshaker"; and the Lil Jon-esque "What's Happnin!"

But the record's first single, "Naggin'," was neither crunked-out nor glorifying strip clubs. It was possible to actually hear *wit* in a group written off from the start as lacking in subtlety or depth. Though it would be easy to characterize "Naggin'" as sexist in its view of male/female roles, it's saved by its sense of humor. Adopting the melody of a playground rhyme ("All the girls in France do the hula hula dance") and the muffled voices of adults on the *Peanuts* cartoons, the Twins chanted, "'Waw, waw, waw, waw, waw'/She talkin' to me like I'm dumb," echoing the pitiful complaint of every man who's ever entered into a relationship with a woman. Who knew the Ying Yang Twins had relationships with women that went beyond a lap dance?

The next track, "Naggin' Pt. II (The Answer)," was even more surprising: An equally funny and incisive female response, offered by lady rappers Flawless and Tha Rhythum (Smurf's sister). "Naggin'," along with the Sammy Sam collaboration, "Calling All Zones"—a sober, even melancholic, tour of Atlanta's disappearing past—suggested the Ying Yang Twins actually had something to say.

The success of "Get Low," then "Salt Shaker"—and the mainstream notoriety that came when Britney Spears pulled Ying Yang to appear on her *In the Zone* album—also suggested the group, confounding expectations, had the wherewithal to endure on the pop charts. By 2004, their popularity was strong enough to sustain a remix album/DVD, *My Brother & Me*, which reached number twelve on the pop chart.

Clearly, though, D-Roc and Kaine still felt misunderstood. Quoting no less an inspiration than Ralph Waldo Emerson, Kaine told *Vibe* magazine, "'To be great is to be misunderstood.'" So in 2005, they took a sharp left turn with *United State of Atlanta*, a record that washed away any taste of the group's "Twurk"-era inanity, and at the same time brought Ying Yang to the top of the charts.

Kaine dispelled any notions that *U.S.A.* would be typical Ying Yang Twins when he solemnly intoned on the dark a cappella introduction, "All Good Things." In fact, each track on the first third of the record packed a surprise: "Fuck the Ying Yang Twins" beat detractors to the punch, offering rare self-deprecation in hip-hop; "Long Time" provided gospel crooning courtesy of Anthony Hamilton and a stab at Ying Yang righteousness; "Live Again" (featuring rock vocalist Adam Levine of Maroon 5) presented the ugly side of strip clubs—desperate women compromising themselves for cash—that once seemed beyond the Twins' comprehension; "Ghetto Classics" confronted social issues including the Iraq war and urban poverty; and "23 Hr. Lock Down" (featuring Bun B of UGK) explored the realities of prison life, and the consequences of criminality. This opening stretch made for great hip-hop by any measure; that it was the Ying Yang Twins was nothing short of astounding.

"I'm more of a soulful person," Kaine explains, "because of what I experienced growing up, and the type of mind games people tried to play from me walking the way I walk. But being in a team, the Ying Yang Twins, [Smurf] told us he was selling sex. In order for me to fuck with that, I had to play the role. I like addressing real-life, serious shit, but we had to create a name. [*U.S.A.*] is more what I want. We hate that people think we don't have brains. I feel like we're the most underrated group out of Atlanta, cause we banging hard as fuck but we're treated like underdogs."

The middle third of *U.S.A.* reverted to more familiar Twins nastiness, but the trio of songs introduced by spoken "Sex Therapy" skits—including the hushed-voice hit, "Wait (The Whisper Song)" and the similar follow-up, "Pull My Hair"—made a leap in maturity by addressing the needs of women in the sexual transaction. More, they introduced a new sound that Smurf—who renamed himself Beat-in-Azz for trademark reasons, then finally became Mr. Collipark—created and called "intimate club music." The diametric opposite of crunk, intimate club music offered laid-back whispers and a minimalist bass-heavy track. Mississippi rapper David Banner became the first outsider to embrace the sound, recruiting Collipark to produce his own hushed track, "Play," which became Banner's biggest hit yet.

"I want to take it in a whole other direction [from crunk]," Mr. Collipark says. "People still want to get physical in the club, but we're grown now. Instead of trying to tell a girl to shake her ass, blah, blah, blah, I want to get up close and personal with the artists I'm doing these records with and ask them, 'What are you telling the girls you pick up in the club?'"

By the final stretch of *U.S.A.*, it was almost a relief to hear Ying Yang reverting to familiar crunk ways, with "Hoes," "Badd" (featuring Houston sensation Mike Jones), "Put That Thang Down" (the obligatory Lil Jon production), and the Atlanta anthem "U.S.A." By then, the point has been made: D-Roc and Kaine have a lot more to offer. Suddenly, the Ying Yang Twins had become the "OutKast of crunk."

Before the Twins returned in 2006 with *Chemically Imbalanced* (the original title was *2 Live Crew*, in tribute to their forebears), D-Roc released a side project with younger brothers, a trio called Da Muzicianz. But more significantly, a third Atlanta subgenre slipped into the void between Lil Jon's crunk and Mr. Collipark's intimate club music. Called snap music because tracks often used finger snaps in place of the snare beat—as Ying Yang's intimate club track, "Wait (The Whisper Song)" had—the sound borrowed crunk's chanting and synth lines while taking a mellow, stripped-down approach. According to Dem Franchize Boyz, the Atlanta quartet that offered snap hits in 2005 and 2006 including "I Think They Like Me" and "Lean

Wit It, Rock Wit It," snap was crunk music that allowed you to dance without spilling the drink in your hands.

A second Atlanta quartet, D4L, offered snap's genre-defining hit: "Laffy
Taffy." Raw and minimalist, like a country cousin to the Neptunes' more
ambitious output, the track featured a two-note riff with a single finger-snap
beat, and a silly conceit about a girl shaking her laffy taffy. Absurdly basic as
a composition, it was somehow infectious enough to reach number one in
early 2006. Where crunk seemed to have run its course by 2006, snap music
stretched its legacy slightly and kept Atlanta rap acts on the pop charts. New
rappers such as College Park's Young Joc (who hit big with "It's Going
Down") and Decatur's Blak Jak served to keep Atlanta front-and-center in
Southern hip-hop as well.

MIAMI BECOMES A HIP-HOP CITY (AGAIN)

In early 2004, when Lil Jon began working on his *Crunk Juice* album, he
felt the need to get away from the distractions of Atlanta. To escape, he
rented a mansion in Miami for several months, where he and his musicians
churned out tracks all night—in between trips to the club for inspiration.
Lil Jon's keyboardist LRoc estimates they made three hundred tracks in all
for *Crunk Juice*. "You have to take yourself out of your normal environment to take something to another level," Lil Jon says. "You have to get
into a different mind state to get your tracks in a different mind state."

The choice of Miami as Jon's home studio away from home was not designed to bring crunk back to its ancestral homeland, the birthplace of bass.
The weather, the water, the women, the clubs, the exotic, international vibe;
all these things made Miami a great place to spend a working vacation. And
Jon was not the only hip-hop star who made Miami a second home. Southerners and Northerners—producers like Timbaland and Scott Storch,
artist/executives from Diddy to Jay-Z, Will Smith to Missy Elliott—have
put some roots down, come to record, shoot videos, or just soak in the
warmth.

Though bass music is gone from the city in all but moments of dance-floor
nostalgia, a decade later Miami once again became a hip-hop city. This time,
however, it's a destination for the entire hip-hop nation, a perfect backdrop
for many of rap's primary images: the scantily clad dancers, the shiny bling,
the steamy clubs. That's what brought *The Source* magazine to set up its annual Source Awards in Miami Beach, and MTV followed with its Video Music Awards. Three decades after top black entertainers were arrested for not
carrying ID cards on the strip, hip-hop now rules South Beach.

Miami has also produced some important local hip-hop acts in the post-bass era—most significantly, Trick Daddy—who, along with former Poison Clan rapper JT Money, defined the transition from early '90s bass to the harder, street sound that now defines Miami hip-hop. Locals love Trick Daddy because he's clearly not a product of Miami Beach, with its nouveau riche hip-hop carpetbaggers. Tricky's from that *other* Miami, the rugged Pork 'N' Beans projects of Liberty City.

Back when he was still Maurice Young, Trick grew up in the projects with his mother and her ten other children. Trouble came early: At thirteen, Trick was kicked out of school and sent to a juvenile detention center for trying to assault a teacher with an iron pipe. At fourteen, he was back in for auto theft, and the year after that, for aggravated assault. When he got out, Trick was sent to live with his dad, Charles Young. "If you're having problems in the projects, either the problem has to leave or the family has to leave. So I didn't want my momma to end up getting kicked out," Trick says.

In the '70s, Charles "Pop" Young and his partner Edward Meriwether were the South District DJs, one of the first generation of mobile sound systems in Miami. Later, they formed one the seminal bass labels, Suntown Records. When Trick moved in with his dad, he started hanging around his oldest half-brother, Hollywood, who had been involved with Suntown and was working with his friend, Ted Lucas, on getting their own operation going.

But Trick wasn't with his dad for long. By sixteen, he was deep into selling drugs, until one night a cop pulled him over to find three kilos of cocaine and a semiautomatic handgun in his car. A judge sentenced him to four years, he got out on probation a year later, then landed back in jail the next month for violating parole.

"We came from a hustling life, so he understood hustling," says Pop, who wound up in jail around the same time. "Because we all had to provide for ourselves. From his brother Hollywood living a street life, it came for Trick to be part of the street as well."

Spending the next two years in prison, Trick developed a skill he didn't know he had. "A lot of cats in there can't read and write, and I used to help them write letters," Trick says. "And they was like, 'Damn, man, you got a way with words.' If somebody's baby momma ain't want to let him talk to his kids, after I write her a letter she'd feel sorry for him, bring the kids to see him, send him a few dollars."

He also started writing rhymes—lots of them. As Pop recalls, "During Trick's incarceration, he sent his lyrics to the house—about twice a week we received lyrics from Trick. He had time to think. He took that time to express his feelings in writing. Sometimes people are not aware of their knowledge until something happens to them."

By the time Trick's term was through, he'd committed himself to rapping. His brother Hollywood was set to invest in his career, but a few months before Trick's release, Hollywood was murdered. The death underscored Trick's determination to get off the streets. "You live by the gun, you die by the gun," he says.

Released from prison to attend his brother's funeral, Trick told Hollywood's friend, Ted Lucas, about his rap plans. Ted, who'd started a label called Slip-N-Slide Records, expressed his support, but had his doubts whether Trick would follow through.

When Trick got his release he went to the Pac Jam, a North Miami teen club owned by the city's rap godfather, Luther Campbell. He entered and won an open-mic contest there, and Luke tapped him to appear on his 1996 single, "Scarred." The record shot to number seven on the rap charts, launching Trick's career. Now convinced that Trick was serious, Lucas signed him to Slip-N-Slide. Within a year, Trick's debut, *Based on a True Story*, arrived. With its two-part title track invoking Hollywood's memory and death in the streets, the record portrayed real life in Liberty City—heavier on truth and consequences than some gangsta fantasy—and the huge regional response sent sales over one hundred thousand copies.

National success followed in 1999, when "Nann Nigga" introduced the rest of the country to Trick and his female foil, Trina, whose hard-core styles revealed how Miami had moved beyond bass-music's party vibe. For Katrina Taylor, the single launched a career as a rapper—a job she'd never considered. Also from Liberty City, Trina began dating Hollywood when she was eighteen. She worked for UPS, then AT&T, and met Ted Lucas when Hollywood took her to the Slip-N-Slide office. Trina grew close to Ted and to Trick, who'd call her from prison to talk about his rap dreams. When Hollywood died, Ted and Trick stayed close to Trina, who decided she was going to sell real estate.

Then one day Trick asked Trina to appear on a song written as a comical dialogue between a man and a woman at a club. Though she'd never rapped before, Trick and Ted had a feeling she was exactly what they needed. "Nobody else talks like Trina," Lucas told the *Miami New Times*. "Nobody else has a slicker mouth than Trina. She was a rapper already and just didn't know it." Her sassy raps helped elevate the song to number three on the rap chart, and launched Trina as a Slide-N-Slide solo artist—the South's own trashy-mouthed counterpart to Lil' Kim.

Across a series of albums tied by their titles—*www.thug.com*; *Book of Thugs: Chapter AK, Verse 47*; *Thugs Are Us*; *Thug Holiday*, and *Thug Matrimony: Married to the Streets*—Trick Daddy reinvented the Miami hip-hop sound as one that was at times recognizably Southern, even crunk, but often wider in scope, combining elements of reggae, house, soul, gospel, and pop. More impressive than the albums was his string of diverse singles, each more mature and sophisticated than its predecessor: the crunked out "Shut Up"; the sing-song and reggae-rolling "I'm a Thug"; the Slip-N-Slide bass revival "Take It to Da House" (based on a sample of Miami legends KC & the Sunshine Band); the lyrically acrobatic and summer grooving "In Da Wind" (featuring OutKast's Big Boi and Cee-Lo); the melancholic, socially conscious "Thug Holiday."

By 2001's *Thugs Are Us*, Trick's albums consistently hit the Top 10 on both the pop and R&B/Hip-Hop charts, but trouble was not yet out of reach. In February 2003, Trick got arrested for pulling a gun on another man after a pick-up basketball game. While still out on bond that September, he again found himself in police custody, arrested for drug possession. After a stint of house arrest, Trick got a break: In exchange for guilty pleas on both charges, Trick walked away with three years supervised probation, anger management classes, and community service.

Trick's determination to stay clean and out of trouble made 2004's *Thug Matrimony* a departure in many ways. Building on the refrain of "Tricky loves the kids" from "In Da Wind," a bunch of songs deal with kids and parenting issues, or actually feature kids. In "These Are the Daze," Trick preaches: "Far as the kids concerned, let 'em live and learn/Let 'em grow to be older than us, teach more than gang banging, drug deals and hold ups/Slow up on your tricking just a little bit, and when they want to get high let them hear this/And let 'em hit it till they OD, cause when they sober up they gonna love and respect us/Now we having more doctors, lawyers, teachers, preachers and deep sea explorers." Both "I Wanna Sing" and "The Children's Song" feature voices of kids from the Betty Wright Children's Choir—a troupe led by Miami's original soul diva, the former protégé of Clarence "Blowfly" Reid and TK Records' Henry Stone.

The old Trick Daddy creeps in with "Menage A Trois" and "J.O.D.D." (Jump on the Dick), or "Thugs About" and "Ain't a Thug." Trick Daddy remains the quintessential Southern hip-hop thug. For Trick, though, "thug" is just about keeping it real, staying connected to the streets, and, like a modern-day bluesman, capturing the pain of the 'hood. On *Thug Matrimony*'s "I Cry," Ron Isley delivers the hook but the spirit is Trick

Daddy's: "No matter how hard I cry it just don't seem loud enough/Lord I hope you're hearing me/This goes out to the lonely streets."

As opposed to the bling-bling of so much hip-hop, South and beyond, Trick doesn't talk much about material possessions. "There's more people in the world with problems than there is with material things," he says.

Less than two years after Trina and the Ying Yang Twins joined Trick on *Thug Matrimony*'s closing track, proclaiming how, "Everybody wanna be down wit the South," that truth hit close to home when Slip-N-Slide's hard-core rapper Rick Ross debuted at number one on the pop chart with his first album, *Port of Miami*. Unlike Trick, Ross—born William Roberts in Carroll City—embraced his city's reputation as a center for drug trafficking and portrayed himself as a crime lord (his rap name paid homage to famed real-life drug kingpin) for the entertainment of the nation.

By the time Trick Daddy returned in late 2006 with his latest installment, *Back by Thug Demand*, Miami had again become a hotbed of up-and-coming talent, with the homegrown super-producer Jim Jonsin shepherding new acts like Pretty Ricky toward the mainstream.

DOWN SOUTH (OF THE BORDER) HIP-HOP

Many would argue Miami was not so much a Southern city as a Latin American city. At least, it was where Latin America met the American South, so it made sense that Miami Latinos integrated Southern hip-hop styles with Spanish influences to create a Dirty South flavor that—combined with Latino rappers from Texas such as South Park Mexican and Chingo Bling—formed what might be termed Southern border hip-hop.

In fact, Spanish-flavored Southern hip-hop goes back nearly as far as the English variety, with Miami bass. Lazaro Mendez's parents came from Cuba three years before he was born in Hollywood, Florida. His mother was a singer in Cuba and his family stayed involved in music in South Florida. In the early '80s, Laz worked with his brother Ray, a mobile DJ, as the Ultra Ray DJs. By 1986, Laz was scratching and mixing on the radio for Miami's Hot 105, then moved to Power 96 in 1989. Soon after arriving, Laz says, "I was messing around with a merengue record and booty record, and I mixed them together and thought, Shit, that sounds good. So that night I got into the radio station and said, I wanna try something. I mixed Clay D's 'Boot the Booty' and Wilfredo Vargas 'El Africano.' The phone lines were insane, because nobody had ever done that."

Hearing how perfectly the merengue melodies and booty bass meshed, Laz brought local rapper Danny D into the studio, laid down a thumping bass track, sampled "El Africano" for the hook, and came up with his 1990 classic "Mami El Negro." While the track, which had English rapping and a Spanish chorus, got played mostly on English radio in Florida, Texas, and California, it also resonated with the second-generation Latinos who were navigating between the American culture they grew up in and their parents' culture. "We gave them the bass music they were into and the Spanish music that their parents were making them listen to at all these parties," Laz says.

A decade later, DJ Laz was still around making records and doing radio when a young Cuban rapper named Armando Perez, aka Pitbull, began bringing around his tracks. Where Laz had combined Latin flavors with bass music, Pitbull mixed his Cuban heritage with a more contemporary Southern rap sound: crunk. Laz heard promise in Pitbull's tracks, but kept sending him back to the studio until, one day, Pitbull brought him his single, "Oye." "Now you got something," Laz told Pit, and put the track on the air that night. "Oye," which slips between English and Spanish rhymes and blends Southern-style chanting with merengue keyboard riffs, was a Miami smash. Among those taking note was Lil Jon, who took Pitbull under his wing and produced his 2004 TVT Records debut, *M.I.A.M.I.—Money Is a Major Issue.*

Like DJ Laz, Pitbull was the American-born son of Cuban immigrants. He grew up all over Miami, in neighborhoods including Westchester, Little Havana, Opa-Locka, Miami Lakes, and South Miami, which exposed him to blacks and Latinos of all backgrounds. He first heard 2 Live Crew as a third grader and loved this early glimpse into nasty music. At sixteen, he wound up at a Miami video shoot for New York rapper DMX and fell into a freestyle battle with the rapper Drag-On from the Ruff Ryders. He caught the ear of record exec Irv Gotti, who stood nearby. Gotti wanted to work with Pit, but he had no written material at that point, only freestyles. Pit started writing raps and, at eighteen, signed with Luther Campbell. The deal lasted only a year, but he learned about the business, and went to work with Miami producers the Diaz Brothers, who made "Oye."

While *M.I.A.M.I.* threw in Spanish lingo and flavors, mostly Pitbull was a Southern crunk rapper. But Pit was also fine playing on stereotypes about Cubans in Miami. After all, if Al Pacino's Cuban American *Scarface* character was powerful enough to inspire the names of rappers in Houston and Memphis—and inspire the rhymes of countless others—why shouldn't he claim *Scarface* as kin?

"We all have Scarfaces, either in our family or our friends' family," Pitbull says. "But the rap game is the new dope game. The music is my cocaine. I go city to city, trying to get you hooked."

Pitbull's follow-up to *M.I.A.M.I.*, late 2006's *El Mariel*, paid more direct tribute to his heritage—its title refers to the Mariel boatlift that brought 125,000 Cuban refugees to South Florida in 1980. Soon after its release, Pit planned to return with *Armando*, a Spanish-only album.

Meanwhile, Spanish-language hip-hop is a boom market in the U.S., much of it revolving around Miami and places on the country's Southern edge. In recent years, the hip-hop-inspired Spanish dance-hall reggae genre called reggaeton has exploded, with artists such as the Miami-raised Tego Calderone flirting with mainstream crossover. It could be that Southern rap's original city may yet be hip-hop's future capital.

chapter 11

HOUSTON REPRISE— THE TURN OF THE SCREW

THINGS IS SLOWER IN THE SOUTH

While Miami's heart beats to a Caribbean-inspired pulse, the uptempo rhythms that bass music introduced to Southern hip-hop are only half of the story. Indeed, Southern hip-hop is bipolar: Literally, it revolves around two distinct poles—the eastern axis around Miami and Atlanta, and the western axis centered on Houston and Memphis (New Orleans being a sort of middle ground influenced by both). It is also bipolar in the clinical sense, because the eastern pole is manic—with hyperactive beats prompting spastic dance-floor gyrations—and the western pole depressed: slow and easy for crawling traffic down sprawling avenues.

Of all Southern hip-hop's flavors, none captured the lazy pace of an oppressively hot and humid day in the big dirty as well as screw music. The warped, slurred concoction—named after its creator, DJ Screw—oozed out of Houston slow as molasses. This was music at the heart of a culture so often characterized by its languid pace.

People generally attribute the South's slower pace to the heat, but that's not the whole story. How, then, to explain the high energy in Miami, where sweat only serves as social lubrication, increasing the tempo? Matt Sonzala, the Houston-based writer and radio host, offers one explanation: the drugs. "Go to Miami and what do you get a ton of? Cocaine. Go to Texas, what do you get a ton of? Mexican weed and pills [and codeine cough syrup]. It's oversimplifying to a certain extent, but the party is different."

It could also be that the choice of drug merely reflects the innate mood of an area; the way people party extends from the way they live. So the question remains why one part of the South sped up hip-hop, while another part slowed it down. The common bonds: Southern rebellion—neither side was content to leave it alone—and the bass that throbs through both extremes.

Having begun with Miami's accelerated tempos, this history of Southern hip-hop comes to its logical conclusion with the tale of how rap music got itself screwed.

THE SOUTHSIDE'S SCREWED-UP EMPIRE

Robert Davis said he got his name DJ Screw because he'd destroy the records he hated by carving into them with a screw. It wasn't his ability to get ladies into bed, and it wasn't because of what he'd become famous for— "screwing" records (he was DJ Screw before he ever slowed down a mix). And screw music, the genre he launched, was named not so much as a description of the sound but in recognition of its creator.

In the late '80s, Screw was living with his dad in Quail Meadows Apartments, down Telephone Road just past the airport, and he kept the place jammed with stacks of records. Impressed with his collection and scratching skills, a fellow DJ named Chill (Andrew Hatton) asked Screw to DJ parties with him. In the early '90s, when 97.9 The Box started up and Chill worked promotions there, he tried to get Screw on air. But Screw DJed backward— turntable one and two rearranged—which required some basic rewiring the station didn't want to do.

By then, though, Screw's reputation as a scratch DJ was spreading, and a couple of Third Ward neighborhood kids approached him about doing some cutting on their demo. The group featured Devin "the Dude" Copeland—who'd go on to have a long career as a gifted but underappreciated solo rapper—as well as blind MC Rob Quest, and Jugg Mugg, collectively known as the Odd Squad. The tracks fell into the hands of Rap-A-Lot's James Prince, who signed the Odd Squad and put out its only album, *Fadanuf Fa Erybody*—a record of laid-back grooves, goofy humor, and stoner ethos that was completely different from anything else the label ever released. By the time the Odd Squad recorded, though, Screw was busy establishing his own legend in Houston.

Various legends circulate about how Screw came to slow down records, but in truth, when Screw first discovered it, he was just doing something all

DJs did: using the turntable's pitch-control knob to beat match (that is, changing the tempos of records so two songs mix well together). Though some claim other DJs were occasionally slowing down records earlier, Screw probably made his discovery no later than 1991 and soon started incorporating slowed songs into his club sets and mix tapes.

People took notice: Slowing records down was a simple gesture, but it created a hazy, dreamlike effect that people liked. It turned upbeat hip-hop into the kind of slow-riding pimpin' music the South had loved for decades. Some liked the way it enabled them to better hear the words and sonic elements in songs. And many screw fans felt like the hypnotic pace complemented the dulling effects of their choice drug—codeine syrup. For all these reasons, Screw's mix tapes established screw music on the Houston underground.

Working out of his house in South Park, off Reveille Street and I-610, Screw created a cottage industry with his distinctive mix tapes. At first, he specialized in personal mixes: A customer could go over to Screw's house, ask for certain songs or styles, and for about ten dollars he'd deliver a tailor-made tape. The early tapes consisted almost entirely of already-released tracks by nationally known acts—2Pac was a fixture, as well as rising locals like UGK—reimagined by Screw and his pitch controller.

But as the mixes grew more popular, Screw took the idea of personalized tapes further, by allowing customers to request shout-outs and inviting neighborhood friends to freestyle over the music—sometimes adding in, for the amusement of southsiders, some disses aimed at the northside. These freestylers were, at first, guys with no ambition of being rappers—they were just friends hanging out, having fun. Among the first to show up on a tape was Screw's brother Al-D, as well as Patrick Hawkins, aka Fat Pat, and Pat's brother, Hawk. Pat, in particular, was already a celebrity in the 'hood, a guy with money and cars (never mind how). He used to lay down personalized shout-outs as needed.

"I'd give shout outs to different people in the neighborhoods," Screw told *Murder Dog* magazine. "I'd make personal tapes. . . . Some of my partners that are locked up right now, they'd come to the house and kick it, watch me make a tape. Might get on the mic, give shout outs. We'd ride around, listen to that in the car. . . . We got some feedback on it, people were likin' it. Everybody was takin' it serious."

The homemade vocals made Screw's mixes more popular, and over time the freestyles and shout-outs evolved into more formal verses. As the vocalists were turning into local rap stars, they started giving Screw original tracks to include in his mixes. In addition to Pat, Hawk, and Al-D, one of the earliest and best-known rappers in Screw's camp was E.S.G., whose original song "Swangin' and Bangin'" began showing up on tapes around 1994. Its success pushed the local cult around Screw to a whole new level.

Born Cedric Hill, E.S.G. (Everyday Street Gangsta) was actually from Opelousas, Louisiana, between Houston and New Orleans. His father lived in Houston, and when he started college in Lafayette, Louisiana, E.S.G. began making trips to H-Town to pursue his rap dreams. Friends suggested he pay a visit to DJ Screw's house to let him hear his songs. "Swangin' and Bangin'" caught Screw's attention: It was a laid-back flute-driven slice of pimp-funk that celebrated the Texas car culture of Cadillacs, candy paint, flashy rims, and white-wall tires—plus "swangin' and bangin'," the practice of turning the steering wheel left and right, often to the beat of a favorite screw song.

Screw started putting "Swangin' and Bangin'" on his mixes, which got the song out to thousands of Screw fans and turned E.S.G. into screw music's first breakout star. E.S.G. released his debut album, *Ocean of Funk*, in 1995 and sold about one hundred thousand copies. Later that year, E.S.G.'s label hooked up with the major distributor Priority Records and compiled more E.S.G. material (including the original and screwed versions of "Swangin'") into a second album, *Sailin' Da South*, which sold twice as much. But by then, E.S.G. was serving a two-and-a-half-year jail stint, which kept him out of the limelight.

Lil' Keke, a rapper from South Park's Herschelwood neighborhood, also launched a successful independent rap career after rising to fame on Screw tapes. Keke was young enough to have grown up on Screw's tapes. Through middle and high school, Keke witnessed the evolution of the screw-music phenomenon and dreamed about having Screw make a tape that featured him one day.

"Ballers from different neighborhoods would get together and have their own tapes made," Keke explained on *Down-South.com*. "Folks from 5th Ward, 3rd Ward, Botany, Dead End, and other 'hoods would have their own tapes out, and people from all over the city would buy them. . . . Every neighborhood that did a tape would have somebody grab the mic and freestyle. And people would talk about who was the best. It would be like: Oh, have you heard so-and-so from Botany, he got flow. . . . And Herschelwood wasn't big in the gangsta department . . . we couldn't go in there and buy out studio time and pay to have a whole bunch of tapes out. . . . So when I was a youngster on the corner I used to say, 'Man when I get my money right I'm going to go over there and make a tape.'"

At around eighteen, Keke finally made it over to Screw's house. By then, appearing on Screw tapes had become so popular, Keke had to make an appointment. When his turn finally came on the mic, Keke ripped so hard that he quickly rivaled Fat Pat as Screw's most popular freestyler. Keke's tapes became Screw's top-sellers, and customers started hiring Keke to appear on their own custom-made tapes. One night over at Screw's house, Keke met up with Fat Pat and they decided to do a track together. "When we made that tape there that night, that's when the Screwed [Up] Click originated," Keke says.

The growing roster of rappers showing up at Screw's house became informally defined as the Screwed Up Click. These included E.S.G. (who was off in jail), Lil' Keke, Fat Pat, Hawk, and Al-D, plus cats like Big Pokey, the Botany Boyz (featuring C-Note), Youngstar, and later, Big Moe and Lil' Flip. By 1995, screw music had become popular around Texas and neighboring states, and was beginning to spill out nationally. So DJ Screw signed with Big Tyme Records, the local label that first put out UGK, and with national distribution through Priority Records, Screw released the first of two *3 'N the Mornin'* CDs, Screw's first commercially available mixes. Vol. 1 concentrated mostly on screwed versions of familiar national tracks, but it was followed soon after with Vol. 2, which featured local rappers—E.S.G., Botany Boyz, Al-D, and Big Moe.

One song from the second mix, Lil' Keke's "Pimp the Pen," became a radio hit. It was yet another milestone in the ascension of DJ Screw, who was by then selling a thousand tapes a week—still directly from his house—and it launched Keke's rap career, solo and as part of the Herschelwood Hardheads. Keke's 1997 debut, *Don't Mess Wit Texas*—featuring a screwed version of the sequel, "Still Pimpin' Pens"—and its 1998 follow-up, *The Commission* (featuring the hit, "South Side"), established him as one of Houston's most popular rap acts.

Even as he began releasing commercial CDs, Screw kept on churning out mix tapes—he's said to have created over a thousand. He continued putting mixes out on "gray tapes" (Maxell metal cassettes) even into the era of CDs and MP3s. He first invested in a handful of cassette duplicators to speed up the process of creating dubs, but eventually he farmed out the job to professional duplication companies. When Screw's operation got too big for his South Park crib, he upgraded to a bigger place in the suburbs, and eventually got another house to use just as a studio. To facilitate his sales, Screw opened a store, Screwed Up Records & Tapes.

At its height in the late '90s, screw music had become an integral part of an entire subculture. Before he opened his store, fans would line up in front of his house, and around the block, to buy his tapes. At first, neighbors called the cops—no one, they figured, could attract so many desperate buyers if they weren't selling a highly addictive, illegal substance. Technically they were right (Screw's mix tapes being bootlegs).

In a February 1997 story in the *Houston Press*, Megan Halverson described the scene at DJ Screw's place: "At eight o'clock almost every night, the privacy gate to DJ Screw's driveway swings open, and cars steadily fill up the street in front of his house. Teenagers and adults—black, Hispanic and occasionally white—line up at the back door's metal security gate to buy from the selection of $10 tapes Screw and his band of 20 in-house rappers (The Screwed Up Click) have just recorded."

Screw culture involved the intermingling of the music with other key elements in the life of his South Houston fans: cars and drugs. Taking cues from E.S.G.'s car anthem, swangin' and bangin' became a key component to a night out cruising the streets with friends, booming screw music from the truck.

Just as closely tied to screw music was the genre's choice intoxicant: Known as syrup, or lean, or "purple stuff," it was any number of drink combinations involving cough syrup with codeine (such as prescription antihistamine Promethazine or over-the-counter cough medicines), sometimes mixed with liquor, but usually diluted with soda such as Sprite or seltzer (and sometimes sweetened with a dissolved Jolly Rancher candy). By custom, syrup was poured into a Styrofoam cup with ice, though that wasn't necessary to achieve the desired effect: a particularly woozy state where senses swirled and everything slowed to a sluggish pace. As much as the drug ecstasy reflected the communal euphoria intended in rave music, or LSD echoed the hallucinatory quality of psychedelic rock, syrup was the ingested counterpart of screw music.

In truth, sipping syrup had been around for generations—DJ Screw neither invented it nor introduced it to his core fans. "It was just a way of life," E.S.G. says. "My daddy says he used to drink it when he was a kid. It's like smoking weed." But it's also impossible to deny the role screw music played in encouraging people to "sip syrup." Some of that was indirect, once people discovered that syrup and screw went together naturally. But there was also a strong element promoting syrup in the music. The liner notes to *3 'N the Mornin'* invite listeners to "Go to that other level by sippin' syrup . . . or whatever gets you to that other level." Two of the tracks mention syrup in the title—"Sippin' Codeine" and "Smokin' and Leanin'"—while other tracks refer to it in lyrics.

Because syrup was available over-the-counter—or prescribed by doctors—users tended to view sipping as safe. But when screw music and its connection to codeine abuse reached the mainstream, the music became controversial—frequently cited in drug-prevention efforts. By then, the music's popularity had grown far beyond codeine users (to whatever extent it was the music's audience to start) and DJ Screw backtracked on his earlier endorsements of the drug.

"'Cause I play my music slow, people think you gotta get high, get fucked up, do drugs, just to listen to my music," Screw told *Murder Dog*. "It ain't like that at all. . . . You don't gotta get high to listen to my music. . . . I'm just bringin' it to you in a different style, where you can hear everything and feel everything. Give you something to ride to."

But there was little indication that the association between codeine abuse and screw music was lessening. By 2000, health reports indicated that codeine use had reached near epidemic proportions in parts of Houston, and sipping syrup was spreading throughout the country. That year, Memphis' Three 6 Mafia teamed with Houston's UGK on the song "Sippin' on Some Syrup," which became a national hit. And the Screwed Up Click remained at the forefront of the drug's glorification.

Leading the pack was Big Moe (Kenneth Moore), a rapper and R&B singer who was probably the S.U.C.'s most musically talented member. After contributing "Sippin' Codeine" to *3 'N the Mornin'*, Moe became the S.U.C.'s go-to guy for singing hooks and guest raps on albums by Hawk, Botany Boyz, E.S.G., Big Pokey, and Fat Pat. With his own debut album in 2000, Big Moe made sipping syrup central in his music. Titled *City of Syrup*, it featured Moe on the cover, pouring purple liquid out of a Styrofoam cup over the Houston skyline. The record's single, "Barre Baby"—its title a reference to a cough syrup brand—was an incredibly catchy ode to being a codeine fiend, complete with children singing the hook. The track actually hit *Billboard*'s R&B/Hip-Hop chart, helping the record sell close to two hundred thousand copies.

City of Syrup's title cut was also addictive—with its harmonica-driven down-home country blues, lightning guest rap from Z-Ro, and infectious singing ("All I wanna do, is bang screw/In the dirty third, the city of syrup, bang screw"). The way Big Moe made some of the most dynamic, accessible hip-hop in Houston made his dangerous message all the more attractive.

As DJ Screw's music reached closer to the mainstream, the Screwed Up Click was becoming an actual group that performed and recorded together. A 1999 compilation, *Blockbleeders*, brought the S.U.C. together as never before, and Screw planned to release his own rap album. "It ain't gonna stop till the casket drop," he promised *Murder Dog*.

And then it stopped. On November 16, 2000, the thirty-year-old Robert Davis Jr. was found dead in his studio after suffering a fatal heart attack. The news shook Houston's hip-hop scene, where Screw had for several years been the dominant figure. The Harris County medical examiner confirmed suspicions that Screw had overdosed on a combination of codeine and other drugs. While he floated just under the radar for much of the country, in his hometown Screw was a true icon, his memory continually invoked even years after his death.

Screwed Up Records & Tapes has kept DJ Screw's substantial body of mix tapes available, while Screw's legacy has grown larger than ever. It became commonplace for Southern rappers (as well as some R&B and rock acts) to release "chopped and screwed" remixes of their albums—*chopped*, referring to the cuts, scratches, pauses, and rewinds that accompany a slowed-down mix. And a new crop of Houston rappers broke nationally relying on many of the elements that defined Screw and the Screwed Up Click.

Even before DJ Screw's death, Screwed Up Click members were slowly entering the mainstream. Except for Scarface's successful solo albums, the mid- and late '90s were a fairly dry period for Houston rappers nationally. An exception came in 1999, when rapper Lil' Troy emerged seemingly out of nowhere to score a hit with "Wanna Be a Baller," which catapulted his debut album, *Sittin' Fat Down South*, into the R&B/Hip-Hop top ten with 1.5 million sales.

The single rolled on a mellow, minimal keyboard track and classic pimp-soul chorus ("Wanna be a baller, shot-caller, 20-inch blades on the Impala . . . /Hit the highway, making money the fly way, but there's got to be a better way"). Though Troy was not directly affiliated with Screw, the song featured S.U.C. rappers Youngstar, Hawk, and most significantly, Fat Pat. A year before the song's release, Fat Pat had been murdered in Houston. Pat's posthumous album, *Ghetto Dreams*, arrived soon after his death and became a big hit locally. Troy, meanwhile, had lifted vocals that Pat—an old neighbor from the Dead End—had recorded years earlier for the Screw-affiliated group Mass 187 (who Troy worked with as well) and fit them onto his track. With Pat's prominent role on "Wanna Be a Baller," Pat became the S.U.C.'s first to cross into the mainstream, albeit after his death. (In 2006, Pat's brother Hawk was murdered as well.)

Though Troy hadn't been heard on record before *Sittin' Fat* appeared on his own Short Stop label (and was picked up nationally by Universal

Records), this was the same Lil' Troy that a decade earlier had been first to release the song "Scarface" by the pre-Geto Boys Scarface, then still known as Akshun. While Troy had continued to dabble in music, he mostly stayed busy with his street hustle: drug dealing. His criminal pursuits caught up with him just as he was putting *Sittin' Fat* together. In the time between his arrest and his trial, Troy released the album, signed a major-label deal, and saw his single shoot up the charts. Then, as the record's popularity peaked in late 1999, Troy was sentenced to eighteen months on a drug-related charge.

The time away put the brakes on Troy's music career, though he attempted to return after his 2001 release with the album, *Back to Ballin'*. He also tried to put out a record by his son, Troy Jr. (aka T2). But Troy's name stayed in the news mostly because of his relationship with Scarface two decades earlier. First, in 2002, Scarface sued Troy for putting old recordings of the "Scarface" track onto *Sittin' Fat*. They settled out of court for a reported $220,000, and Troy followed up with a lawsuit of his own. He sued Scarface for defamation of character after Scarface implied—on the track "G Code," from the Geto Boys' 2005 reunion album, *The Foundation*—that Troy had snitched others out to get a lesser sentence. As part of his response to Scarface, Troy produced an affidavit he claimed proved that Scarface, in fact, had snitched out his cocaine dealer back in 1999.

Meanwhile, another Screwed Up Click member was making moves. Wesley Eric Weston, the rapper known as Lil' Flip, was still only seventeen when he fell in with Screw in the last year or so of the DJ's life. Flip grew up in the southside's Cloverland Park neighborhood, living with his grandparents and attending the Southside Christian Love Baptist Church, where his grandma played piano. A star basketball player at Worthing High School, he turned to rap when that started paying off first. Through a member of the trio H.S.E. (Hustlaz Stackin' Endz), Flip got his break appearing solo on two 1999 local hits: "Diamonds All-N-Yo Face," from *Third Coast Born* by rapper C-Note (of the Cloverland group Botany Boyz), and "Realist Rhymin'" from E.S.G.'s post-prison release, *Shinin' N' Grindin'*.

Flip's affiliation with C-Note brought him to the attention of DJ Screw. After knocking Screw out with a freestyle, Flip got invited to bust on Screw's *Southside Still Holdin'* tape, which showcased Flip going on for what seemed like forever on a classic freestyle. After Flip presented Screw with a plaque recognizing him as the "Best DJ in Texas," Screw returned the favor: At the St. Patrick's Day 2000 release party for Flip's debut album, *The Leprechaun*, Screw gave Flip a plaque anointing him the "Freestyle King." A *Freestyle King* Screw tape soon followed.

The Leprechaun came out on Sucka Free Records, the first product of Lil' Flip's partnership with local concert promoter and family friend, Duane "Humpty Hump" Hobbs. It yielded the local hit "I Can Do That," a humorous old-school boast, as well as the autobiographical "The Biz" and "Dirty Souf," a catchy regional anthem that captures the vibe of South Houston. The album title was Flip's way of representing his 'hood, Cloverland (as in four-leaf clovers and leprechauns), but the cover art—a Lucky Charms cereal box parody with Flip dressed in a bright green tuxedo and top hat—was an odd choice. Looking like a leprechaun, after all, was about as far from "hard" as a Houston MC could get, short of dressing up like the Easter bunny. Still, Sucka Free sold about 150,000 copies of *The Leprechaun* by the time major labels started making serious offers.

Among the many labels pursuing Flip was Def Jam South, the Atlanta-based affiliate run by Houston rap icon Scarface. But in the end, despite 'Face being a fellow southsider and hero, Flip signed with Sony. His major-label debut, *Undaground Legend*, arrived in 2002 and, true to its name, didn't yield any mainstream hits. The single, "This Is the Way We Ball," offered a catchy singsong Southern funk and confident flow that might have heralded a new H-Town star, but the track barely registered nationally. Still, the album—full of soulful hooks sung in (or screwed down to) baritone level—reached number four on the R&B/Hip-Hop chart based on strong regional sales and a discount price. Tracks like "Rulez" and "7–1–3" reveal a flair for disciplined, structured rhyming, and he proves himself a hustler who's respectful of elders on "I Shoulda Listened," "Make Mama Proud," and "R.I.P. Screw," a heartfelt tribute. For good measure, Flip also tries crunk—not entirely successfully—with "Get Crunk" and "What Y'All Wanna Do."

Determined to break bigger on his second try, Flip's 2004 follow-up, *Gotta Feel Me*, perhaps succeeded too well. A less interesting record than its predecessor, *Gotta Feel Me* sounded like Flip was willing to try a little of everything—thug and party, light pop and crunk, sample gimmickry and a slew of guests from all over the South (Ludacris, Three 6 Mafia, David Banner, Pastor Troy) and beyond. Though it diluted the regional flavor that had been a charm for *The Leprechaun* and *Undaground Legend*, the strategy worked: Flip hit the pop charts, twice.

In late spring of 2004, the single "Game Over (Flip)"—which found the rapper flexing over Pac-Man video-game samples—peaked at number four on the rap chart and fifteen pop (Namco, Pac-Man's owner, sued for copyright violation and Sony settled out of court). A few months later a second track, "Sunshine," did even better, climbing to number two on the pop charts. The track featured a catchy guest vocal by R&B singer Lea, who croons the breezy chorus and upstages Flip's standard-issue thug-love rap. While the song elevated *Gotta Feel Me* to platinum status, it also incorrectly pegged Lil' Flip as either a lightweight pop rapper or a faceless, mediocre rapper.

This impression may have made him an easy target of Atlanta rapper T.I.'s wrath when Flip expressed doubts about T.I.'s right to claim "king of the South." Though Flip's opinion might have passed without notice, T.I. saw an opportunity to prove himself and elevated the disagreement into what was the South's most-discussed intraregional beef. With a much-circulated mix-tape track that borrowed a classic hip-hop riff, T.I. offered "99 Problems (Lil' Flip Ain't One)," and then took the stage at a 2004 Atlanta hip-hop festival—with Flip on the bill—and tore into the Houston rapper. Flip shot back with his own freestyle disses, and the battle raged back and forth over several months. It peaked when T.I. and Flip crossed paths in Houston and their crews tussled.

When the beef ran its course both rappers declared it squashed, though in the final tally, T.I. seemed to have gotten the better of Flip. By then, a new generation of Houston rapper was on the rise. With Flip falling out with Sony in 2005 and his album, *I Need Mine*, caught in major delays, it remained to be seen whether Flip would bounce back from the T.I. beef and keep pace with fellow Houstonians. Flip eventually found a new home, like so many other Houstonians, at Warner Bros.' Asylum label, and a revamped *I Need Mine* finally saw release in early 2007.

THE NORTH ALSO RISES

What brought screw music to the mainstream was neither DJ Screw nor the Screwed Up Click, but rather Screw's more media-savvy, crosstown rival-turned-successor, Michael "5000" Watts. Because of screw music's immense local popularity, other DJs—including DJ Tyrone and DJ Marco Polo—inevitably tried it. But Watts was the only one who came close to rivaling Screw himself. And Watts' success helped preserve the music and legend of Screw for people who didn't catch on to slowed-down music until after Screw's death.

Critical to Watts' rise was the fact that he was from the northside. For years, screw fans in north Houston had to sit through the S.U.C. dissing their neighborhood. With Watts, they finally had one of their own to provide the slowed-down sounds they'd come to love. Also, Watts had no interest in Screw's homemade style and direct sales—he put his stuff on CD from the start, used Pro Tools and digital CD mixing for higher fidelity, and sold his mixes in stores. Watts had some important connections to the mass market going in: By the time he started doing slowed-down mixes in 1996, he was working as a DJ for 97.9 The Box, Houston's leading hip-hop station. "I was making regular speed mix tapes and the guys from the neighborhood were begging me to make a slowed-down mix tape," Watts says. "So they finally talked me into it, and I just kept on doing it."

Through his work at The Box and in Houston clubs, Watts had met Screw a few times, but they were not close personally. Publicly, the two had a complicated relationship. Watts never denied Screw had invented screw music—and was always willing to give credit when asked—but he didn't seem to have an overly reverential attitude toward Screw either. Once he found success with slowed-down mixes, Watts saw no problem with adopting screw music as his own style as well. There was, after all, no way to patent this mixing technique—it was fair game to anyone to use.

That didn't mean Watts was free from scrutiny, however. To Screw fans on the southside, Watts was just biting Screw's style—legal, perhaps, but not the most honorable way to build a DJ reputation. "The northside was pretty much happy to have him, and the southside had Screw," says Matt Sonzala, a writer, DJ, and Houston hip-hop authority. "One of the things Screwed Up people say now is, 'Man, they got Michael Watts on the radio. Back then they didn't want to hear no Screw radio shows even though it was the hottest thing in the streets.'"

Resentment between northside and southside was nothing new in Houston hip-hop. The two centers of black life had long accentuated their differences in everything from music to car accessories to hairstyles. Rap battles went back to the very beginning, when South Park Coalition's K-Rino battled Rap-A-Lot's Jukebox. For the most part, violence never erupted between rappers, though that wasn't always the case on the street.

Then, in 1993, former Geto Boys group mates Willie D and Scarface had a confrontation in a club. Less than a year earlier, Willie (a 5th Ward northsider) had left the group on bad terms and Scarface (a southsider) read some of the barbs on Willie's solo album as being directed toward him. "We ran into each other at a club on the southside," Willie told *Rap Pages* three years after the incident. "He came up to me and asked me about it, and I told him to take it however he wanted to take it. He went for his shit, and I went for mine. I was 'bout 199 niggas strong, and he was there deep, and before you know it shots started going off."

Following the shooting, in which Willie says people on both sides were killed, tensions peaked between the northside and southside. They finally subsided when Willie D rejoined the Geto Boys for 1996's *The Resurrection*.

By then, perhaps Houston was too fatigued by the fighting to get riled up about the Watts/Screw rivalry starting to brew. K-Rino, the scene's elder statesman, addressed the north/south divide in his song "You Ain't Real": "You holler northside, southside, leave it alone/killing each other over land that you don't even own."

Still, Watts' popularity grew to a point where—because of his national distribution deal, his record stores sales, and his radio show—he and partner OG Ron C were arguably more famous nationally for making screw music than Screw was. At that point, S.U.C. members began to resent his success. On Screw's later mix tapes, it was common to hear S.U.C. members specify that if DJ Screw didn't make the tape, then it wasn't really a screw tape. Further annoying southsiders was the way Watts seemed willing to embrace the term "chopped and screwed" as a name for his slowed-down mixes (he later stopped using the term). To show their deference to DJ Screw, many southsiders avoided calling their slowed remixes "screwed," because Screw hadn't actually done the mix. Instead, they'd call it "slowed and chopped."

Once Screw died, however, the petty bickering over Watts seemed pointless. Screwed Up Click members even started working with Watts' Swisha House company. Lil' Flip was first to work with Swisha, on OG Ron C's 2001 mix, I-45, and then both the Botany Boyz and Lil' Keke appeared on Watts' mixes. S.U.C. veteran E.S.G. even made an album with up-and-coming Swisha House rapper Slimm Thug, 2001's *Boss Hogg Outlawz*. "You got Pepsi and you got Coke, it's always like that," E.S.G. says, shrugging away the divide between Screw's and Watts' camps.

But just as north and south Houston seemed poised to live happily ever after, an interview with Watts showed up in the underground hip-hop magazine *Murder Dog* quoting him as saying he'd taken screw music to a whole new level. True enough, on a commercial level Watts certainly had brought screw to a wider audience. Still, his words felt like a slight to DJ Screw, and the S.U.C. went on the warpath. Rappers Z-Ro and Al-D shot back first, with the track "Screw Did That" on Z's 2002 album *Life*. Z-Ro was brutal: "Screwed and chopped by who? Probably never met the man . . . /Bitch nigga, you get out of dodge fast/5,000 watts of skills? Naw, 5,000 pounds of trash/Watch what you say in the magazines, ol' fat-ass nigga/Instead of nibblin' off my nigga's cheese, ol' rat ass nigga/I call it like I see it, and I can't be nothing but real/I guess they can't originate, so they do nothing but steal."

Other S.U.C. disses followed, and two years down the line, Z-Ro was still on the subject: "I'ma ride on Watts, until his fat ass apologize for saying what he said about Screw/Look who your style is named after, motherfucker, you're number two," he raps on "That'z Who I Am," from his 2004 Rap-A-Lot debut, *The Life of Joseph W. McVey*.

Surely it was some consolation to Watts that, while the S.U.C. dissed him, he was making a fortune off of slowed-down mixes. In 2000, Eightball & MJG's *Space Age 4 Eva* became the first major-label album to release a chopped and screwed version—and Mike Watts was behind it. Watts launched his Web site around the same time, something Screw never had at his height. "I started getting hits from all over the nation," Watts says. "That's when I knew it was far beyond a local thing."

Watts' syndicated chopped and screwed radio show grew to five cities in Texas and Louisiana, plus an XM Satellite show. And he did mixes for just about everyone in Southern hip-hop—Scarface, Three 6 Mafia, Big Tymers, David Banner, Juvenile, Trillville & Lil' Scrappy, and other groups way beyond Houston, where it was already standard practice to release albums in regular and chopped and screwed formats. With Watts as its foremost practitioner, screw music reached further into mainstream popular culture: MTV Jams started running chopped and screwed videos; Texan soul diva Erykah Badu slowed her video of "Love of My Life" down in tribute to Screw; and L.A. punk supergroup the Transplants became the first notable rock band to make a screwed album.

Meanwhile, the north/south beef subsided as Houston acts began to once again enjoy large-scale mainstream success. "Everybody in Houston goes through that—from age sixteen to twenty-four, that's the age group really tripping on the north/southside rivalry," Houston rap veteran Devin the Dude says. "Once you grow out of it and look at the big picture you're just like, 'Let's try to move units in China, ain't no sense in tripping about somebody across town.'"

While DJ Screw's Screwed Up Click remained a loosely defined group, Swisha House—the label Mike Watts set up in 1997 with his partner G Dash—served as an official organization with a roster of rappers and producers. Swisha House started releasing screwed mix CDs by Watts and OG Ron C, but where Screw never transitioned to creating original music, Swisha House was soon making tracks for its artists.

In late 1999, Swisha House released its first nationally distributed compilation, *The Day Hell Broke Loose*. Featuring the entire Swisha House crew, the set included appearances by rappers Archie Lee, Lil' Mario, Lil' Ron, Billy Cook, and Big Tiger—some who later released Swisha House solo records—as well as one track credited to newcomers Paul Wall and a rapper named Camilean (who later became Chamillionaire). But if any rapper seemed to be highlighted on *Hell Broke Loose*, it was hot northside up-and-comer Slim Thug.

After Michael Watts heard Stayve "Slim Thug" Thomas freestyling at a northside teen club, the eighteen-year-old rapper became one of the first Swisha House acts. It was back in 1999, in the early days of his involvement with Watts, that Slim wrote a freestyle about "still tippin' on fo' fo's, wrapped in fo' Vogues." The flow, which refers to cruising ("tippin'") on 44-spoke rims ("fo' fo's") and Vogue white-wall tires, showed up on a Watts mix and became a popular refrain among Houston's car freaks.

As Slim's star began to rise through Swisha House mixes, he teamed up with veteran S.U.C. rapper E.S.G. By then, E.S.G. had served his two-and-a-half years in jail, got out and signed with Wreckshop, the hot new southside label that was also putting out records by Fat Pat (his posthumous *Ghetto Dreams*) and Big Moe (*City of Syrup*). The pair's first collaboration, from E.S.G.'s 1999 album *Shinin' N' Grindin'*, was an immediate local sensation. "Braids N' Fades" brought together the S.U.C. and Swisha House, the southside and northside, in a strong show of city unity. Between trading off verses praising their respective parts of town, E.S.G. and Slim came together, trading lines on the chorus: "[Slim Thug:] When I come down I be thowin' up the north/[E.S.G.:] And when I come down I be chuckin' up the south/[both:] Swisha House and Wreckshop don't stop, body rockin' in the drop . . . /[Slim Thug:] I heard you on Screw/[E.S.G.:] I heard you on that Michael Watts."

They compare notes on the different highways they ride, the candy paints they prefer, the way they style their hair, and the 'hoods they represent, but ultimately they call for unity, as Slim raps: "The north and south done put it down, it's RIP to our plex [Houston term for 'beef'] . . . /Ain't nothin' but playas in Houston, Tex, whether you got braids or fades/'Cause it don't matter where you from, long as you tryin' to get paid."

The collaboration was so successful, E.S.G. and Slim teamed up again for "Candy Coated Excursion," and hit once more. By then, Slim had stepped away from Swisha House and formed a label with E.S.G. called S.E.S. Entertainment. In 2001, S.E.S. released a full album pairing of the rappers, *Boss Hogg Outlawz*. Though the two soon had a bitter falling out, Slim kept the name and launched his Boss Hogg Outlawz label. He put out his own mix CDs, including *I Represent This*, a compilation of freestyles, as well as an album by his crew, the Boyz-N-Blue (featuring Killa Kyleon). In 2003, Slim teamed up with a second S.U.C. veteran, Lil' Keke, for a duo album called *The Big Unit*.

By 2004, Slim Thug had been prominent in Houston for five years, put out albums with local legends and his crew, and released a series of mix CDs. But Slim had never dropped an actual solo album that defined him as an artist. In truth, he was already making the kind of money he stood to make on a major label (because independents had lower costs and higher profit margins, artists earned more selling fewer records). As he described it, he was "already platinum"—not in actual sales, but he was making as much as a platinum-selling major-label artist made.

But then something changed: The local music distributor, Southwest Wholesale—the company through which virtually all local hip-hop CDs got into stores—shut down in 2003. It left a huge void and made it much more difficult to sell the number of records that allowed independent labels to flourish. Some, including Boss Hogg, tried to use other distributors—including Memphis' Select-O-Hits, which had national reach—but no one knew the Texas market, where the majority of records were sold, as well as Wholesale.

"When we seen that the stuff with Select-O-Hits wasn't really doin' nothin' for us, I said, 'Fuck it—here's what I need to do—I need to sign a deal!,'" Slim told the Web magazine *Soundslam*. "Because people been tryin' to sign me since 2000. It wasn't like I didn't have opportunities to get a deal, but it was just that they were on some crumb shit. . . . I ain't tryin' to do just no regular artist shit. You can't just try to give me $200,000 or $300,000, when that's what I'm makin' in the streets."

So Slim decided to go for the big time. With help from "king of the South" T.I. and UGK legend Bun B, Slim made a demo track called "3 Kings" that anoints him as Houston's next rap star. Over a slowed-down blues guitar and horn sample from Betty Wright's Clarence Reid/Willie Clarke–penned "Secretary," Bun B raps, "Slim Thug you up next to shine and I can't even lie/Wit me and T.I.P you done wrecked 'em this time."

Given Slim's local fame, entrepreneurship, and friends in high places, it wasn't hard to find a good deal with a major. Slim signed with music biz legend Jimmy Iovine's Interscope/Geffen label, which released "3 Kings" as a single in the fall of 2004, but didn't have much success with it. Iovine and Slim agreed that, since Slim was unproven nationally, a big-time producer might help his record. They switched Slim over to the Neptunes' Star Trak label, which had signed a deal with Interscope. But Virginia Beach was a long way from East Texas—geographically and as a Southern hip-hop flavor.

While Slim was first in a new generation of Houston rappers to make a stab at mainstream crossover, a recording process plagued by delays and leaks held his major-label debut back for months. When *Already Platinum* finally arrived in July of 2005, anticipation alone shot it up to a number-two debut on the *Billboard* pop chart. But none of the three advance singles—"3 Kings," then the Neptunes-produced "Like a Boss," then the Jazze Pha–produced "Incredible Feeling"—were strong enough to climb into the Top 40. By the end of 2005, *Already Platinum* hadn't gone platinum.

Ultimately, the record's tragic flaw may have been its fusion. While Pharrell Williams and Chad Hugo were responsible for much of the current era's best pop music, the sound of Slim Thug—the six-and-a-half-foot giant with the slurred baritone and screwed pace—didn't necessarily call for what they had to offer. Tracks like "I Ain't Heard of That (Remix)" and "Like a Boss" were terrific, but they only served to dilute the potency of Houston-style material like "Diamonds" (featuring a slowed-down UGK sample) and the posse track "Boyz N Blue." It seems that, when Slim Thug finally got around to defining himself, he didn't really define himself much at all.

Ironically, what seemed to steal the thunder from Slim Thug's major-label debut was Slim himself. That is, Slim's screwed, disembodied voice booming out from the chorus of "Still Tippin'," the track—credited to Houston rapper Mike Jones—that, in the spring of 2005, finally broke Houston's "post-screw" style into the mainstream.

Though roughly the same age as Slim, Mike Jones didn't catch his break until much later. First known by the Swisha House crew as a guy named Sache (as in Versace) who hustled cell phones, Jones reverted to his real name and started selling mix tapes around 1999. He did it on his own for a couple of years—founding his Ice Age Entertainment company and taking full control of his music's marketing. It was there that Jones discovered his biggest talent—a knack for getting people to remember his otherwise forgettable name: by repeatedly announcing it and his phone number on tapes.

This marketing technique started after he'd heard reports that someone was scamming show promoters by claiming to be Mike Jones and pocketing the upfront fee for shows. "I had heard rumors so I gave my phone number out on a mixtape," Jones told *The Source*. "I said, 'Y'all hit me, man. If anything like that happens again, hit me.' And then after that everything had cooled out. Sometimes people just call me to say whassup or they call me to say they saw my video or they call just asking me what's coming next."

In 2002, Jones took his mixes to the Houston strip clubs, where he created a custom tape for every dancer, using the stripper's favorite tracks and adding in his "Mike Jones!" call-outs. His phone number (the often seen and heard 281-330-8004), his email address, even his instant message account all showed up on his mixes. One night it drew the attention of Mike Watts, who decided to bring Jones into the Swisha House fold.

By then, many from Swisha House's original roster had left, including Slim Thug, Lil' Mario, and Chamillionaire. So Mike Jones quickly became the label's central artist, releasing a collaborative album with Magnificent (aka Magno), *1st Round Draft Pick*, in early 2003. And when Swisha House put together 2004's *The Day Hell Broke Loose, Vol. 2: Major Without a Major Deal*, Mike Jones was featured front and center alongside familiar Swisha House names like Paul Wall, Slim Thug, and Magno.

Among the standout tracks on *Major Without a Major Deal* was "Still Tippin'," a song that sampled the screwed version of Slim Thug's 1999 freestyle: "still tippin' on fo' fo's, wrapped in fo' Vogues." The Swisha House version—which featured a track by the in-house producer T. Farris and verses from Mike Jones, Paul Wall, and Slim Thug himself—was one of two versions in circulation. The other was included on the Rap-A-Lot compilation, *The Day After Hell Broke Loose*, and featured a Southern funk track by producer Bigg Tyme and verses from Jones, Chamillionaire, and Slim. Farris remade the track as a spare, dreamy beat laced with a slinky violin line, and with Chamillionaire—who'd fallen out with Swisha House—replaced by his former rhyme partner, Paul Wall. Rap-A-Lot's version earned some notice in the summer of 2004, but the following spring Swisha House's version exploded as a theme to Houston hip-hop's renaissance.

"Still Tippin'" was the first payoff of the just-inked deal Swisha House had made with Warner Bros. Records. Warner's Lyor Cohen had reanimated the old imprint Asylum as a Southern-heavy hip-hop label, and the deal linked Swisha House—and Rap-A-Lot as well, in a separate deal—with Asylum Records. Mike Jones' solo debut, *Who Is Mike Jones?*, was the first product of the Swisha/Asylum pact—and, hitting number one on the R&B/Hip-Hop album chart, its first hit.

"Still Tippin'" was emblematic of this latest wave from Houston. First, it featured the movement's three biggest stars: Slim Thug (the real star of the song), Mike Jones, and Paul Wall (who had his own Asylum album on the way). Second, it incorporated screw elements—in this case, the slowed chorus. And third, it served as a prelude to the stream of Houston hits and terminology that would roll into the national pop culture over the next year: tippin' down the block with wood grain steering wheels, forty-four rims or spinners, Vogue tires, candy paint and drop tops; sippin' lean with diamonds in the mouth; shouting out "Who is Mike Jones?" and "The People's Champ" and the hook to future hits "Back Then" and "Internet Going Nutz."

Who Is Mike Jones? built up a huge amount of hype before its release, but it largely measured up. It was full of memorable songs, including post-screw cuts like "Screw Dat" and "Back Then" (a loser's revenge fantasy: "back then hoes didn't want me, now I'm hot they all on me"), where Swisha House producer Salih Williams created dynamic, progressive tracks that retain their distinctly Houston feel (note to the Neptunes). *Who Is Mike Jones?* was aggressively accessible, with singing hooks (including original screw crooner Big Moe on the single, "Flossin'") and a something-for-everyone approach that included pimped-out riding songs ("Turning Lane") and eccentric songs ("Cuttin'"), woman-hating songs ("Scandalous Hoes") and conscious raps ("5 Years From Now," which questioned the Iraq War). And for good measure, there was a closing song about Jones' grandma—she first suggested, "Who Is Mike Jones?"

As for the incessant "Mike Jones!" call-outs and other promotional bits, the gimmick wore on the listener long before the record was over. What initially sold Mike Jones—his regular-guy, out-of-nowhere image—became irritating once he established himself as one of Houston's new hit makers, once his phone started attracting a reported fifteen thousand calls per day (good luck getting through now). A new album, *The American Dream*, and a planned autobiographical feature film of the same name will determine whether Mike Jones can move beyond the gimmicks.

Before they were down with Swisha House, Paul Slayton and Hakeem Seriki were just a couple of neighborhood friends going to elementary school together in a lower-middle-class section of northwest Houston. As best friends often do, they had similar interests: by middle school, they loved hip-hop and wanted to rap. Almost from the time DJ Screw first appeared, Paul and Hakeem were fans, though in the years when the Screwed Up Click were dissing the northside, they kept their obsession quiet. It was never an issue, as far as anyone can remember, that Paul happened to be white.

Paul called himself Overflow, but then adopted something simpler: Paul Wall. Hakeem wanted to be the lizard king so he called himself Camilean, then decided he wanted to get paid as well, so it became Chamillionaire. As a way into hip-hop, Paul and Chamillion got jobs doing street promotions, passing out fliers at clubs. While out working one night around 1997, they met Michael Watts. He asked them to promote his new Swisha House mix CDs, so they went to work for Swisha House.

They didn't get to rap on a Swisha House mix for at least another year, when they were about to graduate from high school. Watts agreed to let them bust on a radio spot for his nightly 97.9 The Box mix show. Listeners loved it, so Watts put the spot on one of his mix CDs and Paul and Chamillion became Swisha House regulars. They did freestyles, which paid little, while Paul studied mass communications at the University of Houston and Chamillionaire cut out for Chicago to try and earn some money.

They watched Slim Thug break away and sell mixes through his own label and figured they could do it themselves. So they broke from Swisha House and formed their own Color Changin' Click. By then, Paul had picked up some basic DJ skills from watching Watts, so he did the chopping and screwing while Chamillion and another rapper, 50/50 Twin, added vocals. Things were going so well that in 2001, Paul dropped out of college to focus on music full-time. Chamillion came back from Chicago and they signed as a duo to local label Paid in Full.

Paid in Full was the label started by Watts' coworker at The Box, afternoon drive-time host Madd Hatta. He started the label to put out his own records, which he released as Mista Madd, but he found his biggest success with Paul Wall & Chamillionaire's 2002 debut, *Get Ya Mind Correct*. The record managed to sell 150,000 copies based on its dynamic flow. Chamillion particularly shines, switching between sharp, often humorous, rapping and no-nonsense R&B crooning. But what really makes the record click is the interplay between Paul and Chamillion, who vibe together as only longtime friends can. On "Thinking Thoed" ("throwed" being the Houston hip-hop equivalent of "fly"), Paul actually says, "To tell you the truth, Chamillionaire's better than me, his flip-flop shines a little bit wetter than me/But it don't matter, we're both on the same team." And Cham returns the compliment: "Paul I'm impressed, I thought you was the best/But you just said I was the best so it's a tie, I guess."

Incredibly, given the chemistry they exhibited on *Get Ya Mind Correct*, the normal tensions of spending a lot of time with one person and having to make decisions as a team was breaking Paul and Chamillion apart. When they stopped getting along, they kept it together for a while as a business. But soon they determined that wasn't worth it either. After nearly fifteen years as buddies and partners, they stopped talking completely.

"Our personalities just changed and we just grew up and grew apart," Paul told *Murder Dog*. "Then it started getting so bad . . . the only reason I stayed around was because I gave it everything I had and . . . because of our history together growing up. There was too much stuff going on and it was a real bad situation."

Chamillionaire formed his Chamilitary label, teaming with another former Swisha House member, OG Ron C, who became his DJ. After his triple

CD *Mixtape Messiah* did big business in 2004, Chamillion signed with Universal Records to drop his major-label debut, late 2005's *The Sound of Revenge*. After a slow start, the record took off in 2006 and went platinum with the help of the number-one single, "Ridin'." Cham thanked his fans by offering a *Mixtape Messiah 2* sequel for free on his Web site. Meanwhile, his official follow-up to *Revenge*, called *Ultimate Victory*, was set for early 2007.

Meanwhile, Paul stuck it out a while with Paid in Full. He did a solo album, *The Chick Magnet*, in 2004 and then rounded out the duo's obligation with 2005's *Controversy Sells*, a Paul Wall & Chamillionaire album that pasted together old and new recordings to create what was, essentially, an imaginary collaboration between two people not on speaking terms. But tensions between the former friends never erupted. "The situation between me and Paul is real personal, Paul is like a brother to me," Chamillion explained to *Murder Dog*. "Out of respect for that I don't wanna drop a CD dissing him or anything like that. That chapter of my life is done, I'm moving on."

After his stint at Paid in Full, Paul landed back at Swisha House, which had now grown from a mix CD operation into a full-fledged label. With "Still Tippin'" bubbling throughout the region, Swisha was about to sign its deal with Warner Bros. and Paul Wall was next in line, after Mike Jones, to drop a major-label release.

With an industriousness that matched, if not surpassed, Jones, Paul Wall kept busy between his own recordings as producer of chopped and screwed mixes. They included local cult favorites such as the 1998 album, *Screwed 4 Life*, by the S.U.C. supergroup Dead End Alliance—a record that, oddly, had never been screwed until Paul did it in 2001. He then graduated to doing larger mixes for friends like T.I. (*Urban Legend*) as well as some unlikely candidates (Kanye West's *The College Dropout*, Common's *Be*, and *Haunted Cities* by punk band the Transplants).

Wall also served as the T.I.-led Pimp $quad Click's tour DJ. And he earned a huge reputation as one of the most in-demand designers of grills—the gold- and jewel-encrusted fronts that Southern rappers (and beyond) had taken to wearing on their teeth. He's created grills for Lil Jon, Master P, Chingy, even Kanye West. Partnering with a Vietnamese immigrant jewelry designer named Johnny Dang, Wall opened TV Jewelry, a store in north Houston's Sharpstown Center mall that has grown into a virtual grill factory churning out dozens of fronts each day.

Then in 2005, five months after *Who Is Mike Jones?* and two months after *Already Platinum*, Paul Wall arrived with a post-screw major-label debut of his own: *The People's Champ*. Benefiting from the attention he'd gotten with his predecessors—and perhaps aided slightly in his crossover appeal by his skin color—Paul Wall entered the charts, both pop and urban, at number one. Houston was back on the national hip-hop landscape in a big way—with far more mainstream appeal than the days of the Geto Boys and UGK. Some even began to whisper of Houston's potential to challenge Atlanta's dominance as Southern hip-hop's center—though, in truth, the city never came close to having the music-industry infrastructure that allows Atlanta to succeed.

Reprising almost the exact formula used for "Still Tippin'," Paul Wall recruited Austin-based producer Salih Williams to once again draw a hook from an old screw tape and build a new track around it. This time, Michael Watts suggested he use a nearly ten-year-old freestyle by Big Pokey, from DJ Screw's *June 27* mix. "I'm sitting sideways, boys in a daze/On a Sunday night I might bang me some Maze," goes Pokey's slowed chorus. Like "Still Tippin'," it referenced Houston car culture: "sittin' sideways" referred to one's hunched posture while swerving a 'Lac or Impala down the avenue. The track, "Sittin' Sidewayz," became *The People's Champ*'s first single.

Oddly, the same thing that made Wall's record successful also made it frustrating. It often plays like a beginner's course on Houston hip-hop, with song titles jumping from one key phrase to another: "Sittin' Sidewayz," "Trill," "Sippin' tha Barre," "Got Plex" (*plex* being a local equivalent of "beef"), "Sip-N-Get-High." And with the album's second single, "They Don't Know," Wall manages to catalog the entire scene in two verses, broken up by a wonderful chorus that collages classic Houston quotes (including Fat Pat's line, "Third Coast born, that means we're Texas raised"):

> *What you know about swangers and vogues,*
> *what you know about purple drank?*
> *What you know about poppin' trunk,*
> *with neon lights and candy paint?*
> *What you know about white shirts,*
> *starched down jeans with a razor crease,*
> *Platinum and gold on top our teeth,*
> *big ol' chains with a iced out piece?*
> *You don't know about Michael Watts,*
> *you don't know about DJ Screw,*
> *What you know about 'Man, hold up,'*
> *'I done came down' and 'What it do?'*
> *You don't know about P.A.T.,*
> *what you know about 'Free Pimp C'?*
> *What you know about the Swishahouse,*
> *man, what you know bout the S.U.C.? . . .*

You don't know about chunkin' a deuce,
you don't know 'bout a Southside fade
Down here we be ridin' D's,
but you don't know about choppin' blades
Texas Southern or Prairie View,
what you know about Battle of the Bands?
Down here we got ghetto grub,
like Williams Chicken or Timmy Chan's
You can catch me ridin' swang,
what you know about sippin' syrup?
You don't know about pourin' it up,
purple drank so speech is slurred,
You don't know about the way we talk,
boys say we got country words,
But I don't really care what you heard, '
cause you don't know about the Dirty Third."

Paul Wall had emerged as the great translator of the subculture that brewed in Houston for more than a decade—and he was about as close to an Eminem (that is, a white guy fully accepted within the culture) that the South has created. *The People' Champ* was his classic treatise of how they do things in his hometown—an invaluable road map to a place that thrived for years before anyone on the outside knew about it. But, ultimately, road maps don't make for great literature. For all its local color, Wall's record didn't so much paint a portrait of his world as it just rattled off the signifiers, as if that was enough. *The People's Champ* made Houston hip-hop sound like one big gimmick, when the record should have been a natural extension of the homegrown culture.

LONE STAR SHINING

Signs suggested that Houston's resurgence might wear off on its Texas twin, Dallas—a city that had contributed surprisingly little to the national hip-hop discourse. After earning success making tracks for Lil' Flip, the two Dallas-based Latino brothers who make up the production team Play N Skillz (Juan and Oscar Salinas) got a deal to record their own album, 2004's *The Process*. In addition, Dallas veteran Mr. Pookie and his younger partner Mr. Lucci have made moves to build on their Texas fanbase with a major-label affiliation. And in late 2005, Dallas' hottest local label, T-Town Music—home to the group DSR (Dirty South Rydaz)—signed a deal with Universal/Motown to put out artists such as DSR member Big Tuck (whose major label debut, *The Absolute Truth*, arrived in late 2006).

Meanwhile, as 2005's hype marked Houston as the next hot music mecca, it became increasingly clear that—despite some impressive chart showings—if all Houston had to offer was candy paint, sippin' syrup, and gold grills, the focus would soon turn elsewhere. Chamillionaire's successful debut, *The Sound of Revenge*, offered some deviation from the Houston gimmickry, and so did Lil' Flip's *I Need Mine*—though label conflicts kept that record from seeing release. Both, however, suffered for other reasons.

Still, the explosion of Houston hip-hop helped shine light on H-Town's older generation—whether people like Big Pokey and Fat Pat through prominent appearances in samples, or artists like Devin the Dude who saw their cult status grow by virtue of their hometown affiliation. "Now that they're seeing what Mike Jones and Paul Wall are doing, it's the same shit we've been doing at Screw's house for the last 10 years," E.S.G. says. "Most of us—E.SG., Hawks, Lil Keke, Pokey—were teenagers going to Screw's house. And now we're able to get some of this success, thanks to the newcomers."

Certainly the most prominent of the "old timers" to enjoy his status as a Houston hip-hop god was Bun B, the UGK MC who was biding time doing guest features while his partner Pimp C served out his jail sentence. The exposure from the guest spots and adoration of Southern rap's younger generation built until Bun B had to capitalize on it. In late 2005, Bun's solo debut—called (what else?) *Trill*—appeared as one of the first products of Rap-A-Lot's deal with Warner Bros./Asylum. *Trill*, which boasted a who's who of Southern hip-hop—from Scarface up through Young Jeezy—sounded just as it was intended: The arrival of a pioneer finally getting his due. *Trill*'s companion piece arrived the following summer, when—following Pimp C's release from prison—Rap-A-Lot quickly released his solo album, *Pimpalation*. Back on track, with the double-disc comeback, *UGK Underground Kingz*, the Third Coast originals may finally claim the rewards that have long been just beyond reach.

EPILOGUE

From the vantage point of early 2007, it looks like the era of Southern hip-hop is now over. Not primarily because Southern artists have relinquished their dominance on the pop and urban charts. Indeed, throughout 2006, Southern acts continued to contribute one-third to one-half of all songs on the *Billboard* Hot 100, and about two-thirds of the songs on the Hot Rap Tracks chart—hardly less than its 2003–2004 peak. In fact, Southern hip-hop as a discreet phenomenon may simply have given way to a semipermanent new order where the South is just home base for hip-hop in general—less an exceptional development than a basic rule.

But this sense of establishment has come at a cost. Inevitably, success fosters a self-consciousness that, in pop culture, tends to stultify. The past year has brought two awards shows dedicated solely to Southern rap: the Atlanta-based Dirty Awards, organized by Radio One, and the Orlando-based Ozone Awards, put together by *Ozone* magazine. And in addition to *Ozone*, there is now a second glossy magazine focusing on the region's hip-hop: *Down* magazine (meanwhile, national publications like *XXL*, *Vibe*, and *Murder Dog* remain "bottom" heavy). Certainly, there's no problem giving credit where credit is due, but intense celebration and media oversaturation breed the sort of complacent entitlement that had New Yorkers thinking they ruled hip-hop long after their rappers had run out of fresh ideas.

But more than anything, what's eating away at Southern hip-hop's vibrancy and exceptionalism is the artists themselves. The Dirty South shows signs of rotting from within: If the South still dominates in chart numbers and media focus, its artists seem to be growing less and less distinct from the hip-hop acts in other regions. Georgia quartet Boyz N Da Hood, which debuted in 2005 as a confederation of solo rappers (including Young Jeezy and Jody Breeze), borrowed prominently from early West Coast

337

gangsta rap—particularly Eazy-E and N.W.A.—in name and lyrics. And while Young Buck's *Straight Outta Cashville* (boasting its own N.W.A. reference) manages to retain a Dirty South feel, the Nashville rapper's claim to fame as part of 50 Cent's G-Unit crew makes him seem at times like a token in the G-Unit's drive for intraregional dominance (Eminem's affiliated Shady Records boasts its own Southerner: Atlanta rapper Stat Quo).

While the South has no particular claim to having made objectively *better* or more decent rap across the board than other regions, when it was bad it was at least cheesy, offensive, and just plain awful in its own distinctive way. But the Dirty's descent into a more generalized hip-hop mediocrity of late is typified by its association with "cocaine rap," a subgenre of sorts that entered the lexicon in recent years. It is the term for rappers whose lyrics focus to a large extent on the underworld life of high-stakes drug dealing. Anyone wondering how, exactly, cocaine rap is something new and worthy of distinction—after all, gangsta rappers have been invoking *Scarface* and telling drug tales for decades—has hit upon a sad truth about the levels of self-delusion and cliché that have coincided in hip-hop. If cocaine rap is the best new story hip-hop can offer, the genre is truly in trouble.

While cocaine rappers do not come from one particular region—New Yorkers like Juelz Santana and his Dipset crew have been associated with it, for instance—the style's leading lights are Southerners. There's Florida's Rick Ross, whose 2006 debut, *Port of Miami*, made use of his hometown's reputation as the arrival point for South American narcotics. And there's also Virginia's the Clipse, who returned in late 2006 from label problems with the much-delayed *Hell Hath No Fury*, a critically acclaimed Neptunes production obsessed with the drug trade. But the patron saint of cocaine rap has to be Atlanta's Young Jeezy, whose two official releases have not only staked out his claim to being the "Snowman," they've elevated Jeezy to the short list of the South's most popular new rap stars. (Jeezy landed at the center of controversy in 2006 when promotional T-shirts featuring a snowman were discovered to have a drug connotation and were banned from schools.)

Cocaine rap's rise suggests there's a new crop of Southern rappers who are more similar to East Coast and West Coast rappers than to fellow Third Coasters—at least to the extent that they'd get grouped as cocaine rappers first, Southerners second. The style also suggests that Southerners can now trade in clichés and redundancies in exactly the same way others rappers do.

There are other signs that Southern hip-hop has, to borrow a useful bit of pop lexicography, "jumped the shark." Lil Jon, perhaps stretching his crunk sound beyond its limitations, is planning for a genre-hybrid record called

Crunk Rock. And the Ying Yang Twins, in an odd sign of maturity, split with their cofounder and label head Mr. Collipark (aka DJ Smurf) to go it alone. But the best evidence that the South isn't what it once was came in the second half of 2006, with the surprising shrug that greeted OutKast's most ambitious project to date, the stylized feature film and original soundtrack album *Idlewild*.

It's hard to say exactly why *Idlewild*—as an album and, to a lesser extent, as a movie—fell so quickly off the radar after its promising August 2006, debut. It could have been the timing: Several years passed as the movie project evolved from concept to HBO cable original to full-scale theatrical release, and then the drive to perfect the accompanying album further delayed the release. In the end, nearly three years separated *Idlewild* from its predecessor, *Speakerboxxx/The Love Below*—hardly an eternity, but probably too long for a group at its peak. And still, the rush to get the album—which overlapped with the actual film soundtrack only partially—finished to coincide with the movie premiere may have birthed some of the record's half-baked material.

It also could have been the record label: *Idlewild* was OutKast's first release since L.A. Reid had departed Arista in early 2004, when the company's top artists were transferred over to sister label Jive Records. Fears that Jive (best known in recent years for teen pop) would not know how to properly promote an OutKast album—much less an OutKast *movie*—may have been realized with *Idlewild*. And Andre 3000's disinclination to tour and heavily promote the music didn't help, either.

Of course, it may have also been the music itself: Given OutKast's history, Dre and Big could be forgiven for harboring a notion that, wherever the group went with its music, its audience would keep up and somehow expand along the way. But until *Idlewild*, the movement had always been forward, toward more progressive and expansive sounds. Much of *Idlewild*'s music, however, attempts to keep at least partly in step with the film's Prohibition-era setting: hot jazz, swing, and blues elements lace OutKast's urban pop and hip-hop. It makes sense in the context of the film; even as a new musical direction it could be forgiven as a "back to the roots" experiment (where, after all, to go but backward once you've pushed your genre as far as it can be stretched?). But as a gambit to revisit the pop-chart glory of *Speakerboxxx*? Not likely. The Cab Calloway–inspired "Mighty 'O'" peaked in June of 2006 at number 77 on the Hot 100, while two other tracks—the marching band–driven "Morris Brown" and the 12-bar bluesy "Idlewild Blue"—got just minimal airplay. For the first time, OutKast may have miscalculated its ability to get audiences to come along for the ride.

Ultimately, it was probably a bit of all of that. And this: gravity. There is no way any group can sustain a perpetual rise, as OutKast had done for more than a decade. Who knows, the group's fortunes may rise again, but *Idlewild* simply marks that first album that did not raise the stakes, commercially or artistically, on its predecessors. It could be just a temporary dip, an overly indulgent excursion to be followed by a chastened return to providing the people with what they want. Or, it could mean the end of OutKast.

For a second act, Andre has the head start over Big Boi. He's well on his way to establishing himself as an eclectic actor—from the thriller *Four Brothers* to the Will Ferrell comedy *Semi-Pro* to the kids' fare of *Charlotte's Web*. And with his Cartoon Network vehicle *Class of 3000*—which stars an animated Andre (as Sonny Bridges) leading a group of Atlanta music-school prodigies through surreal adventures and funk symphonies—he may have started the process of tapping into an entirely new audience, and discovering completely new avenues for creativity as he ages slowly out of the hip-hop demographic. As he exits gracefully from his role as part of the Beatles of hip-hop, it could be he's headed for a future as the Bill Cosby of the post-hip-hop generation.

The fall of OutKast, of course, does not by any means spell the death of Southern hip-hop—the group had long since transcended any close association with the genre. Still, we can recall that the group's arrival coincided with the birth of a Southern sensibility in hip-hop, and its peak heralded the era where Southern hip-hop dominated American pop. And so OutKast's descent from the heights (if not outright disappearance) should somehow mark a kind of spiritual death for the genre. If so, then it goes something like this:

Third Coast hip-hop is dead, long live the Dirty South.

NOTES ON SOURCES

As much as possible, I relied foremost on first-hand sources and my own research in compiling the history related in *Third Coast*. To that end, I conducted about a hundred interviews with direct sources, and those sources are quoted and paraphrased throughout the book. At times, it was necessary to go beyond the people I had direct access to and rely on either previous historical research or published materials. In those cases, my practice was to cite the book or publication as part of the text itself. My purpose here, then, is to elaborate informally on the sources that helped me create the story in *Third Coast*.

In the Introduction, I quoted from an article by Dillard University's Mona Lisa Saloy called "African American Oral Traditions in Louisiana," which first appeared in the 1990 Louisiana Folklife Festival booklet. The section on early African American radio DJs relied partially on information in William Barlow's excellent history of that subject, *Voice Over: The Making of Black Radio* (Temple University Press, 1998). For chart information (here and throughout the book), I relied on my own research on Billboard.com's archives and Allmusic.com's chart information. I quoted Juelz Santana from the November 2005 issue of *XXL*, and also included two quotes from Peter Applebome's insightful 1997 book, *Dixie Rising: How the South Is Shaping American Values, Politics and Culture* (Harvest Books).

Chapter 1 came together as the result of several dozen interviews with people involved with early Florida rap, but an extensive early interview with DJ PappaWheelie (as well as reading the articles he'd written on early Miami bass, such as the one at www.electroempire.com/miami.htm) provided an important framework for my research. In addition to my own interview with Miami music pioneer Henry Stone, I found very useful a lengthy interview he did in 2003 with Monica and Mr. C on New York freeform radio station WFMU (archived at www.wfmu.org/playlists/ML2003). I also found useful details about Janet Reno's connection to 2 Live Crew with the help of Heather C. Sarni's article, "Janet Reno: The Early Years and Career of a Pioneering Woman Lawyer," which appears on a Stanford University–affiliated Web site dedicated to women's legal history (womenslegalhistory.stanford.edu). Finally, I got much help in my research on Luther Campbell's legal troubles from two *New Times* articles written by Tristram Korten—one called "One Live Jew" that appeared in the Broward-Palm Beach edition on August 20, 2000, and a second called "Two Live Screwed" from the Miami edition of June 3, 1999.

The information in Chapter 2 is also drawn primarily from my own interviews, and some essential help with the Houston scene came from early interviews and consultations with Matt "So Real" Sonzala, a local DJ, journalist, photographer, and promoter who writes the awesome blog HoustonSoReal (houstonsoreal.blogspot.com). In addition, I borrowed a few key quotes from interviews that ran in the following publications: Vanilla Ice in *Backwash* (www.backwashzine.com/ice.html); the D.O.C. in *Murder Dog* (www.murderdog.com/archives/doc/doc.html); and Andre Benjamin in the April 2005 issue of *Sister2Sister* (www.s2smagazine.com). After some historical perspective, Chapter 3's account of Memphis hip-hop history relied exclusively on my own interviews. Again, though, I owe a great debt to one source in particular: John Shaw (aka J-Dogg), a writer who works at Select-O-Hits and knows more about the scene than anyone I've met.

In part because of the way Hurricane Katrina made everyone more difficult to track down, Chapter 4 (and, to a lesser extent, Chapter 9) relied more heavily than other chapters on second-hand sources. I credit various articles in *XXL*, *Vibe*, *The Source*, and particularly *Murder Dog* for providing important background information. Where I have used quotes that originally appeared in those magazines, they are credited in the text. I also tip my hat to the terrific hip-hop blog Cocaine Blunts (cocaineblunts.com/blunts) for providing a great retrospective of early No Limit records in August of 2005. Some of my information on New Orleans' historic wards, projects, and the general lay of the land (pre-Katrina) came from a very useful site run by the Greater New Orleans Community Data Center (still available in pre-Katrina form at: www.gnocdc.org/prekatrinasite.html). Some useful post-Katrina material came from the New Orleans *Times-Picayune*'s thorough coverage, as well as from the *New York Times* (in particular, "Storm Forces a Hard Look at Troubled Public Housing," by Clifford J. Levy, from November 22, 2005). Finally, I picked up some useful tidbits reading Nik Cohn's piece, "Soljas," that originally appeared in *Granta* before being reprinted in *Da Capo's Best Music Writing of 2002.*

By contrast, the Atlanta sections—Chapter 5 and Chapter 7—rely most heavily on first-hand sources, due to the fact that I was based in Atlanta during most of my years living in the South. However, I must give a prominent credit to Walker Smith, who cowrote Jack (the Rapper) Gibson's autobiography, *The Rise and Fall of the Rapper.* Though the book remains unpublished and Gibson is no longer alive, Gibson's daughter Jamilla Bell kindly put me in touch with Walker, who was glad to share her book with me for my research. I hope more people get to read her fascinating book. Information I got from Rob Tannenbaum's profile of L.A. Reid, "L.A. Comes to New York" (*New York Magazine*, January 29, 2001), also shows up in both chapters 5 and 7. Additional details about Jermaine Dupri's career came from Sonya Murray's reporting in the *Atlanta Journal-Constitution*, and important information about Scarface and Def Jam South came from an article in *Vibe.*

For Chapter 6, I relied on the key players in Virginia to tell their own story, but did some background research on the infamous trio of New York street hustlers A.Z., Rich, and Alpo. The Web site Allhiphop.com ran a story by Odienne Chisolm in September 2002 about the film *Paid in Full*, which fictionalized the threesome's story. I also relied on a series of articles from the Hampton Roads daily paper, *The Virginian-Pilot*, for basic facts about the 1989 Greekfest riot in Virginia Beach. Finally, I was surprised to come across Mosi Reeves' article, "Organic Produce: Will Hip-Hop Studio King of the World Timbaland Someday Be Mr. Universe?" in the April 7, 2005, issue of the *Miami New Times*, which I relied upon for details of Timbaland's excursion into bodybuilding.

In Chapter 8's overview of the African American migration and reverse migration, I relied on a number of sources, including the articles "Black Migration," from *The Reader's Companion to American History* (edited by Eric Foner and John A. Garraty; Houghton Mifflin, 1991), and "The Shifting Patterns of Black Migration From and Into the Nonmetropolitan South, 1965–95," from the U.S. Dept. of Agriculture's *Rural Development Research Report No. 93* (by Glenn V. Fuguitt, John A. Fulton, and Calvin L. Beale). I quote David Banner from the DVD documentary on Southern hip-hop, *Dirty States.* Additional quotes from Banner, along with Field Mob and Bubba Sparxxx, are from *XXL*, and Bubba also gets quoted from the Web sites Allhiphop.com and BallerStatus.net. A Nappy Roots quote comes from *Rolling Stone.* An important source for my background information on

Albany, LaGrange, the Callaway family, and other pieces of Georgia history was the *New Georgia Encyclopedia* (www.georgiaencyclopedia.org/nge). My quote of W.E.B. DuBois' *Souls of Black Folk* is in the public domain, and comes from Chapter 7 of that book ("Of the Black Belt"). It can be read at www.bartleby.com/114.

The first part of Chapter 10, which focuses on Three 6 Mafia, owes a debt (as does all my Memphis research) to John "J-Dogg" Shaw. I also included a great description of Three 6's music written by Kelefa Sanneh in the *Village Voice* of June 21, 2000. The rest of the crunk chapter, with small exceptions, comes from first-hand reporting. The history of screw, told in Chapter 11, relies more heavily on material from *Murder Dog* (including an interview with the deceased DJ Screw) and *Houston Press* (Megan Halverson's February 27, 1997, story "Swangin' and Bangin' . . . and Getting to that Other Level with the Disciples of Screw"), as well as *Down-South.com*, *Rap Pages*, *Soundslam*, and *The Source*.

For a complete list of the first-hand interviews I conducted and used in this book, refer to the acknowledgments, where I thank all my sources for their input.

ACKNOWLEDGMENTS

First, I owe an immeasurable debt to my wife and family for enduring the drain on time and resources to which this book subjected them. To my wife, Danielle, especially, thanks for putting up with me.

Thanks as well to my agent, Paul Bresnick, for making the deal easy, and to my editor at Da Capo, Ben Schafer, for his constant support and encouraging words, even when I suspect he was getting a little exasperated. Same goes for production editor Laura Stine, copy editor Joe Bonyata, and everyone who worked on the book at Perseus. And thanks to Julia Beverly, for her great photography, and to Liana Ponce, for her help with the photos.

Before I go ahead and offer my appreciation to everyone I interviewed for *Third Coast*, I want to single out a few extraordinary sources. Though I had come to know Atlanta's hip-hop community very well from my years working as music editor for the city's alternative weekly, *Creative Loafing*, I had not spent a significant amount of time in any of the other cities on which the book focuses, beyond some work trips and vacations. I was fortunate to locate, early in my research, several key sources that served as a springboard into a deeper understanding of their city—and often helped to provide me access to other sources. For Florida, that source was Joe "DJ PappaWheelie" Gonzalez, a DJ, writer, and bass-music historian exiled in New York City. For Memphis, it was John "J-Dogg" Shaw, a writer and employee of Select-O-Hits Records. And for Houston, it was Matt "SoReal" Sonzala, a writer, photographer, DJ, promoter, and proprietor of the HoustonSoReal blog.

In Virginia, I owe thanks to the rapper Melvin "Magoo" Barcliff, who spent a long night driving me around to key spots in the Tidewater area and telling about the early days of his friends Timbaland, Missy Elliott, and Pharrell Williams. And special thanks as well to Rico Wade in Atlanta, who opened his Dungeon doors and gave his time generously—though I know he has many more stories in him than the ones he shared with me.

Now, I'll break down the big list of everyone else I interviewed by location (and beyond that, in no particular order).

In Florida, thanks to: Clarence "Blowfly" Reid, Luther Campbell, Trick Daddy, Charles Young Sr., Charles Young Jr., Betty Wright, Ted Lucas, Pitbull, Mz. Vet, MC ADE, James McCauley (aka DXJ, Maggotron, etc.), Fresh Kid Ice, Neil Case, Billy Hines, Henry Stone, Disco Rick, Allen Johnston, Bo Crane, DJ Laz, Pretty Tony, DJ Magic Mike, Tom Bowker, and David Noller.

In Houston, thanks to: Willie D, Ready Red, Michael Watts, E.S.G., Lil Troy, DJ Chill, Bun B, Mike Clark, K-Rino, Devin the Dude, Lil Flip. In Memphis, thanks to: Boss King, Devin Steel, Freddy Hydro, Al Kapone, Gangsta Pat, DJ Paul, Juicy J, Nick Scarfo, Eightball, MJG, Crunchy Black, Wes Philips, and Jazze Pha. In New Orleans, thanks to: Gregory D, Mannie Fresh, Bryan "Baby" Williams, Ronald "Slim" Williams, C-Murder, DJ Jubilee, B.G., KLC, Earl Mackie, Shirani at Peaches Records, Robert Shaw, and Anthony Murray. And in Virginia: Teddy Riley, Pharrell Williams, Chad Hugo, Malice, Pusha T, Missy Elliott, Timbaland, Leatrice Pierre (Timbaland's mom), Knottz, and DJ Strez.

In Atlanta, thanks to: Mike "Mr. Collipark/DJ Smurf" Crooms, John Abbey, Tony MF Rock (aka Woodchuck), Speech, Tony Mercedes, Wayne Briggs, Jimmy Brown, MC Shy-D, Jermaine Dupri, Kawan "KP" Prather, Ian Burke, L Rocc, Ryan Cameron, Cecil "DC" Glenn, Kilo, King J, Jason Orr, Jason Geter, Dee Dee Murray, Lil Jon, T.I., Bonecrusher, Pastor Troy, DSGB, Sleepy Brown, Ray Murray, Cee-Lo, Gipp, Khujo, Big Rube, Mr. DJ, Big Boi, Andre Benjamin, Big Sam, Lil Bo, Chuck D, Lil Scrappy, Da Brat, D-Roc, Kaine, Lil Jon's brothers and mom, Rob "Mac" McDowell, Big Oomp, Jamilla Bell (Jack the Rapper's daughter), Gene Griffin, and Bubba Sparxxx.

In none of the above locations, thanks to: David Banner, Prophet from Nappy Roots, Steve Gottlieb, and Orville Hall.

A number of writer friends generously donated their tapes and transcripts for my use in research, and/or helped in some other way. Thanks to David Peisner, Tony Ware, Lang Whitaker, Rhonda Baraka, Ronda Penrice, David Menconi, and Jocelyn Wilson. Thanks as well to the author Walker Smith for sharing with me the unpublished autobiography of Jack "the Rapper" Gibson she cowrote with him shortly before his death.

To the extent that some of the research and writing in *Third Coast* builds upon or borrows from journalism work I had done previously, I must thank my editors for hiring, encouraging, and enabling me, and then for helping shape my copy: At *Creative Loafing*, Ken Edelstein, Suzanne Van Atten, and Hobart Rowland; at *XXL*, Vanessa Satten and David Bry; at *Vibe*, Erik Parker; at *Rolling Stone*, Nathan Brackett; at *Spin*, Sia Michel; and at *Scratch*, Andre Torres.

Finally, you gotta thank the publicists. I dealt with many, but a few stand out as being particularly helpful and reliable. Thanks to Joe Wiggins at TVT, Giovanna Melchiorre at Koch, Vicki Charles at Universal, and Betsy Bolte.

INDEX